2000 SUPPLEMENT TO
CONSTITUTIONAL LAW
THE AMERICAN CONSTITUTION
CONSTITUTIONAL RIGHTS AND LIBERTIES

Eighth Editions

By
Yale Kamisar
Clarence Darrow Distinguished University Professor of Law,
University of Michigan

Jesse H. Choper
Earl Warren Professor of Public Law,
University of California, Berkeley

Steven H. Shiffrin
Professor of Law,
Cornell University

Richard H. Fallon, Jr.
Professor of Law,
Harvard University

AMERICAN CASEBOOK SERIES®

WEST GROUP

ST. PAUL, MINN., 2000

American Casebook Series and the WP symbol are registered trademarks used herein under license.

COPYRIGHT © 1996 By WEST PUBLISHING CO.
COPYRIGHT © 1997, 1998, 1999 By WEST GROUP
COPYRIGHT © 2000 By WEST GROUP
       610 Opperman Drive
       P.O. Box 64526
       St. Paul, MN 55164–0526
       1–800–328–9352

ISBN 0–314–24749–1

TEXT IS PRINTED ON 10% POST CONSUMER RECYCLED PAPER

Preface

This Supplement contains significant developments that have occurred since March 1, 1996—the "cut-off" date of the principal books.

The editorial style of this Supplement follows that of the principal books. In designating the places in the principal books at which the supplementary material is to be inserted, the following abbreviations have been used:

Constitutional Law: Cases, Comments & Questions—CON LAW

The American Constitution: Cases & Materials—AMER CON

Constitutional Rights & Liberties: Cases & Materials—RTS & LIB

Chapter and section titles from the principal books have been reproduced in this Supplement to facilitate identification of the material to be inserted.

YALE KAMISAR
JESSE H. CHOPER
STEVEN H. SHIFFRIN
RICHARD H. FALLON, JR.

July, 2000

*

Table of Contents

Table of Cases

The principal cases are in bold type. Cases cited or discussed in the text are roman type. References are to pages.

2000 SUPPLEMENT TO
CONSTITUTIONAL LAW
THE AMERICAN CONSTITUTION
CONSTITUTIONAL RIGHTS AND LIBERTIES

Eighth Editions

*

NATURE AND SCOPE OF JUDICIAL REVIEW

CONGRESSIONAL REGULATION OF JUDICIAL POWER

CON LAW: P. 47, at end of note 3(b)

Felker v. Turpin, 518 U.S. 651, 116 S.Ct. 2333, 135 L.Ed.2d 827 (1996), per Rehnquist, C.J., unanimously rejected a constitutional challenge to a federal statute withdrawing the Court's appellate jurisdiction in a category of habeas corpus cases involving "successive" petitions. In a concurring opinion, Souter, J., joined by Stevens and Breyer, JJ., reserved the question whether the statute might be held unconstitutional as applied to subsequent cases if, in practice, it stopped the Court from reviewing "divergent interpretations" of a federal statute.

CON LAW: PP. 47–48, at end of footnote d

The Court followed *Yerger*'s interpretive principle that implied repeals of Supreme Court appellate jurisdiction should be disfavored in *Felker v. Turpin*, 518 U.S. 651, 116 S.Ct. 2333, 135 L.Ed.2d 827 (1996). Per Rehnquist, C.J., the Court held, 9–0, that a statute withdrawing its certiorari jurisdiction in certain habeas cases had not affected its authority to review the case before it upon a petition for an original writ of habeas corpus under 28 U.S.C. §§ 2241 and 2254. As in *McCardle*, the availability of an alternative mechanism for the Court to exercise jurisdiction "obviate[d]" any constitutional challenge to the jurisdiction-limiting legislation under Article III, § 2.

NATIONAL LEGISLATIVE POWER

THE NATIONAL COMMERCE POWER

RECENT LIMITATION

CON LAW: P. 112, substitute for *Lopez* to bottom of p. 119
AMER CON: P. 94, substitute for *Lopez* to bottom of p. 101

UNITED STATES v. MORRISON

___ U.S. ___, 120 S.Ct. 1740, 146 L.Ed.2d 658 (2000).

CHIEF JUSTICE REHNQUIST delivered the opinion of the Court.

[Petitioner Brzonkala, alleging that respondent, a fellow student at Virginia Polytechnic Institute, had assaulted and repeatedly raped her, sued him under 42 U.S.C. § 13981 (part of the Violence Against Women Act of 1984) which provides a federal civil remedy for the victims of gender-motivated violence. The United States intervened to defend § 13981's constitutionality.]

As we discussed at length in *United States v. Lopez*, 514 U.S. 549, 115 S.Ct. 1624, 131 L.Ed.2d 626 (1995), our interpretation of the Commerce Clause has changed as our Nation has developed. [I]t suffices to say that, in the years since *Jones & Laughlin*, Congress has had considerably greater latitude in regulating conduct and transactions under the Commerce Clause than our previous case law permitted.

Lopez emphasized, however, that even under our modern, expansive interpretation of the Commerce Clause, Congress' regulatory authority is not without effective bounds. [In] *Jones & Laughlin*, the Court warned that the scope of the interstate commerce power "must be considered in the light of our dual system of government and may not be extended so as to embrace effects upon interstate commerce so indirect and remote that to embrace them, in view of our complex society, would effectually obliterate the distinction between what is national and what is local and create a completely centralized government."

As we observed in *Lopez*, modern Commerce Clause jurisprudence has "identified three broad categories of activity that Congress may regulate under its commerce power." "First, Congress may regulate the use of the channels of interstate commerce" (citing *Heart of Atlanta*; *Darby*). "Second, Congress is empowered to regulate and protect the instrumentalities of interstate commerce, or persons or things in interstate commerce, even though the threat may come only from intrastate activities" (citing *Shreveport Rate Cases*). "Finally, Congress' commerce authority includes the power to regulate those activities having a substantial relation to interstate commerce, i.e., those activities that substantially affect interstate commerce" (citing *Jones & Laughlin*).

Petitioners [seek] to sustain § 13981 as a regulation of activity that substantially affects interstate commerce. Given § 13981's focus on gender-motivated violence wherever it occurs (rather than violence directed at the instrumentalities of interstate commerce, interstate markets, or things or persons in interstate commerce), we agree that this is the proper inquiry.

[In] *Lopez*, we held that the Gun–Free School Zones Act of 1990, 18 U.S.C. § 922(q)(1)(A), which made it a federal crime to knowingly possess a firearm in a school zone, exceeded Congress' authority under the Commerce Clause. Several significant considerations contributed to our decision.

First, we observed that § 922(q) was "a criminal statute that by its terms has nothing to do with 'commerce' or any sort of economic enterprise, however broadly one might define those terms." * * *

Both petitioners and Justice Souter's dissent downplay the role that the economic nature of the regulated activity plays in our Commerce Clause analysis. But a fair reading of *Lopez* shows that the noneconomic, criminal nature of the conduct at issue was central to our decision in that case. See, e.g., ("Even *Wickard*, which is perhaps the most far reaching example of Commerce Clause authority over intrastate activity, involved economic activity in a way that the possession of a gun in a school zone does not"), ("Admittedly, a determination whether an intrastate activity is commercial or noncommercial may in some cases result in legal uncertainty. But, so long as Congress' authority is limited to those powers enumerated in the Constitution, and so long as those enumerated powers are interpreted as having judicially enforceable outer limits, congressional legislation under the Commerce Clause always will engender 'legal uncertainty' "), ("The possession of a gun in a local school zone is in no sense an economic activity that might, through repetition elsewhere,[a] substantially affect any sort of interstate commerce"); see also id. (Kennedy, J., concurring) (stating that *Lopez* did not alter our "practical conception of commercial regulation" and that Congress may "regulate in the commercial sphere on the assumption that we have a single market and a unified purpose to build a stable national economy"), ("Were the Federal Government to take over the regulation of entire areas of traditional state concern, areas having nothing to do with the regulation of commercial activities, the boundaries between the spheres of federal and state authority would blur"), ("[In] a sense any conduct in this interdependent world of ours has an ultimate commercial origin or consequence, but we have not yet said the commerce power may reach so far"). * * *

The second consideration that we found important in analyzing § 922(q) was that the statute contained "no express jurisdictional element which might limit its reach to a discrete set of firearm possessions that additionally have an explicit connection with or effect on interstate commerce." Such a jurisdictional element may establish that the enactment is in pursuance of Congress' regulation of interstate commerce.

Third, we noted that neither § 922(q) "nor its legislative history contains express congressional findings regarding the effects upon interstate commerce of gun possession in a school zone." While "Congress normally is not required to make formal findings as to the substantial burdens that an activity has on interstate commerce," (citing *McClung, Perez*), the existence of such findings may "enable us to evaluate the legislative judgment that the activity in question substantially affects interstate commerce, even though no such substantial effect [is] visible to the naked eye."

---

a. This refers to the "aggregation" principle: that certain activities, although themselves having only a "trivial" impact on interstate commerce (*Wickard*), "contribute in the aggregate a vast volume" (*Fainblatt*).

Finally, our decision in *Lopez* rested in part on the fact that the link between gun possession and a substantial effect on interstate commerce was attenuated. The United States argued that the possession of guns may lead to violent crime, and that violent crime "can be expected to affect the functioning of the national economy in two ways. First, the costs of violent crime are substantial, and, through the mechanism of insurance, those costs are spread throughout the population. Second, violent crime reduces the willingness of individuals to travel to areas within the country that are perceived to be unsafe." The Government also argued that the presence of guns at schools poses a threat to the educational process, which in turn threatens to produce a less efficient and productive workforce, which will negatively affect national productivity and thus interstate commerce.

We rejected these "costs of crime" and "national productivity" arguments because they would permit Congress to "regulate not only all violent crime, but all activities that might lead to violent crime, regardless of how tenuously they relate to interstate commerce." We noted that, under this but-for reasoning: "Congress could regulate any activity that it found was related to the economic productivity of individual citizens: family law (including marriage, divorce, and child custody), for example. Under these theories, [it]is difficult to perceive any limitation on federal power, even in areas such as criminal law enforcement or education where States historically have been sovereign. Thus, if we were to accept the Government's arguments, we are hard pressed to posit any activity by an individual that Congress is without power to regulate."

With these principles underlying our Commerce Clause jurisprudence as reference points, the proper resolution of the present cases is clear. Gender-motivated crimes of violence are not, in any sense of the phrase, economic activity. While we need not adopt a categorical rule against aggregating the effects of any noneconomic activity in order to decide these cases, thus far in our Nation's history our cases have upheld Commerce Clause regulation of intrastate activity only where that activity is economic in nature.

Like the Gun–Free School Zones Act at issue in *Lopez*, § 13981 contains no jurisdictional element establishing that the federal cause of action is in pursuance of Congress' power to regulate interstate commerce. Although *Lopez* makes clear that such a jurisdictional element would lend support to the argument that § 13981 is sufficiently tied to interstate commerce, Congress elected to cast § 13981's remedy over a wider, and more purely intrastate, body of violent crime.[5]

In contrast with the lack of congressional findings that we faced in *Lopez*, § 13981 is supported by numerous findings regarding the serious impact that gender-motivated violence has on victims and their families. But [as] we stated in *Lopez*, " 'Simply because Congress may conclude that a particular activity substantially affects interstate commerce does not necessarily make it so.' " (quoting *Hodel* (Rehnquist, J., concurring in judgment)). Rather, " 'whether particular operations affect interstate commerce sufficiently to come under the constitutional power of Congress to regulate them is ultimately a judicial rather than a

---

5. Title 42 U.S.C. § 13981 is not the sole provision of the Violence Against Women Act of 1994 to provide a federal remedy for gender-motivated crime. Section 40221(a) of the Act creates a federal criminal remedy to punish "interstate crimes of abuse including crimes committed against spouses or intimate partners during interstate travel and crimes committed by spouses or intimate partners who cross State lines to continue the abuse." [The] Courts of Appeals have uniformly upheld this criminal sanction as an appropriate exercise of Congress' Commerce Clause authority, reasoning that the provision properly falls within the first of *Lopez's* categories as it regulates the use of channels of interstate commerce—i.e., the use of the interstate transportation routes through which persons and goods move.

legislative question, and can be settled finally only by this Court.' " (quoting *Heart of Atlanta* (Black, J., concurring)).

In these cases, Congress [found] that gender-motivated violence affects interstate commerce "by deterring potential victims from traveling interstate, from engaging in employment in interstate business, and from transacting with business, and in places involved in interstate commerce; [by] diminishing national productivity, increasing medical and other costs, and decreasing the supply of and the demand for interstate products." Given these findings and petitioners' arguments, the concern that we expressed in *Lopez* that Congress might use the Commerce Clause to completely obliterate the Constitution's distinction between national and local authority seems well founded. The reasoning that petitioners advance seeks to follow the but-for causal chain from the initial occurrence of violent crime (the suppression of which has always been the prime object of the States' police power) to every attenuated effect upon interstate commerce. If accepted, petitioners' reasoning would allow Congress to regulate any crime as long as the nationwide, aggregated impact of that crime has substantial effects on employment, production, transit, or consumption. Indeed, if Congress may regulate gender-motivated violence, it would be able to regulate murder or any other type of violence since gender-motivated violence, as a subset of all violent crime, is certain to have lesser economic impacts than the larger class of which it is a part.[7]

[The] regulation and punishment of intrastate violence that is not directed at the instrumentalities, channels, or goods involved in interstate commerce has always been the province of the States. See, e.g., *Cohens v. Virginia,* (Marshall, C. J.) (stating that Congress "has no general right to punish murder committed within any of the States," and that it is "clear [that] congress cannot punish felonies generally"). Indeed, we can think of no better example of the police power, which the Founders denied the National Government and reposed in the States, than the suppression of violent crime and vindication of its victims. * * *

[The issue of Congress' power to enact § 13981 under § 5 of the fourteenth amendment is discussed at p. 230 of this Supplement.]

JUSTICE THOMAS, concurring.

The majority opinion correctly applies our decision in *Lopez,* and I join it in full. I write separately only to express my view that the very notion of a "substantial effects" test under the Commerce Clause is inconsistent with the original understanding of Congress' powers and with this Court's early Commerce Clause cases.

[Thomas, J.'s concurring opinion in *Lopez* contended:]

["At the time the original Constitution was ratified, 'commerce' consisted of selling, buying, and bartering, as well as transporting for these purposes [in] contradistinction to productive activities such as manufacturing and agriculture.

---

7. Justice Souter's dissent theory [is] remarkable because it undermines this central principle of our constitutional system. As we have repeatedly noted, the Framers crafted the federal system of government so that the people's rights would be secured by the division of power. [No] doubt the political branches have a role in interpreting and applying the Constitution, but ever since *Marbury* this Court has remained the ultimate expositor of the constitutional text. Contrary to Justice Souter's suggestion, [that] from *Gibbons* on, public opinion has been the only restraint on the congressional exercise of the commerce power is true only insofar as it contends that political accountability is and has been the only limit on Congress' exercise of the commerce power within that power's outer bounds. As the language surrounding that relied upon by Justice Souter makes clear, *Gibbons* did not remove from this Court the authority to define that boundary.

Alexander Hamilton, for example, repeatedly treated commerce, agriculture, and manufacturing as three separate endeavors. * * *

["The Constitution not only uses the word 'commerce' in a narrower sense than our case law might suggest, it also does not support the proposition that Congress has authority over all activities that 'substantially affect' interstate commerce. [After] all, if Congress may regulate all matters that substantially affect commerce, there is no need for the Constitution to specify that Congress may enact bankruptcy laws, cl. 4, or coin money and fix the standard of weights and measures, cl. 5, or punish counterfeiters of United States coin and securities, cl. 6. Likewise, Congress would not need the separate authority to establish post offices and post roads, cl. 7, or to grant patents and copyrights, cl. 8, or to 'punish Piracies and Felonies committed on the high Seas,' cl. 10. It might not even need the power to raise and support an Army and Navy, cls. 12 and 13, for fewer people would engage in commercial shipping if they thought that a foreign power could expropriate their property with ease. Indeed, if Congress could regulate matters that substantially affect interstate commerce, there would have been no need to specify that Congress can regulate international trade and commerce with the Indians. As the Framers surely understood, these other branches of trade substantially affect interstate commerce. [An] interpretation of cl. 3 that makes the rest of § 8 superfluous simply cannot be correct."]

By continuing to apply this rootless and malleable standard, however circumscribed, the Court has encouraged the Federal Government to persist in its view that the Commerce Clause has virtually no limits. Until this Court replaces its existing Commerce Clause jurisprudence with a standard more consistent with the original understanding, we will continue to see Congress appropriating state police powers under the guise of regulating commerce.

JUSTICE SOUTER, with whom JUSTICE STEVENS, JUSTICE GINSBURG, and JUSTICE BREYER join, dissenting. * * *

One obvious difference from *Lopez* is the mountain of data assembled by Congress, here showing the effects of violence against women on interstate commerce. Passage of the Act in 1994 was preceded by four years of hearings, which included testimony from physicians and law professors; from survivors of rape and domestic violence; and from representatives of state law enforcement and private business. The record includes reports on gender bias from task forces in 21 States, and we have the benefit of specific factual findings in the eight separate Reports issued by Congress and its committees over the long course leading to enactment.

With respect to domestic violence, Congress received evidence for the following findings:

"Three out of four American women will be victims of violent crimes sometime during their life."

"Violence is the leading cause of injuries to women ages 15 to 44."

"[A]s many as 50 percent of homeless women and children are fleeing domestic violence."

"Since 1974, the assault rate against women has outstripped the rate for men by at least twice for some age groups and far more for others."

"[B]attering 'is the single largest cause of injury to women in the United States.'"

"An estimated 4 million American women are battered each year by their husbands or partners."

"Over 1 million women in the United States seek medical assistance each year for injuries sustained [from] their husbands or other partners."

"Between 2,000 and 4,000 women die every year from [domestic] abuse."

"[A]rrest rates may be as low as 1 for every 100 domestic assaults."

"Partial estimates show that violent crime against women costs this country at least 3 billion—not million, but billion—dollars a year."

"[E]stimates suggest that we spend $5 to $10 billion a year on health care, criminal justice, and other social costs of domestic violence."

The evidence as to rape was similarly extensive, supporting these conclusions:

"[The incidence of] rape rose four times as fast as the total national crime rate over the past 10 years."

"According to one study, close to half a million girls now in high school will be raped before they graduate."

"[One hundred twenty-five thousand] college women can expect to be raped during this—or any—year."

"[T]hree-quarters of women never go to the movies alone after dark because of the fear of rape and nearly 50 percent do not use public transit alone after dark for the same reason."

"[Forty-one] percent of judges surveyed believed that juries give sexual assault victims less credibility than other crime victims."

"Less than 1 percent of all [rape] victims have collected damages."

" '[A]n individual who commits rape has only about 4 chances in 100 of being arrested, prosecuted, and found guilty of any offense.' "

"Almost one-quarter of convicted rapists never go to prison and another quarter received sentences in local jails where the average sentence is 11 months."

"[A]lmost 50 percent of rape victims lose their jobs or are forced to quit because of the crime's severity." * * *

Congress thereby explicitly stated the predicate [quoted in the Court's opinion at p. 5 of this Supplement] for the exercise of its Commerce Clause power. Is its conclusion irrational in view of the data amassed? True, the methodology of particular studies may be challenged, and some of the figures arrived at may be disputed. But the sufficiency of the evidence before Congress to provide a rational basis for the finding cannot seriously be questioned. * * *

The Act would have passed muster at any time between *Wickard* in 1942 and *Lopez* in 1995, a period in which the law enjoyed a stable understanding that congressional power under the Commerce Clause, complemented by the authority of the Necessary and Proper Clause, extended to all activity that, when aggregated, has a substantial effect on interstate commerce. [T]his understanding was secure even against the turmoil at the passage of the Civil Rights Act of 1964, in the aftermath of which the Court not only reaffirmed the cumulative effects and rational basis features of the substantial effects test, but declined to limit the commerce power through a formal distinction between legislation focused on "commerce" and statutes addressing "moral and social wrongs," *Heart of Atlanta.*

The fact that the Act does not pass muster before the Court today is therefore proof, to a degree that *Lopez* was not, that the Court's nominal adherence to the substantial effects test is merely that. [I]t is clear that some congressional conclusions about obviously substantial, cumulative effects on commerce are being assigned lesser values than the once-stable doctrine would assign them. These devaluations are accomplished not by any express repudiation of the substantial effects test or its application through the aggregation of individual conduct, but by supplanting rational basis scrutiny with a new criterion of review.

[The] majority stresses that Art. I, § 8, enumerates the powers of Congress, including the commerce power, an enumeration implying the exclusion of powers not enumerated. It follows, for the majority, [that] some particular subjects arguably within the commerce power can be identified in advance as excluded, on the basis of characteristics other than their commercial effects. Such exclusions come into sight when the activity regulated is not itself commercial or when the States have traditionally addressed it in the exercise of the general police power, conferred under the state constitutions but never extended to Congress under the Constitution of the Nation.

* * * From the fact that Art. I, § 8, cl. 3 grants an authority limited to regulating commerce, it follows only that Congress may claim no authority under that section to address any subject that does not affect commerce. It does not at all follow that an activity affecting commerce nonetheless falls outside the commerce power, depending on the specific character of the activity, or the authority of a State to regulate it along with Congress. My disagreement with the majority is not, however, confined to logic, for history has shown that categorical exclusions have proven as unworkable in practice as they are unsupportable in theory.

Obviously, it would not be inconsistent with the text of the Commerce Clause itself to declare "noncommercial" primary activity beyond or presumptively beyond the scope of the commerce power. That variant of categorical approach is not, however, the sole textually permissible way of defining the scope of the Commerce Clause, and any such neat limitation would at least be suspect in the light of the [necessary and proper clause]. Accordingly, for significant periods of our history, the Court has defined the commerce power as plenary, unsusceptible to categorical exclusions, and this was the view expressed throughout the latter part of the 20th century in the substantial effects test. These two conceptions of the commerce power, plenary and categorically limited, are in fact old rivals, and today's revival of their competition summons up familiar history, a brief reprise of which may be helpful in posing what I take to be the key question going to the legitimacy of the majority's decision to breathe new life into the approach of categorical limitation.

[T]oday's attempt to distinguish between primary activities affecting commerce in terms of the relatively commercial or noncommercial character of the primary conduct proscribed comes with the pedigree of near-tragedy that I outlined in *Lopez*. In the half century following the modern activation of the commerce power with passage of the Interstate Commerce Act in 1887, this Court from time to time created categorical enclaves beyond congressional reach by declaring such activities as "mining," "production," "manufacturing," and union membership to be outside the definition of "commerce" and by limiting application of the effects test to "direct" rather than "indirect" commercial consequences.

Since adherence to these formalistically contrived confines of commerce power in large measure provoked the judicial crisis of 1937, one might reasonably have doubted that Members of this Court would ever again toy with a return to the days before *Jones & Laughlin*, which brought the earlier and nearly disastrous experiment to an end. And yet today's decision can only be seen as a step toward recapturing the prior mistakes. Its revival of a distinction between commercial and noncommercial conduct is at odds with *Wickard*, which repudiated that analysis, and the enquiry into commercial purpose, first intimated by the *Lopez* concurrence (opinion of Kennedy, J.), is cousin to the intent-based analysis employed in *Hammer*, but rejected for Commerce Clause purposes in *Heart of Atlanta* and *Darby*.

Why is the majority tempted to reject the lesson so painfully learned in 1937? An answer emerges from contrasting *Wickard* with one of the predecessor cases it superseded. It was obvious in *Wickard* that growing wheat for consumption right on the farm was not "commerce" in the common vocabulary.[13] [Just] a few years before *Wickard*, however, it had certainly been no less obvious that "mining" practices could substantially affect commerce, even though *Carter Coal* had held mining regulation beyond the national commerce power. When we try to fathom the difference between the two cases, it is clear that they did not go in different directions because the *Carter Coal* Court could not understand a causal connection that the *Wickard* Court could grasp; the difference, rather, turned on the fact that the Court in *Carter Coal* had a reason for trying to maintain its categorical, formalistic distinction, while that reason had been abandoned by the time *Wickard* was decided. The reason was [that the] Court in *Carter Coal* was still trying to create a laissez-faire world out of the 20th-century economy, and formalistic commercial distinctions were thought to be useful instruments in achieving that object.

[Just] as the old formalism had value in the service of an economic conception, the new one is useful in serving a conception of federalism. It is the instrument by which assertions of national power are to be limited in favor of preserving a supposedly discernible, proper sphere of state autonomy to legislate or refrain from legislating as the individual States see fit.* * *

The Court finds it relevant that the statute addresses conduct traditionally subject to state prohibition under domestic criminal law, a fact said to have some heightened significance when the violent conduct in question is not itself aimed directly at interstate commerce or its instrumentalities. Again, history seems to be recycling, for the theory of traditional state concern as grounding a limiting principle has been rejected previously, [and] repudiated in *Garcia* [CON LAW p. 146; AMER CON p. 121], which held that the concept of "traditional governmental function" [was] incoherent, there being no explanation that would make sense of the multifarious decisions placing some functions on one side of the line, some on the other. * * *[14]

13. [The] *Wickard* Court admitted that Filburn's activity "may not be regarded as commerce" but insisted that "it may still, whatever its nature, be reached by Congress if it exerts a substantial economic effect on interstate commerce." The characterization of home wheat production as "commerce" or not is, however, ultimately beside the point. For if substantial effects on commerce are proper subjects of concern under the Commerce Clause, what difference should it make whether the causes of those effects are themselves commercial? The Court's answer is that it makes a difference to federalism, and the legitimacy of the Court's new judicially derived federalism is the crux of our disagreement.

14. The Constitution of 1787 did, in fact, forbid some exercises of the commerce power. Article I, § 9, cl. 6, barred Congress from giving preference to the ports of one State over those of another. More strikingly, the Framers protected the slave trade from federal interference, see Art. I, § 9, cl. 1. [These] reservations demonstrate the plenary nature of the federal power; the exceptions prove the rule. [T]o suppose that enumerated powers must have limits is sensible; to maintain that there exist judicially identifiable areas of state regulation immune to the plenary congressional commerce power even though falling within the limits defined by the substantial effects test is to deny our constitutional history.

The objection to reviving traditional state spheres of action as a consideration in commerce analysis, however, not only rests on the portent of incoherence, but is compounded by a further defect just as fundamental. The defect, in essence, is the majority's rejection of the Founders' considered judgment that politics, not judicial review, should mediate between state and national interests as the strength and legislative jurisdiction of the National Government inevitably increased through the expected growth of the national economy. [quoting Madison (in *Federalist* No. 46), James Wilson, and Marshall, C.J., in *Gibbons*]. The point can be put no more clearly than the Court [in *Garcia*] put it the last time it repudiated the notion that some state activities categorically defied the commerce power as understood in accordance with generally accepted concepts.

The *Garcia* Court's rejection of "judicially created limitations" in favor of the intended reliance on national politics was all the more powerful owing to the Court's explicit recognition that in the centuries since the framing the relative powers of the two sovereign systems have markedly changed. Nationwide economic integration is the norm, the national political power has been augmented by its vast revenues, and the power of the States has been drawn down by the Seventeenth Amendment, eliminating selection of senators by state legislature in favor of direct election. * * *[19]

Amendments that alter the balance of power between the National and State Governments, like the Fourteenth, or that change the way the States are represented within the Federal Government, like the Seventeenth, are not rips in the fabric of the Framers' Constitution, inviting judicial repairs. The Seventeenth Amendment may indeed have lessened the enthusiasm of the Senate to represent the States as discrete sovereignties, but the Amendment did not convert the judiciary into an alternate shield against the commerce power.

The Court [finds] no significance whatever in the state support for the Act based upon the States' acknowledged failure to deal adequately with gender-based violence in state courts, and the belief of their own law enforcement agencies that national action is essential.

The National Association of Attorneys General supported the Act unanimously, and [as] the 1993 Senate Report put it, "The Violence Against Women Act is intended to respond both to the underlying attitude that this violence is somehow less serious than other crime and to the resulting failure of our criminal justice system to address such violence. Its goals are both symbolic and practical." [It] is, then, not the least irony of these cases that the States will be forced to enjoy the new federalism whether they want it or not. * * *

JUSTICE BREYER, with whom JUSTICE STEVENS joins, and with whom JUSTICE SOUTER and JUSTICE GINSBURG join as to Part I–A, dissenting.

No one denies the importance of the Constitution's federalist principles. Its state/federal division of authority protects liberty—both by restricting the burdens that government can impose from a distance and by facilitating citizen participation in government that is closer to home. The question is how the judiciary

---

19. The majority tries to deflect the objection that it blocks an intended political process by explaining that the Framers intended politics to set the federal balance only within the sphere of permissible commerce legislation, whereas we are looking to politics to define that sphere (in derogation even of *Marbury*). * * * Neither Madison nor Wilson nor Marshall, nor the *Jones & Laughlin, Darby, Wickard,* or *Garcia* Courts, suggested that politics defines the commerce power. Nor do we, even though we recognize that the conditions of the contemporary world result in a vastly greater sphere of influence for politics than the Framers would have envisioned. * * *

can [best] impose some meaningful limit, but not too great a limit, upon the scope of the legislative authority that the Commerce Clause delegates to Congress.

A. Consider the problems. The "economic/noneconomic" distinction is not easy to apply. Does the local street corner mugger engage in "economic" activity or "noneconomic" activity when he mugs for money?

The line becomes yet harder to draw given the need for exceptions. The Court itself would permit Congress to aggregate, hence regulate, "noneconomic" activity taking place at economic establishments. See *Heart of Atlanta.* And it would permit Congress to regulate where that regulation is "an essential part of a larger regulation of economic activity, in which the regulatory scheme could be undercut unless the intrastate activity were regulated." cf. Controlled Substances Act (regulating drugs produced for home consumption). Given the former exception, can Congress simply rewrite the present law and limit its application to restaurants, hotels, perhaps universities, and other places of public accommodation? Given the latter exception, can Congress save the present law by including it, or much of it, in a broader "Safe Transport" or "Workplace Safety" act?

More important, why should we give critical constitutional importance to the economic, or noneconomic, nature of an interstate-commerce-affecting cause? If chemical emanations through indirect environmental change cause identical, severe commercial harm outside a State, why should it matter whether local factories or home fireplaces release them? * * *

Most important, the Court's complex rules seem unlikely to help secure the very object that they seek, namely, the protection of "areas of traditional state regulation" from federal intrusion. The Court's rules, even if broadly interpreted, are underinclusive. The local pickpocket is no less a traditional subject of state regulation than is the local gender-motivated assault. Regardless, the Court reaffirms, as it should, Congress' well-established and frequently exercised power to enact laws that satisfy a commerce-related jurisdictional prerequisite—for example, that some item relevant to the federally regulated activity has at some time crossed a state line. *Heart of Atlanta* ("The authority of Congress to keep the channels of interstate commerce free from immoral and injurious uses has been frequently sustained, and is no longer open to question"); see also *Scarborough v. United States*, 431 U.S. 563, 575, 97 S.Ct. 1963, 52 L.Ed.2d 582 (1977) (interpreting [a felon in possession] statute [to] require only that gun passed "in interstate commerce" "at some time," without questioning constitutionality).

And in a world where most everyday products or their component parts cross interstate boundaries, Congress will frequently find it possible to redraft a statute using language that ties the regulation to the interstate movement of some relevant object, thereby regulating local criminal activity or, for that matter, family affairs. See, e.g., Child Support Recovery Act of 1992. Although this possibility does not give the Federal Government the power to regulate everything, it means that any substantive limitation will apply randomly in terms of the interests the majority seeks to protect. How much would be gained, for example, were Congress to reenact the present law in the form of "An Act Forbidding Violence Against Women Perpetrated at Public Accommodations or by Those Who Have Moved in, or through the Use of Items that Have Moved in, Interstate Commerce"? Complex Commerce Clause rules creating fine distinctions that achieve only random results do little to further the important federalist interests that called them into being. That is why modern (pre-*Lopez*) case law rejected them.

* * * We live in a Nation knit together by two centuries of scientific, technological, commercial, and environmental change. Those changes, taken together, mean that virtually every kind of activity, no matter how local, genuinely can affect commerce, or its conditions, outside the State—at least when considered in the aggregate. And that fact makes it close to impossible for courts to develop meaningful subject-matter categories that would exclude some kinds of local activities from ordinary Commerce Clause "aggregation" rules without, at the same time, depriving Congress of the power to regulate activities that have a genuine and important effect upon interstate commerce.

Since judges cannot change the world, * * * Congress, not the courts, must remain primarily responsible for striking the appropriate state/federal balance. Congress is institutionally motivated to do so. Its Members represent state and local district interests. They consider the views of state and local officials when they legislate, and they have even developed formal procedures to ensure that such consideration takes place. See, e.g., Unfunded Mandates Reform Act of 1995. Moreover, Congress often can better reflect state concerns for autonomy in the details of sophisticated statutory schemes than can the judiciary, which cannot easily gather the relevant facts and which must apply more general legal rules and categories.

B.   I would also note [that] attorneys general in the overwhelming majority of States (38) supported congressional legislation, telling Congress that "our experience as Attorneys General strengthens our belief that the problem of violence against women is a national one, requiring federal attention, federal leadership, and federal funds."

Moreover, [Congress] focused the federal law upon documented deficiencies in state legal systems. And it tailored the law to prevent its use in certain areas of traditional state concern, such as divorce, alimony, or child custody. Consequently, the law before us seems to represent an instance, not of state/federal conflict, but of state/federal efforts to cooperate in order to help solve a mutually acknowledged national problem.

[This] Court on occasion has pointed to the importance of procedural limitations in keeping the power of Congress in check. See *Garcia* ("Any substantive restraint on the exercise of Commerce Clause powers must find its justification in the procedural nature of this basic limitation, and it must be tailored to compensate for possible failings in the national political process rather than to dictate a 'sacred province of state autonomy.' ") [Of] course, any judicial insistence that Congress follow particular procedures might itself intrude upon congressional prerogatives and embody difficult definitional problems. But the intrusion, problems, and consequences all would seem less serious than those embodied in the majority's approach.

I continue to agree with Justice Souter that the Court's traditional "rational basis" approach is sufficient. But I recognize that the law in this area is unstable and that time and experience may demonstrate both the unworkability of the majority's rules and the superiority of Congress' own procedural approach—in which case the law may evolve towards a rule that, in certain difficult Commerce Clause cases, takes account of the thoroughness with which Congress has considered the federalism issue. * * *

CON LAW: P. 120, add at end of note
AMER CON: P. 102, add at end of note

JONES v. U.S., ___ U.S. ___, 120 S.Ct. 1904, ___ L.Ed.2d ___ (2000), per GINSBURG, J., unanimously held that the federal arson statute (covering buildings "used [in] any activity affecting interstate or foreign commerce") did not apply to an owner-occupied residence not used for commercial purposes, thus avoiding the constitutional question under the commerce clause. THOMAS, J., joined by Scalia, J., went beyond the facts of this case and "express[ed] no view on the question whether the federal arson statute [is] constitutional in its application to all buildings used for commercial activities."

APPLYING NATIONAL POWERS TO STATE GOVERNMENTS: INTERGOVERNMENTAL IMMUNITIES

STATE IMMUNITY FROM FEDERAL REGULATION

CON LAW: P. 158, after note 3
AMER CON: P. 132, after note 3

PRINTZ v. UNITED STATES

521 U.S. 898, 117 S.Ct. 2365, 138 L.Ed.2d 914 (1997).

JUSTICE SCALIA delivered the opinion of the Court.

The question presented in these cases is whether certain interim provisions of the Brady Handgun Violence Prevention Act, [a detailed federal scheme governing the distribution of firearms,] commanding state and local law enforcement officers to conduct background checks on prospective handgun purchasers and to perform certain related tasks, violate the Constitution.

[T]he Brady Act purports to direct state law enforcement officers to participate, albeit only temporarily, in the administration of a federally enacted regulatory scheme. Regulated firearms dealers are required to forward Brady Forms not to a federal officer or employee, but to the CLEOs ["chief law enforcement officers"], whose obligation to accept those forms is implicit in the duty imposed upon them to make "reasonable efforts" within five days to determine whether the sales reflected in the forms are lawful. While the CLEOs are subjected to no federal requirement that they prevent the sales determined to be unlawful (it is perhaps assumed that their state-law duties will require prevention or apprehension), they are empowered to grant, in effect, waivers of the federally prescribed 5-day waiting period for handgun purchases by notifying the gun dealers that they have no reason to believe the transactions would be illegal.

The petitioners here object to being pressed into federal service, and contend that congressional action compelling state officers to execute federal laws is unconstitutional. Because there is no constitutional text speaking to this precise question, the answer to the CLEOs' challenge must be sought in historical understanding and practice, in the structure of the Constitution, and in the jurisprudence of this Court.

[The Court concluded that the relevant historical practice tends to negate Congress' power to impose federal responsibilities on state officers without the States' consent. "[E]nactments of the early Congresses [contain] no evidence of an assumption that the Federal Government may command the States' executive power in the absence of a particularized constitutional authorization," such as the Extradition Clause of Art IV, Sec. 2. The "early laws establish, at most, that the Constitution was originally understood to permit imposition of an obligation on state judges to enforce federal prescriptions, insofar as those prescriptions related to matters appropriate for the judicial power." Finally, there is "an absence of executive-commandeering statutes [in] our later history as well, at least until very recent years."]

[The dissents disputed each of these points, as well as the meaning of *The Federalist* Nos. 27 and 44. STEVENS, J., concluded: "[T]he majority's opinion consists almost entirely of arguments against the substantial evidence weighing in opposition to its view; the Court's ruling is strikingly lacking in affirmative support. Absent even a modicum of textual foundation for its judicially crafted constitutional rule, there should be a presumption that if the Framers had actually intended such a rule, at least one of them would have mentioned it."]

* * * We turn next to consideration of the structure of the Constitution * * *. We have set forth the historical record in more detail elsewhere, see *New York v. United States,* and need not repeat it here. It suffices to repeat the conclusion: "The Framers explicitly chose a Constitution that confers upon Congress the power to regulate individuals, not States." * * *

This separation of the two spheres is one of the Constitution's structural protections of liberty. [The] power of the Federal Government would be augmented immeasurably if it were able to impress into its service—and at no cost to itself—the police officers of the 50 States.

[F]ederal control of state officers would [also] have an effect upon [the] separation and equilibration of powers between the three branches of the Federal Government itself. The Constitution does not leave to speculation who is to administer the laws enacted by Congress; the President, it says, "shall take Care that the Laws be faithfully executed," personally and through officers whom he appoints. [The] Brady Act effectively transfers this responsibility to thousands of CLEOs in the 50 States, who are left to implement the program without meaningful Presidential control (if indeed meaningful Presidential control is possible without the power to appoint and remove). [T]he power of the President would be subject to reduction, if Congress could act as effectively without the President as with him, by simply requiring state officers to execute its laws.[12] * * *

Finally, and most conclusively in the present litigation, we turn to the prior jurisprudence of this Court. * * *

The Government contends that *New York* is distinguishable on the following ground: unlike the "take title" provisions invalidated there, the background-check provision of the Brady Act does not require state legislative or executive officials to make policy. [But executive] action that has utterly no policymaking component is rare, particularly at an executive level as high as a jurisdiction's chief law-enforcement officer. Is it really true that there is no policymaking involved in deciding, for example, what "reasonable efforts" shall be expended to conduct a background check? It may well satisfy the Act for a CLEO to direct that (a) no background checks will be conducted that divert personnel time from pending felony investigations, and (b) no background check will be permitted to consume more than one-half hour of an officer's time. [Is] this decision whether to devote

---

12. There is not, as the dissent believes, "tension" between the proposition that impressing state police officers into federal service will massively augment federal power, and the proposition that it will also sap the power of the Federal Presidency. It is quite possible to have a more powerful Federal Government that is, by reason of the destruction of its Executive unity, a less efficient one. The dissent is correct that control by the unitary Federal Executive is also sacrificed when States voluntarily administer federal programs, but the condition of voluntary state participation significantly reduces the ability of Congress to use this device as a means of reducing the power of the Presidency.

maximum "reasonable efforts" or minimum "reasonable efforts" not preeminently a matter of policy? It is quite impossible, in short, to draw the Government's proposed line at "no policymaking," and we would have to fall back upon a line of "not too much policymaking." How much is too much is not likely to be answered precisely; and an imprecise barrier against federal intrusion upon state authority is not likely to be an effective one.

Even assuming, moreover, that the Brady Act leaves no "policymaking" discretion with the States, we fail to see how that improves rather than worsens the intrusion upon state sovereignty. Preservation of the States as independent and autonomous political entities is arguably less undermined by requiring them to make policy in certain fields than [by] "reduc[ing] [them] to puppets of a ventriloquist Congress." * * *

The Government also maintains that requiring state officers to perform discrete, ministerial tasks specified by Congress does not violate the principle of *New York* because it does not diminish the accountability of state or federal officials. This argument fails even on its own terms. By forcing state governments to absorb the financial burden of implementing a federal regulatory program, Members of Congress can take credit for "solving" problems without having to ask their constituents to pay for the solutions with higher federal taxes. And even when the States are not forced to absorb the costs of implementing a federal program, they are still put in the position of taking the blame for its burdensomeness and for its defects. Under the present law, for example, it will be the CLEO and not some federal official who stands between the gun purchaser and immediate possession of his gun. And it will likely be the CLEO, not some federal official, who will be blamed for any error (even one in the designated federal database) that causes a purchaser to be mistakenly rejected.

[The] Brady Act, the dissent asserts, is different [from] *New York* because the former is addressed to individuals—namely CLEOs—while the latter were directed to the State itself. That is certainly a difference, but it cannot be a constitutionally significant one. While the Brady Act is directed to "individuals," it is directed to them in their official capacities as state officers; it controls their actions, not as private citizens, but as the agents of the State. * * *

Finally, the Government puts forward a cluster of arguments that can be grouped under the heading: "The Brady Act serves very important purposes, is most efficiently administered by CLEOs during the interim period, and places a minimal and only temporary burden upon state officers." * * * Assuming all the mentioned factors were true, they might be relevant if we were evaluating whether the incidental application to the States of a federal law of general applicability excessively interfered with the functioning of state governments. See, e.g., *Fry; Usery.* But where, as here, it is the whole object of the law to direct the functioning of the state executive, and hence to compromise the structural framework of dual sovereignty, such a "balancing" analysis is inappropriate.[17]

---

17. The dissent observes that "Congress could require private persons, such as hospital executives or school administrators, to provide arms merchants with relevant information about a prospective purchaser's fitness to own a weapon," and that "the burden on police officers [imposed by the Brady Act] would be permissible if a similar burden were also imposed on private parties with access to relevant data." That is undoubtedly true, but it does not advance the dissent's case. The Brady Act does not merely require CLEOs to report information in their private possession. It requires them to provide information that belongs to the State and is available to them only in their official capacity; and to conduct investigations in their official capacity, by examining databases and records that only state officials have access to. In other words, the suggestion that extension of this statute to private citizens

[We] conclude categorically, as we concluded categorically in *New York*: "The Federal Government may not compel the States to enact or administer a federal regulatory program." * * *

JUSTICE O'CONNOR, concurring.

[T]he Court appropriately refrains from deciding [whether] purely ministerial reporting requirements imposed by Congress on state and local authorities pursuant to its Commerce Clause powers are similarly invalid. See, e.g., 42 U.S.C. § 5779(a) (requiring state and local law enforcement agencies to report cases of missing children to the Department of Justice).[a] The provisions invalidated here, however, which directly compel state officials to administer a federal regulatory program, utterly fail to adhere to the design and structure of our constitutional scheme.[b]

JUSTICE STEVENS, with whom JUSTICE SOUTER, JUSTICE GINSBURG, and JUSTICE BREYER join, dissenting. * * *

These cases do not implicate the more difficult questions associated with congressional coercion of state legislatures addressed in *New York*. Nor need we consider the wisdom of relying on local officials rather than federal agents to carry out aspects of a federal program, or even the question whether such officials may be required to perform a federal function on a permanent basis. The question is whether Congress, acting on behalf of the people of the entire Nation, may require local law enforcement officers to perform certain duties during the interim needed for the development of a federal gun control program. * * *

Indeed, since the ultimate issue is one of power, we must consider its implications in times of national emergency. Matters such as the enlistment of air raid wardens, the administration of a military draft, the mass inoculation of children to forestall an epidemic, or perhaps the threat of an international terrorist, may require a national response before federal personnel can be made available to respond. If the Constitution empowers Congress and the President to make an appropriate response, is there anything in the Tenth Amendment, "in historical understanding and practice, in the structure of the Constitution, [or] in the jurisprudence of this Court," that forbids the enlistment of state officers to make that response effective? More narrowly, what basis is there in any of those sources for concluding that it is the Members of this Court, rather than the elected representatives of the people, who should determine whether the Constitution contains the unwritten rule that the Court announces today? * * *

Unlike the First Amendment, which prohibits the enactment of a category of laws that would otherwise be authorized by Article I, the Tenth Amendment [confirms] the principle that the powers of the Federal Government are limited to those affirmatively granted by the Constitution, but it does not purport to limit the scope or the effectiveness of the exercise of powers that are delegated to Congress. Thus, the Amendment provides no support for a rule that immunizes local officials from obligations that might be imposed on ordinary citizens.[2] * * *

would eliminate the constitutional problem posits the impossible.

a. The Court commented that "federal statutes [which] require only the provision of information to the Federal Government, do not involve the precise issue before us [here]."

b. The concurring opinion of Thomas, J., who joined the Court's opinion, is omitted.

2. Recognizing the force of the argument, the Court suggests that this reasoning is in error because—even if it is responsive to the submission that the Tenth Amendment roots the principle set forth by the majority today—it does not answer the possibility that the Court's holding can be rooted in a "principle of state sovereignty" mentioned nowhere in the constitutional text. As a ground for invalidat-

There is not a clause, sentence, or paragraph in the entire text of the Constitution of the United States that supports the proposition that a local police officer can ignore a command contained in a statute enacted by Congress pursuant to an express delegation of power enumerated in Article I. * * *

Recent developments demonstrate that the political safeguards protecting Our Federalism are effective. The majority expresses special concern that were its rule not adopted the Federal Government would be able to avail itself of the services of state government officials "at no cost to itself." But this specific problem of federal actions that have the effect of imposing so-called "unfunded mandates" on the States has been identified and meaningfully addressed by Congress in recent legislation.[18] * * *

Perversely, the majority's rule seems more likely to damage than to preserve the safeguards against tyranny provided by the existence of vital state governments. By limiting the ability of the Federal Government to enlist state officials in the implementation of its programs, the Court creates incentives for the National Government to aggrandize itself. In the name of State's rights, the majority would have the Federal Government create vast national bureaucracies to implement its policies.[c]

JUSTICE BREYER, with whom JUSTICE STEVENS joins, dissenting.

[T]he United States is not the only nation that seeks to reconcile the practical need for a central authority with the democratic virtues of more local control. At least some other countries, facing the same basic problem, have found that local control is better maintained through application of a principle that is the direct opposite of the principle the majority derives from the silence of our Constitution. The federal systems of Switzerland, Germany, and the European Union, for example, all provide that constituent states, not federal bureaucracies, will themselves implement many of the laws, rules, regulations, or decrees enacted by the central "federal" body. * * *

Of course, we are interpreting our own Constitution, [but] their experience may nonetheless cast an empirical light on the consequences of different solutions to a common legal problem. * * *

ing important federal legislation, this argument is remarkably weak. The majority's further claim that, while the Brady Act may be legislation "necessary" to Congress' execution of its undisputed Commerce Clause authority to regulate firearms sales, it is nevertheless not "proper" because it violates state sovereignty, is wholly circular and provides no traction for its argument. [Our] ruling in *New York* that the Commerce Clause does not provide Congress the authority to require States to enact legislation—a power that affects States far closer to the core of their sovereign authority— does nothing to support the majority's unwarranted extension of that reasoning today.

18. The majority also makes the more general claim that requiring state officials to carry out federal policy causes states to "tak[e] the blame" for failed programs. The Court cites no empirical authority to support the proposition. [This] concern is vastly overstated. Unlike state legislators, local government executive officials routinely take action in response to a variety of sources of authority: local ordinance,

state law, and federal law. It doubtless may therefore require some sophistication to discern under which authority an executive official is acting, just as it may not always be immediately obvious what legal source of authority underlies a judicial decision. [But] the majority's rule neither creates nor alters this basic truth. The problem is of little real consequence in any event, because to the extent that a particular action proves politically unpopular, we may be confident that elected officials charged with implementing it will be quite clear to their constituents where the source of the misfortune lies. These cases demonstrate the point. Sheriffs Printz and Mack have made public statements, including their decisions to serve as plaintiffs in these actions, denouncing the Brady Act.

c. Souter, J.'s separate dissent, noting that "in deciding these cases, which I have found closer than I had anticipated, it is *The Federalist* that finally determines my position," is omitted.

RENO v. CONDON, ___ U.S.___, 120 S.Ct. 666, 145 L.Ed.2d 587 (2000), per REHNQUIST, C.J., sustained Congress' power under the commerce clause to pass the Driver's Privacy Protection Act, which bars state motor vehicle departments from disclosing (or selling) personal information (such as name, address, telephone number, vehicle description, Social Security number, medical information, and photograph) required for a driver's license or car registration: "The motor vehicle information which the States have historically sold is used by insurers, manufacturers, direct marketers, and others engaged in interstate commerce [and] is also used in the stream of interstate commerce by various public and private entities for matters related to interstate motoring. Because drivers' information is, in this context, an article of commerce, its sale or release into the interstate stream of business is sufficient to support congressional regulation. * * *

"We agree [that] the DPPA's provisions will require time and effort on the part of state employees, but reject the State's argument that the DPPA violates the principles laid down in either *New York* or *Printz*. * * * Such 'commandeering' [is] an inevitable consequence of regulating a state activity. [That] a State wishing to engage in certain activity must take administrative and sometimes legislative action to comply with federal standards regulating that activity is a commonplace that presents no constitutional defect.

"Like the statute at issue in [*South Carolina v. Baker*, which 'prohibited States from issuing unregistered bonds'], the DPPA does not require the States in their sovereign capacity to regulate their own citizens. The DPPA regulates the States as the owners of databases. It does not require the South Carolina Legislature to enact any laws or regulations, and it does not require state officials to assist in the enforcement of federal statutes regulating private individuals. We accordingly conclude that the DPPA is consistent with the constitutional principles enunciated in *New York* and *Printz*."

Nor does the DPPA "regulate the States exclusively. [It] regulates the universe of entities that participate as suppliers to the market for motor vehicle information–the States as initial suppliers of the information in interstate commerce and private resellers or redisclosers of that information in commerce."

DISTRIBUTION OF FEDERAL POWERS: SEPARATION OF POWERS

PRESIDENTIAL ACTION AFFECTING "CONGRESSIONAL" POWERS

CON LAW: P. 178, at the end of note 2(b)

AMER CON: P. 146, at the end of note 2(b)

Cf. *Minnesota v. Mille Lacs Band of Chippewa Indians*, 526 U.S. 172, 119 S.Ct. 1187, 143 L.Ed.2d 270 (1999) (finding no valid source of authority for an 1850 executive order purporting to require the removal of Chippewa Indians from lands ceded to the United States by an 1837 treaty).

CON LAW: P. 181, after note 6

AMER CON: P. 149, after note 6

7. *Line item veto.* Congress dramatically overhauled the structure established by the Congressional Budget and Impoundment Control Act by enacting the Line Item Veto Act of 1996, which delegated to the President substantially unrestricted authority to "cancel" certain spending and tax benefit measures after he has signed them into law. But the Court held the Line Item Veto Act unconstitutional in *Clinton v. New York*, 524 U.S. 417, 118 S.Ct. 2091, 141 L.Ed.2d 393 (1998), which appears below as a principal case.

CONGRESSIONAL ACTION AFFECTING "PRESIDENTIAL" POWERS

DELEGATION OF RULEMAKING POWER

CON LAW: P. 182, at end of note 1

Compare *Loving v. United States*, 517 U.S. 748, 116 S.Ct. 1737, 135 L.Ed.2d 36 (1996). The Court, per Kennedy, J., held unanimously, on the assumption that its death penalty jurisprudence applied to courts-martial, that it was constitutionally permissible for Congress to delegate to the President responsibility for prescribing aggravating factors warranting capital sentences. Because the assigned duties were "interlinked" with the President's constitutional powers as commander in chief, Congress, which had already defined the underlying capital offense, was not required to supply the President with "further guidance" concerning aggravating factors.[a]

a. Scalia, J., joined by O'Connor, J., concurring in part and concurring in the judgment, declined to join a part of the majority opinion treating English history as a source of relevant separation-of-powers principles in this case. Thomas, J., concurred in the judgment only.

19

CON LAW: P. 189, after note 5
AMER CON: P. 155, after note 5

THE LINE ITEM VETO

CLINTON v. NEW YORK

524 U.S. 417, 118 S.Ct. 2091, 141 L.Ed.2d 393 (1998).

JUSTICE STEVENS delivered the opinion of the Court.

[The Line Item Veto Act, which took effect on January 1, 1997, gives the President the power to "cancel in whole" three types of provisions that have been enacted by Congress and signed into law: "(1) any dollar amount of discretionary budget authority; (2) any item of new direct spending; or (3) any limited tax benefit." After a suit by members of Congress challenging the constitutionality of the Act was dismissed for lack of standing in *Raines v. Byrd*, p. 233 of this Supplement, the President exercised his "line item veto" to nullify the two provisions involved in this case: a section of the Balanced Budget Act of 1997 that waived the federal government's statutory authority to seek recoupment of as much as $2.6 billion in taxes that the State of New York had levied against Medicare providers, and a section of the Taxpayers Relief Act of 1997, which authorized favorable tax treatment of certain parties selling food processing facilities to farmers' cooperatives.]

It is undisputed that the New York case involves an "item of new direct spending" and that the [other] involves a "limited tax benefit" as those terms are defined in the Act. It is also undisputed that each of those provisions had been signed into law pursuant to Article I, § 7, of the Constitution before it was canceled.

The Act requires the President to adhere to precise procedures whenever he exercises his cancellation authority. [He] must [also] determine, with respect to each cancellation, that it will "(i) reduce the Federal budget deficit; (ii) not impair any essential Government functions; and (iii) not harm the national interest." Moreover, he must transmit a special message to Congress notifying it of each cancellation within five calendar days.

A cancellation takes effect upon receipt by Congress of the special message from the President. If, however, a "disapproval bill" pertaining to a special message is enacted into law, the cancellations set forth in that message become "null and void." The Act sets forth a detailed expedited procedure for the consideration of a "disapproval bill," but no such bill was passed for [the] cancellations involved in these cases. A majority vote of both Houses is sufficient to enact a disapproval bill. The Act does not grant the President the authority to cancel a disapproval bill, but he does, of course, retain his constitutional authority to veto such a bill.

With respect to both an item of new direct spending and a limited tax benefit, the cancellation prevents the item "from having legal force or effect."

[There] are important differences between the President's "return" of a bill pursuant to Article I, § 7, and the exercise of the President's cancellation authority pursuant to the Line Item Veto Act. The constitutional return takes place before the bill becomes law; the statutory cancellation occurs after the bill becomes law. The constitutional return is of the entire bill; the statutory cancellation is of only a part. Although the Constitution expressly authorizes the President to play a role in the process of enacting statutes, it is silent on the subject of unilateral Presidential action that either repeals or amends parts of duly enacted statutes.

There are powerful reasons for construing constitutional silence on this profoundly important issue as equivalent to an express prohibition. The procedures governing the enactment of statutes set forth in [Article] I were the product of the great debates and compromises that produced the Constitution itself. [Our] first President understood the text of the Presentment Clause as requiring that he either "approve all the parts of a Bill, or reject it in toto." What has emerged in these cases from the President's exercise of his statutory cancellation powers, however, are truncated versions of two bills that passed both Houses of Congress. They are not the product of the "finely wrought" procedure that the Framers designed.

[Relying] primarily on *Field v. Clark* [CON LAW p. 178; AMER CON p. 146], the Government contends that the cancellations were [not repeals or vetoes in the constitutional sense, but] merely exercises of discretionary authority granted to the President by the Balanced Budget Act and the Taxpayer Relief Act read in light of the previously enacted Line Item Veto Act. [In] *Field*, the Court upheld the constitutionality of the Tariff Act of 1890. That statute contained a "free list" of almost 300 specific articles that were exempted from import duties[, but] directed the President to suspend [the] exemption for sugar, molasses, coffee, tea, and hides "whenever, and so often" as he [determined] that any country producing and exporting those products imposed duties on the agricultural products of the United States that he deemed to be "reciprocally unequal and unreasonable * * *."

[But there are] three critical differences between the power to suspend the exemption from import duties and the power to cancel portions of a duly enacted statute. First, the exercise of the suspension power was contingent upon a condition that did not exist when the Tariff Act was passed: the imposition of "reciprocally unequal and unreasonable" import duties by other countries. In contrast, the exercise of the cancellation power within five days after the enactment of the Balanced Budget and Tax Reform Acts necessarily was based on the same conditions that Congress evaluated when it passed those statutes. Second, under the Tariff Act, when the President determined that the contingency had arisen, he had a duty to suspend; in contrast, [the Line Item Veto Act] did not qualify his discretion to cancel or not to cancel. Finally, whenever the President suspended an exemption under the Tariff Act, he was executing the policy that Congress had embodied in the statute. In contrast, whenever the President cancels an item of new direct spending or a limited tax benefit he is rejecting the policy judgment made by Congress and relying on his own policy judgment.

The Government's reliance upon other tariff and import statutes [that] contain provisions similar to the one challenged in *Field* is unavailing for the same reasons. [In addition, the] cited statutes all relate to foreign trade, and this Court has recognized that in the foreign affairs arena, the President has "a degree of discretion and freedom from statutory restriction which would not be admissible were domestic affairs alone involved." More important, when enacting the statutes discussed in *Field*, Congress itself made the decision to suspend or repeal the particular provisions at issue upon the occurrence of particular events subsequent to enactment, and it left only the determination of whether such events occurred up to the President. The Line Item Veto Act authorizes the President himself to effect the repeal of laws, for his own policy reasons, without observing the procedures set out in Article I, § 7. The fact that Congress intended such a result is of no moment. Although Congress presumably anticipated that the President might cancel some of the items in the Balanced Budget Act and in the Taxpayer Relief Act, Congress cannot alter the procedures set out in Article I, § 7, without amending the Constitution.[40]

Neither are we persuaded by the Government's contention that the President's authority to cancel new direct spending and tax benefit items is no greater than his traditional authority to decline to spend appropriated funds. [The] critical difference between this statute and all of its predecessors [is] that unlike any of them, this Act gives the President the unilateral power to change the text of duly enacted statutes.

[Because] we conclude that the Act's cancellation provisions violate Article I, § 7, [we] find it unnecessary to consider [whether] the Act [impermissibly delegates lawmaking authority to the President].

JUSTICE KENNEDY, concurring.

[To] say the political branches have a somewhat free hand to reallocate their own authority would seem to require acceptance of two premises: first, that the public good demands it, and second, that liberty is not at risk. The former premise is inadmissible. The Constitution's structure requires a stability which transcends the convenience of the moment. The latter premise, too, is flawed. Liberty is always at stake when one or more of the branches seek to transgress the separation of powers. Separation of powers was designed to implement a fundamental insight: concentration of power in the hands of a single branch is a threat to liberty. [If] a citizen who is taxed has the measure of the tax or the decision to spend determined by the Executive alone, without adequate control by the citizen's Representatives in Congress, liberty is threatened.

JUSTICE BREYER, with whom JUSTICE O'CONNOR and JUSTICE SCALIA join as to Part III, dissenting.

III. [When] the President "canceled" the two appropriation measures now before us, he did not repeal any law nor did he amend any law. He simply followed the law, leaving the statutes, as they are literally written, intact.

To understand why one cannot say, literally speaking, that the President has repealed or amended any law, imagine how the provisions of law before us might have been, but were not, written. Imagine that the canceled New York health care tax provision at issue here [had said]:

Section One. Taxes [that] were collected by the State of New York from a health care provider before June 1, 1997 and for which a waiver of provisions [requiring payment] have been sought [are] deemed to be permissible health care related taxes [provided] however that the President may prevent the just-mentioned provision from having legal force or effect if he determines x, y and z.

---

40. The Government argues that the Rules Enabling Act, 28 U.S.C. § 2072(b), permits this Court to "repeal" prior laws without violating Article I, § 7. Section 2072(b) provides that this Court may promulgate rules of procedure for the lower federal courts and that "all laws in conflict with such rules shall be of no further force or effect after such rules have taken effect." See *Sibbach v. Wilson & Co.*, [CON LAW p. 184 n.19; AMER CON p. 150 n.19] (stating that the procedural rules that this Court promulgates, "if they are within the authority granted by Congress, repeal" a prior inconsistent procedural statute). In enacting § 2072(b), however, Congress expressly provided that laws inconsistent with the procedural rules promulgated by this Court would automatically be repealed upon the enactment of new rules in order to create a uniform system of rules for Article III courts. As in the tariff statutes, Congress itself made the decision to repeal prior rules upon the occurrence of a particular event—here, the promulgation of procedural rules by this Court.

(Assume x, y and z to be the same determinations required by the Line Item Veto Act).

Whatever a person might say, or think, about the constitutionality of this imaginary law, [one] could not say that a President who "prevents" the deeming language from "having legal force or effect" has either repealed or amended this particular hypothetical statute. Rather, the President has exercised the power it explicitly delegates to him. He has executed the law, not repealed it.

It could make no significant difference to this linguistic point were the italicized proviso to appear, not as part of what I have called Section One, but, instead, at the bottom of the statute page, say referenced by an asterisk, with a statement that it applies to every spending provision in the act next to which a similar asterisk appears. And that being so, it could make no difference if that proviso appeared, instead, in a different, earlier-enacted law, along with legal language that makes it applicable to every future spending provision picked out according to a specified formula. But, of course, this last-mentioned possibility is this very case.

[Because] one cannot say that the President's exercise of the power the Act grants is, literally speaking, a "repeal" or "amendment," the fact that the Act's procedures differ from the Constitution's exclusive procedures for enacting (or repealing) legislation is beside the point. The Act itself was enacted in accordance with these procedures, and its failure to require the President to satisfy those procedures does not make the Act unconstitutional.

IV. Because I disagree with the Court's holding of literal violation, I must consider whether the Act nonetheless violates Separation of Powers principles.

[One] cannot say that the Act "encroaches" upon Congress' power, when Congress retained the power to insert, by simple majority, into any future appropriations bill, into any section of any such bill, or into any phrase of any section, a provision that says the Act will not apply.

[Nor] can one say the Act's grant of power "aggrandizes" the Presidential office. The grant is limited to the context of the budget. It is limited to the power to spend, or not to spend, particular appropriated items, and the power to permit, or not to permit, specific limited exemptions from generally applicable tax law from taking effect.

[The] "nondelegation" doctrine [raises] a more serious constitutional obstacle here. [The] Constitution permits only those delegations where Congress "shall lay down by legislative act an intelligible principle to which the person or body authorized to [act] is directed to conform." [The standards in the Act] are broad. But this Court has upheld standards that are equally broad, or broader. See, e.g., *National Broadcasting Co. v. United States*, 319 U.S. 190, 63 S.Ct. 997, 87 L.Ed. 1344 (1943) (upholding delegation to Federal Communications Commission to regulate broadcast licensing as "public interest, convenience, or necessity" require).

[Like] statutes delegating power to award broadcast television licenses, [the] Act is aimed at a discrete problem: namely, a particular set of expenditures within the federal budget. [Second], like the award of television licenses, the particular problem involved—determining whether or not a particular amount of money should be spent or whether a particular dispensation from tax law should be granted a few individuals—does not readily lend itself to a significantly more specific standard. [Third], in insofar as monetary expenditure (but not "tax expenditure") is at issue, the President acts in an area where history helps to justify the discretionary power that Congress has delegated. [Congress] has frequently delegated the President the authority to spend, or not to spend, particular sums of money.

[The] "limited tax benefit" question [is] more difficult. [But this] Court has upheld tax statutes [involving tariffs] that delegate to the President the power to change taxes under very broad standards. [These] statutory delegations [have often involved] a duty on imports, which is a tax [that] in the last century was as important then as the income tax is now, for it provided most of the Federal Government's revenues.

[I] recognize that the Act before us is novel. [But the] Constitution, in my view, authorizes Congress and the President to try novel methods in this way.

JUSTICE SCALIA, with whom JUSTICE O'CONNOR joins, and with whom JUSTICE BREYER joins as to Part III, concurring in part and dissenting in part.

III. [Although the Court should rule that there is no party before it with standing to challenge the President's authority to cancel a "limited tax benefit,"] I agree [that] the New York appellees have standing to challenge the President's cancellation of [an] "item of new direct spending."

Article I, § 7 of the Constitution obviously prevents the President from canceling a law that Congress has not authorized him to cancel. But that is not this case. [Article I, § 7] no more categorically prohibits the Executive reduction of congressional dispositions in the course of implementing statutes that authorize such reduction, than it categorically prohibits the Executive augmentation of congressional dispositions in the course of implementing statutes that authorize such augmentation—generally known as substantive rulemaking.

[I] turn, then, to [whether] Congress's authorizing the President to cancel an item of spending [violates the non-delegation doctrine by giving] him a power that our history and traditions show must reside exclusively in the Legislative Branch. [Insofar] as the degree of political, "law-making" power conferred upon the Executive is concerned, there is not a dime's worth of difference between Congress's authorizing the President to cancel a spending item, and Congress's authorizing money to be spent on a particular item at the President's discretion. And the latter has been done since the Founding of the Nation. From 1789–1791, the First Congress made lump-sum appropriations for the entire Government— "sums not exceeding" specified amounts for broad purposes. From a very early date Congress also made permissive individual appropriations, leaving the decision whether to spend the money to the President's unfettered discretion.

[The] short of the matter is this: Had the Line Item Veto Act authorized the President to "decline to spend" any item of spending contained in the Balanced Budget Act of 1997, there is not the slightest doubt that authorization would have been constitutional. The title of the Line Item Veto Act, which was perhaps designed to simplify for public comprehension, or perhaps merely to comply with the terms of a campaign pledge, has succeeded in faking out the Supreme Court. The President's action it authorizes in fact is not a line-item veto and thus does not offend Art. I, § 7; and insofar as the substance of that action is concerned, it is no different from what Congress has permitted the President to do since the formation of the Union.

CONTROL OVER APPOINTMENT AND
REMOVAL OF OFFICERS

CON LAW: P. 204, at the end of note 3

AMER CON: P. 166, at the end of note 2

(c) EDMOND v. UNITED STATES, 520 U.S. 651, 117 S.Ct. 1573, 137 L.Ed.2d 917 (1997), upheld the authority of the Secretary of Transportation to appoint civilian members of the Coast Guard Court of Criminal Appeals, which hears appeals from courts martial. The Court, per SCALIA, J., reasoned that Coast Guard Court of Criminal Appeals judges were "inferior" officers, subject to appointment by heads of departments, because they were supervised by the Judge Advocate General, who could remove them without cause, and by the Court of Appeals for the Armed Forces, which has appellate jurisdiction over Coast Guard Court of Criminal Appeals judgments: "Generally speaking, the term 'inferior officer' connotes a relationship with some higher ranking officer or officers below the President: Whether one is an inferior officer depends upon whether he has a superior."

Is the rationale of *Edmond*, as advanced by Scalia, J., consistent with *Morrison v. Olson*, from which Scalia, J., dissented? Who is the independent counsel's "superior"?

EXECUTIVE PRIVILEGE AND IMMUNITY

CON LAW: P. 219, at the end of note 5

AMER CON: P. 175, at the end of note 5

CLINTON v. JONES, 520 U.S. 681, 117 S.Ct. 1636, 137 L.Ed.2d 945 (1997). Paula Jones, a former Arkansas state employee, filed a civil suit against President Bill Clinton, seeking damages for acts allegedly committed while Clinton was governor of Arkansas. More specifically, Jones alleged that then-Governor Clinton arranged for her to be brought to a suite in a hotel, where he had just addressed a conference for which Jones provided staff support, and made " 'abhorrent' sexual advances that she vehemently rejected." Claiming that defending the suit would interfere with his performance of the presidential office, Clinton sought to have the suit dismissed without prejudice, and the statute of limitations tolled, until the expiration of his term.

The Court, per STEVENS, J., unanimously rejected Clinton's claims and held that the suit could go forward, notwithstanding the holding of *Nixon v. Fitzgerald* that the President is absolutely immune from suits for civil damages based on official Presidential acts. "[Clinton's] principal submission—that 'in all but the most exceptional cases,' the Constitution affords the President temporary immunity from civil damages litigation arising out of events that occurred before he took office—cannot be sustained. [The] principal rationale for affording certain public servants immunity from suits for money damages arising out of their official acts" is to "enabl[e] such officials to perform their designated functions effectively without fear that a particular decision may give rise to personal liability. [This] reasoning provides no support for an immunity for unofficial conduct [including conduct occurring before Clinton became President].

"Petitioner's strongest argument * * * relies on separation of powers principles. [He] contends that this particular case—as well as the potential additional litigation that [it] may spawn—may impose an unacceptable burden on the

President's time and energy, and thereby impair the effective performance of his office. [But this] predictive judgment finds little support in either history or the relatively narrow compass of the issues raised in this particular case. [In] the more than 200 year history of the Republic, only three sitting Presidents have been subjected to suits for their private actions. [It therefore] seems unlikely that a deluge of such litigation will ever engulf the Presidency. As for the case at hand, if properly managed by the District Court, it appears to us highly unlikely to occupy any substantial amount of petitioner's time.

"[Of] greater significance, petitioner errs by presuming that interactions between the Judicial Branch and the Executive, even quite burdensome interactions, necessarily rise to the level of constitutionally forbidden impairment of the Executive's ability to perform its constitutionally mandated functions. [We] have long held that when the President takes official action, the Court has the authority to determine whether he has acted within the law. [E.g., *Youngstown.*] [If] the Judiciary may severely burden the Executive Branch by reviewing the legality of the President's official conduct, and if it may direct appropriate process to the President himself [e.g., United States v. Nixon], it must follow that the federal courts have power to determine the legality of his unofficial conduct."

Having found that Clinton lacked any constitutional immunity from Jones' suit, the Court went on to consider whether "a stay of either trial or discovery might be justified [in the discretion of the District Court] by considerations that do not require the recognition of any constitutional immunity. The District Court has broad discretion to stay proceedings as an incident to its power to control its own docket [and] potential burdens on the President [are] appropriate matters for the District Court to evaluate in its management of the case. The high respect that is owed to the Office of the Chief Executive [is] a matter that should inform the conduct of the entire proceeding, including the timing and scope of discovery."

Nonetheless, "the proponent of a stay bears the burden of establishing its need." And so far there was "nothing in the record to enable a judge to assess the potential harm that may ensue from scheduling the trial promptly after discovery is concluded."

Breyer, J., concurred in the judgment only. He agreed "that the Constitution does not automatically grant the President an immunity from civil lawsuits based upon his private conduct." But "once the President sets forth and explains a conflict between judicial proceeding and public duties, [the] Constitution permits a judge to schedule a trial in an ordinary civil damages action [only] within the constraints of a constitutional principle—a principle that forbids a federal judge in such a case to interfere with the President's discharge of his public duties." Breyer, J., was less "sanguine" than the majority that permitting suits against sitting Presidents would not lead to a proliferation of such actions and the threat of significant impositions on the President's time. He therefore thought that "ordinary case-management principles are unlikely to prove sufficient" and would make clear that the Constitution does "not grant a single judge more than a very limited power to second guess a President's reasonable determination (announced in open court) of his scheduling needs, nor could [the Constitution] permit the issuance of a trial scheduling order that would significantly interfere with the President's discharge of his duties."

STATE POWER TO REGULATE

CASES AND DOCTRINE

CON LAW: P. 244, at the end of note 3

AMER CON: P. 190, at the end of note 3

CAMPS NEWFOUND/OWATONNA, INC. v. TOWN OF HARRISON, 520 U.S. 564, 117 S.Ct. 1590, 137 L.Ed.2d 852 (1997), held that a Maine statute providing a general property tax exemption for charitable institutions, but withholding the exemption from charitable institutions operated principally for the benefit of non-residents, violates the Commerce Clause. The tax was challenged by the operators of a summer camp for children of the Christian Science faith, about 95% of whose campers are not Maine residents. Dividing 5–4, the Court, per STEVENS, J., viewed the tax as facially discriminatory against interstate commerce. The camp was selling a product that included "in part the natural beauty of Maine itself"; the statute created a financial incentive for the camp and other charitable institutions to prefer state residents over out-of-staters. Reasoning that the statute would be virtually per se illegal as applied to for-profit activities, Stevens, J., saw no reason to make an exception for not-for-profit organizations.

The majority rejected the argument that the "discriminatory tax exemption [at issue] is, in economic reality, no different from a discriminatory subsidy of those charities that cater principally to local needs" and should therefore be upheld. "Assuming, arguendo, that [a] direct subsidy benefitting only those nonprofits serving principally Maine residents would be permissible, our cases do not sanction a tax exemption serving similar ends. [E.g., *New Energy Co. of Indiana v. Limbach*.]"

SCALIA, J., joined by Rehnquist, C.J., and Thomas and Ginsburg, JJ., dissented. "[T]he provision at issue here is [narrowly] designed [to] compensate or subsidize those organizations that contribute to the public fisc by dispensing public benefits the state might otherwise provide." So understood, the statute did not facially discriminate against interstate commerce; any effect on interstate commerce was "indirect." In any event, the selective exemption was "supported by such traditional and important state interests that it survives scrutiny [even] under the 'virtually per se rule of invalidity.'" Alternatively, the state interests would support recognition of a " 'domestic charity' exception [to] the negative Commerce Clause."

THOMAS, J., joined by Scalia, J., and in part by Rehnquist, C.J., argued in a separate dissent that the Court should "abandon" its negative Commerce Clause jurisprudence. He suggested that the Court had developed its doctrine partly in response to the perception that it was "necessary to check [discriminatory] state measures contrary to the perceived spirit, if not the actual letter, of the Constitution." Rather than continuing with "policy-laden decisionmaking" that is unsupported by the constitutional text, the Court should consider whether there is not a textual prohibition against certain forms of discriminatory taxation in the Import–

Export Clause, Art. I, § 10, cl. 2, which provides that "[n]o state shall, without the Consent of Congress, lay any Imposts or Duties on Imports or Exports." Although the Court found this provision applicable only to foreign trade in *Woodruff v. Parham*, 75 U.S. (8 Wall.) 123 (1869), Thomas, J., argued that *Woodruff* "was, in all likelihood, wrongly decided" and ought to be reconsidered. Because the Import–Export Clause would not plausibly forbid the property tax at issue, the constitutional challenge should be rejected.

————

Ohio imposes general sales and use taxes on natural gas purchases from all sellers, except regulated utilities that meet the state's definition of a "natural gas company." Does the differential treatment of sales by regulated utilities, all of which are in-state entities, and other "marketers," many from other states, violate the Commerce Clause? In GENERAL MOTORS CORP. v. TRACY, 519 U.S. 278, 117 S.Ct. 811, 136 L.Ed.2d 761 (1997), the Court, per SOUTER, J., held that it does not: regulated utilities and other sellers are sufficiently different to warrant different treatment; the former serve "captive" markets of small consumers that the latter cannot reach and are subject to a variety of regulatory obligations—including obligations to provide costly services—that the latter are not. Even insofar as regulated gas companies and unregulated "marketers" compete for the same, non-captive customers (such as large corporations), "a number of reasons support a decision to give greater weight to the captive market and the local utilities' singular role in serving it" and thus to treat the disparity of tax treatment as constitutionally permissible. "First and most important, we must recognize an obligation to proceed cautiously lest we imperil the delivery by regulated [gas companies] of [gas and services] to the noncompetitive captive market. Second, as a court we lack the expertness and the institutional resources necessary to predict the effects of judicial intervention invalidating Ohio's tax scheme on the utilities' capacity to serve this captive market."

STEVENS, J., dissenting, would have upheld the challenged tax scheme as applied to sales of "bundled" gas and services in non-competitive, captive markets but not as applied to the competitive market for sales of "unbundled" gas to large customers.

INTERSTATE PRIVILEGES AND IMMUNITIES CLAUSE

CON LAW: P. 279, after note 2

AMER CON: P. 212, after note 2

In LUNDING v. NEW YORK STATE TAX APPEALS TRIBUNAL, 522 U.S. 287, 118 S.Ct. 766, 139 L.Ed.2d 717 (1998), the Court invalidated a New York statute that effectively denied non-resident taxpayers a state income tax deduction for alimony payments that was available to resident taxpayers. The 6–3 majority, per O'CONNOR, J., found that the state had advanced no justification for the disparate treatment adequate to satisfy the applicable standard, which it stated as follows: "[W]hen confronted with a challenge under the Privileges and Immunities Clause to a law distinguishing between residents and nonresidents, a State may defend its position by demonstrating that '(i) there is a substantial reason for the difference in treatment; and (ii) the discrimination practiced against nonresidents bears a substantial relationship to the State's objective.'" Ginsburg, J., joined by Rehnquist, C.J., and Kennedy, J., dissented.

THE EFFECT OF FEDERAL REGULATION: PREEMPTION

CON LAW: P. 285, at the end of note 2

When a federal statute establishing safety standards includes a provision expressly preserving "common law" remedies, and thereby negatives a possible inference of "express" pre-emption, should a defendant have to bear a "special burden" in order to establish that a state tort standard nonetheless impliedly conflicts with the objectives of the federal statute or its implementing regulations? Rejecting a dissenting argument to this effect, the Court, per BREYER, J., applied "ordinary" standards and upheld an implied pre-emption claim under the National Traffic and Motor Vehicle Safety Act in GEIER v. HONDA MOTOR CO., ___ U.S. ___, 120 S.Ct. 1913, ___ L.Ed.2d ___ (2000). According to the majority, the purpose of a 1984 federal implementing rule was to encourage automobile manufacturers to experiment with a variety of passive restraint devices; a state tort action asserting that it was negligent not to equip a vehicle with airbags in the 1987 model year would be in conflict with this objective. Stevens, J., joined by Souter, Thomas, and Ginsburg, JJ., dissented.

CON LAW: P. 286, at end of note 5

The Court again divided about the scope of an express preemption clause in MEDTRONIC, INC. v. LOHR, 518 U.S. 470, 116 S.Ct. 2240, 135 L.Ed.2d 700 (1996). A section of the Medical Device Amendments of 1976 provides that no state may establish or maintain "any requirement" that "is different from, or in addition to," any requirement of the Federal Food, Drug, and Cosmetic Act. In an opinion by STEVENS, J.,[a] a five-member majority agreed that application of the preemption clause should be informed by "the assumption that the historic police powers of the States were not to be superseded by the Federal Act unless that was the clear and manifest purpose of Congress." Writing only for a plurality on this point, Justice Stevens further found that state common law liability rules would "rare[ly,]" if ever, be specific enough in their application to particular medical devices to count as preempted "requirements" within the meaning of the federal statute. BREYER, J., concurring, thought that common law rules would be preempted "requirements" in some cases, but agreed that the particular common law rules in issue—imposing liability for the design and sale of a faulty heart pacemaker—were not "different from, or in addition to" any sufficiently specific federal requirements for the preemption clause to be triggered. In reaching their conclusions, both Stevens and Breyer, JJ., gave substantial weight to the interpretations expressed in regulations promulgated by the federal Food and Drug Administration.

O'CONNOR, J., joined by Rehnquist, C.J., and Scalia and Thomas, JJ., argued in partial dissent that substantive state liability standards for negligent manufacture and failure to warn were preempted; agency regulations suggesting the contrary deserved no deference. O'Connor, J., agreed with the majority, however, that plaintiffs' defective design claims were not in addition to or different from any applicable federal regulations and that state liability rules establishing standards identical or parallel to applicable federal standards also escaped preemption.

---

a. The opinion of Stevens, J., was joined in its entirety by Kennedy, Souter, and Ginsburg, JJ., and in part by Breyer, J., who also concurred entirely in the judgment.

SUBSTANTIVE PROTECTION OF ECONOMIC INTERESTS

ORIGINS OF SUBSTANTIVE DUE PROCESS

CON LAW: P. 325, at end of note 3

AMER CON: P. 224 end of note 3

RTS & LIB: P. 56, at end of note 3

However, does the Court's reliance on the privileges and immunities clause of the fourteenth amendment in *Saenz v. Roe*, discussed at pp. 84, 214 of this Supplement, signal that this long-ignored provision may become a new source of protection for individual rights?

"TAKING" OF PROPERTY INTERESTS

"TAKING" THROUGH REGULATION

CON LAW: P. 362, after note 9 add new notes

AMER CON: P. 253, after note 8 add new notes

Violation of the Takings Clause vs. violations of due process. Consider Eastern Enterprises v. Apfel, 524 U.S. 498, 118 S. Ct. 2131, 141 L.Ed.2d 451 (1998): As a signatory to various coal wage agreements executed between 1947 and 1964, petitioner Eastern Enterprises (Eastern) made substantial contributions to funds providing health benefits to miners and their dependents. In 1965 Eastern ceased its coal mining operations (transferring these operations to a subsidiary). Thus, Eastern neither participated in negotiations nor agreed to make contributions in connection with benefit plans established under agreements made in the 1970s, agreements suggesting for the first time an industry commitment to the funding of lifetime health benefits for both retirees and their family members.[a]

The decline in coal production, the retirement of a generation of miners, and rapid acceleration in health care caused serious financial problems for the 1950 and 1974 Benefit Plans. As more coal operators abandoned the Benefit Plans, the remaining signatories were forced to absorb the increasing cost of covering retirees left behind by existing employers. Ultimately Congress passed the Coal Industry Retiree Health Benefit Act of 1992 (Coal Act), providing for benefits to retirees by merging the 1950 and 1974 Benefit Plans into a new fund (Combined Fund) financed by annual premiums assessed against "signatory coal operators," i.e., coal operators that signed any agreement requiring contributions to the 1950 or 1974 Benefit Plans. The Commissioner of Social Security assigned Eastern the

---

a. Although Eastern's subsidiary continued mining coal until 1987, according to the plurality opinion by O'Connor, J., "Eastern's liability under the Act bears no relationship to [the] ownership of [its subsidiary]; the Act assigns Eastern responsibility for benefits relating to miners that Eastern itself, not [its subsidiary], employed, while [the subsidiary] would be assigned the responsibility for any miners that it had employed."

obligation for Combined Fund premiums respecting some 1,000 retired miners who had worked for the company before 1966. Eastern responded by suing the Commissioner, as well as the Combined Fund, asserting that the Coal Act violated both substantive due process and the Takings clause.

Although a 5–4 majority struck down the Coal Act as applied to Eastern, the justices making up the majority disagreed over the basis for the Act's invalidation. O'CONNOR, J., joined by Rehnquist, C.J., and Scalia and Thomas JJ., concluded that forcing Eastern "to bear the expense of lifetime health benefits for miners based on [the company's] activities decades before those benefits were promised" violated the Takings Clause.[b] She recognized that prior decisions "make clear that Congress has considerable leeway to fashion economic legislation, including the power to affect contractual commitments between private parties," but maintained that the Court's decisions left open the possibility that legislation might violate the Takings Clause "if it imposes severe retroactive liability on a limited class of parties that could not have anticipated the liability, and the extent of that liability is substantially disproportionate to the parties' experience. [The] Coal Act's allocation scheme, as applied to Eastern, presents such a case." When, continued the plurality opinion, a legislative solution to a problem "singles out certain employers to bear a burden that is substantial in amount, based on the employers' conduct far in the past, and unrelated to any commitment that the employers made or to any injury they caused, the governmental action implicates fundamental principles of fairness underlying the Taking Clause."[c]

Concurring in the judgment and dissenting in part, KENNEDY, J., rejected the O'Connor plurality's Takings Clause analysis. He concluded that the Coal Act "must be invalidated as contrary to essential due process principles, without regard to the Takings Clause." The Clause does not apply, he maintained, because the challenged Act "regulates the former mine owner without regard to property. It does not operate upon or alter an identified property interest, and is not applicable to or measured by a property interest. [The] law simply imposes an obligation to perform an act, the payment of benefits. The statute is indifferent as to how the regulated entity elects to comply or the property it uses to do so. To the extent it affects property interests, it does so in a manner similar to many laws; but until today, none were thought to constitute takings."

"Although we have been hesitant to subject economic legislation to due process scrutiny as a general matter" observed Kennedy, J., "the Court has given careful consideration to due process challenges to legislation with retroactive effects. As today's plurality opinion notes, for centuries our law has harbored a singular distrust of retroactive statutes. [The] Court's due process jurisprudence reflects this distrust. [It] is no accident that the primary retroactivity precedents upon which today's plurality opinion relies in its takings analysis were grounded in due process."

b. At one point O'Connor, J., noted that the Constitution "expresses concern with retroactive laws through several of its provisions, including the Ex Post Facto and Takings Clauses." Although Thomas, J., joined O'Connor, J.'s opinion in full, he wrote separately to emphasize that the Ex Post Facto Clause even more clearly than the Takings Clause "reflects the principle that 'retrospective laws are, indeed, generally unjust.'" Although the Court had long ago considered the Ex Post Facto clause to apply only in the criminal context, Justice Thomas expressed a willingness to re-consider these precedents in order to "determine whether a retroactive civil law that passes muster under our current Taking Clause jurisprudence is nevertheless unconstitutional under the Ex Post Facto Clause."

c. Because of its determination that the Coal Act's allocation scheme violates the Takings Clause as applied to Eastern, the plurality saw no need to address Eastern's due process claim. It noted, however, that "this Court has expressed concerns about using the Due Process clause to invalidate economic legislation."

Kennedy, J., acknowledged that the Court had upheld the imposition of liability on former employers based on past employment relationships, but "the statutes at issue were remedial, designed to impose an 'actual measurable cost of [the employer's] business' which the employer had been able to avoid in the past. *Usery v. Turner Elkhorn Mining Co.* [The] Coal Act, however, does not serve this purpose. Eastern was once in the coal business and employed many of the beneficiaries, but it was not responsible for their expectation of lifetime health benefits or for the perilous financial condition of the 1950 and 1974 Plans which put the benefits in jeopardy. [This] case is far outside the bounds of retroactivity permissible under our law."

When one takes into account Breyer, J.'s dissenting opinion, Kennedy, J.'s view of the appropriate constitutional provision in a case such as this commands a majority of the Court. Although BREYER, J., joined by Stevens, Souter and Ginsburg, JJ., thought the Coal Act constitutional, "as a preliminary matter" he agreed with Justice Kennedy that "the plurality views this case through the wrong legal lens." The Takings Clause does not apply, maintained Breyer, because "[t]he 'private property' upon which the Clause traditionally has focused is a specific interest in physical or intellectual property." However, the instant case involves not such an interest "but an ordinary liability to pay money, and not to the government, but to third parties."

"Insofar as the plurality avoids reliance upon the Due Process Clause for fear of resurrecting *Lochner* and related doctrines of 'substantive due process,'" continued Breyer, J., "that fear is misplaced. [To] find that the Due process Clause protects against this kind of fundamental unfairness—that it protects against an unfair allocation of public burdens through this kind of specially arbitrary retroactive means—is to read the Clause in light of a basic purpose: the fair application of law. [It] is not to resurrect long-discredited substantive notions of 'freedom of contract.'"

However, Breyer, J., did *not* consider it "fundamentally unfair to require Eastern to make future payments for health care costs of retired miners and their families, on the basis of Eastern's past association with these miners." For one thing the liability imposed upon Eastern "extends only to miners whom Eastern itself employed." Moreover, "the record shows that pre–1965 statements and other conduct led management to understand, and labor legitimately to expect, that health care benefits for retirees and their dependents would continue to be provided." Finally, "Eastern continued to obtain profits from the coal mining industry long after 1965, for it operated a wholly-owned coal-mining subsidiary [until] the late 1980s."[d]

Is interest earned in client funds that is paid to foundations financing legal services for low-income individuals the "private property" of the client for purposes of the Takings Clause? Texas, like 48 other states, has adopted an Interest on Lawyers Trust Account (IOLTA) program. Under these programs an attorney who receives client funds must place them in a separate, interest-bearing, federally authorized account upon determining that the funds could not reasonably be expected to earn interest for the client or that any interest which might be earned is unlikely to be sufficient to offset the cost of establishing and maintaining the account. IOLTA interest income is paid to foundations that finance legal services

---

d. In a separate dissent, Stevens, J., joined by Souter, Ginsburg and Breyer, JJ. emphasized that "there was an implicit understanding on both sides of the bargaining table that the operators would provide the miners with lifetime health benefits. It was this understanding that kept the mines in operation and enabled Eastern to earn handsome profits before it transferred its coal business to a wholly-owned subsidiary."

for low-income persons. In PHILLIPS v. WASHINGTON LEGAL FOUNDATION, 524 U.S. 156, 118 S.Ct. 1925, 141 L.Ed.2d 174 (1998), a 5–4 majority, per REHNQUIST, C.J., held that the interest earned on client funds held in IOLTA accounts is the "private property" of the client for Takings Clause purposes. However, the Court "express[ed] no view as to whether these funds have been 'taken' by the States" nor "the amount of 'just compensation,' if any, due respondents."

"Because the Constitution protects rather than creates property interests," observed the Court, "the existence of a property interest is determined by reference to 'existing rules or understandings that stem from an independent source such as state law.'" The firmly embedded and widely held view that "interest follows principal" applies in Texas.

Dissenting, SOUTER, J., joined by Stevens, Ginsburg and Breyer, JJ., maintained that "the Court's limited enquiry has led it to announce an essentially abstract proposition [that] may ultimately turn out to have no significance in resolving the real issue, [which] is whether [the IOLTA] scheme violated the Takings Clause":

"The Court recognizes three distinct issues implicated by a takings claim: whether the interest asserted by the plaintiff is property, whether the government has taken that property, and whether the plaintiff has been denied just compensation for the taking. [By addressing] only the first of these questions [the Court has] postponed consideration of the most salient fact relied upon by petitioners in contesting [the] Fifth Amendment claim: that the respondent client would effectively be barred from receiving any net interest on his funds subject to the state IOLTA rule by the combination of an unchallenged federal banking state and regulation [and other rules]. If it should turn out that within the meaning of the Fifth Amendment, the IOLTA scheme had not taken the property recognized today, or if it should turn out that the 'just compensation' for any taking was zero, then there would be no practical consequence for purposes of the Fifth Amendment in recognizing a client's property right in the interest in the first place; any such recognition would be an inconsequential abstraction."

In a separate dissent, BREYER, J., joined by Stevens, Souter and Ginsburg, JJ., criticized the Court's use of the truism that "interest follows principal": "The Question Presented is whether 'interest earned on client trust funds' [which] would 'not earn interest' in the absence of a special 'IOLTA program' amounts to a 'property interest of the client or lawyer' for purposes [of the] Takings Clause. [The] truism [that 'interest follows the principal'] does not help because the Question Presented assumes circumstances that differ dramatically from those in which interest is ordinarily at issue. Ordinarily, principal is capable of generating interest for whoever holds it. Here, by the very terms of the question, we must assume that (because of pre-existing federal law) the client's principal could not generate interest without IOLTA intervention. That is to say, the client could not have had an expectation of receiving interest without intervention. [Thus] the question is whether 'interest,' *earned only as a result of IOLTA rules* and earned upon otherwise *barren* client principal, 'follows principal.'"

PROTECTION OF INDIVIDUAL RIGHTS: DUE PROCESS, THE BILL OF RIGHTS, AND NONTEXTUAL CONSTITUTIONAL RIGHTS

THE NATURE AND SCOPE OF FOURTEENTH AMENDMENT DUE PROCESS; APPLICABILITY OF THE BILL OF RIGHTS TO THE STATES

BODILY EXTRACTIONS: ANOTHER LOOK AT THE "DUE PROCESS" AND "SELECTIVE INCORPORATION" APPROACHES

CON LAW: P. 385, after note 3

AMER CON: P. 269, after note 3

RTS & LIB: P. 116, after note 3

4. The "shocks-the-conscience" test and substantive due process claims. Applying the "shocks-the-conscience" test first articulated in the *Rochin* case, SACRAMENTO v. LEWIS, 523 U.S. 833, 118 S.Ct. 1708, 140 L.Ed.2d 1043 (1988), held, per SOUTER, J., that a police officer did not violate substantive due process by causing death through "reckless indifference" to, or "reckless disregard" for, a person's life in a high-speed automobile chase of a speeding motorcyclist. (The chase resulted in the death of the motorcyclist's passenger when the police car skidded into the passenger after the cycle had tipped over). In such circumstances, concluded the Court, "only a purpose to cause harm unrelated to the legitimate object of arrest will satisfy the element of arbitrary conduct shocking to the conscience, necessary for a due process violation [and for police liability under 42 U.S.C. § 1983]."

The Court recalled that it had held in *Graham v. Connor*, 490 U.S. 386, 109 S.Ct. 1865, 104 L.Ed.2d 443 (1989), that "where a particular amendment provides an explicit textual source of constitutional protection against a particular sort of government behavior, that Amendment, not the more generalized notion of substantive due process, must be the guide for analyzing [claims of substantive due process violations]." But the "more-specific-provision" rule of *Graham* did not bar respondents' lawsuit because neither the high-speed chase of the motorcycle nor the accidental killing of the motorcycle passenger constituted a Fourth Amendment "seizure." (Such a "seizure" occurs only when there is a governmentally caused termination of an individual's freedom of movement *"through means intentionally applied."*) The Court then addressed respondents' substantive due process claim:

"Since the time of our early explanations of due process, we have understood the core of the concept to be protection against arbitrary action * * *. Our cases dealing with abusive executive action have repeatedly emphasized that only the most egregious official conduct can be said to be 'arbitrary in the constitutional sense' * * *.

"[F]or half a century now we have spoken of the cognizable level of executive abuse of power as that which shocks the conscience. We first put the test this way in *Rochin* * * *. In the intervening years we have repeatedly adhered to *Rochin's* benchmark.* * * Most recently, in *Collins v. Harker Heights,* 503 U. S. 115, 112 S. Ct. 1061, 117 L.Ed. 2d 261 (1992), we said again that the substantive component of the Due Process Clause is violated by executive action only when it 'can properly be characterized as arbitrary, or conscience shocking, in a constitutional sense.'

The Court emphasized that much turns on the particular context in which the executive misconduct arises. Thus, in a prison custodial situation, when the state has rendered an individual unable to care for himself, and at the same time fails to provide for his basic needs, "the point of the conscience-shocking is reached" when injuries are produced by reckless or grossly negligent executive conduct. On the other hand, "deliberate indifference does not suffice for constitutional liability (albeit under the Eighth Amendment) even in prison circumstances when a prisoner's claim arises not from normal custody but from response to a violent disturbance." Continued the Court:

"Like prison officials facing a riot, the police on an occasion calling for fast action have obligations that tend to tug against each other. Their duty is to restore and maintain lawful order, while not exacerbating disorder more than necessary to do their jobs. They are supposed to act decisively and to show restraint at the same moment, and their decisions have to be made 'in haste, under pressure, and frequently without the luxury of a second chance.' [A] police officer deciding whether to give chase must balance on one hand the need to stop a suspect and show that flight from the law is no way to freedom, and, on the other, the high-speed threat to everyone within stopping range, be they suspects, their passengers, other drivers, or bystanders.

"To recognize a substantive due process violation in these circumstances when only mid-level fault has been shown [i.e., something more than simple negligence, but something less than intentional misconduct] would be to forget that liability for deliberate indifference to inmate welfare rests upon the luxury enjoyed by prison officials of having time to make unhurried judgments, upon the chance for repeated reflection, largely uncomplicated by the pulls of competing obligations. When such extended opportunities to do better are teamed with protracted failure even to care, indifference is truly shocking. But when unforeseen circumstances demand an officer's instant judgment, even precipitate recklessness fails to inch close enough to harmful purpose to spark the shock that implicates 'the large concerns of the governors and the governed.' Just as a purpose to cause harm is needed for Eighth Amendment liability in a riot case, so it ought to be needed for Due Process liability in a pursuit case. Accordingly, we hold that high-speed chases with no intent to harm suspects physically or to worsen their legal plight do not give rise to liability under the Fourteenth Amendment, redressible by an action under § 1983. * * * Regardless whether Smith's behavior offended the reasonableness held up by tort law or the balance struck in law enforcement's own codes of sound practice, it does not shock the conscience * * *."a

a. Kennedy, J., joined by O'Connor, J. joined the opinion of the Court, but also wrote separately. They "share[d] Justice Scalia's con-cerns about using the phrase 'shocks the conscience' in a manner suggesting that it is a self-defining test." The phrase, they observed,

Concurring in the judgment, SCALIA, J., joined by Thomas, J. would not have decided the case by applying the "shocks-the-conscience" test but "on the ground that respondents offer no textual or historical support for their alleged due process right." The concurring Justices maintained that in *Washington v. Glucksberg*, p. 57 of this Supplement (upholding a criminal prohibition against physician-assisted suicide), "the Court specifically rejected the method of substantive-due-process analysis employed by Justice Souter in that case, which is the very same method employed by Justice Souter in his opinion for the Court today." Scalia, J., continued:

"Adhering to our decision in *Glucksberg,* rather than ask whether the police conduct here at issue shocks my unelected conscience, I would ask whether our Nation has traditionally protected the right respondents assert.* * * I agree with the Court's conclusion that [respondents' complaint] asserts a substantive right to be free from 'deliberate or reckless indifference to life in a high-speed automobile chase aimed at apprehending a suspected offender.' Respondents provide no textual or historical support for this alleged due process right, [and] I would 'decline to fashion a new due process right out of thin air.' Nor have respondents identified any precedential support. Indeed, precedent is to the contrary * * *.

"[To] hold, as respondents urge, that all government conduct deliberately indifferent to life, liberty, or property, violates the Due Process Clause would make 'the Fourteenth Amendment a font of tort law to be superimposed upon whatever systems may already be administered by the States.' [If] the people [of] California would prefer a system that renders police officers liable for reckless driving during high-speed pursuits, '[t]hey may create such a system [by] changing the tort law of the State in accordance with the regular lawmaking process.' For now, they prefer not to [do so]. It is the prerogative of a self-governing people to make that legislative choice. [For] judges to overrule [the] democratically adopted policy judgment [of the people of California and their elected representatives] on the ground that it shocks *their* consciences is not judicial review but judicial governance."

"has the unfortunate connotation of a standard laden with subjective assessments. In that respect, it must be viewed with considerable skepticism."

CONSTITUTIONAL–CRIMINAL PROCEDURE

POLICE INTERROGATION AND CONFESSIONS

Can Congress "Repeal" Miranda?

AMER CON: P. 403, add to discussion of § 3501

DICKERSON v. UNITED STATES

___ U.S. ___, 120 S.Ct. 2326, ___ L.Ed.2d ___, (2000).

CHIEF JUSTICE REHNQUIST delivered the opinion of the Court.

[In] the wake of [*Miranda*], Congress enacted 18 U.S.C. § 3501, which in essence laid down a rule that the admissibility of [a custodial suspect's] statements should turn only on whether or not they were voluntarily made. We hold that *Miranda*, being a constitutional decision of this Court, may not be in effect overruled by an Act of Congress, and we decline to overrule *Miranda* ourselves. We therefore hold that *Miranda* and its progeny in this Court govern the admissibility of statements made during custodial interrogation in both state and federal courts.

* * * Prior to *Miranda*, we evaluated the admissibility of a suspect's confession under a voluntariness test. [Over] time, our cases recognized two constitutional bases for the requirement that a confession be voluntary to be admitted into evidence: the Fifth Amendment right against self-incrimination and the Due Process Clause of the Fourteenth Amendment. See, *e.g.*, *Bram v. United States* (1897) (stating that the voluntariness test "is controlled by that portion of the Fifth Amendment * * * commanding that no person 'shall be compelled in any criminal case to be a witness against himself ' "); *Brown v. Mississippi*, (1936) (reversing a criminal conviction under the Due Process Clause because it was based on a confession obtained by physical coercion).

While *Bram* was decided before *Brown* and its progeny, for the middle third of the 20th century our cases based the rule against admitting coerced confessions primarily, if not exclusively, on notions of due process. We applied the due process voluntariness test in "some 30 different cases decided during the era that intervened between *Brown* and *Escobedo v. Illinois*." Those cases refined the test into an inquiry that examines "whether a defendant's will was overborne" by the circumstances surrounding the giving of a confession. The due process test takes into consideration "the totality of all the surrounding circumstances—both the characteristics of the accused and the details of the interrogation." * * *

We have never abandoned this due process jurisprudence, and thus continue to exclude confessions that were obtained involuntarily. But our decisions in *Malloy* and *Miranda* changed the focus of much of the inquiry in determining the admissibility of suspects' incriminating statements. In *Malloy*, we held that the Fifth Amendment's Self–Incrimination Clause is incorporated in the Due Process

Clause of the Fourteenth Amendment and thus applies to the States. We decided *Miranda* on the heels of *Malloy*. * * *

Two years after *Miranda* was decided, Congress enacted § 3501. * * *

Given § 3501's express designation of voluntariness as the touchstone of admissibility, its omission of any warning requirement, and the instruction for trial courts to consider a nonexclusive list of factors relevant to the circumstances of a confession, we agree with the Court of Appeals that Congress intended by its enactment to overrule *Miranda*. Because of the obvious conflict between our decision in *Miranda* and § 3501, we must address whether Congress has constitutional authority to thus supersede *Miranda*. If Congress has such authority, § 3501's totality-of-the-circumstances approach must prevail over *Miranda*'s requirement of warnings; if not, that section must yield to *Miranda*'s more specific requirements.

The law in this area is clear. This Court has supervisory authority over the federal courts, and we may use that authority to prescribe rules of evidence and procedure that are binding in those tribunals. However, the power to judicially create and enforce nonconstitutional "rules of procedure and evidence for the federal courts exists only in the absence of a relevant Act of Congress." Congress retains the ultimate authority to modify or set aside any judicially created rules of evidence and procedure that are not required by the Constitution.

But Congress may not legislatively supersede our decisions interpreting and applying the Constitution. See, *e.g.*, *Boerne v. Flores* [this Supplement, p. 222]. This case therefore turns on whether the *Miranda* Court announced a constitutional rule or merely exercised its supervisory authority to regulate evidence in the absence of congressional direction. [Relying] on the fact that we have created several exceptions to *Miranda*'s warnings requirement and that we have repeatedly referred to the *Miranda* warnings as "prophylactic," *Quarles*, and "not themselves rights protected by the Constitution," *Tucker*, the Court of Appeals concluded that the protections announced in *Miranda* are not constitutionally required.

We disagree * * *, although we concede that there is language in some of our opinions that supports the view taken by that court. But first and foremost of the factors on the other side—that *Miranda* is a constitutional decision—is that both *Miranda* and two of its companion cases applied the rule to proceedings in state courts—to wit, Arizona, California, and New York. Since that time, we have consistently applied *Miranda*'s rule to prosecutions arising in state courts. It is beyond dispute that we do not hold a supervisory power over the courts of the several States. With respect to proceedings in state courts, our "authority is limited to enforcing the commands of the United States Constitution."

The *Miranda* opinion itself begins by stating that the Court granted certiorari "to explore some facets of the problems [of] applying the privilege against self-incrimination to in-custody interrogation, *and to give concrete constitutional guidelines for law enforcement agencies and courts to follow*" (emphasis added). In fact, the majority opinion is replete with statements indicating that the majority thought it was announcing a constitutional rule. Indeed, the Court's ultimate conclusion was that the unwarned confessions obtained in the four cases before the Court in *Miranda* "were obtained from the defendant under circumstances that did not meet constitutional standards for protection of the privilege."

Additional support for our conclusion that *Miranda* is constitutionally based is found in the *Miranda* Court's invitation for legislative action to protect the constitutional right against coerced self-incrimination. [The] Court emphasized that it could not foresee "the potential alternatives for protecting the privilege which might be devised by Congress or the States," and it accordingly opined that the Constitution would not preclude legislative solutions that differed from the prescribed *Miranda* warnings but which were "at least as effective in apprising accused persons of their right of silence and in assuring a continuous opportunity to exercise it."

[Various decisions carving out exceptions to *Miranda*] illustrate the principle—not that *Miranda* is not a constitutional rule—but that no constitutional rule is immutable. No court laying down a general rule can possibly foresee the various circumstances in which counsel will seek to apply it, and the sort of modifications represented by these cases are as much a normal part of constitutional law as the original decision.

[The] dissent argues that it is judicial overreaching for this Court to hold § 3501 unconstitutional unless we hold that the *Miranda* warnings are required by the Constitution, in the sense that nothing else will suffice to satisfy constitutional requirements. But we need not go farther than *Miranda* to decide this case. In *Miranda*, the Court noted that reliance on the traditional totality-of-the-circumstances test raised a risk of overlooking an involuntary custodial confession, a risk that the Court found unacceptably great when the confession is offered in the case in chief to prove guilt. The Court therefore concluded that something more than the totality test was necessary. Section 3501 reinstates the totality test as sufficient. [The statute] therefore cannot be sustained if *Miranda* is to remain the law.

Whether or not we would agree with *Miranda*'s reasoning and its resulting rule, were we addressing the issue in the first instance, the principles of stare decisis weigh heavily against overruling it now.

* * * *Miranda* has become embedded in routine police practice to the point where the warnings have become part of our national culture. [While] we have overruled our precedents when subsequent cases have undermined their doctrinal underpinnings, we do not believe that this has happened to the *Miranda* decision. If anything, our subsequent cases have reduced the impact of the *Miranda* rule on legitimate law enforcement while reaffirming the decision's core ruling that unwarned statements may not be used as evidence in the prosecution's case in chief.

The disadvantage of the *Miranda* rule is that statements which may be by no means involuntary, made by a defendant who is aware of his "rights," may nonetheless be excluded and a guilty defendant go free as a result. But experience suggests that the totality-of-the-circumstances test which § 3501 seeks to revive is more difficult than *Miranda* for law enforcement officers to conform to, and for courts to apply in a consistent manner. The requirement that *Miranda* warnings be given does not, of course, dispense with the voluntariness inquiry. But * * * "[c]ases in which a defendant can make a colorable argument that a self-incriminating statement was 'compelled' despite the fact that the law enforcement authorities adhered to the dictates of *Miranda* are rare."

In sum, we conclude that *Miranda* announced a constitutional rule that Congress may not supersede legislatively. Following the rule of *stare decisis*, we decline to overrule *Miranda* ourselves. * * *

JUSTICE SCALIA, with whom JUSTICE THOMAS joins, dissenting.

Those to whom judicial decisions are an unconnected series of judgments that produce either favored or disfavored results will doubtless greet today's decision as a paragon of moderation, since it declines to overrule *Miranda*. Those who understand the judicial process will appreciate that today's decision is not a reaffirmation of *Miranda*, but a radical revision of the most significant element of *Miranda* (as of all cases): the rationale that gives it a permanent place in our jurisprudence.

Marbury v. Madison held that an Act of Congress will not be enforced by the courts if what it prescribes violates the Constitution of the United States. That was the basis on which *Miranda* was decided. One will search today's opinion in vain, however, for a statement (surely simple enough to make) that what § 3501 prescribes—the use at trial of a voluntary confession, even when a *Miranda* warning or its equivalent has failed to be given—violates the Constitution. The reason the statement does not appear is not only (and perhaps not so much) that it would be absurd, inasmuch as § 3501 excludes from trial precisely what the Constitution excludes from trial, viz., compelled confessions; but also that Justices whose votes are needed to compose today's majority are on record as believing that a violation of *Miranda* is *not* a violation of the Constitution. And so, to justify today's agreed-upon result, the Court must adopt a significant *new*, if not entirely comprehensible, principle of constitutional law. As the Court chooses to describe that principle, statutes of Congress can be disregarded, not only when what they prescribe violates the Constitution, but when what they prescribe contradicts a decision of this Court that "announced a constitutional rule." As I shall discuss in some detail, the only thing that can possibly mean in the context of this case is that this Court has the power, not merely to apply the Constitution but to expand it, imposing what it regards as useful "prophylactic" restrictions upon Congress and the States. That is an immense and frightening antidemocratic power, and it does not exist.

It takes only a small step to bring today's opinion out of the realm of power-judging and into the mainstream of legal reasoning: The Court need only go beyond its carefully couched iterations that "*Miranda* is a constitutional decision," that "*Miranda* is constitutionally based," that *Miranda* has "constitutional underpinnings," and come out and say quite clearly: "We reaffirm today that custodial interrogation that is not preceded by *Miranda* warnings or their equivalent violates the Constitution of the United States." It cannot say that, because a majority of the Court does not believe it. The Court therefore acts in plain violation of the Constitution when it denies effect to this Act of Congress.

It was once possible to characterize the so-called *Miranda* rule as resting (however implausibly) upon the proposition that what the statute here before us permits—the admission at trial of un-*Mirandized* confessions—violates the Constitution. That is the fairest reading of the *Miranda* case itself. [Having] extended the privilege into the confines of the station house, the Court liberally sprinkled throughout its sprawling 60–page opinion suggestions that, because of the compulsion inherent in custodial interrogation, the privilege was violated by any statement thus obtained that did not conform to the rules set forth in *Miranda*, or some functional equivalent. * * *

So understood, *Miranda* was objectionable for innumerable reasons, not least the fact that cases spanning more than 70 years had rejected its core premise that, absent the warnings and an effective waiver of the right to remain silent and of the (thitherto unknown) right to have an attorney present, a statement obtained pursuant to custodial interrogation was necessarily the product of compulsion.

Moreover, history and precedent aside, the decision in *Miranda*, if read as an explication of what the Constitution *requires*, is preposterous. There is, for example, simply no basis in reason for concluding that a response to the very first question asked, by a suspect who already *knows* all of the rights described in the *Miranda* warning, is anything other than a volitional act. And even if one assumes that the elimination of compulsion absolutely requires informing even the most knowledgeable suspect of his right to remain silent, it cannot conceivably require the right to have *counsel* present. There is a world of difference, which the Court recognized under the traditional voluntariness test but ignored in *Miranda*, between compelling a suspect to incriminate himself and preventing him from foolishly doing so of his own accord. Only the latter (which is *not* required by the Constitution) could explain the Court's inclusion of a right to counsel and the requirement that it, too, be knowingly and intelligently waived. Counsel's presence is not required to tell the suspect that he *need* not speak; the interrogators can do that. The only good reason for having counsel there is that he can be counted on to advise the suspect that he *should* not speak.

Preventing foolish (rather than compelled) confessions is likewise the only conceivable basis for the rules that courts must exclude any confession elicited by questioning conducted, without interruption, after the suspect has indicated a desire to stand on his right to remain silent or initiated by police after the suspect has expressed a desire to have counsel present. Nonthreatening attempts to persuade the suspect to reconsider that initial decision are not, without more, enough to render a change of heart the product of anything other than the suspect's free will. Thus, what is most remarkable about the *Miranda* decision—and what made it unacceptable as a matter of straightforward constitutional interpretation in the *Marbury* tradition—is its palpable hostility toward the act of confession *per se*, rather than toward what the Constitution abhors, *compelled* confession.

[For] these reasons, and others more than adequately developed in the *Miranda* dissents and in the subsequent works of the decision's many critics, any conclusion that a violation of the *Miranda* rules *necessarily* amounts to a violation of the privilege against compelled self-incrimination can claim no support in history, precedent, or common sense, and as a result would at least presumptively be worth reconsidering even at this late date. But that is unnecessary, since the Court has (thankfully) long since abandoned the notion that failure to comply with *Miranda*'s rules is itself a violation of the Constitution.

As the Court today acknowledges, since *Miranda* we have explicitly, and repeatedly, interpreted that decision as having announced, not the circumstances in which custodial interrogation runs afoul of the Fifth or Fourteenth Amendment, but rather only "prophylactic" rules that go beyond the right against compelled self-incrimination. Of course the seeds of this "prophylactic" interpretation of *Miranda* were present in the decision itself. [In] subsequent cases, the seeds have sprouted and borne fruit: The Court has squarely concluded that it is possible—indeed not uncommon—for the police to violate *Miranda* without also violating the Constitution.

[In light of cases such as *Michigan v. Tucker* (1974), *New York v. Quarles* (1984) and *Oregon v. Elstad* (1985),] it is simply no longer possible for the Court to conclude, even if it wanted to, that a violation of *Miranda*'s rules is a violation of the Constitution. But [that] is what is required before the Court may disregard a law of Congress governing the admissibility of evidence in federal court. The Court today insists that the *decision* in *Miranda* is a "constitutional" one, that it has "constitutional underpinnings," a "constitutional basis" and a "constitutional origin," that it was "constitutionally based," and that it announced a "constitutional rule." It is fine to play these word games; but what makes a decision "constitutional" in the only sense relevant here—in the sense that renders it impervious to supersession by congressional legislation such as § 3501—is the determination that the Constitution *requires* the result that the decision announces and the statute ignores. By disregarding congressional action that concededly does not violate the Constitution, the Court flagrantly offends fundamental principles of separation of powers, and arrogates to itself prerogatives reserved to the representatives of the people.

[The] Court asserts that *Miranda* must be a "constitutional decision" announcing a "constitutional rule," and thus immune to congressional modification, because we have since its inception applied it to the States. If this argument is meant as an invocation of *stare decisis*, it fails because, though it is true that our cases applying *Miranda* against the States must be reconsidered if *Miranda* is not required by the Constitution, it is likewise true that our cases (discussed above) based on the principle that *Miranda* is *not* required by the Constitution will have to be reconsidered if it *is*. So the *stare decisis* argument is a wash.

[There] was available to the Court a means of reconciling the established proposition that a violation of *Miranda* does not itself offend the Fifth Amendment with the Court's assertion of a right to ignore the present statute. That means of reconciliation was argued strenuously by both petitioner and the United States, who were evidently more concerned than the Court is with maintaining the coherence of our jurisprudence. It is not mentioned in the Court's opinion because, I assume, a majority of the Justices intent on reversing believes that incoherence is the lesser evil. They may be right.

Petitioner and the United States contend that there is nothing at all exceptional, much less unconstitutional, about the Court's adopting prophylactic rules to buttress constitutional rights, and enforcing them against Congress and the States. Indeed, the United States argues that "prophylactic rules are now and have been for many years a feature of this Court's constitutional adjudication." That statement is not wholly inaccurate, if by "many years" one means since the mid–1960's. However, in their zeal to validate what is in my view a lawless practice, the United States and petitioner greatly overstate the frequency with which we have engaged in it.

[What] the Court did in *Miranda* (assuming, as later cases hold, that *Miranda* went beyond what the Constitution actually requires) is in fact extraordinary. That the Court has, on rare and recent occasion, repeated the mistake does not transform error into truth, but illustrates the potential for future mischief that the error entails. [The] power with which the Court would endow itself under a "prophylactic" justification for *Miranda* goes far beyond what it has permitted Congress to do under authority of [U.S. Const., Amdt. 14, § 5].

I applaud [the] refusal of the Justices in the majority to enunciate this boundless doctrine of judicial empowerment as a means of rendering today's decision rational. In nonetheless joining the Court's judgment, however, they overlook two truisms: that actions speak louder than silence, and that (in judge-made law at least) logic will out. Since there is in fact no other principle that can reconcile today's judgment with the post-*Miranda* cases that the Court refuses to abandon, what today's decision will stand for, whether the Justices can bring themselves to say it or not, is the power of the Supreme Court to write a prophylactic, extraconstitutional Constitution, binding on Congress and the States. * * *

* * * I am not convinced by petitioner's argument that *Miranda* should be preserved because the decision occupies a special place in the "public's consciousness." As far as I am aware, the public is not under the illusion that we are infallible. I see little harm in admitting that we made a mistake in taking away from the people the ability to decide for themselves what protections (beyond those required by the Constitution) are reasonably affordable in the criminal investigatory process. And I see much to be gained by reaffirming for the people the wonderful reality that they govern themselves * * *.

Today's judgment converts *Miranda* from a milestone of judicial overreaching into the very Cheops' Pyramid (or perhaps the Sphinx would be a better analogue) of judicial arrogance. In imposing its Court-made code upon the States, the original opinion at least *asserted* that it was demanded by the Constitution. Today's decision does not pretend that it is—and yet *still* asserts the right to impose it against the will of the people's representatives in Congress. Far from believing that *stare decisis* compels this result, I believe we cannot allow to remain on the books even a celebrated decision—*especially* a celebrated decision—that has come to stand for the proposition that the Supreme Court has power to impose extraconstitutional constraints upon Congress and the States. This is not the system that was established by the Framers, or that would be established by any sane supporter of government by the people.

I dissent from today's decision, and, until § 3501 is repealed, will continue to apply it in all cases where there has been a sustainable finding that the defendant's confession was voluntary.

THE RIGHT OF "PRIVACY" (OR "AUTONOMY" OR "PERSONHOOD")

THE COURT REAFFIRMS "THE ESSENTIAL HOLDING OF *ROE*"

CON LAW: P. 500, after note 7
AMER CON: P. 575, after note 4
RTS & LIB: P. 406, after note 7

"*Partial-birth abortion.*" At issue in STENBERG v. CARHART, ___ U.S. ___, 120 S.Ct. 2597, ___ L.E2d ___, (2000), was a Nebraska statute that prohibited, except where "necessary to save the life of the mother," a medical procedure that abortion opponents call "partial-birth abortion."[a] The statute defined "partial-birth abortion" as "an abortion procedure in which the person performing the abortion partially delivers vaginally a living unborn child before killing the unborn child and completing the delivery." It further defined "partially delivers vaginally a living unborn child before killing [it]" to mean "deliberately and intentionally delivering into the vagina a living unborn child, *or a substantial portion thereof*, for the purpose of performing a procedure [that] will kill [and] does kill the unborn child." (Emphasis added.)

According to defenders of the Nebraska statute, it was meant to ban a specific procedure known in the medical profession as dilation and extraction (D & X). In this procedure, used after 16 weeks of pregnancy, when the fetal skull becomes too large to pass through the cervix, the doctors extracts the fetal body, feet first, up

---

a. A violation of the statute was punishable by as much as 20 years' imprisonment. The law also provided for the automatic revocation of a doctor's license to practice medicine in Nebraska.

to the head; collapses the skull with a sharp instrument; and then extracts the whole fetus through the cervix. D & X can be distinguished from a more commonly used abortion procedure, dilation and evaluation (D & E), which after the 15th week of pregnancy involves dismemberment of the fetus or the collapse of fetal parts to facilitate evacuation from the uterus. But dismemberment often does not occur until an arm or leg has been pulled into the vagina. Thus the Nebraska statute's definition of "partial-birth abortion" seemed to prohibit D & E as well as the less frequently used D & X.

A 5–4 majority, BREYER, J., joined by Stevens, O'Connor, Souter, and Ginsburg, J.J., held the statute unconstitutional "for at least two independent reasons": (1) it "lacks any exception 'for the preservation of the health of the mother,'" *Planned Parenthood v. Casey* (joint opinion of O'Connor, Kennedy and Souter, J.J.); and (2) it "imposes an undue burden on the woman's ability to chose a D & E abortion, thereby unduly burdening the right to choose abortion itself. *Casey*."

As for the statute's failure to include an exception for the preservation of the health of the mother: "Justice Thomas says that [our cases] limit [the need for an exception to preserve the health of the mother] to situations where the pregnancy *itself* creates a threat to health. He is wrong. [Our cases,] reaffirmed in *Casey*, recognize that a State cannot subject women's health to significant risks both in that context, *and also* where state regulations force women to use riskier methods of abortion. [Our cases] make clear that a risk to a woman's health is the same whether it happens to arise from regulating a particular method of abortion, or barring abortion entirely. * * *

"Nebraska responds that the law does not require a health exception unless there is a need for such an exception. And here there is no such need, it says. It argues that 'safe alternatives remain available' and 'a ban on partial-birth abortion/D & X would create no risk to the health of women.' The problem for Nebraska is that the parties strongly contested this factual question in the trial court below; and the findings and evidence support Dr. Carhart. The State fails to demonstrate that banning D & X without a health exception may not create significant health risks for women, because the record shows that significant medical authority supports the proposition that in some circumstances, D & X would be the safest procedure.

"[The] upshot is a District Court finding that D & X significantly obviates health risks in certain circumstances, a highly plausible record-based explanation of why that might be so, a division of opinion among some medical experts over whether D & X is generally safer, and an absence of controlled medical studies that would help answer these medical questions. Given these medically related evidentiary circumstances, we believe the law requires a health exception."

"The word 'necessary' in *Casey*'s phrase 'necessary, in appropriate medical judgment, for the preservation of the life or health of the mother,' cannot refer to an absolute necessity or to absolute proof. Medical treatments and procedures are often considered appropriate (or inappropriate) in light of estimated comparative health risks (and health benefits) in particular cases. Neither can that phrase require unanimity of medical opinion. Doctors often differ in their estimation of comparative health risks and appropriate treatment. And *Casey*'s words 'appropriate medical judgment' must embody the judicial need to tolerate responsible differences of medical opinion—differences of a sort that [the statements of the] American Medical Association [supporting Nebraska] and [the] American College of Obstetricians and Gynecologists [supporting respondent Dr. Carhart] indicate are present here.

"[Where] a significant body of medical opinion believes a procedure may bring with it greater safety for some patients and explains the medical reasons supporting that view, we cannot say that the presence of a different view by itself proves the contrary. Rather, the uncertainty means a significant likelihood that those who believe that D & X is a safer abortion method in certain circumstances may turn out to be right. If so, then the absence of a health exception will place women at an unnecessary risk of tragic health consequences. If they are wrong, the exception will simply turn out to have been unnecessary.

"In sum, Nebraska has not convinced us that a health exception is 'never necessary to preserve the health of women.' Rather, a statute that altogether forbids D & X creates a significant health risk. The statute consequently must contain a health exception. This is not to say, as Justice Thomas and Justice Kennedy claim, that a State is prohibited from proscribing an abortion procedure whenever a particular physician deems the procedure preferable. [But] where substantial medical authority supports the proposition that banning a particular abortion procedure could endanger women's health, *Casey* requires the statute to include a health exception when the procedure is 'necessary, in appropriate medical judgment, for the preservation of the life or health of the mother.' Requiring such an exception in this case is no departure from *Casey*, but simply a straightforward application of its holding."

As for the conclusion that the statute unduly burdens a woman's right to choose abortion:

"Nebraska does not deny that the statute imposes an 'undue burden' [upon a woman's right to terminate her pregnancy before viability] *if* it applies to the more commonly used D & E procedure as well as to D & X. And we agree with the Eighth Circuit that it does so apply.

"[The] statute forbids 'deliberately and intentionally delivering into the vagina a living unborn child, or a substantial portion thereof, for the purpose of performing a procedure that the person performing such procedure knows will kill the unborn child.' We do not understand how one could distinguish, using this language, between D & E (where a foot or arm is drawn through the cervix) and D & X (where the body up to the head is drawn through the cervix). Evidence before the trial court makes clear that D & E will often involve a physician pulling a 'substantial portion' of a still living fetus, say, an arm or leg, into the vagina prior to the death of the fetus.

"[Even] if the statute's basic aim is to ban D & X, its language makes clear that it also covers a much broader category of procedures. The language does not track the medical differences between D & E and D & X—though it would have been a simple matter, for example, to provide an exception for the performance of D & E and other abortion procedures Nor does the statute anywhere suggest that its application turns on whether a portion of the fetus' body is drawn into the vagina as part of a process to extract an intact fetus after collapsing the head as opposed to a process that would dismember the fetus. Thus, the dissenters' argument that the law was generally intended to bar D & X can be both correct and irrelevant. The relevant question is *not* whether the legislature wanted to ban D & X; it is whether the law was intended to apply *only* to D & X. The plain language covers both procedures. [Both] procedures can involve the introduction of a 'substantial portion' of a still living fetus, through the cervix, into the vagina—the very feature of an abortion that leads Justice Thomas to characterize such a procedure as involving 'partial birth.' "

[The Court then declined to accept as authoritative the Nebraska Attorney General's view that the statute banned only the D & X abortion procedure, pointing out that under Nebraska law the Attorney General's interpretation of state law does not bind the state courts or, apparently, elected county attorneys. Moreover, even if the Court gave the Attorney General's views "substantial weight," it still would have to reject his interpretation for it conflicts with the statutory language.]

"In sum, using this law some present prosecutors and future Attorneys General may choose to pursue physicians who use D & E procedures, the most commonly used methods for performing previability second trimester abortions. All those who perform abortion procedures using that method must fear prosecution, conviction, and imprisonment. The result is an undue burden upon the woman's right to make an abortion decision."

O'CONNOR, J., wrote a concurring opinion observing that "[c]ontrary to the assertions of Justice Kennedy and Justice Thomas, the need for a health exception does not arise from 'the individual views of Dr. Carhart and his supporters.' Rather, as the majority explains, where, as here, 'a significant body of medical opinion believes a procedure may bring with it greater safety for some patients and explains the medical reasons supporting that view,' then Nebraska cannot say that the procedure will not, in some circumstances, be 'necessary to preserve the life or health of the mother.' " As for the statute's other constitutional defect, its wording is such that "it is not possible to interpret the statute's language as applying only to the D & X procedure."

She deemed it "important to note that, unlike Nebraska, some other states have enacted statutes more narrowly tailored to proscribing the D & X procedure alone. [By] restricting their prohibitions to the D & X procedure exclusively, the Kansas Utah, and Montana statutes avoid a principal defect of the Nebraska law.

"[If] there were adequate alternative methods for a woman safely to obtain an abortion before viability, it is unlikely that prohibiting the D & X procedure alone would 'amount in practical terms to a substantial obstacle to a woman seeking an abortion.' *Casey* (joint opinion). Thus, a ban on partial-birth abortion that only proscribed the D & X method of abortion and that included an exception to preserve the life and health of the mother would be constitutional in my view."[b]

Concurring Justice STEVENS, joined by Ginsburg, J., observed: "Although much ink is spilled today describing the gruesome nature of late-term abortion procedures, that rhetoric does not provide me a *reason* to believe that the procedure Nebraska here claims it seeks to ban is more brutal, more gruesome, or less respectful of 'potential life' than the equally gruesome procedure Nebraska claims it still allows. [The] notion that either of these two equally gruesome procedures performed at this late stage of gestation is more akin to infanticide than the other, or that the State furthers any legitimate interest by banning one but not the other, is simply irrational."

b. Some proponents of partial-birth abortion bans were not encouraged by Justice O'Connor's concurring opinion. They viewed the need for an exception to preserve the health of the murder a "trap" for them: If the exception were too narrow it would be struck down; on the other hand, if it were too broad, e.g., it included factors like a woman's age, psychological or emotional condition, doctors could invoke the exceptions routinely. See William Glaberson, *Foes of Abortion Start New Effort after Court Loss*, N.Y. Times, June 30, 2000, p. 1.

Concurring Justice Ginsburg, joined by Stevens, J., wrote separately to emphasize that the Nebraska law "does not save any fetus from destruction, for it targets only 'a *method* of performing abortion.' " As Chief Judge Posner said of a similar law, she observed, "the law prohibits the [abortion] procedure because the State legislators seek to chip away at the private choice shielded by *Roe*, even as modeled by *Casey*. [As] stated by Chief Judge Posner, 'if a statute burdens constitutional rights and all that can be said on its behalf is that it is the vehicle that legislators have chosen for expressing their hostility to those rights, the burden is undue.' *Hope Clinic v. Ryan*, 195 F.3d 857, 881 (7th Cir. 1999) (dissenting opinion)."

Scalia, J., dissenting, was "optimistic enough to believe that *Stenberg* v. *Carhart* will be assigned its rightful place in the history of this Court's jurisprudence beside *Korematsu* and *Dred Scott*. The method of killing a human child— one cannot even accurately say an entirely unborn human child—proscribed by this statute is so horrible that the most clinical description of it evokes a shudder of revulsion. And the Court must know (as most state legislatures banning this procedure have concluded) that demanding a 'health exception'—which requires the abortionist to assure himself that, in his expert medical judgment, this method is, in the case at hand, marginally safer than others (how can one prove the contrary beyond a reasonable doubt?)—is to give live-birth abortion free rein. The notion that the Constitution * * * prohibits the States from simply banning this visibly brutal means of eliminating our half-born posterity is quite simply absurd.

"[The] two lengthy dissents in this case have, appropriately enough, set out to establish that today's result does not follow from this Court's most recent pronouncement on the matter of abortion, *Casey*. It would be unfortunate, however, if those who disagree with the result were induced to regard it as merely a regrettable misapplication of *Casey*. It is not that, but is *Casey's* logical and entirely predictable consequence. To be sure, the Court's construction of this statute so as to make it include procedures other than live-birth abortion involves not only a disregard of fair meaning, but an abandonment of the principle that even ambiguous statutes should be interpreted in such fashion as to render them valid rather than void. *Casey* does not permit *that* jurisprudential novelty—which must be chalked up to the Court's inclination to bend the rules when any effort to limit abortion, or even to speak in opposition to abortion, is at issue.

"But the Court gives a second and independent reason for invalidating this humane (not to say anti-barbarian) law: That it fails to allow an exception for the situation in which the abortionist believes that this live-birth method of destroying the child might be safer for the woman. (As pointed out by Justice Thomas, and elaborated upon by Justice Kennedy, there is no good reason to believe this is ever the case, but—who knows?—it sometime *might* be.)

"[In] my dissent in *Casey*, I wrote that the 'undue burden' test made law by the joint opinion created a standard that was 'as doubtful in application as it is unprincipled in origin' * * *. Today's opinion is the proof. As long as we are debating this issue of necessity for a health-of-the-mother exception on the basis of *Casey*, it is really quite impossible for us dissenters to contend that the majority is *wrong* on the law—any more than it could be said that one is *wrong in law* to support or oppose the death penalty, or to support or oppose mandatory minimum sentences. The most that we can honestly say is that we disagree with the majority on their policy-judgment-couched-as-law. And those who believe that a 5– to–4 vote on a policy matter by unelected lawyers should not overcome the judgment of 30 state legislatures have a problem, not with the *application* of *Casey*, but with its *existence*. *Casey* must be overruled.

"[If] only for the sake of its own preservation, the Court should return this matter to the people—where the Constitution, by its silence on the subject, left it—and let *them* decide, State by State, whether this practice should be allowed. *Casey* must be overruled."

KENNEDY, J., joined by Rehnquist, C.J., dissented: "The Court's decision today, in my submission, repudiates [the central premise of *Casey* that the States retain a critical role in legislating on the subject of abortion] by invalidating a statute advancing critical state interests, even though the law denies no woman the right to choose an abortion and places no undue burden upon the right. The legislation is well within the State's competence to enact. Having concluded Nebraska's law survives the scrutiny dictated by a proper understanding of *Casey*, I dissent from the judgment invalidating it.

"The Court's failure to accord any weight to Nebraska's interest in prohibiting partial-birth abortion is erroneous and undermines its discussion and holding. The Court's approach in this regard is revealed by its description of the abortion methods at issue, which the Court is correct to describe as 'clinically cold or callous.' The majority views the procedures from the perspective of the abortionist, rather than from the perspective of a society shocked when confronted with a new method of ending human life. * * * Repeated references [by the majority] to sources understandable only to a trained physician may obscure matters for persons not trained in medical terminology. Thus it seems necessary at the outset to set forth what may happen during an abortion."

"[As] described by Dr. Carhart, the D & E procedure requires the abortionist to use instruments to grasp a portion (such as a foot or hand) of a developed and living fetus and drag the grasped portion out of the uterus into the vagina. Dr. Carhart uses the traction created by the opening between the uterus and vagina to dismember the fetus, tearing the grasped portion away from the remainder of the body.

"[The] other procedure implicated today is called 'partial-birth abortion' or the D & X. [In] the D & X, the abortionist initiates the woman's natural delivery process by causing the cervix of the woman to be dilated, sometimes over a sequence of days. The fetus' arms and legs are delivered outside the uterus while the fetus is alive; witnesses to the procedure report seeing the body of the fetus moving outside the woman's body. At this point, the abortion procedure has the appearance of a live birth. [With] only the head of the fetus remaining in utero, the abortionist tears open the skull. According to [a] leading proponent of the procedure, the appropriate instrument to be used at this stage of the abortion is a pair of scissors. Witnesses report observing the portion of the fetus outside the woman react to the skull penetration. The abortionist then inserts a suction tube and vacuums out the developing brain and other matter found within the skull.

"[Of] the two described procedures, Nebraska seeks only to ban the D & X. In light of the description of the D & X procedure, it should go without saying that Nebraska's ban on partial-birth abortion furthers purposes States are entitled to pursue. Dr. Carhart nevertheless maintains the State has no legitimate interest in forbidding the D & X. As he interprets the controlling cases in this Court, the only two interests the State may advance through regulation of abortion are in the health of the woman who is considering the procedure and in the life of the fetus she carries. The Court, as I read its opinion, accedes to his views, misunderstanding *Casey* and the authorities it confirmed. * * *

"*Casey* is premised on the States having an important constitutional role in defining their interests in the abortion debate. It is only with this principle in mind that Nebraska's interests can be given proper weight. The State's brief describes its interests as including concern for the life of the unborn and 'for the partially-born,' in preserving the integrity of the medical profession, and in 'erecting a barrier to infanticide.' A review of *Casey* demonstrates the legitimacy of these policies. The Court should say so. * * *

"*Casey* demonstrates that the interests asserted by the State are legitimate and recognized by law. It is argued, however, that a ban on the D & X does not further these interests. This is because, the reasoning continues, the D & E method, which Nebraska claims to be beyond its intent to regulate, can still be used to abort a fetus and is no less dehumanizing than the D & X method. While not adopting the argument in express terms, the Court indicates tacit approval of it by refusing to reject it in a forthright manner. Rendering express what is only implicit in the majority opinion, Justice Stevens and Justice Ginsburg are forthright in declaring that the two procedures are indistinguishable and that Nebraska has acted both irrationally and without a proper purpose in enacting the law. The issue is not whether members of the judiciary can see a difference between the two procedures. It is whether Nebraska can. The Court's refusal to recognize Nebraska's right to declare a moral difference between the procedure is a dispiriting disclosure of the illogic and illegitimacy of the Court's approach to the entire case."

"Nebraska was entitled to find the existence of a consequential moral difference between the procedures. We are referred to substantial medical authority that D & X perverts the natural birth process to a greater degree than D & E, commandeering the live birth process until the skull is pierced. American Medical Association (AMA) publications describe the D & X abortion method as 'ethically wrong.' The D & X differs from the D & E because in the D & X the fetus is 'killed *outside* of the womb' where the fetus has 'an autonomy which separates it from the right of the woman to choose treatments for her own body.' Witnesses to the procedure relate that the fingers and feet of the fetus are moving prior to the piercing of the skull; when the scissors are inserted in the back of the head, the fetus' body, wholly outside the woman's body and alive, reacts as though startled and goes limp. D & X's stronger resemblance to infanticide means Nebraska could conclude the procedure presents a greater risk of disrespect for life and a consequent greater risk to the profession and society, which depend for their sustenance upon reciprocal recognition of dignity and respect. The Court is without authority to second-guess this conclusion."

THOMAS, J., joined by Rehnquist, C.J., and Scalia, J., dissented: "Abortion is a unique act, in which a woman's exercise of control over her own body ends, depending on one's view, human life or potential human life. Nothing in our Federal Constitution deprives the people of this country of the right to determine whether the consequences of abortion to the fetus and to society outweigh the burden of an unwanted pregnancy on the mother. Although a State *may* permit abortion, nothing in the Constitution dictates that a State *must* do so.

"[Although] in *Casey* the separate opinions of the Chief Justice and Justice Scalia urging the Court to overrule *Roe* did not command a majority, seven Members of that Court, including six Members sitting today, acknowledged that

States have a legitimate role in regulating abortion and recognized the States' interest in respecting fetal life at all stages of development. [The] joint opinion [concluded] that prior case law 'went too far' in 'undervaluing the State's interest in potential life' and in 'striking down [some] abortion regulations which in no real sense deprived women of the ultimate decision.' *Roe* and subsequent cases, according to the joint opinion, had wrongly 'treated all governmental attempts to influence a woman's decision on behalf of the potential life within her as unwarranted,' a treatment that was 'incompatible with the recognition that there is a substantial state interest in potential life throughout pregnancy.' Accordingly, the joint opinion held that so long as state regulation of abortion furthers legitimate interests—that is, interests not designed to strike at the right itself—the regulation is invalid only if it imposes an undue burden on a woman's ability to obtain an abortion, meaning that it places a *substantial obstacle* in the woman's path.

"[The] standard set forth in the *Casey* joint opinion has no historical or doctrinal pedigree. The standard is a product of its authors' own philosophical views about abortion, and it should go without saying that it has no origins in or relationship to the Constitution and is, consequently, as illegitimate as the standard it purported to replace. Even assuming, however, as I will for the remainder of this dissent, that *Casey's* fabricated undue-burden standard merits adherence (which it does not), today's decision is extraordinary. Today, the Court inexplicably holds that the States cannot constitutionally prohibit a method of abortion that millions find hard to distinguish from infanticide and that the Court hesitates even to describe.

"This holding cannot be reconciled with *Casey*'s undue-burden standard, as that standard was explained to us by the authors of the joint opinion, and the majority hardly pretends otherwise. In striking down this statute—which express-es a profound and legitimate respect for fetal life and which leaves unimpeded several other safe forms of abortion—the majority opinion gives the lie to the promise of *Casey* that regulations that do no more than 'express profound respect for the life of the unborn are permitted, if they are not a substantial obstacle to the woman's exercise of the right to choose' whether or not to have an abortion. Today's decision is so obviously irreconcilable with *Casey*'s explication of what its undue-burden standard requires, let alone the Constitution, that it should be seen for what it is, a reinstitution of the pre-*Webster* abortion-on-demand era in which the mere invocation of 'abortion rights' trumps any contrary societal interest. If this statute is unconstitutional under *Casey*, then *Casey* meant nothing at all, and the Court should candidly admit it.

"[In] the almost 30 years since *Roe*, this Court has never described the various methods of aborting a second-or third-trimester fetus. From reading the majority's sanitized description, one would think that this case involves state regulation of a widely accepted routine medical procedure. Nothing could be further from the truth. The most widely used method of abortion during this stage of pregnancy is so gruesome that its use can be traumatic even for the physicians and medical staff who perform it. And the particular procedure at issue in this case, 'partial birth abortion,' so closely borders on infanticide that 30 States have attempted to ban it. * * *

"There is no question that the State of Nebraska has a valid interest—one not designed to strike at the right itself—in prohibiting partial birth abortion.

Casey itself noted that States may 'express profound respect for the life of the unborn.' States may, without a doubt, express this profound respect by prohibiting a procedure that approaches infanticide, and thereby dehumanizes the fetus and trivializes human life. The AMA has recognized that this procedure is 'ethically different from other destructive abortion techniques because the fetus, normally twenty weeks or longer in gestation, is killed *outside* the womb. The "partial birth" gives the fetus an autonomy which separates it from the right of the woman to choose treatments for her own body.' Thirty States have concurred with this view.

"[The] next question, therefore, is whether the Nebraska statute is unconstitutional because it does not contain an exception that would allow use of the procedure whenever 'necessary in appropriate medical judgment, for the preservation of [the] health of the mother.' According to the majority, such a health exception is required here because there is a 'division of opinion among some medical experts over whether D & X is generally safer [than D & E], and an absence of controlled medical studies that would help answer these medical questions.' In other words, unless a State can conclusively establish that an abortion procedure is no safer than other procedures, the State cannot regulate that procedure without including a health exception. Justice O'Connor agrees. The rule set forth by the majority and Justice O'Connor dramatically expands on our prior abortion cases and threatens to undo *any* state regulation of abortion procedures.

"[In] *Roe* and *Casey*, the Court stated that the State may 'regulate, and even proscribe, abortion except where it is necessary, in appropriate medical judgment, for the preservation of the life or health of the mother.' *Casey* said that a health exception must be available if '*continuing her pregnancy* would constitute a threat' to the woman. (emphasis added). Under these cases, if a State seeks to prohibit abortion, even if only temporarily or under particular circumstances, as *Casey* says that it may, the State must make an exception for cases in which the life or health of the mother is endangered by continuing the pregnancy. These cases addressed only the situation in which a woman must obtain an abortion because of some threat to her health from continued pregnancy. But *Roe* and *Casey* say nothing at all about cases in which a physician considers one prohibited method of abortion to be preferable to permissible methods. Today's majority and Justice O'Connor twist *Roe* and *Casey* to apply to the situation in which a woman desires—for whatever reason—an abortion and wishes to obtain the abortion by some particular method. In other words, the majority and Justice O'Connor fail to distinguish between cases in which health concerns require a woman to obtain an abortion and cases in which health concerns cause a woman who desires an abortion (for whatever reason) to prefer one method over another.

"We were reassured repeatedly in *Casey* that not all regulations of abortion are unwarranted and that the States may express profound respect for fetal life. Under *Casey*, the regulation before us today should easily pass constitutional muster. But the Court's abortion jurisprudence is a particularly virulent strain of constitutional exegesis. And so today we are told that 30 States are prohibited from banning one rarely used form of abortion that they believe to border on infanticide. It is clear that the Constitution does not compel this result."

FAMILY LIVING ARRANGEMENTS, PARENTAL RIGHTS, AND THE "RIGHT TO MARRY"

CON LAW: P. 505, after note 2

AMER CON: P.580 , after note 2

RTS & LIB: P. 411, after note 2

Non-parental visitation rights vs. rights of parents to make decisions concerning the care, custody, and control of their children. At issue in TROXEL v. GRANVILLE, ___ U.S. ___, 120 S.Ct. 2054, ___ L.Ed.2d ___ (2000), was a Washington statute, § 26.10.160(3), that permitted "[a]ny person" to petition for visitation rights "at any time" and authorized state superior courts to grant such rights whenever "visitation may serve the best interest of the child." The Troxels petitioned for the right to visit their deceased son's two daughters. Greenville, the girls' mother, did not oppose all visitation, but objected to the amount sought by the girls' grandparents (two weekends of overnight visitation per month and two weeks of visitation each summer). She asked the court to order one day of visitation per month with no overnight stay. The superior court ordered more visitation than Granville desired, and she appealed.

The Washington Supreme Court struck down the statute on its face for two reasons: (1) the Constitution permits a state to interfere with the rights of parents to rear their children only to prevent harm or potential harm to a child and the statute fails that standard "because it recognizes no threshold showing of harm"; (2) by allowing "any person" to petition for forced visitation of a child at "any time," with the only requirement being that the visitation serve "the best interest of the child," the statute sweeps too broadly. The U.S. Supreme Court affirmed, but, as dissenting Justice Stevens noted, it did not endorse either the holding or the reasoning of the state supreme court. There was no opinion of the Court. The principal opinion was written by O'CONNOR, J., joined by Rehnquist, C.J., and Ginsburg and Breyer, JJ. The plurality found the statute "as applied in this case" unconstitutional:

"The liberty interest at issue in this case—the interest of parents in the care, custody, and control of their children—is perhaps the oldest of the fundamental liberty interests recognized by this Court. [The Court then discussed *Meyer v. Nebraska* (1923); *Pierce v. Society of Sisters* (1925); and *Prince v. Massachusetts* (1944). Next it discussed, e.g., *Stanley v. Illinois* (1972); *Wisconsin v. Yoder* (1972); and *Quilloin v. Walcott* (1978.)] In light of this extensive precedent, it cannot now be doubted that the Due Process Clause of the Fourteenth Amendment protects the fundamental right of parents to make decisions concerning the care, custody, and control of their children.

"[The Washington statute], as applied to Granville and her family in this case, unconstitutionally infringes on that fundamental parental right. [The statute] is breathtakingly broad. [Its] language effectively permits any third party seeking visitation to subject any decision by a parent concerning visitation of the parent's children to state-court review. Once [the] matter is placed before a judge, a parent's decision that visitation would not be in the child's best interest is accorded no deference. [The statute] places the best-interest determination solely in the hands of the judge. [Thus,] in practical effect, in the State of Washington, a court can disregard and overturn *any* decision by a fit custodial parent concerning visitation whenever a third party affected by the decision files a visitation petition, based solely on the judge's determination of the child's best interests.

" * * * The Superior Court's order was not founded on any special factors that might justify the State's interference with Granville's fundamental right to make decisions concerning the rearing of her two daughters. To be sure, this case involves a visitation petition filed by grandparents soon after the death of their son [,but] the combination of several factors here compels our conclusion that [the statute], as applied, exceeded the bounds of the Due Process Clause.

"First, the Troxels did not allege, and no court has found, that Granville was an unfit parent. That aspect of the case is important for there is a presumption that fit parents act in the best interests of their children. * * *

"The problem here is [that the Superior Court] gave no special weight at all to Granville's determination of her daughters' best interests. More importantly, it appears that the Superior Court applied exactly the opposite presumption. [The judge's remarks indicate that he] [i]n effect * * * placed on Granville, the fit custodial parent, the burden of *disproving* that visitation would be in the best interest of her daughters. [If] a fit parent's decision of the kind at issue here becomes subject to judicial review, the court must accord at least some special weight to the parents' own determination.

"Finally, we note that there is no allegation that Granville ever sought to cut off visitation entirely. Rather, the present dispute originated when Granville informed the Troxels that she would prefer to restrict their visitation with [the girls] to one short visit per month and special holidays. * * *

Considered together with the Superior Court's reasons for awarding visitation to the Troxels, the combination of these factors demonstrates that the visitation order in this case was an unconstitutional infringement on Granville's fundamental right to make decisions concerning the care, custody, and control of her two daughters. [The circumstances] show that this case involves nothing more than a simple disagreement between the Washington Superior Court and Granville concerning her children's best interest. [The] Due Process Clause does not permit a State to infringe on the fundamental right of parents to make childrearing decisions simply because a state judge believes a 'better' decision could be made. Neither the Washington [statute] generally [nor] the Superior Court in this specific case required anything more. Accordingly, we hold that [the statute], as applied in this case, is unconstitutional.

"Because we rest our decision on the sweeping breadth of [the statute] and the application of that broad, unlimited power in this case, we do not consider the primary constitutional question passed on by the Washington Supreme Court— whether the Due Process Clause requires all nonparental visitation statutes to include a showing of harm or potential harm to the child as a condition precedent to granting visitation. We do not, and need not, define today the precise scope of the parental due process right in the visitation context."

The plurality also saw no reason to remand the case for further proceedings: "[I]t is apparent that the entry of the visitation order in this case violated the Constitution. We should say so now, without forcing the parties into additional litigation that would further burden Granville's parental right."

SOUTER, J., "concur[red] in the judgment affirming the decision of the Supreme Court of Washington, whose facial invalidation of its own statute is consistent with the Court's prior cases addressing the substantive interests at stake." He saw no error in the state supreme court's second reason for invalidating the statute—"because the state statute authorizes any person at any time to request (and a judge to award) visitation rights, subject only to the State's particular best-interests standard, [it] sweeps too broadly and is unconstitutional on its face. Consequently, there is no need to decide whether harm is required or to consider the precise scope of the parent's right or its necessary protections."

THOMAS, J., also concurred in the judgment, "agree[ing] with the plurality that the Court's recognition of a fundamental right of parents to direct the upbringing of their children resolves this case." He "would apply strict scrutiny to infringements of fundamental rights. Here, the State of Washington lacks even a legitimate governmental interest—to say nothing of a compelling one—in second-guessing a fit parent's decision regarding visitation with third parties."

He "note[d] that neither party has argued that our substantive due process cases were wrongly decided and that the original understanding of the Due Process Clause precludes judicial enforcement of unenumerated rights under that constitutional provision." Thus, he "express[ed] no view on the merits of this matter."

Dissenting Justice STEVENS maintained that the state supreme court "erred in its federal constitutional analysis because neither the provision granting 'any person' the right to petition the court for visitation nor the absence of a provision requiring a 'threshold ... finding of harm to the child' provides a sufficient basis for holding that the statute is invalid in all its applications." He "believe[d] that a facial challenge should fail whenever a statute has 'a plainly legitimate sweep.' Under the Washington statute, there are plainly any number of cases—indeed, one suspects, the most common to arise—in which the 'person' among 'any' seeking visitation is a once-custodial caregiver, an intimate relation, or even a genetic parent."

As for "the second key aspect of the Washington Supreme Court's holding—that the Federal Constitution requires a showing of actual or potential 'harm' to the child before a court may order visitation continued over a parent's objections"—this, maintained Stevens, J., "finds no support in the Court's case law":

"A parent's rights with respect to her child [have] never been regarded as absolute, but rather are limited by the existence of an actual, developed relationship with a child, and are tied to the presence or absence of some embodiment of family. [While] this Court has not yet had occasion to elucidate the nature of a child's liberty interests in preserving established familial or family-like bonds, it seems to me extremely likely that, to the extent parents and families have fundamental liberty interests in preserving such intimate relationships, so, too, do children have these interests, and so, too, must their interests be balanced in the equation. At a minimum, our prior cases recognizing that children are, generally speaking, constitutionally protected actors require that this Court reject any suggestion that when it comes to parental rights, children are so much chattel.

" * * * It is indisputably the business of the States, rather than a federal court employing a national standard, to assess in the first instance the relative importance of the conflicting interests that give rise to disputes such as this. Far from guaranteeing that parents' interests will be trammeled in the sweep of cases arising under the statute, the Washington law merely gives an individual—with whom a child may have an established relationship—the procedural right to ask the State to act as arbiter, through the entirely well-known best-interests standard, between the parent's protected interests and the child's. It seems clear to me that the Due Process Clause of the Fourteenth Amendment leaves room for States to consider the impact on a child of possibly arbitrary parental decisions that neither serve nor are motivated by the best interests of the child."

SCALIA, J., who wrote a separate dissenting opinion, thought it "entirely compatible with the commitment to representative democracy set forth in the founding documents to argue, in legislative chambers or in electoral campaigns, that the state has *no power* to interfere with parents' authority over the rearing of their children," but did "not believe that the power which the Constitution confers upon me *as a judge* entitles me to deny legal effect to laws that (in my view) infringe upon what is (in my view) that unenumerated right." Continued Scalia:

"Only three holdings of this Court rest in whole or in part upon a substantive constitutional right of parents to direct the upbringing of their children [citing *Meyer v. Nebraska* (1923), *Pierce v. Society of Sisters* (1925) and *Wisconsin v. Yoder* (1972)]—two of them from an era rich in substantive due process holdings that have since been repudiated. The sheer diversity of today's opinions persuades me that the theory of unenumerated parental rights underlying these three cases has small claim to *stare decisis* protection. A legal principle that can be thought to produce such diverse outcomes in the relatively simply case before us here is not a legal principle that has induced substantial reliance. While I would not now overrule these earlier cases (that has not been urged), neither would I extend the theory upon which they rested to this new context.

"Judicial vindication of 'parental rights' under a Constitution that does not even mention them requires (as Justice Kennedy's opinion rightly points out) not only a judicially crafted definition of parents, but also—unless, as no one believes, the parental rights are to be absolute—judicially approved assessments of 'harm to the child' and judicially defined graduations of other persons (grandparents, extended family, adoptive family in an adoption later found to be invalid, long-term guardians, etc.) who may have some claim against the wishes of the parents. If we embrace this unenumerated right, I think it obvious [that] we will be ushering in a new regime of judicially prescribed, and federally prescribed, family law. I have no reason to believe that federal judges will be better at this than state legislatures; and state legislatures have the great advantages of doing harm in a more circumscribed area, of being able to correct their mistakes in a flash, and of being removable by the people."

KENNEDY, J., who wrote a third dissenting opinion, maintained that the state supreme court's "first theory"—that the challenged statute is fatally defective because "it allows an award of visitation to a nonparent without a finding that harm to the child would result if visitation were withheld"—"is too broad to be correct, as it appears to contemplate that the best interests of the child standard may not be applied in any visitation case." Given the error he saw in the state court's "central conclusion," he thought "that court should have the first opportunity to reconsider this case." Thus, he would remand the case to the state court for further proceedings.

Justice Kennedy's "principal concern" was that the states court's holding "seems to proceed from the assumption that the parent or parents who resist visitation have always been the child's primary caregivers and that the third parties who seek visitation have no legitimate and established relationship with the child. That idea, in turn, appears influenced by the concept that the conventional nuclear family ought to establish the visitation standard for every domestic relations case. As we all know, this is simply not the structure or prevailing condition in many households. * * *

"Cases are sure to arise—perhaps a substantial number of cases—in which a third party, by acting in a caregiving role over a significant period of time, has developed a relationship with a child which is not necessarily subject to absolute parental veto. * * * Indeed, contemporary practice should give us some pause before rejecting the best interests of the child standard in all third-party visitation cases, as the Washington court has done. The standard has been recognized for many years as a basic tool of domestic relations law in visitation proceedings. [The third-party visitation statutes enacted by all 50 states] include a variety of methods for limiting parents' exposure to third-party visitation petitions and for ensuring parental decisions are given respect. Many States limit the identity of permissible petitioners by restricting visitation petitions to grandparents or by requiring petitioners to show a substantial relationship with a child, or both.

[In] light of the inconclusive historical record and case law, as well as the almost universal adoption of the best interests standard for visitation disputes, I would be hard pressed to conclude the right to be free of such review in all cases is itself 'implicit in the concept of ordered liberty.' In my view, it would be more appropriate to conclude that the constitutionality of the applications of the best interests standard depends on more specific factors. In short, a fit parent's rights vis-à-vis a complete stranger is one thing; her right vis-à-vis another parent or a *de facto* parent may be another."

CRITICISM OF *BOWERS v. HARDWICK*

CON LAW: P. 527, after note 7 add new note

AMER CON: P. 601, after note 5 add new note

RTS & LIB: P. 433, after note 7 add new note

8. *Are Romer and Hardwick reconcilable?* Compare *Hardwick* with *Romer v. Evans,* p. 204 of this Supplement, holding that a voter-initiated state constitutional amendment prohibiting state or local governments from acting to protect the status of persons based on their "homosexual, lesbian or bisexual orientation" violates the Equal Protection Clause: "[I]n making a general announcement that gays and lesbians shall not have any particular protections from the law," the amendment inflicts injuries on them "that outrun and belie any legitimate justifications that may be claimed for it"; "it is a classification of persons undertaken for its own sake, something the Equal Protection Clause does not permit." The 6–3 majority did not mention *Hardwick,* but the dissent did. It maintained that the majority had "contradict[ed]" *Hardwick* and "place[d] the prestige of this institution behind the proposition that opposition to homosexuality is as reprehensible as racial or religious bias." Do you share the *Romer* dissenters' view of the Court's holding? Why (not)?

THE "RIGHT TO DIE"

IS THERE A CONSTITUTIONAL RIGHT TO PHYSICIAN–ASSISTED SUICIDE?

WASHINGTON v. GLUCKSBERG

521 U.S. 702, 117 S.Ct. 2258, 138 L.Ed.2d 772 (1997).

CON LAW: P. 542, delete pp. 542–50 and substitute following

AMER CON: P. 615, delete pp. 615–23 and substitute following

RTS & LIB: P. 447, delete pp. 447–55 and substitute following

CHIEF JUSTICE REHNQUIST delivered the opinion of the Court.

The question presented in this case is whether Washington's prohibition against "caus[ing]" or "aid[ing]" a suicide offends the Fourteenth Amendment to the United States Constitution. We hold that it does not.

[Respondents, four physicians who declare they would assist terminally ill, suffering patients in ending their lives if not for Washington's assisted-suicide ban, along with three gravely ill patients, who have since died, and Compassion in Dying, a nonprofit organization that counsels people considering physician-assisted suicide, sought a declaration that Washington's statute is, on its face, unconstitutional. Respondents] asserted "the existence of a liberty interest protected by the Fourteenth Amendment which extends to a personal choice by a mentally competent, terminally ill adult to commit physician-assisted suicide." Relying primarily on *Casey* and *Cruzan*, the District Court agreed and concluded that Washington's assisted suicide ban is unconstitutional because it "places an undue burden on the exercise of [that] constitutionally protected liberty interest." [5]

A panel of the Court of Appeals for the Ninth Circuit reversed, emphasizing that "[i]n the two hundred and five years of our existence no constitutional right to aid in killing oneself has ever been asserted and upheld by a court of final jurisdiction." The Ninth Circuit reheard the case en banc, reversed the panel's decision [8–3], and affirmed the District Court. Like the District Court, the Court of Appeals emphasized our *Casey* and *Cruzan* decisions. The court [concluded] that "the Constitution encompasses a due process liberty interest in controlling the time and manner of one's death—that there is, in short, a constitutionally-recognized 'right to die.'" After "[w]eighing and then balancing" this interest against Washington's various interests, the court held that the State's assisted-suicide ban was unconstitutional "as applied to terminally ill competent adults who wish to hasten their deaths with medication prescribed by their physicians." * * *

We begin, as we do in all due-process cases, by examining our Nation's history, legal traditions, and practices. In almost every State—indeed, in almost every western democracy—it is a crime to assist a suicide. The States' assisted-suicide bans are not innovations. Rather, they are longstanding expressions of the States' commitment to the protection and preservation of all human life. * * * Indeed, opposition to and condemnation of suicide—and, therefore, of

---

5. The District Court determined that *Casey's* "undue burden" standard, not the standard from *United States v. Salerno*, 481 U.S. 739, 107 S.Ct. 2095, 95 L.Ed.2d 697 (1987) (requiring a showing that "no set of circumstances exists under which the [law] would be valid"), governed the plaintiffs' facial challenge to the assisted-suicide ban.

assisting suicide—are consistent and enduring themes of our philosophical, legal, and cultural heritages.

More specifically, for over 700 years, the Anglo–American common-law tradition has punished or otherwise disapproved of both suicide and assisting suicide.

[For] the most part, the early American colonies adopted the common-law approach. [Over] time, however, [the] colonies abolished [the] harsh common-law penalties [such as forfeiture of the suicide's property. However,] the movement away from the common law's harsh sanctions did not represent an acceptance of homicide, [but] reflected the growing consensus that it was unfair to punish the suicide's family for his wrongdoing.

[That] suicide remained a grievous, though nonfelonious, wrong is confirmed by the fact that colonial and early state legislatures and courts did not retreat from prohibiting assisting suicide. [And] the prohibitions against assisted suicide never contained exceptions for those who were near death. [In] this century, the [American Law Institute's] Model Penal Code also prohibited "aiding" suicide, prompting many States to enact or revise their assisted-suicide bans. The Code's drafters observed that "the interests in the sanctity of life that are represented by the criminal homicide laws are threatened by one who expresses a willingness to participate in taking the life of another, even though the act may be accomplished with the consent, or at the request, of the suicide victim."

Though deeply rooted, the States' assisted-suicide bans have in recent years been reexamined and, generally, reaffirmed. Because of advances in medicine and technology, Americans today are increasingly likely to die in institutions, from chronic illnesses. Public concern and democratic action are therefore sharply focused on how best to protect dignity and independence at the end of life, with the result that there have been many significant changes in state laws and in the attitudes these laws reflect. Many States, for example, now permit "living wills," surrogate health-care decisionmaking, and the withdrawal or refusal of life-sustaining medical treatment. At the same time, however, voters and legislators continue for the most part to reaffirm their States' prohibitions on assisting suicide.

The Washington statute at issue in this case was enacted in 1975 as part of a revision of that State's criminal code. Four years later, Washington passed its Natural Death Act, which specifically stated that the "withholding or withdrawal of life-sustaining treatment [shall] not, for any purpose, constitute a suicide" and that "[n]othing in this chapter shall be construed to condone, authorize, or approve mercy killing * * *." In 1991, Washington voters rejected a ballot initiative which, had it passed, would have permitted a form of physician-assisted suicide. Washington then added a provision to the Natural Death Act expressly excluding physician-assisted suicide.

California voters rejected an assisted-suicide initiative similar to Washington's in 1993. On the other hand, in 1994, voters in Oregon enacted, also through ballot initiative, that State's "Death With Dignity Act," which legalized physician-assisted suicide for competent, terminally ill adults. Since the Oregon vote, many proposals to legalize assisted-suicide have been and continue to be introduced in the States' legislatures, but none has been enacted. And just last year, Iowa and Rhode Island joined the overwhelming majority of States explicitly prohibiting assisted suicide. Also, on April 30, 1997, President Clinton signed the Federal Assisted Suicide Funding Restriction Act of 1997, which prohibits the use of federal funds in support of physician-assisted suicide.

Thus, the States are currently engaged in serious, thoughtful examinations of physician-assisted suicide and other similar issues. For example, New York State's Task Force on Life and the Law—an ongoing, blue-ribbon commission composed of doctors, ethicists, lawyers, religious leaders, and interested laymen— was convened in 1984 and commissioned with "a broad mandate to recommend public policy on issues raised by medical advances." Over the past decade, the Task Force has recommended laws relating to end-of-life decisions, surrogate pregnancy, and organ donation. After studying physician-assisted suicide, however, the Task Force unanimously concluded that "[l]egalizing assisted suicide and euthanasia would pose profound risks to many individuals who are ill and vulnerable. [T]he potential dangers of this dramatic change in public policy would outweigh any benefit that might be achieved."

Attitudes toward suicide itself have changed, [but] our laws have consistently condemned, and continue to prohibit, assisting suicide. Despite changes in medical technology and notwithstanding an increased emphasis on the importance of end-of-life decision-making, we have not retreated from this prohibition. Against this backdrop of history, tradition, and practice, we now turn to respondents' constitutional claim.

The Due Process Clause guarantees more than fair process, and the "liberty" it protects includes more than the absence of physical restraint. [The] Clause also provides heightened protection against government interference with certain fundamental rights and liberty interests. In a long line of cases, we have held that, in addition to the specific freedoms protected by the Bill of Rights, the "liberty" specially protected by the Due Process Clause includes the rights to marry, to have children, to direct the education and upbringing of one's children, to marital privacy, to use contraception, to bodily integrity, and to abortion. We have also assumed, and strongly suggested, that the Due Process Clause protects the traditional right to refuse unwanted lifesaving medical treatment. *Cruzan.*

But we "ha[ve] always been reluctant to expand the concept of substantive due process because guideposts for responsible decisionmaking in this unchartered area are scarce and open-ended." By extending constitutional protection to an asserted right or liberty interest, we, to a great extent, place the matter outside the arena of public debate and legislative action. We must therefore "exercise the utmost care whenever we are asked to break new ground in this field," lest the liberty protected by the Due Process Clause be subtly transformed into the policy preferences of the members of this Court.

Our established method of substantive-due-process analysis has two primary features: First, we have regularly observed that the Due Process Clause specially protects those fundamental rights and liberties which are, objectively, "deeply rooted in this Nation's history and tradition." * * * Second, we have required in substantive-due-process cases a "careful description" of the asserted fundamental liberty interest. * * *

Justice Souter, relying on Justice Harlan's dissenting opinion in *Poe v. Ullman,* would largely abandon this restrained methodology, and instead ask "whether [Washington's] statute sets up one of those 'arbitrary impositions' or 'purposeless restraints' at odds with the Due Process Clause of the Fourteenth Amendment." [17] In our view, however, the development of this Court's substan-

---

17. In Justice Souter's opinion, Justice Harlan's *Poe* dissent supplies the "modern justification" for substantive-due-process review. But although Justice Harlan's opinion has often been cited in due-process cases, we have never abandoned our fundamental-rights-based tive-due-process jurisprudence, described briefly above, has been a process whereby the outlines of the "liberty" specially protected by the Fourteenth Amendment—never fully clarified, to be sure, and perhaps not capable of being fully clarified—have at least been carefully refined by concrete examples involving fundamental rights found to be deeply rooted in our legal tradition. This approach tends to rein in the subjective elements that are necessarily present in due-process judicial review. In addition, by establishing a threshold requirement—that a challenged state action implicate a fundamental right—before requiring more than a reasonable relation to a legitimate state interest to justify the action, it avoids the need for complex balancing of competing interests in every case.

Turning to the claim at issue here, the Court of Appeals stated that "[p]roperly analyzed, the first issue to be resolved is whether there is a liberty interest in determining the time and manner of one's death" or, in other words, "[i]s there a right to die?" Similarly, respondents assert a "liberty to choose how to die" and a right to "control of one's final days," and describe the asserted liberty as "the right to choose a humane, dignified death" and "the liberty to shape death." As noted above, we have a tradition of carefully formulating the interest at stake in substantive-due-process cases. For example, although *Cruzan* is often described as a "right to die" case, we were, in fact, more precise: we assumed that the Constitution granted competent persons a "constitutionally protected right to refuse lifesaving hydration and nutrition." [The] Washington statute at issue in this case prohibits "aid[ing] another person to attempt suicide" and, thus, the question before us is whether the "liberty" specially protected by the Due Process Clause includes a right to commit suicide which itself includes a right to assistance in doing so.

We now inquire whether this asserted right has any place in our Nation's traditions. Here, as discussed above, we are confronted with a consistent and almost universal tradition that has long rejected the asserted right, and continues explicitly to reject it today, even for terminally ill, mentally competent adults. To hold for respondents, we would have to reverse centuries of legal doctrine and practice, and strike down the considered policy choice of almost every State.

[Respondents] contend, however, that the liberty interest they assert *is* consistent with this Court's substantive-due-process line of cases, if not with this Nation's history and practice. Pointing to *Casey* and *Cruzan*, respondents read our jurisprudence in this area as reflecting a general tradition of "self-sovereignty" and as teaching that the "liberty" protected by the Due Process Clause includes "basic and intimate exercises of personal autonomy." According to respondents, our liberty jurisprudence, and the broad, individualistic principles it reflects, protects the "liberty of competent, terminally ill adults to make end-of-life decisions free of undue government interference." The question presented in this case, however, is whether the protections of the Due Process Clause include a right to commit suicide with another's assistance. With this "careful description" of respondents' claim in mind, we turn to *Casey* and *Cruzan*. * * *

analytical method. Just four Terms ago, six of the Justices now sitting joined the Court's opinion in *Reno v. Flores,* 507 U.S. 292, 113 S.Ct. 1439, 123 L.Ed.2d 1 (1993); *Poe* was not even cited. And in *Cruzan,* neither the Court's nor the concurring opinions relied on *Poe;* rather, we concluded that the right to refuse unwanted medical treatment was so rooted in our history, tradition, and practice as to require special protection under the Fourteenth Amendment. True, the Court relied on Justice Harlan's dissent in *Casey,* but, as *Flores* demonstrates, we did not in so doing jettison our established approach. Indeed, to read such a radical move into the Court's opinion in *Casey* would seem to fly in the face of that opinion's emphasis on stare decisis.

Respondents contend that in *Cruzan* we "acknowledged that competent, dying persons have the right to direct the removal of life-sustaining medical treatment and thus hasten death" and that "the constitutional principle behind recognizing the patient's liberty to direct the withdrawal of artificial life support applies at least as strongly to the choice to hasten impending death by consuming lethal medication."

[The] right assumed in *Cruzan*, however, was not simply deduced from abstract concepts of personal autonomy. Given the common-law rule that forced medication was a battery, and the long legal tradition protecting the decision to refuse unwanted medical treatment, our assumption was entirely consistent with this Nation's history and constitutional traditions. The decision to commit suicide with the assistance of another may be just as personal and profound as the decision to refuse unwanted medical treatment, but it has never enjoyed similar legal protection. Indeed, the two acts are widely and reasonably regarded as quite distinct. In *Cruzan* itself, we recognized that most States outlawed assisted suicide—and even more do today—and we certainly gave no intimation that the right to refuse unwanted medical treatment could be somehow transmuted into a right to assistance in committing suicide.

Respondents also rely on *Casey*. [The] Court of Appeals, like the District Court, found *Casey* " 'highly instructive' " and " 'almost prescriptive' " for determining " 'what liberty interest may inhere in a terminally ill person's choice to commit suicide' ": "Like the decision of whether or not to have an abortion, the decision how and when to die is one of 'the most intimate and personal choices a person may make in a lifetime,' a choice 'central to personal dignity and autonomy.' " Similarly, respondents emphasize the statement in *Casey* that: "At the heart of liberty is the right to define one's own concept of existence, of meaning, of the universe, and of the mystery of human life. Beliefs about these matters could not define the attributes of personhood were they formed under compulsion of the State."

By choosing this language, the Court's opinion in *Casey* described, in a general way and in light of our prior cases, those personal activities and decisions that this Court has identified as so deeply rooted in our history and traditions, or so fundamental to our concept of constitutionally ordered liberty, that they are protected by the Fourteenth Amendment. [That] many of the rights and liberties protected by the Due Process Clause sound in personal autonomy does not warrant the sweeping conclusion that any and all important, intimate, and personal decisions are so protected, and *Casey* did not suggest otherwise.

The history of the law's treatment of assisted suicide in this country has been and continues to be one of the rejection of nearly all efforts to permit it. That being the case, our decisions lead us to conclude that the asserted "right" to assistance in committing suicide is not a fundamental liberty interest protected by the Due Process Clause. The Constitution also requires, however, that Washington's assisted-suicide ban be rationally related to legitimate government interests. This requirement is unquestionably met here. As the court below recognized, Washington's assisted-suicide ban implicates a number of state interests.

First, Washington has an "unqualified interest in the preservation of human life." *Cruzan*. The State's prohibition on assisted suicide, like all homicide laws, both reflects and advances its commitment to this interest.

[The] Court of Appeals also recognized Washington's interest in protecting life, but held that the "weight" of this interest depends on the "medical condition and the wishes of the person whose life is at stake." Washington, however, has rejected this sliding-scale approach and, through its assisted-suicide ban, insists that all persons' lives, from beginning to end, regardless of physical or mental condition, are under the full protection of the law. [As] we have previously affirmed, the States "may properly decline to make judgments about the 'quality' of life that a particular individual may enjoy," *Cruzan*. This remains true, as *Cruzan* makes clear, even for those who are near death.

Relatedly, all admit that suicide is a serious public-health problem, especially among persons in otherwise vulnerable groups. [Those] who attempt suicide—terminally ill or not—often suffer from depression or other mental disorders. [But research indicates] that many people who request physician-assisted suicide withdraw that request if their depression and pain are treated. The New York Task Force, however, expressed its concern that, because depression is difficult to diagnose, physicians and medical professionals often fail to respond adequately to seriously ill patients' needs. Thus, legal physician-assisted suicide could make it more difficult for the State to protect depressed or mentally ill persons, or those who are suffering from untreated pain, from suicidal impulses.

The State also has an interest in protecting the integrity and ethics of the medical profession. [The] American Medical Association, like many other medical and physicians' groups, has concluded that "[p]hysician-assisted suicide is fundamentally incompatible with the physician's role as healer." [And] physician-assisted suicide could, it is argued, undermine the trust that is essential to the doctor-patient relationship by blurring the time-honored line between healing and harming.

[Next,] the State has an interest in protecting vulnerable groups—including the poor, the elderly, and disabled persons—from abuse, neglect, and mistakes. The Court of Appeals dismissed [this] concern, [but we] have recognized [the] real risk of subtle coercion and undue influence in end-of-life situations. *Cruzan*. Similarly, the New York Task Force warned that "[l]egalizing physician-assisted suicide would pose profound risks to many individuals who are ill and vulnerable. [The] risk of harm is greatest for the many individuals in our society whose autonomy and well-being are already compromised by poverty, lack of access to good medical care, advanced age, or membership in a stigmatized social group." [If] physician-assisted suicide were permitted, many might resort to it to spare their families the substantial financial burden of end-of-life health-care costs.

The State's interest here goes beyond protecting the vulnerable from coercion; it extends to protecting disabled and terminally ill people from prejudice, negative and inaccurate stereotypes, and "societal indifference." The State's assisted-suicide ban reflects and reinforces its policy that the lives of terminally ill, disabled, and elderly people must be no less valued than the lives of the young and healthy, and that a seriously disabled person's suicidal impulses should be interpreted and treated the same way as anyone else's.

Finally, the State may fear that permitting assisted suicide will start it down the path to voluntary and perhaps even involuntary euthanasia. [The] Court of Appeal's decision, and its expansive reasoning, provide ample support for the State's concerns. The court noted, for example, that the "decision of a duly appointed surrogate decision maker is for all legal purposes the decision of the patient himself"; that "in some instances, the patient may be unable to self-administer the drugs [and] administration by the physician [may] be the only way the patient may be able to receive them"; and that not only physicians, but also family members and loved ones, will inevitably participate in assisting suicide. Thus, it turns out that what is couched as a limited right to "physician-assisted suicide" is likely, in effect, a much broader license, which could prove extremely difficult to police and contain.[23] Washington's ban on assisting suicide prevents such erosion.

This concern is further supported by evidence about the practice of euthanasia in the Netherlands. The Dutch government's own [1990 study] suggests that, despite the existence of various reporting procedures, euthanasia in the Netherlands has not been limited to competent, terminally ill adults who are enduring physical suffering, and that regulation of the practice may not have prevented abuses in cases involving vulnerable persons, including severely disabled neonates and elderly persons suffering from dementia. * * * Washington, like most other States, reasonably ensures against this risk by banning, rather than regulating, assisting suicide.

We need not weigh exactingly the relative strengths of these various interests. They are unquestionably important and legitimate, and Washington's ban on assisted suicide is at least reasonably related to their promotion and protection. We therefore hold that [the challenged Washington statute] does not violate the Fourteenth Amendment, either on its face or "as applied to competent, terminally ill adults who wish to hasten their deaths by obtaining medication prescribed by their doctors."[24] * * *

Throughout the Nation, Americans are engaged in an earnest and profound debate about the morality, legality, and practicality of physician-assisted suicide. Our holding permits this debate to continue, as it should in a democratic society. * * *

JUSTICE O'CONNOR, concurring.*

[The] Court frames the issue in this case as whether the Due Process Clause of the Constitution protects a "right to commit suicide which itself includes a right to assistance in doing so," and concludes that our Nation's history, legal traditions, and practices do not support the existence of such a right. I join the Court's opinions because I agree that there is no generalized right to "commit suicide." But respondents urge us to address the narrower question whether a

---

23. Justice Souter concludes that "[t]he case for the slippery slope is fairly made out here, not because recognizing one due process right would leave a court with no principled basis to avoid recognizing another, but because there is a plausible case that the right claimed would not be readily containable by reference to facts about the mind that are matters of difficult judgment, or by gatekeepers who are subject to temptation, noble or not." We agree that the case for a slippery slope has been made out, [but] we also recognize the reasonableness of the widely expressed skepticism about the lack of a principled basis for confining the right. See Brief for United States as Amicus Curiae ("Once a legislature abandons a categorical prohibition against physician-assisted suicide, there is no obvious stopping point) * * *."

24. Justice Stevens states that "the Court does conceive of respondents' claim as a facial challenge—addressing not the application of the statute to a particular set of plaintiffs before it, but the constitutionality of the statute's categorical prohibition...." We emphasize that we today reject the Court of Appeals'

specific holding that the statute is unconstitutional "as applied" to a particular class. Justice Stevens agrees with this holding, but would not "foreclose the possibility that an individual plaintiff seeking to hasten her death, or a doctor whose assistance was sought, could prevail in a more particularized challenge." Our opinion does not absolutely foreclose such a claim. However, given our holding that the Due Process Clause of the Fourteenth Amendment does not provide heightened protection to the asserted liberty interest in ending one's life with a physician's assistance, such a claim would have to be quite different from the ones advanced by respondents here.

* Justice Ginsburg concurs in the Court's judgments substantially for the reasons stated in this opinion. Justice Breyer joins this opinion except insofar as it joins the opinion of the Court.

[Justice O'Connor's opinion also constitutes her concurring opinion in the companion case of *Vacco v. Quill.*]

mentally competent person who is experiencing great suffering has a constitutionally cognizable interest in controlling the circumstances of his or her imminent death. I see no need to reach that question in the context of the facial challenges to the New York and Washington laws at issue here. [The] parties and *amici* agree that in these States a patient who is suffering from a terminal illness and who is experiencing great pain has no legal barriers to obtaining medication, from qualified physicians, to alleviate that suffering, even to the point of causing unconsciousness and hastening death. In this light, even assuming that we would recognize such an interest, I agree that the State's interests in protecting those who are not truly competent or facing imminent death, or those whose decisions to hasten death would not truly be voluntary, are sufficiently weighty to justify a prohibition against physician-assisted suicide.

Every one of us at some point may be affected by our own or a family member's terminal illness. There is no reason to think the democratic process will not strike the proper balance between the interests of terminally ill, mentally competent individuals who would seek to end their suffering and the State's interests in protecting those who might seek to end life mistakenly or under pressure. As the Court recognizes, States are presently undertaking extensive and serious evaluation of physician-assisted suicide and other related issues. In such circumstances, "[the] challenging task of crafting appropriate procedures for safeguarding * * * liberty interests is entrusted to the 'laboratory' of the States [in] the first instance." *Cruzan* (O'Connor, J., concurring) (citing *New State Ice Co. v. Liebmann* (1932)).

In sum, there is no need to address the question whether suffering patients have a constitutionally cognizable interest in obtaining relief from the suffering that they may experience in the last days of their lives. There is no dispute that dying patients in Washington and New York can obtain palliative care, even when doing so would hasten their deaths. The difficulty in defining terminal illness and the risk that a dying patient's request for assistance in ending his or her life might not be truly voluntary justifies the prohibitions on assisted suicide we uphold here.

JUSTICE STEVENS, concurring in the judgments.[a]

[The] morality, legality, and practicality of capital punishment have been the subject of debate for many years. In 1976, this Court upheld the constitutionality of the practice in cases coming to us from Georgia, Florida, and Texas. In those cases we concluded that a State does have the power to place a lesser value on some lives than on others; there is no absolute requirement that a State treat all human life as having an equal right to preservation. Because the state legislatures had sufficiently narrowed the category of lives that the State could terminate, and had enacted special procedures to ensure that the defendant belonged in that limited category, we concluded that the statutes were not unconstitutional on their face. In later cases coming to us from each of those States, however, we found that some applications of the statutes were unconstitutional.

Today, the Court decides that Washington's statute prohibiting assisted suicide is not invalid "on its face," that is to say, in all or most cases in which it might be applied. That holding, however, does not foreclose the possibility that some applications of the statute might well be invalid. * * *

History and tradition provide ample support for refusing to recognize an open-ended constitutional right to commit suicide. Much more than the State's

a. This opinion also constitutes Justice Stevens's concurring opinion in *Vacco v. Quill*.

paternalistic interest in protecting the individual from the irrevocable conse- quences of an ill-advised decision motivated by temporary concerns is at stake. There is truth in John Donne's observation that "No man is an island." [The] value to others of a person's life is far too precious to allow the individual to claim a constitutional entitlement to complete autonomy in making a decision to end that life. Thus, I fully agree with the Court that the "liberty" protected by the Due Process Clause does not include a categorical "right to commit suicide which itself includes a right to assistance in doing so."

But just as our conclusion that capital punishment is not always unconstitu- tional did not preclude later decisions holding that it is sometimes impermissibly cruel, so is it equally clear that a decision upholding a general statutory prohibi- tion of assisted suicide does not mean that every possible application of the statute would be valid.

[The *Cruzan* Court] assumed that the interest in liberty protected by the Fourteenth Amendment encompassed the right of a terminally ill patient to direct the withdrawal of life-sustaining treatment. [That] assumption [was] supported by the common-law tradition protecting the individual's general right to refuse unwanted medical treatment. [However,] [g]iven the irreversible nature of her illness and the progressive character of her suffering, Nancy Cruzan's interest in refusing medical care was incidental to her more basic interest in controlling the manner and timing of her death. * * * I insist that the source of Nancy Cruzan's right to refuse treatment was not just a common-law rule. Rather, this right is an aspect of a far broader and more basic concept of freedom that is even older than the common law. This freedom embraces, not merely a person's right to refuse a particular kind of unwanted treatment, but also her interest in dignity, and in determining the character of the memories that will survive long after her death.

[Thus,] the common-law right to protection from battery, which included the right to reject medical treatment in most circumstances, did not mark "the outer limits of the substantive sphere of liberty" that supported the Cruzan family's decision to hasten Nancy's death. *Casey.* [Whatever] the outer limits of the concept may be, it definitely includes protection for matters "central to personal dignity and autonomy." *Casey.*

[The] *Cruzan* case demonstrated that some state intrusions on the right to decide how death will be encountered are also intolerable. The now-deceased plaintiffs in this action may in fact have had a liberty interest even stronger than Nancy Cruzan's because, not only were they terminally ill, they were suffering constant and severe pain. Avoiding intolerable pain and the indignity of living one's final days incapacitated and in agony is certainly "[a]t the heart of [the] liberty [to] define one's own concept of existence, of meaning, of the universe, and of the mystery of human life."

[Although] there is no absolute right to physician-assisted suicide, *Cruzan* makes it clear that some individuals who no longer have the option of deciding whether to live or to die because they are already on the threshold of death have a constitutionally protected interest that may outweigh the State's interest in preserving life at all costs. The liberty interest at stake in a case like this differs from, and is stronger than, both the common-law right to refuse medical treat- ment and the unbridled interest in deciding whether to live or die. It is an interest in deciding how, rather than whether, a critical threshold shall be crossed.

The state interests supporting a general rule banning the practice of physi- cian-assisted suicide do not have the same force in all cases. First and foremost of these interests is the " 'unqualified interest in the preservation of human life,' " which is equated with " 'the sanctity of life' " * * * Properly viewed, however, this interest is not a collective interest that should always outweigh the interests of a person who because of pain, incapacity, or sedation finds her life intolerable, but rather, an aspect of individual freedom.

[Allowing] the individual, rather than the State, to make judgments " 'about the "quality" of life that a particular individual may enjoy' " does not mean that the lives of terminally-ill, disabled people have less value than the lives of those who are healthy. Rather, it gives proper recognition to the individual's interest in choosing a final chapter that accords with her life story, rather than one that demeans her values and poisons memories of her. See Brief for Bioethicists as Amici Curiae; see also Ronald Dworkin, *Life's Dominion* 213 (1993). * * *

Similarly, the State's legitimate interests in preventing suicide, protecting the vulnerable from coercion and abuse, and preventing euthanasia are less significant in this context. I agree that the State has a compelling interest in preventing persons from committing suicide because of depression, or coercion by third parties. But the State's legitimate interest in preventing abuse does not apply to an individual who is not victimized by abuse, who is not suffering from depression, and who makes a rational and voluntary decision to seek assistance in dying. * * *

Relatedly, the State and *amici* express the concern that patients whose physical pain is inadequately treated will be more likely to request assisted suicide. Encouraging the development and ensuring the availability of adequate pain treatment is of utmost importance; palliative care, however, cannot alleviate all pain and suffering. [An] individual adequately informed of the care alternatives thus might make a rational choice for assisted suicide. For such an individual, the State's interest in preventing potential abuse and mistake is only minimally implicated.

The final major interest asserted by the State is its interest in preserving the traditional integrity of the medical profession. The fear is that a rule permitting physicians to assist in suicide is inconsistent with the perception that they serve their patients solely as healers. But for some patients, it would be a physician's refusal to dispense medication to ease their suffering and make their death tolerable and dignified that would be inconsistent with the healing role. [Furthermore,] because physicians are already involved in making decisions that hasten the death of terminally ill patients—through termination of life support, withholding of medical treatment, and terminal sedation—there is in fact significant tension between the traditional view of the physician's role and the actual practice in a growing number of cases.[12]

[Unlike] the Court of Appeals, I would not say as a categorical matter that these state interests are invalid as to the entire class of terminally ill, mentally competent patients. I do not, however, foreclose the possibility that an individual plaintiff seeking to hasten her death, or a doctor whose assistance was sought, could prevail in a more particularized challenge. Future cases will determine whether such a challenge may succeed.

12. I note that there is evidence that a significant number of physicians support the practice of hastening death in particular situations. A survey published in the New England Journal of Medicine, found that 56% of responding doctors in Michigan preferred legalizing assisted suicide to an explicit ban. In a survey of Oregon doctors, 60% of the responding doctors supported legalizing assisted suicide for terminally ill patients. Another study showed that 12% of physicians polled in Washington State reported that they had been asked by their terminally ill patients for prescriptions to hasten death, and that, in the year prior to the study, 24% of those physicians had complied with such requests. * * *

[There] remains room for vigorous debate about the outcome of particular cases that are not necessarily resolved by the opinions announced today. How such cases may be decided will depend on their specific facts. In my judgment, however, it is clear that the so-called "unqualified interest in the preservation of human life" is not itself sufficient to outweigh the interest in liberty that may justify the only possible means of preserving a dying patient's dignity and alleviating her intolerable suffering.

JUSTICE SOUTER, concurring in the judgment.

[The] question is whether the statute sets up one of those "arbitrary impositions" or "purposeless restraints" at odds with the Due Process Clause of the Fourteenth Amendment. *Poe v. Ullman* (Harlan, J., dissenting). I conclude that the statute's application to the doctors has not been shown to be unconstitutional, but I write separately to give my reasons for analyzing the substantive due process claims as I do, and for rejecting this one.

[In] their brief to this Court, [the four physicians who brought this challenge to the Washington statute] claim not that they ought to have a right generally to hasten patients' imminent deaths, but only to help patients who have made "personal decisions regarding their own bodies, medical care, and, fundamentally, the future course of their lives," and who have concluded responsibly and with substantial justification that the brief and anguished remainders of their lives have lost virtually all value to them. Respondents fully embrace the notion that the State must be free to impose reasonable regulations on such physician assistance to ensure that the patients they assist are indeed among the competent and terminally ill and that each has made a free and informed choice in seeking to obtain and use a fatal drug.

In response, the State argues that the interest asserted by the doctors is beyond constitutional recognition because it has no deep roots in our history and traditions. But even aside from that, without disputing that the patients here were competent and terminally ill, the State insists that recognizing the legitimacy of doctors' assistance of their patients as contemplated here would entail a number of adverse consequences that the Washington Legislature was entitled to forestall. The nub of this part of the State's argument is not that such patients are constitutionally undeserving of relief on their own account, but that any attempt to confine a right of physician assistance to the circumstances presented by these doctors is likely to fail.

First, the State argues that the right could not be confined to the terminally ill. Even assuming a fixed definition of that term, the State observes that it is not always possible to say with certainty how long a person may live. It asserts that "[t]here is no principled basis on which [the right] can be limited to the prescription of medication for terminally ill patients to administer to themselves" when the right's justifying principle is as broad as " 'merciful termination of suffering' " (citing Yale Kamisar, *Are Laws Against Assisted Suicide Unconstitutional?*, Hastings Center Report 32, 36–37 (May–June 1993)). Second, the State argues that the right could not be confined to the mentally competent, observing that a person's competence cannot always be assessed with certainty, and suggesting further that no principled distinction is possible between a competent patient acting independently and a patient acting through a duly appointed and competent surrogate. Next, according to the State, such a right might entail a right to or at least merge in practice into "other forms of life-ending assistance," such as euthanasia. Finally, the State believes that a right to physician assistance could not easily be distinguished from a right to assistance from others, such as friends, family, and other health-care workers. The State thus argues that recognition of the substantive due process right at issue here would jeopardize the lives of others outside the class defined by the doctors' claim, creating risks of irresponsible suicides and euthanasia, whose dangers are concededly within the State's authority to address.

[The] persistence of substantive due process in our cases points to the legitimacy of the modern justification for such judicial review found in Justice Harlan's dissent in *Poe*,[4] [while] the acknowledged failures of some of these cases point with caution to the difficulty raised by the present claim.

[Justice Harlan's *Poe* dissent] is important for three things that point to our responsibilities today. The first is Justice Harlan's respect for the tradition of substantive due process review itself, and his acknowledgment of the Judiciary's obligation to carry it on. For two centuries American courts, and for much of that time this Court, have thought it necessary to provide some degree of review over the substantive content of legislation under constitutional standards of textual breadth. [This] enduring tradition of American constitutional practice is, in Justice Harlan's view, nothing more than what is required by the judicial authority and obligation to construe constitutional text and review legislation for conformity to that text. * * *

Following the first point of the *Poe* dissent, on the necessity to engage in the sort of examination we conduct today, the dissent's second and third implicitly address those cases, already noted, that are now condemned with virtual unanimity as disastrous mistakes of substantive due process review. The second of the dissent's lessons is a reminder that the business of such review is not the identification of extratextual absolutes but scrutiny of a legislative resolution (perhaps unconscious) of clashing principles, each quite possibly worthy in and of itself, but each to be weighed within the history of our values as a people. It is a comparison of the relative strengths of opposing claims that informs the judicial task, not a deduction from some first premise. Thus informed, judicial review still has no warrant to substitute one reasonable resolution of the contending positions for another, but authority to supplant the balance already struck between the contenders only when it falls outside the realm of the reasonable.

[Justice Harlan's] approach calls for a court to assess the relative "weights" or dignities of the contending interests, and to this extent the judicial method is familiar to the common law. Common law method is subject, however, to two important constraints in the hands of a court engaged in substantive due process review. First, such a court is bound to confine the values that it recognizes to those truly deserving constitutional stature, either to those expressed in constitutional text, or those exemplified by "the traditions from which [the Nation] developed," or revealed by contrast with "the traditions from which it broke." *Poe* (Harlan, J., dissenting).

[The] second constraint, again, simply reflects the fact that constitutional review, not judicial lawmaking, is a court's business here. [It] is only when the legislation's justifying principle, critically valued, is so far from being commensurate with the individual interest as to be arbitrarily or pointlessly applied that the statute must give way. Only if this standard points against the statute can the individual claimant be said to have a constitutional right. * * *[10]

---

4. The status of the Harlan dissent in *Poe v. Ullman* is shown by the Court's adoption of its result in *Griswold* and by the Court's acknowledgment of its status and adoption of its reasoning in *Casey*. * * *

10. Our cases have used various terms to refer to fundamental liberty interests [and] at

[Justice] Harlan of course assumed that adjudication under the Due Process Clauses is like any other instance of judgment dependent on common-law method, being more or less persuasive according to the usual canons of critical discourse. [When] identifying and assessing the competing interests of liberty and authority, for example, the breadth of expression that a litigant or a judge selects in stating the competing principles will have much to do with the outcome and may be dispositive. As in any process of rational argumentation, we recognize that when a generally accepted principle is challenged, the broader the attack the less likely it is to succeed. The principle's defenders will, indeed, often try to characterize any challenge as just such a broadside, perhaps by couching the defense as if a broadside attack had occurred. So the Court in *Dred Scott* treated prohibition of slavery in the Territories as nothing less than a general assault on the concept of property.

Just as results in substantive due process cases are tied to the selections of statements of the competing interests, the acceptability of the results is a function of the good reasons for the selections made. It is here that the value of common-law method becomes apparent, for the usual thinking of the common law is suspicious of the all-or-nothing analysis that tends to produce legal petrification instead of an evolving boundary between the domains of old principles. Common-law method tends to pay respect instead to detail, seeking to understand old principles afresh by new examples and new counterexamples.

[So,] in *Poe,* Justice Harlan viewed it as essential to the plaintiffs' claimed right to use contraceptives that they sought to do so within the privacy of the marital bedroom. This detail in fact served two crucial and complementary functions, and provides a lesson for today. It rescued the individuals' claim from a breadth that would have threatened all state regulation of contraception or intimate relations; extramarital intimacy, no matter how privately practiced, was outside the scope of the right Justice Harlan would have recognized in that case. It was, moreover, this same restriction that allowed the interest to be valued as an aspect of a broader liberty to be free from all unreasonable intrusions into the privacy of the home and the family life within it, a liberty exemplified in constitutional provisions such as the Third and Fourth Amendments,. in prior decisions of the Court involving unreasonable intrusions into the home and family life, and in the then-prevailing status of marriage as the sole lawful locus of intimate relations.[11] The individuals' interest was therefore at its peak in *Poe,* because it was supported by a principle that distinguished of its own force

times we have also called such an interest a "right" even before balancing it against the government's interest, see, e.g., *Roe v. Wade; Carey v. Population Services Int'l.* * * * Precision in terminology, however, favors reserving the label "right" for instances in which the individual's liberty interest actually trumps the government's countervailing interests; only then does the individual have anything legally enforceable as against the state's attempt at regulation.

11. Thus, as the *Poe* dissent illustrates, the task of determining whether the concrete right claimed by an individual in a particular case falls within the ambit of a more generalized protected liberty requires explicit analysis when what the individual wants to do could arguably be characterized as belonging to different strands of our legal tradition requiring

different degrees of constitutional scrutiny. See also Laurence H. Tribe & Michael C. Dorf, *Levels of Generality in the Definition of Rights,* 57 U.Chi.L.Rev. 1057, 1091 (1990) (abortion might conceivably be assimilated either to the tradition regarding women's reproductive freedom in general, which places a substantial burden of justification on the State, or to the tradition regarding protection of fetuses, as embodied in laws criminalizing feticide by someone other than the mother, which generally requires only rationality on the part of the State). Selecting among such competing characterizations demands reasoned judgment about which broader principle, as exemplified in the concrete privileges and prohibitions embodied in our legal tradition, best fits the particular claim asserted in a particular case.

between areas in which government traditionally had regulated (sexual relations outside of marriage) and those in which it had not (private marital intimacies), and thus was broad enough to cover the claim at hand without being so broad as to be shot-through by exceptions.

On the other side of the balance, the State's interest in *Poe* was not fairly characterized simply as preserving sexual morality, or doing so by regulating contraceptive devices. [It] was assumed that the State might legitimately enforce limits on the use of contraceptives through laws regulating divorce and annulment, or even through its tax policy, *ibid.,* but not necessarily be justified in criminalizing the same practice in the marital bedroom, which would entail the consequence of authorizing state enquiry into the intimate relations of a married couple who chose to close their door.

The same insistence on exactitude lies behind questions, in current terminology, about the proper level of generality at which to analyze claims and counterclaims, and the demand for fitness and proper tailoring of a restrictive statute is just another way of testing the legitimacy of the generality at which the government sets up its justification. We may therefore classify Justice Harlan's example of proper analysis in any of these ways: as applying concepts of normal critical reasoning, as pointing to the need to attend to the levels of generality at which countervailing interests are stated, or as examining the concrete application of principles for fitness with their own ostensible justifications. But whatever the categories in which we place the dissent's example, it stands in marked contrast to earlier cases whose reasoning was marked by comparatively less discrimination, and it points to the importance of evaluating the claims of the parties now before us with comparable detail. For here we are faced with an individual claim not to a right on the part of just anyone to help anyone else commit suicide under any circumstances, but to the right of a narrow class to help others also in a narrow class under a set of limited circumstances. And the claimants are met with the State's assertion, among others, that rights of such narrow scope cannot be recognized without jeopardy to individuals whom the State may concededly protect through its regulations.

Respondents claim that a patient facing imminent death, who anticipates physical suffering and indignity, and is capable of responsible and voluntary choice, should have a right to a physician's assistance in providing counsel and drugs to be administered by the patient to end life promptly. They accordingly claim that a physician must have the corresponding right to provide such aid, contrary to the provisions of [state law]. I do not understand the argument to rest on any assumption that rights either to suicide or to assistance in committing it are historically based on such. Respondents, rather, acknowledge the prohibition of each historically, but rely on the fact that to a substantial extent the State has repudiated that history. The result of this, respondents say, is to open the door to claims of such a patient to be accorded one of the options open to those with different, traditionally cognizable claims to autonomy in deciding how their bodies and minds should be treated.

[The] principal significance of [the history of suicide] in the State of Washington, according to respondents, lies in its repudiation of the old tradition to the extent of eliminating the criminal suicide prohibitions. Respondents do not argue that the State's decision goes further, to imply that the State has repudiated any legitimate claim to discourage suicide or to limit its encouragement. The reasons for the decriminalization, after all, may have had more to do with difficulties of law enforcement than with a shift in the value ascribed to life in various circumstances or in the perceived legitimacy of taking one's own. Thus it may indeed make sense for the State to take its hands off suicide as such, while continuing to prohibit the sort of assistance that would make its commission easier. Decriminalization does not, then, imply the existence of a constitutional liberty interest in suicide as such; it simply opens the door to the assertion of a cognizable liberty interest in bodily integrity and associated medical care that would otherwise have been inapposite so long as suicide, as well as assisting a suicide, was a criminal offense.

* * * Constitutional recognition of the right to bodily integrity underlies the assumed right, good against the State, to require physicians to terminate artificial life support, *Cruzan,* [and] the affirmative right to obtain medical intervention to cause abortion, see *Casey.* It is, indeed, in the abortion cases that the most telling recognitions of the importance of bodily integrity and the concomitant tradition of medical assistance have occurred. [The] analogies between the abortion cases and this one are several. Even though the State has a legitimate interest in discouraging abortion, the Court recognized a woman's right to a physician's counsel and care. Like the decision to commit suicide, the decision to abort potential life can be made irresponsibly and under the influence of others, and yet the Court has held in the abortion cases that physicians are fit assistants. Without physician assistance in abortion, the woman's right would have too often amounted to nothing more than a right to self-mutilation, and without a physician to assist in the suicide of the dying, the patient's right will often be confined to crude methods of causing death, most shocking and painful to the decedent's survivors.

There is, finally, one more reason for claiming that a physician's assistance here would fall within the accepted tradition of medical care in our society, and the abortion cases are only the most obvious illustration of the further point. While the Court has held that the performance of abortion procedures can be restricted to physicians, the Court's opinion in *Roe* recognized the doctors' role in yet another way. For, in the course of holding that the decision to perform an abortion called for a physician's assistance, the Court recognized that the good physician is not just a mechanic of the human body whose services have no bearing on a person's moral choices, but one who does more than treat symptoms, one who ministers to the patient. [This] idea of the physician as serving the whole person is a source of the high value traditionally placed on the medical relationship. Its value is surely as apparent here as in the abortion cases, for just as the decision about abortion is not directed to correcting some pathology, so the decision in which a dying patient seeks help is not so limited.

[Respondents] argue that the State has in fact already recognized enough evolving examples of this tradition of patient care to demonstrate the strength of their claim. Washington, like other States, authorizes physicians to withdraw life-sustaining medical treatment and artificially delivered food and water from patients who request it, even though such actions will hasten death. The State permits physicians to alleviate anxiety and discomfort when withdrawing artificial life-supporting devices by administering medication that will hasten death even further. And it generally permits physicians to administer medication to patients in terminal conditions when the primary intent is to alleviate pain, even when the medication is so powerful as to hasten death and the patient chooses to receive it with that understanding.

The argument supporting respondents' position thus progresses through three steps of increasing forcefulness. First, it emphasizes the decriminalization of suicide. Reliance on this fact is sanctioned under the standard that looks not only to the tradition retained, but to society's occasional choices to reject traditions of the legal past. See *Poe* (Harlan, J., dissenting). [The] second step in the argument is to emphasize that the State's own act of decriminalization gives a freedom of choice much like the individual's option in recognized instances of bodily autonomy. One of these, abortion, is a legal right to choose in spite of the interest a State may legitimately invoke in discouraging the practice, just as suicide is now subject to choice, despite a state interest in discouraging it. The third step is to emphasize that respondents claim a right to assistance not on the basis of some broad principle that would be subject to exceptions if that continuing interest of the State's in discouraging suicide were to be recognized at all. Respondents base their claim on the traditional right to medical care and counsel, subject to the limiting conditions of informed, responsible choice when death is imminent, conditions that support a strong analogy to rights of care in other situations in which medical counsel and assistance have been available as a matter of course. There can be no stronger claim to a physician's assistance than at the time when death is imminent, a moral judgment implied by the State's own recognition of the legitimacy of medical procedures necessarily hastening the moment of impending death.

In my judgment, the importance of the individual interest here, as within that class of "certain interests" demanding careful scrutiny of the State's contrary claim, see *Poe,* cannot be gainsaid. Whether that interest might in some circumstances, or at some time, be seen as "fundamental" to the degree entitled to prevail is not, however, a conclusion that I need draw here, for I am satisfied that the State's interests [are] sufficiently serious to defeat the present claim that its law is arbitrary or purposeless.

The State has put forward several interests to justify the Washington law as applied to physicians treating terminally ill patients, even those competent to make responsible choices: protecting life generally, discouraging suicide even if knowing and voluntary, and protecting terminally ill patients from involuntary suicide and euthanasia, both voluntary and nonvoluntary.

It is not necessary to discuss the exact strengths of the first two claims of justification in the present circumstances, for the third is dispositive for me. That third justification is different from the first two, for it addresses specific features of respondents' claim, and it opposes that claim not with a moral judgment contrary to respondents', but with a recognized state interest in the protection of nonresponsible individuals and those who do not stand in relation either to death or to their physicians as do the patients whom respondents describe. The State claims interests in protecting patients from mistakenly and involuntarily deciding to end their lives, and in guarding against both voluntary and involuntary euthanasia. [The] argument is that a progression would occur, obscuring the line between the ill and the dying, and between the responsible and the unduly influenced, until ultimately doctors and perhaps others would abuse a limited freedom to aid suicides by yielding to the impulse to end another's suffering under conditions going beyond the narrow limits the respondents propose. The State thus argues, essentially, that respondents' claim is not as narrow as it sounds, simply because no recognition of the interest they assert could be limited to vindicating those interests and affecting no others. The State says that the claim, in practical effect, would entail consequences that the State could, without doubt, legitimately act to prevent.

[The State argues] that dependence on the vigilance of physicians will not be enough. First, the lines proposed here (particularly the requirement of a knowing and voluntary decision by the patient) would be more difficult to draw than the lines that have limited other recently recognized due process rights. Limiting a state from prosecuting use of artificial contraceptives by married couples posed no practical threat to the State's capacity to regulate contraceptives in other ways that were assumed at the time of *Poe* to be legitimate; the trimester measurements of *Roe* and the viability determination of *Casey* were easy to make with a real degree of certainty. But the knowing and responsible mind is harder to assess.[16] Second, this difficulty could become the greater by combining with another fact within the realm of plausibility, that physicians simply would not be assiduous to preserve the line. They have compassion, and those who would be willing to assist in suicide at all might be the most susceptible to the wishes of a patient, whether the patient were technically quite responsible or not. Physicians, and their hospitals, have their own financial incentives, too, in this new age of managed care. Whether acting from compassion or under some other influence, a physician who would provide a drug for a patient to administer might well go the further step of administering the drug himself; so, the barrier between assisted suicide and euthanasia could become porous, and the line between voluntary and involuntary euthanasia as well.[17] The case for the slippery slope is fairly made out here, not because recognizing one due process right would leave a court with no principled basis to avoid recognizing another, but because there is a plausible case that the right claimed would not be readily containable by reference to facts about the mind that are matters of difficult judgment, or by gatekeepers who are subject to temptation, noble or not.

Respondents propose an answer to all this, the answer of state regulation with teeth. Legislation proposed in several States, for example, would authorize physician-assisted suicide but require two qualified physicians to confirm the patient's diagnosis, prognosis, and competence; and would mandate that the patient make repeated requests witnessed by at least two others over a specified time span; and would impose reporting requirements and criminal penalties for various acts of coercion.

But at least at this moment there are reasons for caution in predicting the effectiveness of the teeth proposed. Respondents' proposals, as it turns out, sound much like the guidelines now in place in the Netherlands, the only place where experience with physician-assisted suicide and euthanasia has yielded empirical evidence about how such regulations might affect actual practice. [There] is, however, a substantial dispute today about what the Dutch experience

---

16. While it is also more difficult to assess in cases involving limitations on life incidental to pain medication and the disconnection of artificial life support, there are reasons to justify a lesser concern with the punctilio of responsibility in these instances. The purpose of requesting and giving the medication is presumably not to cause death but to relieve the pain so that the State's interest in preserving life is not unequivocally implicated by the practice; and the importance of pain relief is so clear that there is less likelihood that relieving pain would run counter to what a responsible patient would choose, even with the consequences for life expectancy. As for ending artificial life support, the State again may see its interest in preserving life as weaker here than in the general case just because artificial life support preserves life when nature would

not; and, because such life support is a frequently offensive bodily intrusion, there is a lesser reason to fear that a decision to remove it would not be the choice of one fully responsible. Where, however, a physician writes a prescription to equip a patient to end life, the prescription is written to serve an affirmative intent to die (even though the physician need not and probably does not characteristically have an intent that the patient die but only that the patient be equipped to make the decision). The patient's responsibility and competence are therefore crucial when the physician is presented with the request.

17. Again, the same can be said about life support and shortening life to kill pain, but the calculus may be viewed as different in these instances, as noted just above.

shows. Some commentators marshall evidence that the Dutch guidelines have in practice failed to protect patients from involuntary euthanasia and have been violated with impunity. This evidence is contested. The day may come when we can say with some assurance which side is right, but for now it is the substantiality of the factual disagreement, and the alternatives for resolving it, that matter. They are, for me, dispositive of the due process claim at this time.

I take it that the basic concept of judicial review with its possible displacement of legislative judgment bars any finding that a legislature has acted arbitrarily when the following conditions are met: there is a serious factual controversy over the feasibility of recognizing the claimed right without at the same time making it impossible for the State to engage in an undoubtedly legitimate exercise of power; facts necessary to resolve the controversy are not readily ascertainable through the judicial process; but they are more readily subject to discovery through legislative factfinding and experimentation. It is assumed in this case, and must be, that a State's interest in protecting those unable to make responsible decisions and those who make no decisions at all entitles the State to bar aid to any but a knowing and responsible person intending suicide, and to prohibit euthanasia. How, and how far, a State should act in that interest are judgments for the State, but the legitimacy of its action to deny a physician the option to aid any but the knowing and responsible is beyond question.

The capacity of the State to protect the others if respondents were to prevail is, however, subject to some genuine question, underscored by the responsible disagreement over the basic facts of the Dutch experience. This factual controversy is not open to a judicial resolution with any substantial degree of assurance at this time. [While] an extensive literature on any subject can raise the hopes for judicial understanding, the literature on this subject is only nascent. Since there is little experience directly bearing on the issue, the most that can be said is that whichever way the Court might rule today, events could overtake its assumptions, as experimentation in some jurisdictions confirmed or discredited the concerns about progression from assisted suicide to euthanasia.

Legislatures, on the other hand, have superior opportunities to obtain the facts necessary for a judgment about the present controversy. [Moreover,] their mechanisms include the power to experiment, moving forward and pulling back as facts emerge within their own jurisdictions. * * *

I do not decide here what the significance might be of legislative foot-dragging in ascertaining the facts going to the State's argument that the right in question could not be confined as claimed. [Now,] it is enough to say that our examination of legislative reasonableness should consider the fact that the Legislature of the State of Washington is no more obviously at fault than this Court is in being uncertain about what would happen if respondents prevailed today. We therefore have a clear question about which institution, a legislature or a court, is relatively more competent to deal with an emerging issue as to which facts currently unknown could be dispositive. The answer has to be, for the reasons already stated, that the legislative process is to be preferred. There is a closely related further reason as well.

One must bear in mind that the nature of the right claimed, if recognized as one constitutionally required, would differ in no essential way from other constitutional rights guaranteed by enumeration or derived from some more definite textual source than "due process." An unenumerated right should not therefore be recognized, with the effect of displacing the legislative ordering of things, without the assurance that its recognition would prove as durable as the recognition of those other rights differently derived. To recognize a right of lesser promise would simply create a constitutional regime too uncertain to bring with it the expectation of finality that is one of this Court's central obligations in making constitutional decisions.

Legislatures, however, are not so constrained. The experimentation that should be out of the question in constitutional adjudication displacing legislative judgments is entirely proper, as well as highly desirable, when the legislative power addresses an emerging issue like assisted suicide. The Court should accordingly stay its hand to allow reasonable legislative consideration. While I do not decide for all time that respondents' claim should not be recognized, I acknowledge the legislative institutional competence as the better one to deal with that claim at this time.

JUSTICE GINSBURG, concurring in the judgments.

I concur in the Court's judgments in these cases substantially for the reasons stated by Justice O'Connor in her concurring opinion.

JUSTICE BREYER, concurring in the judgments.

I believe that Justice O'Connor's views, which I share, have greater legal significance than the Court's opinion suggests. I join her separate opinion, except insofar as it joins the majority. And I concur in the judgments. I shall briefly explain how I differ from the Court.

I agree with the Court in *Vacco v. Quill,* [infra] that the articulated state interests justify the distinction drawn between physician assisted suicide and withdrawal of life-support. I also agree [that] the critical question in both of the cases before us is whether "the 'liberty' specially protected by the Due Process Clause includes a right" of the sort that the respondents assert. *Washington v. Glucksberg.* I do not agree, however, with the Court's formulation of that claimed "liberty" interest. The Court describes it as a "right to commit suicide with another's assistance." But I would not reject the respondents' claim without considering a different formulation, for which our legal tradition may provide greater support. That formulation would use words roughly like a "right to die with dignity." But irrespective of the exact words used, at its core would lie personal control over the manner of death, professional medical assistance, and the avoidance of unnecessary and severe physical suffering—combined.

As Justice Souter points out, Justice Harlan's dissenting opinion in *Poe* offers some support for such a claim. In that opinion, Justice Harlan referred to the "liberty" that the Fourteenth Amendment protects as including "a freedom from all substantial arbitrary impositions and purposeless restraints" and also as recognizing that "*certain interests* require particularly careful scrutiny of the state needs asserted to justify their abridgment." The "certain interests" to which Justice Harlan referred may well be similar (perhaps identical) to the rights, liberties, or interests that the Court today, as in the past, regards as "fundamental."

Justice Harlan concluded that marital privacy was such a "special interest." He found in the Constitution a right of "privacy of the home"—with the home, the bedroom, and "intimate details of the marital relation" at its heart—by examining the protection that the law had earlier provided for related, but not identical, interests described by such words as "privacy," "home," and "family." The respondents here essentially ask us to do the same. They argue that one can find a "right to die with dignity" by examining the protection the law has provided for related, but not identical, interests relating to personal dignity, medical treatment, and freedom from state-inflicted pain.

I do not believe, however, that this Court need or now should decide whether or a not such a right is "fundamental." That is because, in my view, the avoidance of severe physical pain (connected with death) would have to comprise an essential part of any successful claim and because, as Justice O'Connor points out, the laws before us do not *force* a dying person to undergo that kind of pain. Rather, the laws of New York and of Washington do not prohibit doctors from providing patients with drugs sufficient to control pain despite the risk that those drugs themselves will kill. And under these circumstances the laws of New York and Washington would overcome any remaining significant interests and would be justified, regardless.

Medical technology, we are repeatedly told, makes the administration of pain-relieving drugs sufficient, except for a very few individuals for whom the ineffectiveness of pain control medicines can mean, not pain, but the need for sedation which can end in a coma. We are also told that there are many instances in which patients do not receive the palliative care that, in principle, is available, but that is so for institutional reasons or inadequacies or obstacles, which would seem possible to overcome, and which do *not* include *a prohibitive set of laws*.

This legal circumstance means that the state laws before us do not infringe directly upon the (assumed) central interest (what I have called the core of the interest in dying with dignity) as, by way of contrast, the state anticontraceptive laws at issue in *Poe* did interfere with the central interest there at stake—by bringing the State's police powers to bear upon the marital bedroom.

Were the legal circumstances different—for example, were state law to prevent the provision of palliative care, including the administration of drugs as needed to avoid pain at the end of life—then the law's impact upon serious and otherwise unavoidable physical pain (accompanying death) would be more directly at issue. And as Justice O'Connor suggests, the Court might have to revisit its conclusions in these cases.

VACCO v. QUILL
521 U.S. 793, 117 S.Ct. 2293, 138 L.Ed.2d 834 (1997).

CHIEF JUSTICE REHNQUIST delivered the opinion of the Court.

In New York, as in most States, it is a crime to aid another to commit or attempt suicide, but patients may refuse even lifesaving medical treatment. The question presented by this case is whether New York's prohibition on assisting suicide therefore violates the Equal Protection Clause of the Fourteenth Amendment. We hold that it does not.

[Respondent New York physicians] assert that although it would be "consistent with the standards of [their] medical practice[s]" to prescribe lethal medication for "mentally competent, terminally ill patients" who are suffering great pain and desire a doctor's help in taking their own lives, they are deterred from doing so by New York's ban on assisting suicide. Respondents, and three gravely ill patients who have since died, [maintain] that because New York permits a competent person to refuse life-sustaining medical treatment, and because the refusal of such treatment is "essentially the same thing" as physician-assisted suicide, New York's assisted-suicide ban violates the Equal Protection Clause.

The District Court disagreed, [but the] Court of Appeals for the Second Circuit reversed, [concluding that] "New York law does not treat equally all competent persons who are in the final stages of fatal illness and wish to hasten their deaths," because "those in the final stages of terminal illness who are on life-support systems are allowed to hasten their deaths by directing the removal of such systems; but those who are similarly situated, except for the previous attachment of life-sustaining equipment, are not allowed to hasten death by self-administering prescribed drugs." In the court's view, "[t]he ending of life by [the withdrawal of life-support systems] is *nothing more nor less than assisted suicide*" (emphasis added). The Court of Appeals then examined whether this supposed unequal treatment was rationally related to any legitimate state interests,[5] and concluded that [it was not].

[The] Equal Protection Clause [embodies] a general rule that States must treat like cases alike but may treat unlike cases accordingly. If a legislative classification or distinction "neither burdens a fundamental right nor targets a suspect class, we will uphold [it] so long as it bears a rational relation to some legitimate end." *Romer v. Evans* [p. 86 of this Supplement].

New York's statutes outlawing assisting suicide [neither] infringe fundamental rights nor involve suspect classifications. [These] laws are therefore entitled to a "strong presumption of validity."

On their faces, neither New York's ban on assisting suicide nor its statutes permitting patients to refuse medical treatment treat anyone differently than anyone else or draw any distinctions between persons. *Everyone,* regardless of physical condition, is entitled, if competent, to refuse unwanted lifesaving medical treatment; *no one* is permitted to assist a suicide. Generally speaking, laws that apply evenhandedly to all "unquestionably comply" with the Equal Protection Clause.

The Court of Appeals, however, concluded that some terminally ill people—those who are on life-support systems—are treated differently than those who are not, in that the former may "hasten death" by ending treatment, but the latter may not "hasten death" through physician-assisted suicide. This conclusion depends on the submission that ending or refusing lifesaving medical treatment "is nothing more nor less than assisted suicide." Unlike the Court of Appeals, we think the distinction between assisting suicide and withdrawing life-sustaining treatment, a distinction widely recognized and endorsed in the medical profession and in our legal traditions, is both important and logical; it is certainly rational.

The distinction comports with fundamental legal principles of causation and intent. First, when a patient refuses life-sustaining medical treatment, he dies from an underlying fatal disease or pathology; but if a patient ingests lethal medication prescribed by a physician, he is killed by that medication. * * *

Furthermore, a physician who withdraws, or honors a patient's refusal to begin, life-sustaining medical treatment purposefully intends, or may so intend, only to respect his patient's wishes and "to cease doing useless and futile or degrading things to the patient when [the patient] no longer stands to benefit from them." The same is true when a doctor provides aggressive palliative care; in some cases, painkilling drugs may hasten a patient's death, but the physician's purpose and intent is, or may be, only to ease his patient's pain. A doctor who assists a suicide, however, "must, necessarily and indubitably, intend primarily that the patient be made dead." Similarly, a patient who commits suicide with a

---

5. The court acknowledged that because New York's assisted-suicide statutes "do not impinge on any fundamental rights [or] involve suspect classifications," they were subject only to rational-basis judicial scrutiny.

doctor's aid necessarily has the specific intent to end his or her own life, while a patient who refuses or discontinues treatment might not.

[The] law has long used actors' intent or purpose to distinguish between two acts that may have the same result. * * * Put differently, the law distinguishes actions taken "because of" a given end from actions taken "in spite of" their unintended but foreseen consequences.

[Given] these general principles, it is not surprising that many courts, including New York courts, have carefully distinguished refusing life-sustaining treatment from suicide. * * * Similarly, the overwhelming majority of state legislatures have drawn a clear line between assisting suicide and withdrawing or permitting the refusal of unwanted lifesaving medical treatment by prohibiting the former and permitting the latter. And "nearly all states expressly disapprove of suicide and assisted suicide either in statutes dealing with durable powers of attorney in health-care situations, or in 'living will' statutes." Thus, even as the States move to protect and promote patients' dignity at the end of life, they remain opposed to physician-assisted suicide.

New York is a case in point. The State enacted its current assisted-suicide statutes in 1965.[10] Since then, New York has acted several times to protect patients' common-law right to refuse treatment [but] reaffirmed the line between "killing" and "letting die." * * * More recently, the New York State Task Force on Life and the Law studied assisted suicide and euthanasia and, in 1994, unanimously recommended against legalization.

[This] Court has also recognized, at least implicitly, the distinction between letting a patient die and making that patient die. In *Cruzan* our assumption of a right to refuse treatment was grounded not, as the Court of Appeals supposed, on the proposition that patients have a general and abstract "right to hasten death," but on well established, traditional rights to bodily integrity and freedom from unwanted touching. In fact, we observed that "the majority of States in this country have laws imposing criminal penalties on one who assists another to commit suicide." *Cruzan* therefore provides no support for the notion that refusing life-sustaining medical treatment is "nothing more nor less than suicide."

For all these reasons, we disagree with respondents' claim that the distinction between refusing lifesaving medical treatment and assisted suicide is "arbitrary" and "irrational."[11] [By] permitting everyone to refuse unwanted medical treatment while prohibiting anyone from assisting a suicide, New York law follows a longstanding and rational distinction.

New York's reasons for recognizing and acting on this distinction—including prohibiting intentional killing and preserving life; preventing suicide; maintaining physicians' role as their patients' healers; protecting vulnerable people from

---

10. It has always been a crime, either by statute or under the common law, to assist a suicide in New York. See Marzen, O'Dowd, Crone, & Balch, *Suicide: A Constitutional Right?*, 24 Duquesne L.Rev. 1, 205–210 (1985) (Appendix).

11. Respondents also argue that the State irrationally distinguishes between physician-assisted suicide and "terminal sedation," a process respondents characterize as "induc[ing] barbiturate coma and then starv[ing] the person to death." Petitioners insist, however, that " '[a]lthough proponents of physician-assisted suicide and euthanasia contend that terminal sedation is covert physician-assisted suicide or euthanasia, the concept of sedating pharmacotherapy is based on informed consent and the principle of double effect.' " Just as a State may prohibit assisting suicide while permitting patients to refuse unwanted lifesaving treatment, it may permit palliative care related to that refusal, which may have the foreseen but unintended "double effect" of hastening the patient's death.

indifference, prejudice, and psychological and financial pressure to end their lives; and avoiding a possible slide towards euthanasia—are discussed in greater detail in our opinion in *Glucksberg*. These valid and important public interests easily satisfy the constitutional requirement that a legislative classification bear a rational relation to some legitimate end.[13] * * *

[The concurring opinions of Justices O'Connor, Stevens, Ginsburg and Breyer in *Glucksberg*, supra, also constitute their concurring opinions in *Vacco v. Quill*. The portion of Justice Steven's opinion addressing the equal protection issue is set forth below.]

JUSTICE STEVENS, concurring in the judgments. * * *

In New York, a doctor must respect a competent person's decision to refuse or to discontinue medical treatment even though death will thereby ensue, but the same doctor would be guilty of a felony if she provided her patient assistance in committing suicide. Today we hold that the Equal Protection Clause is not violated by the resulting disparate treatment of two classes of terminally ill people who may have the same interest in hastening death. I agree that the distinction between permitting death to ensue from an underlying fatal disease and causing it to occur by the administration of medication or other means provides a constitutionally sufficient basis for the State's classification. Unlike the Court, however, I am not persuaded that in all cases there will in fact be a significant difference between the intent of the physicians, the patients or the families in the two situations.

There may be little distinction between the intent of a terminally-ill patient who decides to remove her life-support and one who seeks the assistance of a doctor in ending her life; in both situations, the patient is seeking to hasten a certain, impending death. The doctor's intent might also be the same in prescribing lethal medication as it is in terminating life support. A doctor who fails to administer medical treatment to one who is dying from a disease could be doing so with an intent to harm or kill that patient. Conversely, a doctor who prescribes lethal medication does not necessarily intend the patient's death—rather that doctor may seek simply to ease the patient's suffering and to comply with her wishes. The illusory character of any differences in intent or causation is confirmed by the fact that the American Medical Association unequivocally endorses the practice of terminal sedation—the administration of sufficient dosages of pain-killing medication to terminally ill patients to protect them from excruciating pain even when it is clear that the time of death will be advanced. The purpose of terminal sedation is to ease the suffering of the patient and comply with her wishes, and the actual cause of death is the administration of heavy doses of lethal sedatives. This same intent and causation may exist when a doctor complies with a patient's request for lethal medication to hasten her death.[15]

---

13. Justice Stevens observes that our holding today "does not foreclose the possibility that some applications of the New York statute may impose an intolerable intrusion on the patient's freedom." This is true, but, as we observe in *Glucksberg*, a particular plaintiff hoping to show that New York's assisted-suicide ban was unconstitutional in his particular case would need to present different and considerably stronger arguments than those advanced by respondents here.

15. If a doctor prescribes lethal drugs to be self-administered by the patient, it not at all clear that the physician's intent is that the patient "be made dead." Many patients prescribed lethal medications never actually take them; they merely acquire some sense of control in the process of dying that the availability of those medications provides.

Thus, although the differences the majority notes in causation and intent between terminating life-support and assisting in suicide support the Court's rejection of the respondents' facial challenge, these distinctions may be inapplicable to particular terminally ill patients and their doctors. Our holding today in *Vacco v. Quill* that the Equal Protection Clause is not violated by New York's classification, just like our holding in *Washington v. Glucksberg* that the Washington statute is not invalid on its face, does not foreclose the possibility that some applications of the New York statute may impose an intolerable intrusion on the patient's freedom.

There remains room for vigorous debate about the outcome of particular cases that are not necessarily resolved by the opinions announced today. How such cases may be decided will depend on their specific facts. In my judgment, however, it is clear that the so-called "unqualified interest in the preservation of human life" is not itself sufficient to outweigh the interest in liberty that may justify the only possible means of preserving a dying patient's dignity and alleviating her intolerable suffering.

JUSTICE SOUTER, concurring in the judgment.

Even though I do not conclude that assisted suicide is a fundamental right entitled to recognition at this time, I accord the claims raised by the patients and physicians in this case and *Washington v. Glucksberg* a high degree of importance, requiring a commensurate justification. The reasons that lead me to conclude in *Glucksberg* that the prohibition on assisted suicide is not arbitrary under the due process standard also support the distinction between assistance to suicide, which is banned, and practices such as termination of artificial life support and death-hastening pain medication, which are permitted. * * *

Notes and Questions

1. *Preventing pain relief; the "double effect" principle.* Providing medication to terminally ill people knowing that it will have a "double effect"—reduce the patient's pain and hasten death—is widely accepted by the medical profession. Many physicians and bioethicists seem to believe that providing risky pain relief is always justifiable, regardless of how certain or probable the risk of death may be. Recently, however, two law professors have maintained that as a matter of criminal law the physician's motive or desire to relieve pain does not automatically or necessarily justify the administration of pain relief. Norman Cantor & George Thomas, *Pain Relief, Acceleration of Death, and Criminal Law*, 6 Kennedy Inst. of Ethics J. 107 (June, 1996). They argue that if, for example, the situation were such that no analgesic dosage could provide pain relief without also causing prompt death (or if under the circumstances it was almost certain that the required analgesic dosage would cause death) the physician who administered the analgesic would be criminally liable for the resulting death even though death was not intended. According to the authors, as defined by the Model Penal Code these deaths would be "knowing" homicides (acting with awareness that one's conduct is "practically certain" to bring about a particular result). Moreover, according to the authors, if it were *highly likely* that the administration of an analgesic would cause prompt death (for example a 75–90% chance), the physician who used the painkillers that caused the death would also be criminally liable (for having acted "recklessly").

Suppose, inspired by the Cantor–Thomas article, a state legislature criminalized the use of medication designed to relieve severe pain when it is highly likely (or more probable than not) that administration of such pain relief would cause death. In such an event, how many members of the Supreme Court would be inclined to "revisit" the questions raised by the physician-assisted suicide cases? See Robert A. Burt, *The Supreme Court Speaks—Not Assisted Suicide but a Constitutional Right to Palliative Care*, 337 New Eng. J. Med, 1234 (1997); Lawrence O. Gostin, *Deciding Life and Death in the Courtroom*, 278 JAMA 1523, 1527–28 (1997); Yale Kamisar, *On the Meaning and Impact of the Physician–Assisted Suicide Cases*, 82 Minn. L. Rev. 895, 904–09 (1998).

2. *Judicial "minimalism" and the 1997 physician-assisted suicide cases.* As he explains at considerable length in his book, *One Case at a Time: Judicial Minimalism on the Supreme Court* (1999), Professor Cass R. Sunstein is a strong proponent of judicial "minimalism." As a general matter, this approach leaves important questions unresolved by saying no more than necessary to justify the outcome of a case. (Judicial "maximalism," on the other hand, is the practice of deciding cases in a way that establishes broad rules for the future.)

Professor Sunstein maintains (p. 89) that because "it is extremely difficult to produce any verbal formula that is satisfying, consistent with current law, and adequate to resolve the issue of physician-assisted suicide, * * * the best and appropriately minimalist route is for the Court simply to assume that the right qualifies as fundamental and to proceed from there to the question of justification." According to Sunstein, although Rehnquist, C.J., rejected this approach, the five justices who wrote concurring opinions did not.[a] "In good minimalist fashion," these five justices "left open the question whether people facing pain and imminent death" may have a constitutional right to physician-assisted suicide and "[t]he Court was right not to decide that question" (p. 76).[b]

Professor Sunstein criticizes Rehnquist, C.J., for writing "the ambitious, emphatically nonminimalist opinion that he and Justice Scalia have been (unsuccessfully) urging on the Court in the abortion cases—an opinion that would limit the right of privacy, and indeed all fundamental rights under the due process clause, to those rights that are 'deeply rooted' in our long-standing traditions and practices" (Preface, p. xii).

But consider Jeffrey Rosen, *The Age of Mixed Results*, (essay review of Sunstein's book), The New Republic, June 28, 1999, pp. 43, 46: "[W]hy is Rehnquist's opinion 'emphatically nonminimalist'? The conventional tools of legal interpretation—text, history, tradition, constitutional structure, and judicial precedent—all fail to support the claim that there is a fundamental right to physician-assisted suicide, even to alleviate great pain when death is imminent. By recognizing the weakness of the argument for a judicially created right to die, and by removing the courts from the debate entirely, Rehnquist's approach would seem to preserve the largest space for democratic deliberation."

"Yet Sunstein prefers the far more elusive approach of Justice O'Connor, who stressed that the Court had not decided whether or not a competent person

---

a. Professor Sunstein is well aware that five justices signed the Chief Justice's opinion, but he observes that O'Connor, J., who signed the Chief Justice's opinion, "wrote one of her characteristic separate opinions, * * * caution[ing] that the Court had not decided whether a competent person experiencing great suffering had a constitutional right to control the circumstances of an imminent death. That issue remained to be decided on another day." (Preface, p. xii) "What this means," continues Sunstein, "is that a majori-

ty of five justices on the Court has signaled the possible existence of a right to physician-assisted suicide in compelling circumstances—and thus a five-justice majority has rejected the whole approach in Rehnquist's opinion (for a five-justice majority)." (Ibid.)

b. Sunstein adds, however, that when and if it is forced to decide that question, the Court should conclude that "the state has sufficient reason to override the individual interest even in such extreme cases" (p. 76).

experiencing great suffering might have a constitutional right to control the circumstances of imminent death. * * *"

"Sunstein, like O'Connor, says that the Court should assume that the right to physician-assisted suicide is 'presumptively protected' in medically hopeless cases, but should also hold that the state's interests are sufficiently strong to override it. Why is this opaque holding more 'minimalist' than Rehnquist's far less intrusive alternative? Since neither Sunstein nor O'Connor explains the reasons that might persuade the Court to recognize a presumptive right to die under medically hopeless conditions, all this has the feel of a fiat, and it raises the specter that the Court might create other unenumerated rights in the future with similarly thin support in text, history, and precedent. Wasn't it precisely this threat of an untethered court inventing constitutional rights without coherent explanations that the minimalist project was designed to avoid?"

3. *The significance of the informally agreed-upon "right" to assisted suicide, especially in compelling cases.* A number of prominent commentators opposed to the legalization of physician-assisted suicide (e.g., John Arras, Ezekiel Emanuel and Mark Siegler) defend the flat prohibition partly on the ground that it is *not really* a flat ban—that the availability of informal practice and informally agreed-upon "rights," especially in the most compelling cases, *reduces the pressure* to legalize these practices formally. But which way does "the availability of informal practice" cut? See the discussion in Yale Kamisar, *Physician–Assisted Suicide: The Problems Presented by the Compelling, Heartwrenching Case,* 88 J.Crim.L. & Crim. 1121 (1998).

4. *What next?* Should the question of whether and how physician-assisted suicide (PAS) is to be legalized be left to state legislatures? Consider Charles H. Baron, *Pleading for Physician–Assisted Suicide in the Courts,* 19 W. New Eng. L.Rev. 371, 373, 389, 398–99 (1997) (written before the Supreme Court's PAS decisions):

"Both courts and legislatures have played important roles in the development of contemporary American law regarding the 'right to die,' but many of the most significant first steps were taken by the courts [discussing, inter alia, *In re Quinlan,* 70 N.J. 10, 355 A.2d 647 (1976); *Superintendent of Belchertown State School v. Saikewicz,* 373 Mass. 728, 370 N.E.2d 417 (1977); *In re Conroy,* 98 N.J. 321, 486 A.2d 1209 (1985); and *Brophy v. New England Sinai Hospital,* 398 Mass. 417, 497 N.E.2d 626 (1986)]."

"[Until the 1990s] the law of the right to die in New Jersey was governed entirely by principles and procedures developed by New Jersey courts, out of decisions in cases that cried out for recognition of a right to die on the facts presented. At each step along the way, the New Jersey Supreme Court described itself as being forced to act, at least in part, in the face of the legislature's failure to do so—going so far as to establish, on its own authority, the legality of living wills and durable powers of attorney for health care. [Even] in states where comprehensive right to die legislation has been enacted, courts have been required to fashion common law as part of the comprehensive package of rules governing the right to die."

"[The] various state supreme courts that have bottomed the right to die on various provisions of their state constitutions and the federal constitutions [have] continually urged the state legislatures to develop comprehensive rules for dealing with the issues that were raised. Indeed, as time has passed, the state supreme courts have emphasized the constitutional aspects less and have used state common law increasingly—in part, presumably, to provide a greater scope of experimentation for state legislatures. The New Jersey Supreme Court, for example, beginning [in 1985], has relied primarily upon the common law principles of informed consent, and only secondarily upon the constitutional right to privacy."

"[The] fears that have kept state legislatures from leading the way in developing the right to die law in the past still seem to haunt the corridors of our legislative assemblies. Oregon has thus far been the only state to legalize [PAS] by legislation, and that law was enacted through a citizen initiative vote—not by the normal legislative process."

5. *After Glucksberg and Quill, how will PAS proponents fare in the state courts? Krischer v. McIver*, 697 So.2d 97 (Fla. 1997), indicates that they may meet heavy resistance. About six months *before* the U.S. Supreme Court's decisions in the PAS cases, a Florida trial court held that a terminally ill AIDS patient was entitled, under the Privacy Amendment of the Florida Constitution, to determine the time and manner of his death and that, in order to do so, he had the right to seek and obtain the assistance of his physician in committing suicide. However, a few weeks *after* the U.S. Supreme Court's PAS decisions, the Florida Supreme Court reversed the trial court (5–1).

Since Florida's Privacy Amendment establishes a right much broader in scope than that of the U.S. Constitution, the Florida Supreme Court could have distinguished *Glucksberg* and *Quill* quite easily. Instead, however, the Court quoted at length from Rehnquist C.J.'s opinion in *Glucksberg* and from the New York Task Force Report on assisted suicide and euthanasia, a report that recommended unanimously that New York's total ban against assisted suicide and euthanasia be maintained. (Rehnquist, C.J., had also relied heavily on the New York report.) After balking at arguments frequently made by PAS proponents, the Florida Supreme Court concluded: "By broadly construing the privacy amendment to include the right to assisted suicide, we would run the risk of arrogating to ourselves those powers to make social policy that as a constitutional matter belong only to the legislature."

6. *The second-degree murder conviction of Dr. Kevorkian.* In March of 1999, after having assisted, by his own count, in over 100 suicides, and after been acquitted of assisted suicide in several previous cases, Dr. Jack Kevorkian was convicted of second-degree murder (and sentenced to 10 to 25 years in prison) for administering a lethal injection to Lou Gehrig's disease patient Thomas Youk. *The New York Times* editorialized, March 27, 1999, p. A26: "Most advocates of physician-assisted suicide hold as a first principle that the patient must be the one in full control. The Oregon laws that have legalized assisted suicide, for example, honor that principle. Dr. Kevorkian's mercy killing violates it. Previous juries have let him off the hook for assisting in suicides. But this jury drew the line at direct killing."

Is this the message of the Kevorkian conviction? How significant was it that a videotape of Kevorkian injecting Youk with a lethal dose was shown on CBS's "60 Minutes" in a segment in which Kevorkian dared prosecutors to charge him? How significant was it that the trial judge ruled that the issue of whether Mr. Youk consented to his death was irrelevant and that the jury never heard Youk's wife or mother or brother tell how grateful they were that Kevorkian was available? How significant was it that in all the previous cases Dr. Kevorkian had been represented by Geoffrey Fieger, a prominent trial attorney, but in the Youk case he represented himself?

Many opponents of assisted suicide applauded Kevorkian's conviction and hoped that it signaled a change in public attitude. However, as pointed out in Charles H. Baron, *Assisted Dying*, Trial, July 1999, at 44, recent opinion polls in the United States indicate that this is not so: "[These polls] show a high and increasing level of support for legalization and regulation of physician-assisted suicide. A Field poll taken after [Kevorkian's] conviction shows that support in California has increased in the last two years from 70 percent to 75 percent (from 61 percent to 68 percent among Roman Catholics). An ABC News poll showed that 55 percent of the public disagreed with the jury's verdict [in the trial of Dr. Kevorkian for the death of Mr. Youk], and only 39 percent agreed."

7. The Supreme Court's rulings in *Glucksberg* and *Quill* have generated a considerable amount of commentary. See, e.g., *Symposium: Physician–Assisted Suicide: Facing Death after* Glucksberg *and* Quill, 82 Minn. L. Rev. 885–1101 (1998) (contributions by Howard Brody, Robert Burt, Ezekiel Emanual, Yale Kamisar, Patricia King, Sylvia Law, Kathryn Tucker, Leslie Wolf and Susan Wolf); Lawrence Gostin, note 1 supra; Martha Minow, *Which Question? Which Lie? Reflections on the Physician–Assisted Suicide Case*, 1997 Sup. Ct. Rev. 1; David Orentlicher, *The Supreme Court and Physician–Assisted Suicide—Rejecting Assisted Suicide, but Embracing Euthanasia*, 337 New Eng. J. Med. 1236 (1997); Note, 111 Harv. L. Rev. 237 (1997); Robert A Sedler, *Abortion, Physician–Assisted Suicide and the Constitution*, 12 Notre Dame J. L., Ethics & Pub. Policy 529 (1998); Sunstein, note 2 supra.

THE RIGHT TO TRAVEL

CON LAW: P. 555, add after note 4

RTS & LIB: P. 461, add after note 4

5. *The three different components of the right to travel.* In SAENZ v. ROE, discussed at greater length at pp. 30, 214 of this Supplement, in the course of holding that state welfare programs may not restrict new residents, for the first year they live in the state, to the welfare benefits they would have received in the state of their prior residence, a 7–2 majority, per STEVENS, J., observed: "The 'right to travel' discussed in our cases embraces at least three different components. It protects the right of a citizen of one State to enter and to leave another State, the right to be treated as a welcome visitor rather than an unfriendly alien when temporarily present in the second State, and, for those travelers who elect to become permanent residents, the right to be treated like other citizens of that State. * * *

"What is at issue in this case [is the] third aspect of the right to travel—the right of the newly arrived citizen to the same privilege and immunities enjoyed by other citizens of the same State. That right is protected not only by the new arrival's status as a state citizen, but also by her status as a citizen of the United States. That additional source of protection is plainly identified in the opening words of the Fourteenth Amendment: ' * * * No State shall make or enforce any law which shall abridge the privileges or immunities of citizens of the United States.' Despite fundamentally differing views concerning the coverage of the Privileges or Immunities Clause of the Fourteenth Amendment, most notably expressed in the majority and dissenting opinions in the *Slaughter–House Cases*, it has always been common ground that this Clause protects the third component of the right to travel."

PROCEDURAL DUE PROCESS IN NON–CRIMINAL CASES

DEPRIVATION OF "LIBERTY" AND "PROPERTY" INTERESTS

CON LAW: P. 595, add after note 6 (b)

RTS & LIB: P. 502, add after note 6 (b)

(c) COLLEGE SAVINGS BANK v. FLORIDA PREPAID POSTSECONDARY EDUCATION EXPENSE BOARD, 527 U.S. 666, 119 S.Ct. 2219, 144 L.Ed.2d 605 (1999): Petitioner markets and sells certificates of deposit designed to finance college costs. When respondent, a Florida state entity, began its own tuition prepayment program, petitioner filed suit, alleging that by its false and misleading advertising respondent had violated the Lanham Act and that the Trademark Remedy Clarification Act (TRCA) had subjected states to suits brought under the Lanham Act. Congress's abrogation of sovereign immunity in the TRCA was effective, argued petitioner, since it was enacted to enforce the Fourteenth Amendment's Due Process Clause. The Court, per SCALIA, J., disagreed: "[The] object of valid [legislation under § 5 of the fourteenth amendment] must be the carefully delimited remediation or prevention of constitutional violations. Petitioner claims [that] Congress enacted the TRCA to remedy and prevent state deprivations without due process of two species of 'property' rights: (1) a right to be free from a business competitor's false advertising about its own product, and (2) a more generalized right to be secure in one's business interests. Neither of these qualifies as a property right protected by the Due Process Clause.

"As to the first: The hallmark of a protected property interest is the right to exclude others. [The] Lanham Act may well contain provisions that protect constitutionally cognizable property interests—notably, its provisions dealing with infringement of trademarks, which are the 'property' of the new owner because he can exclude others from using them. [The] Lanham Act's false-advertising provisions, however, bear no relationship to any right to exclude; and Florida Prepaid's alleged misrepresentations concerning its own products intruded upon no interest over which petitioner had exclusive dominion. * * *

"Petitioner's second assertion of a property interest rests upon an argument [that] businesses are 'property' within the meaning of the Due Process Clause, and that Congress legislates under § 5 when it passes a law that prevents state interference with business (which false advertising does). The assets of a business (including its good will) unquestionably are property, and any state taking of those assets is unquestionably a 'deprivation' under the Fourteenth Amendment. But business in the sense of the activity of doing business, or the activity of making a profit, is not property in the ordinary sense—and it is only that, and not any business asset, which is impinged upon by a competitor's false advertising."

Stevens, Souter, Ginsburg and Breyer, JJ., dissented from the Court's opinion, but only Stevens, J., expressed disagreement with this part.

CON LAW: P. 597, end of note 7

RTS & LIB: P. 504, end of note 7

It is not easy to reconcile KANSAS v. HENDRICKS, 521 U.S. 346, 117 S.Ct. 2072, 138 L.Ed.2d 501 (1997), with *Foucha*. In 1994, the year Hendricks was scheduled to complete his 10–year prison term for taking "indecent liberties" with two 13–year old boys, Kansas enacted the Sexually Violent Predators Act (SVPA), establishing procedures for civilly committing persons who, because of a "mental abnormality" or a "personality disorder," are likely to commit "predatory acts of sexual violence." The legislature explained in the preamble to the new law that it did not consider the existing involuntary civil commitment statute adequate to deal with SVPs because such persons "do not have a mental disease or defect that renders them appropriate for involuntary commitment." The Act was invoked for the first time against Hendricks, just before he was scheduled to be released from prison.

The state did not deny that Supreme Court precedents seemed to require that a person subject to civil commitment be "mentally ill," but argued that the Court had not constitutionalized any particular definition of the term. Hendricks, continued the state, was diagnosed as having pedophilia—a condition the psychiatric profession classifies as a "mental disorder" and a condition that Hendricks admitted made him unable to control the urge to molest children.

The Court, per THOMAS, J. (who had dissented in *Foucha*), concluded that the Kansas statute satisfied the "mental Illness" requirement, pointing out that no case had ever required state legislatures to adopt any particular nomenclature in drafting civil commitment statutes. Breyer, J., joined by Stevens, Souter, and Ginsburg, JJ., dissented on other grounds,[a] but supported the majority on the substantive due process issue. Hendricks's abnormality, emphasized Breyer, J., "does not consist simply of a long course of antisocial behavior, but rather it includes a specific, serious and highly unusual inability to control his actions. [The] law traditionally has considered this kind of abnormality akin to insanity for purposes of confinement."

CON LAW: P. 598, at end of note 8 (a)
RTS & LIB: P. 505, at end of note 8 (a)

How, if at all, can *College Savings Bank*, p. 85 of this Supplement, be reconciled with *Zimmerman Brush*?

---

a. Because the SVPA did not provide Hendricks (or others like him) any treatment until after he completed his prison term and only inadequate treatment then the dissenters maintained that the Act was really "an effort to inflict further punishment" upon Hendricks in violation of the Ex Post Facto Clause. However the majority rejected the ex post facto claim because it considered the SVPA civil in nature and confinement under it not tantamount to "punishment."

FREEDOM OF EXPRESSION AND ASSOCIATION

REPUTATION AND PRIVACY

EMOTIONAL DISTRESS

CON LAW: P. 690, after note 1

AMER CON: P. 700, after note 1

RTS & LIB: P. 597, after note 1

SCHENCK v. PRO–CHOICE NETWORK OF WESTERN NEW YORK, 519 U.S. 357, 117 S.Ct. 855, 137 L.Ed.2d 1 (1997), per REHNQUIST, C.J., maintained that an injunction ordering abortion protesters to cease and desist from "counseling" women entering abortion clinics, who indicate they do not wish to be counseled, could not be sustained in order to protect privacy: "As [a] general matter, we have indicated that in public debate our own citizens must tolerate insulting, and often outrageous, speech in order to provide adequate breathing space to the freedoms protected by the First Amendment."[a]

DISCLOSURE OF PRIVATE FACTS

CON LAW: p. 696, after note 2

AMER CON: p. 706, after note 2

RTS & LIB: P. 603, after note 2

3. *Media ride-alongs.* WILSON v. LAYNE, 526 U.S. 603, 119 S.Ct. 1692, 143 L.Ed.2d 818 (1999), per REHNQUIST, C.J., held that privacy considerations outweighed the interests served by having *Washington Post* reporters accompany police in executing an arrest warrant in the home: "Respondents argue that the presence of the *Washington Post* reporters in the Wilsons' home [served] a number of legitimate law enforcement purposes. They first assert that officers should be able to exercise reasonable discretion about when it would 'further their law enforcement mission to permit members of the news media to accompany them in executing a warrant.' But this claim ignores the importance of the right of residential privacy at the core of the Fourth Amendment. It may well be that media ride-alongs further the law enforcement objectives of the police in a general

---

a. This portion of the injunction was sustained on other grounds. Demonstrators had previously engaged in physical intimidation against women and their escorts. The lower court ordered demonstrators to stay 15 feet away from doorways, driveways, and driveway entrances except for two sidewalk counselors in order to accommodate free speech rights. The Court observed that the counselors, if ordered to desist, and other demonstrators could present their messages outside the 15-foot buffer zone and that their consignment to that area was a result of their own previous intimidation. Agreeing with the Court that the privacy ground had no merit and finding no other basis in the lower court's findings to support the cease and desist rule (once the counselors had already been admitted within the 15-foot zone), Scalia, J., joined by Kennedy and Thomas, JJ., dissenting would have upheld this portion of the injunction.

sense, but that is not the same as furthering the purposes of the search. Were such generalized 'law enforcement objectives' themselves sufficient to trump the Fourth Amendment, the protections guaranteed by that Amendment's text would be significantly watered down.''

"Respondents next argue that the presence of third parties could serve the law enforcement purpose of publicizing the government's efforts to combat crime, and facilitate accurate reporting on law enforcement activities. There is certainly language in our opinions interpreting the First Amendment which points to the importance of 'the press' in informing the general public about the administration of criminal justice. *Cox Broadcasting.* [No] one could gainsay the truth of these observations, or the importance of the First Amendment in protecting press freedom from abridgement by the government. But the Fourth Amendment also protects a very important right, and in the present case it is in terms of that right that the media ride-alongs must be judged.

"Surely the possibility of good public relations for the police is simply not enough, standing alone, to justify the ride-along intrusion into a private home. And even the need for accurate reporting on police issues in general bears no direct relation to the constitutional justification for the police intrusion into a home in order to execute a felony arrest warrant.

"Finally, respondents argue that the presence of third parties could serve in some situations to minimize police abuses and protect suspects, and also to protect the safety of the officers. While it might be reasonable for police officers to themselves videotape home entries as part of a 'quality control' effort to ensure that the rights of homeowners are being respected, or even to preserve evidence, such a situation is significantly different from the media presence in this case. The *Washington Post* reporters in the Wilsons' home were working on a story for their own purposes. They were not present for the purpose of protecting the officers, much less the Wilsons. A private photographer was acting for private purposes, as evidenced in part by the fact that the newspaper and not the police retained the photographs. Thus, although the presence of third parties during the execution of a warrant may in some circumstances be constitutionally permissible, the presence of these third parties was not.''

"The reasons advanced by respondents, taken in their entirety, fall short of justifying the presence of media inside a home. We hold that it is a violation of the Fourth Amendment for police to bring members of the media or other third parties into a home during the execution of a warrant when the presence of the third parties in the home was not in aid of the execution of the warrant.[a]

SHOULD NEW CATEGORIES BE CREATED?

HARM TO CHILDREN AND THE OVERBREADTH DOCTRINE

CON LAW: P. 737, add to fn. 26

AMER CON: P. 747, add to fn. 26

RTS & LIB: P. 644, add to note fn. 26

[Scalia, J., dissenting in *Chicago v. Morales*, 527 U.S. 41, S.Ct. 1849, 144 L.Ed.2d. 67 (1999), argues that in order to avoid advisory

---

a. Stevens, J., concurring in part and dissenting in part, agreed that media ride-alongs violated the fourth amendment, but dissented on a different issue.

opinions, federal courts should limit themselves to as applied attacks, but that if they
insist on considering

facial attacks, they should insist that a statute be unconstitutional in all its applications before declaring it unconstitutional. Are either of these positions acceptable?]

IS SOME PROTECTED SPEECH LESS EQUAL THAN OTHER PROTECTED SPEECH?
NEAR OBSCENE SPEECH

CON LAW: P. 800, substitute for Barnes
AMER CON: P. 810, substitute for Barnes
RTS & LIB: P. 707, substitute for Barnes

Five years after *Renton*, the Court held that an Indiana statute prohibiting the knowing or intentional appearing in a public place in a state of nudity could constitutionally be applied to require that female dancers at a minimum wear "pasties" and a "G-string" when they dance. *Barnes v. Glen Theatre, Inc.*, 501 U.S. 560, 111 S.Ct. 2456, 115 L.Ed.2d 504 (1991). The Justices upholding the ordinance were divided upon the rationale for doing so. Rehnquist, C.J., joined by O'Connor and Kennedy, JJ., applied the *O'Brien* test, characterized the statute as a "public indecency" statute, and concluded that the interests in order and morality justified the statute. Souter, J., concurring, also applied the *O'Brien* test, but concluded that the statute was justified by the "secondary effects" of prostitution, sexual assaults, and other criminal activity even though he recognized that the secondary effects justification had not been articulated by the Indiana legislature or its courts. Scalia, J., argued against the plurality that the interest in morality was not substantial enough to pass muster under *O'Brien*; nonetheless, he voted to uphold the statute by repudiating the *O'Brien* test. He argued that when a general law is directed at conduct, not specifically against expression, it is subject to no first amendment test even if it is applied against expression. White, joined by Marshall, Blackmun, and Stevens, J., dissenting, argued that the Indiana statute was directed at expression and did not survive close scrutiny.

The fragmented character of the *Barnes* majority created interpretive difficulties for the Pennsylvania Supreme Court in considering an ordinance of Erie, Pennsylvania. Like Indiana, Erie, Pennsylvania, enacted an ordinance making it a offense to knowingly or intentionally appear in public in a "state of nudity." Unlike Indiana, however, the Erie city council made it clear that nude dancing was a special concern in its passage of the ordinance. The preamble to the ordinance stated that "Council specifically wishes to adopt the concept of Public Indecency prohibited by the laws of the State of Indiana, which was approved by the U.S. Supreme Court in *Barnes v. Glen Theatre Inc.*, * * * for the purpose of limiting a recent increase in nude live entertainment within the City" which led to prostitution and other crime.

Pap's A.M., a Pennsylvania corporation, operated "Kandyland," an Erie establishment featuring nude erotic dancing by women. To comply with the ordinance, as written, these dancers had to wear, at a minimum, "pasties" and a "G-string." Pap's filed suit against Erie and city officials, seeking declaratory relief and a permanent injunction against the ordinance's enforcement. The Pennsylvania Supreme Court was unable to find a lowest common denominator uniting the *Barnes* majority; so it felt free to reach an independent judgment, and proceeded to find that the Erie ordinance, although also directed at secondary effects, was primarily directed at expression and did not survive close scrutiny.

CITY OF ERIE v. PAP'S A.M., ___ U.S. ___, 120 S.Ct. 1382, 146 L.Ed.2d 265 (2000), per O'CONNOR, J. joined by Rehnquist, C.J., Kennedy, and Breyer, JJ., concluded that the application of the ordinance to prevent nude dancing was constitutional:[a] "Being 'in a state of nudity' is not an inherently expressive condition. As we explained in *Barnes*, however, nude dancing of the type at issue here is expressive conduct, although we think that it falls only within the outer ambit of the First Amendment's protection. * * *

"In *Barnes*, we analyzed an almost identical statute, holding that Indiana's public nudity ban did not violate the First Amendment, although no five Members of the Court agreed on a single rationale for that conclusion. We now clarify that government restrictions on public nudity such as the ordinance at issue here should be evaluated under the framework set forth in *O'Brien* for content-neutral restrictions on symbolic speech. * * *

"The ordinance here, like the statute in *Barnes*, is on its face a general prohibition on public nudity. By its terms, the ordinance regulates conduct alone. It does not target nudity that contains an erotic message; rather, it bans all public nudity, regardless of whether that nudity is accompanied by expressive activity. And like the statute in *Barnes*, the Erie ordinance replaces and updates provisions of an 'Indecency and Immorality' ordinance that has been on the books since 1866, predating the prevalence of nude dancing establishments such as Kandyland. * * *

"Although the Pennsylvania Supreme Court acknowledged that one goal of the ordinance was to combat the negative secondary effects associated with nude dancing establishments, the court concluded that the ordinance was nevertheless content based, relying on Justice White's position in dissent in *Barnes* for the proposition that a ban of this type *necessarily* has the purpose of suppressing the erotic message of the dance. Because the Pennsylvania court agreed with Justice White's approach, it concluded that the ordinance must have another, 'unmentioned' purpose related to the suppression of expression. That is, the Pennsylvania court adopted the dissent's view in *Barnes* that '[s]ince the State permits the dancers to perform if they wear pasties and G-strings but forbids nude dancing, it is precisely because of the distinctive, expressive content of the nude dancing performances at issue in this case that the State seeks to apply the statutory prohibition.' A majority of the Court rejected that view in *Barnes*, and we do so again here.

"Respondent's argument that the ordinance is 'aimed' at suppressing expression through a ban on nude dancing—an argument that respondent supports by pointing to statements by the city attorney that the public nudity ban was not intended to apply to 'legitimate' theater productions—is really an argument that the city council also had an illicit motive in enacting the ordinance. As we have said before, however, this Court will not strike down an otherwise constitutional statute on the basis of an alleged illicit motive. In light of the Pennsylvania court's determination that one purpose of the ordinance is to combat harmful secondary effects, the ban on public nudity here is no different from the ban on burning draft registration cards in *O'Brien*, where the Government sought to prevent the means of the expression and not the expression of antiwar sentiment itself.

"Justice Stevens argues that the ordinance enacts a complete ban on expression. We respectfully disagree with that characterization. The public nudity ban

---

a. O'Connor, J., rebuffed a contention that the case was moot. Scalia, J., joined by Thomas, J., would have sustained the mootness claim. Stevens, J., joined by Ginsburg, J., did not address the issue.

certainly has the effect of limiting one particular means of expressing the kind of erotic message being disseminated at Kandyland. But simply to define what is being banned as the 'message' is to assume the conclusion. We did not analyze the regulation in *O'Brien* as having enacted a total ban on expression. Instead, the Court recognized that the regulation against destroying one's draft card was justified by the Government's interest in preventing the harmful 'secondary effects' of that conduct (disruption to the Selective Service System), even though that regulation may have some incidental effect on the expressive element of the conduct. Because this justification was unrelated to the suppression of O'Brien's antiwar message, the regulation was content neutral. Although there may be cases in which banning the means of expression so interferes with the message that it essentially bans the message, that is not the case here. * * *

"Similarly, even if Erie's public nudity ban has some minimal effect on the erotic message by muting that portion of the expression that occurs when the last stitch is dropped, the dancers at Kandyland and other such establishments are free to perform wearing pasties and G-strings. Any effect on the overall expression is de minimis. And as Justice Stevens eloquently stated for the plurality in *Young* v. *American Mini Theatres, Inc.,* 'even though we recognize that the First Amendment will not tolerate the total suppression of erotic materials that have some arguably artistic value, it is manifest that society's interest in protecting this type of expression is of a wholly different, and lesser, magnitude than the interest in untrammeled political debate,' and 'few of us would march our sons or daughters off to war to preserve the citizen's right to see' specified anatomical areas exhibited at establishments like Kandyland. If States are to be able to regulate secondary effects, then *de minimis* intrusions on expression such as those at issue here cannot be sufficient to render the ordinance content based. See *Clark* v. *Community for Creative Non–Violence*; *Ward* v. *Rock Against Racism* (even if regulation has an incidental effect on some speakers or messages but not others, the regulation is content neutral if it can be justified without reference to the content of the expression).

"This case is, in fact, similar to *O'Brien, Community for Creative Non–Violence,* and *Ward.* The justification for the government regulation in each case prevents harmful 'secondary' effects that are unrelated to the suppression of expression. See, e.g., *Ward* v. *Rock Against Racism* (noting that '[t]he principal justification for the sound-amplification guideline is the city's desire to control noise levels at bandshell events, in order to retain the character of [the adjacent] Sheep Meadow and its more sedate activities,' and citing *Renton* for the proposition that '[a] regulation that serves purposes unrelated to the content of expression is deemed neutral, even if it has an incidental effect on some speakers or messages but not others'). While the doctrinal theories behind 'incidental burdens' and 'secondary effects' are, of course, not identical, there is nothing objectionable about a city passing a general ordinance to ban public nudity (even though such a ban may place incidental burdens on some protected speech) and at the same time recognizing that one specific occurrence of public nudity—nude erotic dancing—is particularly problematic because it produces harmful secondary effects.

"[W]e conclude that Erie's ordinance is justified under *O'Brien.* [E]rie's efforts to protect public health and safety are clearly within the city's police powers. * * * The asserted interests of regulating conduct through a public nudity ban and of combating the harmful secondary effects associated with nude dancing are undeniably important. And in terms of demonstrating that such secondary effects pose a threat, the city need not 'conduct new studies or produce evidence independent of that already generated by other cities' to demonstrate the problem of secondary effects, 'so long as whatever evidence the city relies upon is reasonably believed to be relevant to the problem that the city addresses.' *Renton.* * * * Erie could reasonably rely on the evidentiary foundation set forth in *Renton* and *American Mini Theatres* to the effect that secondary effects are caused by the presence of even one adult entertainment establishment in a given neighborhood. See *Renton* (indicating that reliance on a judicial opinion that describes the evidentiary basis is sufficient). In fact, Erie expressly relied on *Barnes* and its discussion of secondary effects, including its reference to *Renton* and *American Mini Theatres.* * * *

"In any event, Erie also relied on its own findings. The preamble to the ordinance states that 'the Council of the City of Erie *has, at various times over more than a century, expressed its findings* that certain lewd, immoral activities carried on in public places for profit are highly detrimental to the public health, safety and welfare, and lead to the debasement of both women and men, promote violence, public intoxication, prostitution and other serious criminal activity.' The city council members, familiar with commercial downtown Erie, are the individuals who would likely have had first-hand knowledge of what took place at and around nude dancing establishments in Erie, and can make particularized, expert judgments about the resulting harmful secondary effects. Analogizing to the administrative agency context, it is well established that, as long as a party has an opportunity to respond, an administrative agency may take official notice of such 'legislative facts' within its special knowledge, and is not confined to the evidence in the record in reaching its expert judgment. Here, Kandyland has had ample opportunity to contest the council's findings about secondary effects—before the council itself, throughout the state proceedings, and before this Court. Yet to this day, Kandyland has never challenged the city council's findings or cast any specific doubt on the validity of those findings. Instead, it has simply asserted that the council's evidentiary proof was lacking. In the absence of any reason to doubt it, the city's expert judgment should be credited.

"Justice Souter, however, would require Erie to develop a specific evidentiary record supporting its ordinance[,] and he agrees that the ordinance should therefore be evaluated under *O'Brien. O'Brien*, of course, required no evidentiary showing at all that the threatened harm was real. But that case is different, *Justice Souter* contends, because in *O'Brien* 'there could be no doubt' that a regulation prohibiting the destruction of draft cards would alleviate the harmful secondary effects flowing from the destruction of those cards.

"But whether the harm is evident to our 'intuition,' is not the proper inquiry. If it were, we would simply say there is no doubt that a regulation prohibiting public nudity would alleviate the harmful secondary effects associated with nude dancing. * * * Justice Souter attempts to denigrate the city council's conclusion that the threatened harm was real, arguing that we cannot accept Erie's findings because the subject of nude dancing is 'fraught with some emotionalism,' Yet surely the subject of drafting our citizens into the military is 'fraught' with more emotionalism than the subject of regulating nude dancing.

"As to [whether] the regulation furthers the government interest—it is evident that, since crime and other public health and safety problems are caused by the presence of nude dancing establishments like Kandyland, a ban on such nude dancing would further Erie's interest in preventing such secondary effects. To be sure, requiring dancers to wear pasties and G-strings may not greatly reduce these secondary effects, but *O'Brien* requires only that the regulation further the interest in combating such effects. [It may] be true that a pasties and

G-string requirement would not be as effective as, for example, a requirement that the dancers be fully clothed, but the city must balance its efforts to address the problem with the requirement that the restriction be no greater than necessary to further the city's interest.

"[The requirement that the restriction be] no greater than is essential to the furtherance of the government interest—is satisfied as well. The ordinance regulates conduct, and any incidental impact on the expressive element of nude dancing is *de minimis*. The requirement that dancers wear pasties and G-strings is a minimal restriction in furtherance of the asserted government interests, and the restriction leaves ample capacity to convey the dancer's erotic message. Justice Souter points out that zoning is an alternative means of addressing this problem. It is far from clear, however, that zoning imposes less of a burden on expression than the minimal requirement implemented here. In any event, since this is a content-neutral restriction, least restrictive means analysis is not required.

"We hold, therefore, that Erie's ordinance is a content-neutral regulation that is valid under *O'Brien*. Accordingly, the judgment of the Pennsylvania Supreme Court is reversed, and the case is remanded for further proceedings not inconsistent with this opinion."

SCALIA, J., joined by Thomas., J., concurred: "I agree that the decision of the Pennsylvania Supreme Court must be reversed, but disagree with the mode of analysis the Court has applied. The city of Erie self-consciously modeled its ordinance on the public nudity statute we upheld against constitutional challenge in *Barnes*. [In] *Barnes*, I voted to uphold the challenged Indiana statute 'not because it survives some lower level of First Amendment scrutiny, but because, as a general law regulating conduct and not specifically directed at expression, it is not subject to First Amendment scrutiny at all.' Erie's ordinance, too, by its terms prohibits not merely nude dancing, but the act—irrespective of whether it is engaged in for expressive purposes—of going nude in public. The facts that a preamble to the ordinance explains that its purpose, in part, is to 'limi[t] a recent increase in nude live entertainment,' that city councilmembers in supporting the ordinance commented to that effect, and that the ordinance includes in the definition of nudity the exposure of devices simulating that condition, neither make the law any less general in its reach nor demonstrate that what the municipal authorities *really* find objectionable is expression rather than public nakedness. As far as appears (and as seems overwhelmingly likely), the preamble, the councilmembers' comments, and the chosen definition of the prohibited conduct simply reflect the fact that Erie had recently been having a public nudity problem not with streakers, sunbathers or hot-dog vendors, but with lap dancers.

"There is no basis for the contention that the ordinance does not apply to nudity in theatrical productions such as Equus or Hair. Its text contains no such limitation. It was stipulated in the trial court that no effort was made to enforce the ordinance against a production of Equus involving nudity that was being staged in Erie at the time the ordinance became effective. Notwithstanding Justice Stevens' assertion to the contrary, however, neither in the stipulation, nor elsewhere in the record, does it appear that the city was aware of the nudity—and before this Court counsel for the city attributed nonenforcement not to a general exception for theatrical productions, but to the fact that no one had complained. One instance of nonenforcement—against a play already in production that prosecutorial discretion might reasonably have 'grandfathered'—does not render this ordinance discriminatory on its face. To be sure, in the trial court counsel for the city said that '[t]o the extent that the expressive activity that is contained in

[such] productions rises to a higher level of protected expression, they would not be [covered],'—but he rested this assertion upon the provision in the preamble that expressed respect for 'fundamental Constitutional guarantees of free speech and free expression.' [What] he was saying there [was] essentially what he said at oral argument before this Court: that the ordinance would not be enforceable against theatrical productions if the Constitution forbade it. Surely that limitation does not cause the ordinance to be not generally applicable, in the relevant sense of being *targeted* against expressive conduct.

"Moreover, even were I to conclude that the city of Erie had specifically singled out the activity of nude dancing, I still would not find that this regulation violated the First Amendment unless I could be persuaded (as on this record I cannot) that it was the communicative character of nude dancing that prompted the ban. When conduct other than speech itself is regulated, it is my view that the First Amendment is violated only '[w]here the government prohibits conduct precisely because of its communicative attributes.' Here, even if one hypothesizes that the city's object was to suppress only nude dancing, that would not establish an intent to suppress what (if anything) nude dancing communicates. I do not feel the need, as the Court does, to identify some 'secondary effects' associated with nude dancing that the city could properly seek to eliminate. (I am highly skeptical, to tell the truth, that the addition of pasties and g-strings will at all reduce the tendency of establishments such as Kandyland to attract crime and prostitution, and hence to foster sexually transmitted disease.) The traditional power of government to foster good morals (*bonos mores*), and the acceptability of the traditional judgment (if Erie wishes to endorse it) that nude public dancing *itself* is immoral, have not been repealed by the First Amendment.

SOUTER, J., concurred in part and dissented in part: "I [agree] with the analytical approach that the plurality employs in deciding this case. Erie's stated interest in combating the secondary effects associated with nude dancing establishments is an interest unrelated to the suppression of expression under *O'Brien*, and the city's regulation is thus properly considered under the *O'Brien* standards. I do not believe, however, that the current record allows us to say that the city has made a sufficient evidentiary showing to sustain its [regulation].[1]

"[I]ntermediate scrutiny requires a regulating government to make some demonstration of an evidentiary basis for the harm it claims to flow from the expressive activity, and for the alleviation expected from the restriction imposed. That evidentiary basis may be borrowed from the records made by other governments if the experience elsewhere is germane to the measure under consideration and actually relied upon. I will assume, further, that the reliance may be shown by legislative invocation of a judicial opinion that accepted an evidentiary foundation as sufficient for a similar regulation. What is clear is that the evidence of reliance must be a matter of demonstrated fact, not speculative supposition.

"By these standards, the record before us today is deficient in its failure to reveal any evidence on which Erie may have relied, either for the seriousness of the threatened harm or for the efficacy of its chosen remedy. The plurality does the best it can with the materials to hand, but the pickings are slim. [T]he ordinance's preamble assert[s] that over the course of more than a century the

---

1. [We] do not require Congress to create a record in the manner of an administrative agency, and we accord its findings greater respect than those of agencies. We might likewise defer less to a city council than we would to Congress. The need for evidence may be espe- cially acute when a regulation is content based on its face and is analyzed as content neutral only because of the secondary effects doctrine. And it may be greater when the regulation takes the form of a ban, rather than a time, place, or manner restriction.

city council had expressed 'findings' of detrimental secondary effects flowing from lewd and immoral profitmaking activity in public places. But however accurate the recital may be and however honestly the councilors may have held those conclusions to be true over the years, the recitation does not get beyond conclusions on a subject usually fraught with some emotionalism. The plurality recognizes this, of course, but seeks to ratchet up the value of mere conclusions by analogizing them to the legislative facts within an administrative agency's special knowledge, on which action is adequately premised in the absence of evidentiary challenge. The analogy is not obvious * * *. [I]t is one thing to accord administrative leeway as to predictive judgments in applying 'elusive concepts' to circumstances where the record is inconclusive and 'evidence [is] difficult to compile,' and quite another to dispense with evidence of current fact as a predicate for banning a subcategory of expression.[3] [T]he invocation of *Barnes* in one paragraph of the preamble to Erie's ordinance [does not] suffice. The plurality opinion in *Barnes* made no mention of evidentiary showings at all, and though my separate opinion did make a pass at the issue, I did not demand reliance on germane evidentiary demonstrations, whether specific to the statute in question or developed elsewhere. To invoke *Barnes*, therefore, does not indicate that the issue of evidence has been addressed.

"There is one point, however, on which an evidentiary record is not quite so hard to find, but it hurts, not helps, the city. The final *O'Brien* requirement is that the incidental speech restriction be shown to be no greater than essential to achieve the government's legitimate purpose. To deal with this issue, we have to ask what basis there is to think that the city would be unsuccessful in countering any secondary effects by the significantly lesser restriction of zoning to control the location of nude dancing, thus allowing for efficient law enforcement, restricting effects on property values, and limiting exposure of the public. The record shows that for 23 years there has been a zoning ordinance on the books to regulate the location of establishments like Kandyland, but the city has not enforced it. [Even] on the plurality's view of the evidentiary burden, this hurdle to the application of *O'Brien* requires an evidentiary response. * * *

"While respondent did claim that the evidence before the city council was insufficient to support the ordinance, Erie's reply urged us not to consider the question, apparently assuming that *Barnes* authorized us to disregard it. The question has not been addressed, and in that respect this case has come unmoored from the general standards of our First Amendment jurisprudence.

"Careful readers, and not just those on the Erie City Council, will of course realize that my partial dissent rests on a demand for an evidentiary basis that I failed to make when I concurred in *Barnes, supra*. I should have demanded the evidence then, too, and my mistake calls to mind Justice Jackson's foolproof explanation of a lapse of his own, when he quoted Samuel Johnson, 'Ignorance, sir, ignorance.' *McGrath* v. *Kristensen*, 340 U. S. 162, 178, 71 S.Ct. 224, 95 L.Ed. 173 (1950) (concurring opinion). I may not be less ignorant of nude dancing than I was nine years ago, but after many subsequent occasions to think further about the needs of the First Amendment, I have come to believe that a government must toe the mark more carefully than I first insisted.

---

3. The proposition that the presence of nude dancing establishments increases the incidence of prostitution and violence is amenable to empirical treatment, and the city councilors who enacted Erie's ordinance are in a position to look to the facts of their own community's experience as well as to experiences elsewhere. Their failure to do so is made all the clearer by one of the *amicus* briefs, largely devoted to the argument that scientifically sound studies show no such correlation.

"The record before us now does not permit the conclusion that Erie's ordinance is reasonably designed to mitigate real harms. This does not mean that the required showing cannot be made, only that, on this record, Erie has not made it. I would remand to give it the opportunity to do so. Accordingly, although I join with the plurality in adopting the *O'Brien* test, I respectfully dissent from the Court's disposition of the case."

STEVENS, J., joined by Ginsburg, J., dissented: "Far more important than the question whether nude dancing is entitled to the protection of the First Amendment are the dramatic changes in legal doctrine that the Court endorses today. Until now, the 'secondary effects' of commercial enterprises featuring indecent entertainment have justified only the regulation of their location. For the first time, the Court has now held that such effects may justify the total suppression of protected speech. Indeed, the plurality opinion concludes that admittedly trivial advancements of a State's interests may provide the basis for censorship. The Court's commendable attempt to replace the fractured decision in *Barnes* with a single coherent rationale is strikingly unsuccessful; it is supported neither by precedent nor by persuasive reasoning.

"As the preamble to Ordinance No. 75–1994 candidly acknowledges, the council of the city of Erie enacted the restriction at issue 'for the purpose of limiting a recent increase in nude live entertainment within the City.' Prior to the enactment of the ordinance, the dancers at Kandyland performed in the nude. As the Court recognizes, after its enactment they can perform precisely the same dances if they wear 'pasties and G-strings.' In both instances, the erotic messages conveyed by the dancers to a willing audience are a form of expression protected by the First Amendment. Despite the similarity between the messages conveyed by the two forms of dance, they are not identical.

"If we accept Chief Judge Posner's evaluation of this art form, see *Miller v. South Bend*, 904 F.2d 1081, 1089–1104 (7th Cir. 1990) (en banc), the difference between the two messages is significant. The plurality assumes, however, that the difference in the content of the message resulting from the mandated costume change is 'de minimis.' Although I suspect that the patrons of Kandyland are more likely to share Chief Judge Posner's view than the plurality's, for present purposes I shall accept the assumption that the difference in the message is small. The crucial point to remember, however, is that whether one views the difference as large or small, nude dancing still receives First Amendment protection, even if that protection lies only in the 'outer ambit' of that Amendment. Erie's ordinance, therefore, burdens a message protected by the First Amendment. If one assumes that the same erotic message is conveyed by nude dancers as by those wearing miniscule costumes, one means of expressing that message is banned;[2] if one assumes that the messages are different, one of those messages is banned. In either event, the ordinance is a total ban.

"The Court relies on the so-called 'secondary effects' test to defend the ordinance. The present use of that rationale, however, finds no support whatsoever in our precedents. Never before have we approved the use of that doctrine to justify a total ban on protected First Amendment expression. On the contrary, we have been quite clear that the doctrine would not support that end. * * *[3], [4]

2. Although nude dancing might be described as one protected "means" of conveying an erotic message, it does not follow that a protected message has not been totally banned simply because there are other, similar ways to convey erotic messages. A State's prohibition of a particular book, for example, does not fail to be a total ban simply because other books conveying a similar message are available.

3. The Court contends *Ward* shows that we have used the secondary effects rationale to justify more burdensome restrictions than

4. See note 4 on page 97.

"The reason we have limited our secondary effects cases to zoning and declined to extend their reasoning to total bans is clear and straightforward: A dispersal that simply limits the places where speech may occur is a minimal imposition whereas a total ban is the most exacting of restrictions. The State's interest in fighting presumed secondary effects is sufficiently strong to justify the former, but far too weak to support the latter, more severe burden. Yet it is perfectly clear that in the present case—to use Justice Powell's metaphor in *American Mini Theatres*—the city of Erie has totally silenced a message the dancers at Kandyland want to convey. The fact that this censorship may have a laudable ulterior purpose cannot mean that censorship is not censorship. For these reasons, the Court's holding rejects the explicit reasoning in *American Mini Theatres* and *Renton* and the express holding in *Schad*. * * *

"The Court's mishandling of our secondary effects cases is not limited to its approval of a total ban. It compounds that error by dramatically reducing the degree to which the State's interest must be furthered by the restriction imposed on speech, and by ignoring the critical difference between secondary effects caused by speech and the incidental effects on speech that may be caused by a regulation of conduct.

"In what can most delicately be characterized as an enormous understatement, the plurality concedes that 'requiring dancers to wear pasties and G-strings may not greatly reduce these secondary effects.' To believe that the mandatory addition of pasties and a G-string will have *any* kind of noticeable impact on secondary effects requires nothing short of a titanic surrender to the implausible. * * * It is one thing to say [that] *O'Brien* is more lenient than the 'more demanding standard' we have imposed in cases such as *Texas* v. *Johnson*. It is quite another to say that the test can be satisfied by nothing more than the mere possibility of *de minimis* effects on the neighborhood.

"The Court is also mistaken in equating our secondary effects cases with the 'incidental burdens' doctrine applied in cases such as *O'Brien*; and it aggravates the error by invoking the latter line of cases to support its assertion that Erie's ordinance is unrelated to speech. The incidental burdens doctrine applies when 'speech' and 'nonspeech' elements are combined in the same course of conduct, and the government's interest in regulating the latter justifies incidental burdens on the former. *O'Brien*. Secondary effects, on the other hand, are indirect consequences of protected speech and may justify regulation of the places where that speech may occur. See *American Mini Theatres*. When a State enacts a

---

those approved in *Renton* and *American Mini Theatres*. That argument is unpersuasive for two reasons. First, as in the two cases just mentioned, the regulation in *Ward* was as a time, place, and manner restriction. Second, [*Ward*] is not a secondary effects case.

4. We [held] in *Renton* that in enacting its adult theater zoning ordinance, the city of Renton was permitted to rely on a detailed study conducted by the city of Seattle that examined the relationship between zoning controls and the secondary effects of adult theaters. (It was permitted to rely as well on 'the "detailed findings" summarized' in an opinion of the Washington Supreme Court to the same effect.) Renton, having identified the same problem in its own city as that experienced in Seattle, quite logically drew on Seattle's experience and adopted a similar solution. But if Erie is relying on the Seattle study as well, its use of that study is most peculiar. After identifying a problem in its own city similar to that in Seattle, Erie has implemented a solution (pasties and G-strings) bearing no relationship to the efficacious remedy identified by the Seattle study (dispersal through zoning).

But the city of Erie, of course, has not in fact pointed to any study by anyone suggesting that the adverse secondary effects of commercial enterprises featuring erotic dancing depends in the slightest on the precise costume warn by the performers—it merely assumes it to be so. If the city is permitted simply to assume that a slight addition to the dancers' costumes will sufficiently decrease secondary effects, then presumably the city can require more and more clothing as long as any danger of adverse effects remains.

regulation, it might focus on the secondary effects of speech as its aim, or it might concentrate on nonspeech related concerns, having no thoughts at all with respect to how its regulation will affect speech—and only later, when the regulation is found to burden speech, justify the imposition as an unintended incidental consequence. But those interests are not the same, and the Court cannot ignore their differences and insist that both aims are equally unrelated to speech simply because Erie might have 'recogniz[ed]' that it could possibly have had either aim in mind. One can think of an apple and an orange at the same time; that does not turn them into the same fruit.

"Of course, the line between governmental interests aimed at conduct and unrelated to speech, on the one hand, and interests arising out of the effects of the speech, on the other, may be somewhat imprecise in some cases. In this case, however, we need not wrestle with any such difficulty because Erie has expressly justified its ordinance with reference to secondary effects. Indeed, if Erie's concern with the effects of the message were unrelated to the message itself, it is strange that the only means used to combat those effects is the suppression of the message. For these reasons, the Court's argument that 'this case is similar to O'Brien,' is quite wrong, as are its citations to *Clark* v. *Community for Creative Non–Violence*, and *Ward*, neither of which involved secondary effects. The Court cannot have its cake and eat it too—either Erie's ordinance was not aimed at speech and the Court may attempt to justify the regulation under the incidental burdens test, or Erie has aimed its law at the secondary effects of speech, and the Court can try to justify the law under that doctrine. But it cannot conflate the two with the expectation that Erie's interests aimed at secondary effects will be rendered unrelated to speech by virtue of this doctrinal polyglot.

"Correct analysis of the issue in this case should begin with the proposition that nude dancing is a species of expressive conduct that is protected by the First Amendment. As Chief Judge Posner has observed, nude dancing fits well within a broad, cultural tradition recognized as expressive in nature and entitled to First Amendment protection. [It] is pure sophistry to reason from the premise that the regulation of the nudity component of nude dancing is unrelated to the message conveyed by nude dancers. Indeed, both the text of the ordinance and the reasoning in the Court's opinion make it pellucidly clear that the city of Erie has prohibited nude dancing *'precisely because of its communicative attributes.'* Barnes (White, J., dissenting).

"The censorial purpose of Erie's ordinance precludes reliance on the judgment in *Barnes* as sufficient support for the Court's holding today. [As] its preamble forthrightly admits, the ordinance's 'purpose' is to 'limi[t]' a protected form of speech; its invocation of *Barnes* cannot obliterate that professed aim.

"Erie's ordinance differs from the statute in *Barnes* in another respect. [In] an earlier proceeding in this case, the Court of Common Pleas asked Erie's counsel 'what effect would this ordinance have on theater . . . productions such as Equus, Hair, O[h!] Calcutta[!]? Under your ordinance would these things be prevented . . .?' Counsel responded: 'No, they wouldn't, Your Honor.' Indeed, as *stipulated* in the record, the city permitted a production of Equus to proceed without prosecution, even after the ordinance was in effect, and despite its awareness of the nudity involved in the production. Even if, in light of its broad applicability, the statute in *Barnes* was not aimed at a particular form of speech, Erie's ordinance is quite different. As presented to us, the ordinance is deliberately targeted at Kandyland's type of nude dancing (to the exclusion of plays like Equus), in terms of both its applicable scope and the city's enforcement.[14]

"This narrow aim is confirmed by the expressed views of the Erie City Councilmembers who voted for the ordinance. The four city councilmembers who approved the measure (of the six total councilmembers) each stated his or her view that the ordinance was aimed specifically at nude adult entertainment, and not at more mainstream forms of entertainment that include total nudity, nor even at nudity in general. One lawmaker observed: 'We're not talking about nudity. We're not talking about the theater or art * * * * We're talking about what is indecent and immoral* * * * We're not prohibiting nudity, we're prohibiting nudity when it's used in a lewd and immoral fashion.' * * * In my view, we need not strain to find consistency with more general purposes when the most natural reading of the record reflects a near obsessive preoccupation with a single target of the law.[16]

"It is clear beyond a shadow of a doubt that the Erie ordinance was a response to a more specific concern than nudity in general, namely, nude dancing of the sort found in Kandyland.[18] Given that the Court has not even tried to defend the ordinance's total ban on the ground that its censorship of protected speech might be justified by an overriding state interest, it should conclude that the ordinance is patently invalid."

COMMERCIAL SPEECH

CON LAW: P. 822, substitute for Central Hudson, Posadas, and notes thereafter

AMER CON: P. 832, after note 5

RTS & LIB: P. 729, substitute for Central Hudson, Posadas, and notes thereafter

14. Justice Scalia [states] that even if the ordinance singled out nude dancing, he would not strike down the law unless the dancing was singled out because of its message. He opines that here, the basis for singling out Kandyland is morality. But since the 'morality' of the public nudity in Hair is left untouched by the ordinance, while the 'immorality' of the public nudity in Kandyland is singled out, the distinction cannot be that 'nude public dancing *itself* is immoral.' Rather, the only arguable difference between the two is that one's message is more immoral than the other's.

16. The Court dismisses this evidence, declaring that it 'will not strike down an otherwise constitutional statute on the basis of an alleged illicit motive.' *O'Brien* [said] only that we would not strike down a law 'on the *assumption* that a wrongful purpose or motive has caused the power to be exerted,' (emphasis added; internal quotation marks omitted), and that statement was due to our recognition that it is a 'hazardous matter' to determine the actual intent of a body as large as Congress 'on the basis of what fewer than a handful of Congressmen said about [a law],' [We] need not base our inquiry on an 'assumption,' nor must we infer the collective intent of a large

body based on the statements of a few, for we have in the record the actual statements of all the

18. The Court states that Erie's ordinance merely 'replaces and updates provisions of an "Indecency and Immorality" ordinance' from the mid–19th century, just as the statute in *Barnes* did. * * * The record does indicate that Erie's Ordinance No. 75–1994 updates an older ordinance of similar import. Unfortunately, that old regulation is not in the record. [From] statements of one councilmember, it can reasonably be inferred that the old ordinance was merely a residential zoning restriction, not a total ban. If that is so, it leads to the further question why Erie felt it necessary to shift to a total ban in 1994.

But even if the Court's factual contention is correct, it does not undermine the points I have made in the text. The inference [of motivation] supposedly rebutted in *Barnes* stemmed from the *timing* of the enactment. Here, however, the inferences I draw depend on the text of the ordinance, its preamble, its scope and enforcement, and the comments of the councilmembers. These do not depend on the timing of the ordinance's enactment.

44 LIQUORMART, INC. v. RHODE ISLAND

517 U.S. 484, 116 S.Ct. 1495, 134 L.Ed.2d 711 (1996).

JUSTICE STEVENS announced the judgment of the Court and delivered the opinion of the Court with respect to Parts I, II, VII,[a] and VIII,[b] an opinion with respect to Parts III and V, in which JUSTICE KENNEDY, JUSTICE SOUTER, and JUSTICE GINSBURG join, an opinion with respect to Part VI, in which JUSTICE KENNEDY, JUSTICE THOMAS, and JUSTICE GINSBURG join, and an opinion with respect to Part IV, in which JUSTICE KENNEDY and JUSTICE GINSBURG join. * * *

I

In 1956, the Rhode Island Legislature enacted two separate prohibitions against advertising the retail price of alcoholic beverages. The first applies to vendors licensed in Rhode Island as well as to out-of-state manufacturers, wholesalers, and shippers. It prohibits them from "advertising in any manner whatsoever" the price of any alcoholic beverage offered for sale in the State; the only exception is for price tags or signs displayed with the merchandise within licensed premises and not visible from the street. The second statute applies to the Rhode Island news media. It contains a categorical prohibition against the publication or broadcast of any advertisements—even those referring to sales in other States—that "make reference to the price of any alcoholic beverages." * * *

III

Advertising has been a part of our culture throughout our history. Even in colonial days, the public relied on "commercial speech" for vital information about the market. Early newspapers displayed advertisements for goods and services on their front pages, and town criers called out prices in public squares. Indeed, commercial messages played such a central role in public life prior to the Founding that Benjamin Franklin authored his early defense of a free press in support of his decision to print, of all things, an advertisement for voyages to Barbados.

In accord with the role that commercial messages have long played, the law has developed to ensure that advertising provides consumers with accurate information about the availability of goods and services. In the early years, the common law, and later, statutes, served the consumers' interest in the receipt of accurate information in the commercial market by prohibiting fraudulent and misleading advertising. It was not until the 1970's, however, that this Court held that the First Amendment protected the dissemination of truthful and nonmisleading commercial messages about lawful products and services. See generally Alex Kozinski & Stuart Banner, *The Anti–History and Pre–History of Commercial Speech*, 71 Texas L.Rev. 747 (1993). * * *

[O]ur early cases uniformly struck down several broadly based bans on truthful, nonmisleading commercial speech, each of which served ends unrelated to consumer protection.[8] Indeed, one of those cases [*Linmark*] expressly likened

---

a. Scalia, Kennedy, Souter, Thomas, and Ginsburg, JJ., joined parts I, II, and VII of the Stevens, J., opinion. Section VII concluded that the twenty-first amendment does not qualify the first. The same conclusion was reached in O'Connor, J.'s concurring opinion joined by Rehnquist, C.J., Souter and Breyer, JJ.

b. Scalia, Kennedy, Souter, and Ginsburg, JJ., joined part VIII of the Stevens, J.'s opinion.

8. See *Bates* (ban on lawyer advertising); *Carey* (ban on contraceptive advertising); *Linmark* (ban on "For Sale" signs); *Virginia Bd. of Pharmacy* (ban on prescription drug prices); *Bigelow* (ban on abortion advertising). Although *Linmark* involved a prohibition against a particular means of advertising the sale of one's home, we treated the restriction as if it were a complete ban because it did not leave open "satisfactory" alternative channels of communication.

the rationale that *Virginia Pharmacy Bd.* employed to the one that Justice Brandeis adopted in his concurrence in *Whitney v. California*[:] "the remedy to be applied is more speech, not enforced silence. Only an emergency can justify repression." * * *

At the same time, our early cases recognized that the State may regulate some types of commercial advertising more freely than other forms of protected speech. * * *

In *Central Hudson Gas & Elec. Corp. v. Public Serv. Comm'n of N.Y.*, 447 U.S. 557, 100 S.Ct. 2343, 65 L.Ed.2d 341 (1980), we took stock of our developing commercial speech jurisprudence. In that case, we considered a regulation "completely" banning all promotional advertising by electric utilities. Our decision acknowledged the special features of commercial speech but identified the serious First Amendment concerns that attend blanket advertising prohibitions that do not protect consumers from commercial harms.[c]

Five Members of the Court recognized that the state interest in the conservation of energy was substantial, and that there was "an immediate connection between advertising and demand for electricity." Nevertheless, they concluded that the regulation was invalid because the Commission had failed to make a showing that a more limited speech regulation would not have adequately served the State's interest.[9]

In reaching its conclusion, the majority explained that although the special nature of commercial speech may require less than strict review of its regulation, special concerns arise from "regulations that entirely suppress commercial speech in order to pursue a nonspeech-related policy." *Id.* n. 9. In those circumstances, "a ban on speech could screen from public view the underlying governmental policy." As a result, the Court concluded that "special care" should attend the review of such blanket bans, and it pointedly remarked that "in recent years this Court has not approved a blanket ban on commercial speech unless the speech itself was flawed in some way, either because it was deceptive or related to unlawful activity."[10]

IV

[W]hen a State entirely prohibits the dissemination of truthful, nonmisleading commercial messages for reasons unrelated to the preservation of a fair bargaining process, there is far less reason to depart from the rigorous review that the First Amendment generally demands. * * *

---

c. *Central Hudson* referred to commercial speech as "expression related solely to the economic interests of the speaker and its audience." Was the speech in *Central Hudson* solely in the economic interests of the speaker and its audience? Is the *Central Hudson* locution broader or narrower than the category of promoting a commercial transaction? Reconsider this question in connection with the *Greenmoss* case, CON LAW, p. 832; AMER CON, p. 832; RTS & LIB, p. 739.

9. In other words, the regulation failed the fourth step in the four-part inquiry that the majority announced in its opinion. It wrote: "In commercial speech cases, then, a four-part analysis has developed. At the outset, we must determine whether the expression is protected by the First Amendment. For commercial speech to come within that provision, it at least must concern lawful activity and not be misleading. Next, we ask whether the asserted governmental interest is substantial. If both inquiries yield positive answers, we must determine whether the regulation directly advances the governmental interest asserted, and whether it is not more extensive than is necessary to serve that interest."

10. The Justices concurring in the judgment adopted a somewhat broader view. They expressed "doubt whether suppression of information concerning the availability and price of a legally offered product is ever a permissible way for the State to 'dampen' the demand for or use of the product." Indeed, Justice Blackmun believed that even "though 'commercial' speech is involved, such a regulation strikes at the heart of the First Amendment."

The special dangers that attend complete bans on truthful, nonmisleading commercial speech cannot be explained away by appeals to the "commonsense distinctions" that exist between commercial and noncommercial speech. Regulations that suppress the truth are no less troubling because they target objectively verifiable information, nor are they less effective because they aim at durable messages. As a result, neither the "greater objectivity" nor the "greater hardiness" of truthful, nonmisleading commercial speech justifies reviewing its complete suppression with added deference. * * *

Precisely because bans against truthful, nonmisleading commercial speech rarely seek to protect consumers from either deception or overreaching, they usually rest solely on the offensive assumption that the public will respond "irrationally" to the truth. The First Amendment directs us to be especially skeptical of regulations that seek to keep people in the dark for what the government perceives to be their own good.

V

[Although] the record suggests that the price advertising ban may have some impact on the purchasing patterns of temperate drinkers of modest means, the State has presented no evidence to suggest that its speech prohibition will significantly reduce market-wide consumption. Indeed, the District Court's considered and uncontradicted finding on this point is directly to the contrary. Moreover, the evidence suggests that the abusive drinker will probably not be deterred by a marginal price increase, and that the true alcoholic may simply reduce his purchases of other necessities. * * *

As is evident, any conclusion that elimination of the ban would significantly increase alcohol consumption would require us to engage in the sort of "speculation or conjecture" that is an unacceptable means of demonstrating that a restriction on commercial speech directly advances the State's asserted interest. Such speculation certainly does not suffice when the State takes aim at accurate commercial information for paternalistic ends.

The State also cannot satisfy the requirement that its restriction on speech be no more extensive than necessary. It is perfectly obvious that alternative forms of regulation that would not involve any restriction on speech would be more likely to achieve the State's goal of promoting temperance. As the State's own expert conceded, higher prices can be maintained either by direct regulation or by increased taxation. Per capita purchases could be limited as is the case with prescription drugs. Even educational campaigns focused on the problems of excessive, or even moderate, drinking might prove to be more effective.

As a result, even under the less than strict standard that generally applies in commercial speech cases, the State has failed to establish a "reasonable fit" between its abridgment of speech and its temperance goal. *Board of Trustees v. Fox*, 492 U.S. 469, 109 S.Ct. 3028, 106 L.Ed.2d 388 (1989);[d] see also *Rubin v.*

d. *Fox*, per Scalia, J., joined by Rehnquist, C.J., White, Stevens, O'Connor, and Kennedy, JJ., in the course of considering a provision that operated to bar commercial organizations from making sales demonstrations in students' dormitory rooms, held that the *Central Hudson* test did not require government to foreclose the possibility of all less restrictive alternatives. The university sought to promote an educational rather than a commercial atmosphere and to prevent commercial exploitation. Scalia, J., characterized these interests as substantial, but stated that it was enough if the fit between means and ends were "reasonable." It did not need to be "perfect." Like time, place, and manner regulations, however, the relationship between means and ends had to be "narrowly tailored to achieve the desired objective." Under that standard, as interpreted (see *Ward*, CON LAW, p. 894; AMER CON, p. 894; RTS & LIB, p. 801), government may not "'burden substantially more speech than is necessary to

Coors Brewing Co., 514 U.S. 476, 115 S.Ct. 1585, 131 L.Ed.2d 532 (1995)(explaining that defects in a federal ban on alcohol advertising are "further highlighted by the availability of alternatives that would prove less intrusive to the First Amendment's protections for commercial speech").[e] It necessarily follows that the price advertising ban cannot survive the more stringent constitutional review that *Central Hudson* itself concluded was appropriate for the complete suppression of truthful, nonmisleading commercial speech.

VI

The State responds by arguing that it merely exercised appropriate "legislative judgment" in determining that a price advertising ban would best promote temperance. Relying on the *Central Hudson* analysis set forth in *Posadas de Puerto Rico Associates v. Tourism Co. of P. R.*, 478 U.S. 328, 106 S.Ct. 2968, 92 L.Ed.2d 266 (1986), and *United States v. Edge Broadcasting Co.*, 509 U.S. 418, 113 S.Ct. 2696, 125 L.Ed.2d 345 (1993), Rhode Island first argues that, because expert opinions as to the effectiveness of the price advertising ban "go both ways," the Court of Appeals correctly concluded that the ban constituted a "reasonable choice" by the legislature. The State next contends that precedent requires us to give particular deference to that legislative choice because the State could, if it chose, ban the sale of alcoholic beverages outright. See *Posadas*. Finally, the State argues that deference is appropriate because alcoholic beverages are so-called "vice" products. We consider each of these contentions in turn.

The State's first argument fails to justify the speech prohibition at issue. Our commercial speech cases recognize some room for the exercise of legislative judgment. See *Metromedia*. However, Rhode Island errs in concluding that *Edge* and *Posadas* establish the degree of deference that its decision to impose a price advertising ban warrants.

In *Edge*, we upheld a federal statute that permitted only those broadcasters located in States that had legalized lotteries to air lottery advertising. The statute was designed to regulate advertising about an activity that had been deemed illegal in the jurisdiction in which the broadcaster was located. Here, by contrast, the commercial speech ban targets information about entirely lawful behavior.[f]

Posadas is more directly relevant. There, a five-Member majority held that, under the *Central Hudson* test, it was "up to the legislature" to choose to reduce gambling by suppressing in-state casino advertising rather than engaging in educational speech. Rhode Island argues that this logic demonstrates the constitu-

further the government's legitimate interest,' " but need not foreclose "all conceivable alternatives." Scalia, J., argued that to have a more demanding test in commercial speech than that used for time, place, and manner regulations would be inappropriate because time, place, and manner regulations can apply to political speech.

e. *Rubin* held that a federal provision prohibiting the display of alcoholic content on beer labels violated the first amendment. The Court argued among other things that the overall federal scheme was irrational in that it prohibited alcoholic beverage advertising from mentioning alcoholic content in many circumstances and required disclosures of alcoholic content in the labeling of wines in some circumstances.

f. *Edge* upheld federal legislation prohibiting the broadcast of lottery advertising if the broadcaster were located in a state that does not permit lotteries even in circumstances where 92% of the broadcaster's audience resided in a state that permitted lotteries and where the advertisement was for the lottery in the state where it was legal.

Greater New Orleans Broadcasting v. United States, 527 U.S. 173, 119 S.Ct. 1923, 144 L.Ed.2d 161 (1999), held that the congressional ban on the broadcasting of lottery information could not constitutionally be applied to advertisements of casino gambling when the broadcaster was located in a state where such gambling was legal. In addition, as in *Rubin*, fn. e, the Court objected to the lack of rationale for many of the exceptions to the legislation.

tionality of its own decision to ban price advertising in lieu of raising taxes or employing some other less speech-restrictive means of promoting temperance.

The reasoning in *Posadas* does support the State's argument, but, on reflection, we are now persuaded that *Posadas* erroneously performed the First Amendment analysis. The casino advertising ban was designed to keep truthful, nonmisleading speech from members of the public for fear that they would be more likely to gamble if they received it. * * *

Because the 5–to–4 decision in *Posadas* marked such a sharp break from our prior precedent, and because it concerned a constitutional question about which this Court is the final arbiter, we decline to give force to its highly deferential approach.

Instead, in keeping with our prior holdings, we conclude that a state legislature does not have the broad discretion to suppress truthful, nonmisleading information for paternalistic purposes that the *Posadas* majority was willing to tolerate. * * *

We also cannot accept the State's second contention, which is premised entirely on the "greater-includes-the-lesser" reasoning endorsed toward the end of the majority's opinion in *Posadas*. * * * The majority concluded that it would "surely be a strange constitutional doctrine which would concede to the legislature the authority to totally ban a product or activity, but deny to the legislature the authority to forbid the stimulation of demand for the product or activity through advertising on behalf of those who would profit from such increased demand." * * *

Although we do not dispute the proposition that greater powers include lesser ones, we fail to see how that syllogism requires the conclusion that the State's power to regulate commercial activity is "greater" than its power to ban truthful, nonmisleading commercial speech. Contrary to the assumption made in *Posadas*, we think it quite clear that banning speech may sometimes prove far more intrusive than banning conduct. As a venerable proverb teaches, it may prove more injurious to prevent people from teaching others how to fish than to prevent fish from being sold.[19] Similarly, a local ordinance banning bicycle lessons may curtail freedom far more than one that prohibits bicycle riding within city limits. In short, we reject the assumption that words are necessarily less vital to freedom than actions, or that logic somehow proves that the power to prohibit an activity is necessarily "greater" than the power to suppress speech about it.

As a matter of First Amendment doctrine, the *Posadas* syllogism is even less defensible. The text of the First Amendment makes clear that the Constitution presumes that attempts to regulate speech are more dangerous than attempts to regulate conduct.

[J]ust as it is perfectly clear that Rhode Island could not ban all obscene liquor ads except those that advocated temperance, we think it equally clear that its power to ban the sale of liquor entirely does not include a power to censor all advertisements that contain accurate and nonmisleading information about the price of the product. As the entire Court apparently now agrees, the statements in the *Posadas* opinion on which Rhode Island relies are no longer persuasive.

---

19. "Give a man a fish, and you feed him for a day. Teach a man to fish, and you feed him for a lifetime." *The International Thesau-* *rus of Quotations* 646 (compiled by R. Tripp 1970).

Finally, we find unpersuasive the State's contention that, under *Posadas* and *Edge*, the price advertising ban should be upheld because it targets commercial speech that pertains to a "vice" activity.

[T]he scope of any "vice" exception to the protection afforded by the First Amendment would be difficult, if not impossible, to define. Almost any product that poses some threat to public health or public morals might reasonably be characterized by a state legislature as relating to "vice activity". Such characterization, however, is anomalous when applied to products such as alcoholic beverages, lottery tickets, or playing cards, that may be lawfully purchased on the open market. The recognition of such an exception would also have the unfortunate consequence of either allowing state legislatures to justify censorship by the simple expedient of placing the "vice" label on selected lawful activities, or requiring the federal courts to establish a federal common law of vice. * * *

VIII

Because Rhode Island has failed to carry its heavy burden of justifying its complete ban on price advertising, we conclude that R.I. Gen. Laws §§ 3–8–7 and 3–8–8.1, as well as Regulation 32 of the Rhode Island Liquor Control Administration, abridge speech in violation of the First Amendment as made applicable to the States by the Due Process Clause of the Fourteenth Amendment. * * *

JUSTICE SCALIA, concurring in part and concurring in the judgment.

I share Justice Thomas's discomfort with the *Central Hudson* test, which seems to me to have nothing more than policy intuition to support it. I also share Justice Stevens' aversion towards paternalistic governmental policies that prevent men and women from hearing facts that might not be good for them. On the other hand, it would also be paternalism for us to prevent the people of the States from enacting laws that we consider paternalistic, unless we have good reason to believe that the Constitution itself forbids them. I will take my guidance as to what the Constitution forbids, with regard to a text as indeterminate as the First Amendment's preservation of "the freedom of speech," and where the core offense of suppressing particular political ideas is not at issue, from the long accepted practices of the American people.

The briefs and arguments of the parties in the present case provide no illumination on that point; understandably so, since both sides accepted *Central Hudson*. The amicus brief on behalf of the American Advertising Federation et al. did examine various expressions of view at the time the First Amendment was adopted; they are consistent with First Amendment protection for commercial speech, but certainly not dispositive. I consider more relevant the state legislative practices prevalent at the time the First Amendment was adopted, since almost all of the States had free-speech constitutional guarantees of their own, whose meaning was not likely to have been different from the federal constitutional provision derived from them. Perhaps more relevant still are the state legislative practices at the time the Fourteenth Amendment was adopted, since it is most improbable that that adoption was meant to overturn any existing national consensus regarding free speech. Indeed, it is rare that any nationwide practice would develop contrary to a proper understanding of the First Amendment itself—for which reason I think also relevant any national consensus that had formed regarding state regulation of advertising after the Fourteenth Amendment, and before this Court's entry into the field. The parties and their amici provide no evidence on these points.

Since I do not believe we have before us the wherewithal to declare *Central Hudson* wrong—or at least the wherewithal to say what ought to replace it—I must resolve this case in accord with our existing jurisprudence, which [would] prohibit the challenged regulation. * * * [A]ccordingly [I] join Parts I, II, VII, and VIII of Justice Stevens' opinion.

JUSTICE THOMAS, concurring in Parts I, II, VI, and VII, and concurring in the judgment.

In cases such as this, in which the government's asserted interest is to keep legal users of a product or service ignorant in order to manipulate their choices in the marketplace, the balancing test adopted in *Central Hudson* should not be applied, in my view. Rather, such an "interest" is per se illegitimate and can no more justify regulation of "commercial" speech than it can justify regulation of "noncommercial" speech. * * *

Although the Court took a sudden turn away from *Virginia Pharmacy Bd.* in *Central Hudson*, it has never explained why manipulating the choices of consumers by keeping them ignorant is more legitimate when the ignorance is maintained through suppression of "commercial" speech than when the same ignorance is maintained through suppression of "noncommercial" speech. * * *

JUSTICE O'CONNOR, with whom THE CHIEF JUSTICE, JUSTICE SOUTER, and JUSTICE BREYER join, concurring in the judgment. * * *

I agree with the Court that Rhode Island's price-advertising ban is invalid. I would resolve this case more narrowly, however, by applying our established *Central Hudson* test to determine whether this commercial-speech regulation survives First Amendment scrutiny. * * *

The fit between Rhode Island's method and [its goal of reducing consumption] is not reasonable. If the target is simply higher prices generally to discourage consumption, the regulation imposes too great, and unnecessary, a prohibition on speech in order to achieve it. The State has other methods at its disposal— methods that would more directly accomplish this stated goal without intruding on sellers' ability to provide truthful, nonmisleading information to customers. * * * A tax, for example, is not normally very difficult to administer and would have a far more certain and direct effect on prices, without any restriction on speech. The principal opinion suggests further alternatives, such as limiting per capita purchases or conducting an educational campaign about the dangers of alcohol consumption. The ready availability of such alternatives—at least some of which would far more effectively achieve Rhode Island's only professed goal, at comparatively small additional administrative cost—demonstrates that the fit between ends and means is not narrowly tailored. Too, this regulation prevents sellers of alcohol from communicating price information anywhere but at the point of purchase. No channels exist at all to permit them to publicize the price of their products.

Respondents point for support to *Posadas*. The closer look that we have required since *Posadas* comports better with the purpose of the analysis set out in *Central Hudson*, by requiring the State to show that the speech restriction directly advances its interest and is narrowly tailored. Under such a closer look, Rhode Island's price-advertising ban clearly fails to pass muster.

Because Rhode Island's regulation fails even the less stringent standard set out in *Central Hudson*, nothing here requires adoption of a new analysis for the evaluation of commercial speech regulation. [Because] we need go no further, I would not here undertake the question whether the test we have employed since *Central Hudson* should be displaced. * * *

CONCEIVING AND RECONCEIVING THE STRUCTURE OF FIRST AMENDMENT DOCTRINE: HATE SPEECH REVISITED—AGAIN

CON LAW: P. 850, add to note 3

AMER CON: P. 849, add to note 3

RTS & LIB: P. 757, add to note 3

See also *Davis v. Monroe County Board of Educ.*, 526 U.S. 629, 119 S.Ct. 1661, 143 L.Ed.2d 839 (1999) (Kennedy, J., dissenting).

FAIR ADMINISTRATION OF JUSTICE AND THE FIRST AMENDMENT AS SWORD

CON LAW: P. 890, add to note 2

AMER CON: P. 880, add to note 2

RTS & LIB: P. 797, add to note 2

For the conclusion that the police may generally not invite members of the media to accompany them in executing an arrest warrant in the home without violating the fourth amendment, see *Wilson v. Layne*, 526 U.S. 603, 119 S.Ct. 1692, 143 L.Ed.2d 818 (1998).

CON LAW: P. 891, add to note 4

AMER CON: P. 880, add to note 4

RTS & LIB: P. 798, add to note 4

California law provides that state and local law enforcement agencies shall make public:

"[T]he current address of every individual arrested by the agency and the current address of the victim of a crime, where the requester declares under penalty of perjury that the request is made for a scholarly, journalistic, political, or governmental purpose, or that the request is made for investigation purposes by a licensed private investigator ... except that the address of the victim of [certain crimes] shall remain confidential. Address information obtained pursuant to this paragraph shall not be used directly or indirectly to sell a product or service to any individual or group of individuals, and the requester shall execute a declaration to that effect under penalty of perjury."

Constitutional? See *Los Angeles Police Department v. United Reporting Publishing Corp.*, ___ U.S. ___, 120 S.Ct. 483, 145 L.Ed.2d 451 (1999) (law may not be challenged on its face; remanded for as applied attack).

GOVERNMENT PROPERTY AND THE PUBLIC FORUM

FOUNDATION CASES

MANDATORY ACCESS

CON LAW: P. 894, add to note 3

AMER CON: P. 883, add to note 3

RTS & LIB: P. 801, add to note 3

CHICAGO v. MORALES, 527 U.S. 41, 119 S.Ct. 1849, 144 L.Ed.2d 67 (1999), per STEVENS, J., joined by Souter and Ginsburg, JJ., in dictum contended that an ordinance ordering street gang members and associates loitering in a public place to disperse upon an officer's order did not violate the first amendment although it was void for vagueness under the due process clause: "Because the term 'loiter' is defined as remaining in one place 'with no apparent purpose,' it is [clear] that it does not prohibit any form of conduct that is apparently intended to convey a message. By its terms, the ordinance is inapplicable to assemblies that are designed to demonstrate a group's support of, or opposition to, a particular point of view. Its impact on the social contact between gang members and others does not impair the First Amendment 'right of association' that our cases have recognized."[b]

NEW FORUMS

CON LAW: P. 909, after note 4

AMER CON: P. 898, after note 4

RTS & LIB: P. 816, after note 4

A Colorado statute regulates speech-related conduct within 100 feet of the entrance to any health care facility. The specific section of the statute that is challenged, Colo. Rev. Stat. § 18–9–122(3) (1999), makes it unlawful within the regulated areas for any person to "knowingly approach" within eight feet of another person, without that person's consent, "for the purpose of passing a leaflet or handbill to, displaying a sign to, or engaging in oral protest, education, or counseling with such other person." HILL v. COLORADO, ___ U.S. ___, 120 S.Ct. 2480, ___ L.Ed.3d ___, (2000), per STEVENS, J., upheld the statute: "Although the statute [at issue] prohibits speakers from approaching unwilling listeners, it does not require a standing speaker to move away from anyone passing by. Nor does it place any restriction on the content of any message that anyone may wish to communicate to anyone else, either inside or outside the regulated areas. It does, however, make it more difficult to give unwanted advice, particularly in the form of a handbill or leaflet, to persons entering or leaving medical facilities.

"The question is whether the First Amendment rights of the speaker are abridged by the protection the statute provides for the unwilling listener.

"Before confronting the question whether the Colorado statute reflects an acceptable balance between the constitutionally protected rights of law-abiding

b. Breyer, Kennedy, and O'Connor, JJ., in separate concurring opinions agreed with Stevens, J.'s vagueness conclusion, but did not address the first amendment question. Scalia, J., and Thomas, J., joined by Rehnquist, C.J. and Scalia, J., dissented on the vagueness issue, but agreed with the conclusion that no first amendment right was at stake.

speakers and the interests of unwilling listeners, it is appropriate to examine the competing interests at stake. A brief review of both sides of the dispute reveals that each has legitimate and important concerns.

"The First Amendment interests of petitioners are clear and undisputed. As a preface to their legal challenge, petitioners emphasize three propositions. First, they accurately explain that the areas protected by the statute encompass all the public ways within 100 feet of every entrance to every health care facility everywhere in the State of Colorado. There is no disagreement on this point, even though the legislative history makes it clear that its enactment was primarily motivated by activities in the vicinity of abortion clinics. Second, they correctly state that their leafletting, sign displays, and oral communications are protected by the First Amendment. The fact that the messages conveyed by those communications may be offensive to their recipients does not deprive them of constitutional protection. Third, the public sidewalks, streets, and ways affected by the statute are 'quintessential' public forums for free speech. Finally, although there is debate about the magnitude of the statutory impediment to their ability to communicate effectively with persons in the regulated zones, that ability, particularly the ability to distribute leaflets, is unquestionably lessened by this statute.

"On the other hand, petitioners do not challenge the legitimacy of the state interests that the statute is intended to serve. It is a traditional exercise of the States' 'police powers to protect the health and safety of their citizens.' That interest may justify a special focus on unimpeded access to health care facilities and the avoidance of potential trauma to patients associated with confrontational protests. See *Madsen.* Moreover, as with every exercise of a State's police powers, rules that provide specific guidance to enforcement authorities serve the interest in even-handed application of the law. Whether or not those interests justify the particular regulation at issue, they are unquestionably legitimate.

"It is also important when conducting this interest analysis to recognize the significant difference between state restrictions on a speaker's right to address a willing audience and those that protect listeners from unwanted communication. This statute deals only with the latter. * * *

"The unwilling listener's interest in avoiding unwanted communication has been repeatedly identified in our cases. It is an aspect of the broader 'right to be let alone' that one of our wisest Justices characterized as 'the most comprehensive of rights and the right most valued by civilized men.' *Olmstead v. United States* (Brandeis, J., dissenting). The right to avoid unwelcome speech has special force in the privacy of the home, *Rowan v. Post Office Dept.,* and its immediate surroundings, *Frisby v. Schultz,* but can also be protected in confrontational settings. Thus, this comment on the right to free passage in going to and from work applies equally—or perhaps with greater force—to access to a medical facility:

"[We] are a social people, and the accosting by one of another in an inoffensive way and an offer by one to communicate and discuss information with a view to influencing the other's action, are not regarded as aggression or a violation of that other's rights. If, however, the offer is declined, as it may rightfully be, then persistence, importunity, following and dogging, become unjustifiable annoyance and obstruction which is likely soon to savor of intimidation. From all of this the person sought to be influenced has a right to be free, and his employer has a right to have him free. *American Steel Foundries v. Tri–City Central Trades Council,* 257 U. S. 184, 204 (1921).* * *

"The dissenters argue that we depart from precedent by recognizing a 'right to avoid unpopular speech in a public forum,' We, of course, are not addressing whether there is such a 'right.' Rather, we are merely noting that our cases have repeatedly recognized the interests of unwilling listeners in situations where 'the degree of captivity makes it impractical for the unwilling viewer or auditor to avoid exposure.' * * *[25]

'As we explained in *Ward v. Rock Against Racism*: 'The principal inquiry in determining content neutrality, in speech cases generally and in time, place, or manner cases in particular, is whether the government has adopted a regulation of speech because of disagreement with the message it conveys.'

"The Colorado statute passes that test * * *. Petitioners contend that an individual near a health care facility who knowingly approaches a pedestrian to say 'good morning' or to randomly recite lines from a novel would not be subject to the statute's restrictions. Because the content of the oral statements made by an approaching speaker must sometimes be examined to determine whether the knowing approach is covered by the statute, petitioners argue that the law is 'content-based' * * *.

"It is common in the law to examine the content of a communication to determine the speaker's purpose. Whether a particular statement constitutes a threat, blackmail, an agreement to fix prices, a copyright violation, a public offering of securities, or an offer to sell goods often depends on the precise content of the statement. We have never held, or suggested, that it is improper to look at the content of an oral or written statement in order to determine whether a rule of law applies to a course of conduct. With respect to the conduct that is the focus of the Colorado statute, it is unlikely that there would often be any need to know exactly what words were spoken in order to determine whether 'sidewalk counselors' are engaging in 'oral protest, education, or counseling' rather than pure social or random conversation.

"Theoretically, of course, cases may arise in which it is necessary to review the content of the statements made by a person approaching within eight feet of an unwilling listener to determine whether the approach is covered by the statute. But that review need be no more extensive than a determination of whether a general prohibition of 'picketing' or 'demonstrating' applies to innocuous speech. The regulation of such expressive activities, by definition, does not cover social, random, or other everyday communications. See *Webster's Third New International Dictionary* 600, 1710 (1993) (defining 'demonstrate' as 'to make a public display of sentiment for or against a person or cause' and 'picket' as an effort 'to persuade or otherwise influence'). Nevertheless, we have never suggested that the kind of cursory examination that might be required to exclude casual conversation from the coverage of a regulation of picketing would be problematic. * * *

"The Colorado statute's regulation of the location of protests, education, and counseling [places] no restrictions on—and clearly does not prohibit—either a particular viewpoint or any subject matter that may be discussed by a speaker.

---

25. Furthermore, whether there is a 'right' to avoid unwelcome expression is not before us in this case. The purpose of the Colorado statute is not to protect a potential listener from hearing a particular message. It is to protect those who seek medical treatment from the potential physical and emotional harm suffered when an unwelcome individual delivers a message (whatever its content) by physically approaching an individual at close range, i.e., within eight feet. In offering protection from that harm, while maintaining free access to health clinics, the State pursues interests constitutionally distinct from the freedom from unpopular speech to which Justice Kennedy refers.

Rather, it simply establishes a minor place restriction on an extremely broad category of communications with unwilling listeners. Instead of drawing distinctions based on the subject that the approaching speaker may wish to address, the statute applies equally to used car salesmen, animal rights activists, fundraisers, environmentalists, and missionaries. Each can attempt to educate unwilling listeners on any subject, but without consent may not approach within eight feet to do so.

"The dissenters, nonetheless, contend that the statute is not 'content neutral.' As Justice Scalia points out, the vice of content-based legislation in this context is that 'it lends itself' to being 'used for invidious thought-control purposes.' But a statute that restricts certain categories of speech only lends itself to invidious use if there is a significant number of communications, raising the same problem that the statute was enacted to solve, that fall outside the statute's scope, while others fall inside. E.g., *Mosley*. Here, the statute's restriction seeks to protect those who enter a health care facility from the harassment, the nuisance, the persistent importuning, the following, the dogging, and the implied threat of physical touching that can accompany an unwelcome approach within eight feet of a patient by a person wishing to argue vociferously face-to-face and perhaps thrust an undesired handbill upon her. The statutory phrases, 'oral protest, education, or counseling,' distinguish speech activities likely to have those consequences from speech activities (such as Justice Scalia's 'happy speech' that are most unlikely to have those consequences. The statute does not distinguish among speech instances that are similarly likely to raise the legitimate concerns to which it responds. Hence, the statute cannot be struck down for failure to maintain 'content neutrality,' or for 'underbreadth.'

"Also flawed is Justice Kennedy's theory that a statute restricting speech becomes unconstitutionally content based because of its application 'to the specific locations where that discourse occurs,' A statute prohibiting solicitation in airports that was motivated by the aggressive approaches of Hari–Krishnas does not become content based solely because its application is confined to airports—'the specific location where that discourse occurs.' A statute making it a misdemeanor to sit at a lunch counter for an hour without ordering any food would also not be 'content based' even if it were enacted by a racist legislature that hated civil rights protesters (although it might raise separate questions about the State's legitimate interest at issue).

"Similarly, the contention that a statute is 'viewpoint based' simply because its enactment was motivated by the conduct of the partisans on one side of a debate is without support. The antipicketing ordinance upheld in *Frisby v. Schultz*, a decision in which both of today's dissenters joined, was obviously enacted in response to the activities of antiabortion protesters who wanted to protest at the home of a particular doctor to persuade him and others that they viewed his practice of performing abortions to be murder. We nonetheless summarily concluded that the statute was content neutral."

STEVENS, J., maintained that the statute was a reasonable place regulation: "The three types of communication regulated by § 18–9–122(3) are the display of signs, leafletting, and oral speech. The 8–foot separation between the speaker and the audience should not have any adverse impact on the readers' ability to read signs displayed by demonstrators. In fact, the separation might actually aid the pedestrians' ability to see the signs by preventing others from surrounding them and impeding their view. Furthermore, the statute places no limitations on the number, size, text, or images of the placards. And, as with all of the restrictions, the 8–foot zone does not affect demonstrators with signs who remain in place.

"With respect to oral statements, the distance certainly can make it more difficult for a speaker to be heard, particularly if the level of background noise is high and other speakers are competing for the pedestrian's attention. Notably, the statute places no limitation on the number of speakers or the noise level, including the use of amplification equipment, although we have upheld such restrictions in past cases. [T]he statute allows the speaker to remain in one place, and other individuals can pass within eight feet of the protester without causing the protester to violate the statute. Finally, here there is a 'knowing' requirement that protects speakers 'who thought they were keeping pace with the targeted individual' at the proscribed distance from inadvertently violating the statute.

"It is also not clear that the statute's restrictions will necessarily impede, rather than assist, the speakers' efforts to communicate their messages. The statute might encourage the most aggressive and vociferous protesters to moderate their confrontational and harassing conduct, and thereby make it easier for thoughtful and law-abiding sidewalk counselors like petitioners to make themselves heard. But whether or not the 8–foot interval is the best possible accommodation of the competing interests at stake, we must accord a measure of deference to the judgment of the Colorado Legislature. Once again, it is worth reiterating that only attempts to address unwilling listeners are affected.

"The burden on the ability to distribute handbills is more serious because it seems possible that an 8–foot interval could hinder the ability of a leafletter to deliver handbills to some unwilling recipients. The statute does not, however, prevent a leafletter from simply standing near the path of oncoming pedestrians and proffering his or her material, which the pedestrians can easily accept. And, as in all leafletting situations, pedestrians continue to be free to decline the tender. * * *

"Justice Kennedy [argues] that the statute leaves petitioners without adequate means of communication. This is a considerable overstatement. The statute seeks to protect those who wish to enter health care facilities, many of whom may be under special physical or emotional stress, from close physical approaches by demonstrators. In doing so, the statute takes a prophylactic approach; it forbids all unwelcome demonstrators to come closer than eight feet. We recognize that by doing so, it will sometimes inhibit a demonstrator whose approach in fact would have proved harmless. But the statute's prophylactic aspect is justified by the great difficulty of protecting, say, a pregnant woman from physical harassment with legal rules that focus exclusively on the individual impact of each instance of behavior, demanding in each case an accurate characterization (as harassing or not harassing) of each individual movement within the 8–foot boundary. Such individualized characterization of each individual movement is often difficult to make accurately. A bright-line prophylactic rule may be the best way to provide protection, and, at the same time, by offering clear guidance and avoiding subjectivity, to protect speech itself. * * *

"Petitioners argue that § 18–9–122(3) is invalid because it is 'overbroad.' There are two parts to petitioners' 'overbreadth' argument. On the one hand, they argue that the statute is too broad because it protects too many people in too many places, rather than just the patients at the facilities where confrontational speech had occurred. Similarly, it burdens all speakers, rather than just persons with a history of bad conduct. On the other hand, petitioners also contend that the statute is overbroad because it 'bans virtually the universe of protected expression, including displays of signs, distribution of literature, and mere verbal statements.'

"The first part of the argument does not identify a constitutional defect. The fact that the coverage of a statute is broader than the specific concern that led to its enactment is of no constitutional significance. What is important is that all persons entering or leaving health care facilities share the interests served by the statute. It is precisely because the Colorado Legislature made a general policy choice that the statute is assessed under the constitutional standard set forth in *Ward*, rather than a more strict standard. See *Madsen* * * * In this case, it is not disputed that the regulation affects protected speech activity, the question is thus whether it is a 'reasonable restrictio[n] on the time, place, or manner of protected speech.' * * *

"The second part of the argument is based on a misreading of the statute and an incorrect understanding of the overbreadth doctrine. As we have already noted, § 18–9–122(3) simply does not 'ban' any messages, and likewise it does not 'ban' any signs, literature, or oral statements. It merely regulates the places where communications may occur.[Petitioners] have not persuaded us that the impact of the statute on the conduct of other speakers will differ from its impact on their own sidewalk counseling. Like petitioners' own activities, the conduct of other protesters and counselors at all health care facilities are encompassed within the statute's 'legitimate sweep.' Therefore, the statute is not overly broad.

"Petitioners also claim that § 18–9–122(3) is unconstitutionally vague. * * * [This] concern is ameliorated by the fact that § 18–9–122(3) contains a scienter requirement. The statute only applies to a person who 'knowingly' approaches within eight feet of another, without that person's consent, for the purpose of engaging in oral protest, education, or counseling. The likelihood that anyone would not understand any of those common words seems quite remote. * * *

"The judgment of the Colorado Supreme Court is affirmed."

Souter, J., joined by O'Connor, Ginsburg, & Breyer, JJ., concurred:"I join the opinion of the Court and add this further word. The key to determining whether Colo. Rev. Stat. § 18–9–122(3) (1999), makes a content-based distinction between varieties of speech lies in understanding that content-based discriminations are subject to strict scrutiny because they place the weight of government behind the disparagement or suppression of some messages, whether or not with the effect of approving or promoting others. * * *

"Concern about employing the power of the State to suppress discussion of a subject or a point of view is not, however, raised in the same way when a law addresses not the content of speech but the circumstances of its delivery. The right to express unpopular views does not necessarily immunize a speaker from liability for resorting to otherwise impermissible behavior meant to shock members of the speaker's audience, see *United States v. O'Brien* (burning draft card), or to guarantee their attention, see *Kovacs v. Cooper* (sound trucks);*Frisby v. Schultz* (residential picketing); *Heffron v. International Soc. for Krishna Consciousness, Inc.*(soliciting). Unless regulation limited to the details of a speaker's delivery results in removing a subject or viewpoint from effective discourse (or otherwise fails to advance a significant public interest in a way narrowly fitted to that objective), a reasonable restriction intended to affect only the time, place, or manner of speaking is perfectly valid. * * *

"It is important to recognize that the validity of punishing some expressive conduct, and the permissibility of a time, place, or manner restriction, does not depend on showing that the particular behavior or mode of delivery has no association with a particular subject or opinion. Draft card burners disapprove of the draft, see *O'Brien*, and abortion protesters believe abortion is morally wrong, *Madsen*. There is always a correlation with subject and viewpoint when the law regulates conduct that has become the signature of one side of a controversy. But that does not mean that every regulation of such distinctive behavior is content based as First Amendment doctrine employs that term. The correct rule, rather, is captured in the formulation that a restriction is content based only if it is imposed because of the content of the speech. * * *

"No one disputes the substantiality of the government's interest in protecting people already tense or distressed in anticipation of medical attention (whether an abortion or some other procedure) from the unwanted intrusion of close personal importunity by strangers. The issues dividing the Court, then, go to the content neutrality of the regulation, its fit with the interest to be served by it, and the availability of other means of expressing the desired message (however offensive it may be even without physically close communication).

"Each of these issues is addressed principally by the fact that subsection (3) simply does not forbid the statement of any position on any subject. It does not declare any view as unfit for expression within the 100–foot zone or beyond it. What it forbids, and all it forbids, is approaching another person closer than eight feet (absent permission) to deliver the message. * * *

"This is not to say that enforcement of the approach restriction will have no effect on speech; of course it will make some difference. The effect of speech is a product of ideas and circumstances, and time, place, and manner are circumstances. The question is simply whether the ostensible reason for regulating the circumstances is really something about the ideas. Here, the evidence indicates that the ostensible reason is the true reason. * * *

"The matter of proper tailoring to limit no more speech than necessary to vindicate the public interest deserves a few specific comments * * *. Subsection (3) could possibly be applied to speakers unlike the present petitioners, who might not know that the entrance to the facility was within 100 feet, or who might try to engage people within 100 feet of a health facility other than a physician's office or hospital, or people having no business with the facility. These objections do not, however, weigh very heavily on a facial challenge like this. The specter of liability on the part of those who importune while oblivious of the facility is laid to rest by the requirement that a defendant act 'knowingly.' While it is true that subsection (3) was not enacted to protect dental patients, I cannot say it goes beyond the State's interest to do so; someone facing an hour with a drill in his tooth may reasonably be protected from the intrusive behavior of strangers who are otherwise free to speak. While some mere passersby may be protected needlessly, I am skeptical about the number of health care facilities with substantial pedestrian traffic within 100 feet of their doors but unrelated to the business conducted inside. Hence, I fail to see danger of the substantial overbreadth required to be shown before a statute is struck down out of concern for the speech rights of those not before the Court.

"As for the claim of vagueness, at first blush there is something objectionable. Those who do not choose to remain stationary may not approach within eight feet with a purpose, among others, of 'engaging in oral protest, education, or counseling.' While that formula excludes liability for enquiring about the time or the bus schedule within eight feet, 'education' does not convey much else by way of limitation. But that is not fatal here. What is significant is not that the word fails to limit clearly, but that it pretty clearly fails to limit very much at all. It succeeds in naturally covering any likely address by one person approaching another on a street or parking lot outside a building entrance (aside from common social greetings, protests, or requests for assistance). Someone planning to spread a message by accosting strangers is likely to understand the statute's application to 'education.' And just because the coverage is so obviously broad, the discretion given to the police in deciding whether to charge an offense seems no greater than the prosecutorial discretion inherent in any generally applicable criminal statute.''

Scalia, J., joined by Thomas, J., dissented: "What is before us [is] a speech regulation directed against the opponents of abortion, and it therefore enjoys the benefit of the 'ad hoc nullification machine' that the Court has set in motion to push aside whatever doctrines of constitutional law stand in the way of that highly favored practice. Having deprived abortion opponents of the political right to persuade the electorate that abortion should be restricted by law, the Court today continues and expands its assault upon their individual right to persuade women contemplating abortion that what they are doing is wrong. Because, like the rest of our abortion jurisprudence, today's decision is in stark contradiction of the constitutional principles we apply in all other contexts, I dissent.* * *

"Whatever may be said about the restrictions on the other types of expressive activity, the regulation as it applies to oral communications is obviously and undeniably content-based. A speaker wishing to approach another for the purpose of communicating any message except one of protest, education, or counseling may do so without first securing the other's consent. Whether a speaker must obtain permission before approaching within eight feet—and whether he will be sent to prison for failing to do so—depends entirely on *what he intends to say* when he gets there. I have no doubt that this regulation would be deemed content-based *in an instant* if the case before us involved antiwar protesters, or union members seeking to 'educate' the public about the reasons for their strike. * * *

"The Court asserts that this statute is not content-based for purposes of our First Amendment analysis because it neither (1) discriminates among viewpoints nor (2) places restrictions on 'any subject matter that may be discussed by a speaker.' Ante, at 18. But we have never held that the universe of content-based regulations is limited to those two categories, and such a holding would be absurd. Imagine, for instance, special place-and-manner restrictions on all speech except that which 'conveys a sense of contentment or happiness.' This 'happy speech' limitation would not be 'viewpoint-based'—citizens would be able to express their joy in equal measure at either the rise or fall of the NASDAQ, at either the success or the failure of the Republican Party—and would not discriminate on the basis of subject matter, since gratification could be expressed about anything at all. Or consider a law restricting the writing or recitation of poetry—neither viewpoint-based nor limited to any particular subject matter. Surely this Court would consider such regulations to be 'content-based' and deserving of the most exacting scrutiny.

" 'The vice of content-based legislation—what renders it deserving of the high standard of strict scrutiny—is not that it is always used for invidious, thought-control purposes, but that it lends itself to use for those purposes.' A restriction that operates only on speech that communicates a message of protest, education, or counseling presents exactly this risk. When applied, as it is here, at the entrance to medical facilities, it is a means of impeding speech against abortion. The Court's confident assurance that the statute poses no special threat to First Amendment freedoms because it applies alike to 'used car salesmen, animal rights activists, fundraisers, environmentalists, and missionaries,' is a wonderful replication (except for its lack of sarcasm) of Anatole France's observation that '[t]he law, in its majestic equality, forbids the rich as well as the poor to sleep under bridges * * * *' This Colorado law is no more targeted at used car salesmen, animal rights activists, fund raisers, environmentalists, and missionaries than French vagrancy law was targeted at the rich. We know what the Colorado legislators, by their careful selection of content ('protest, education, and counseling'), were taking aim at, for they set it forth in the statute itself: the 'right to protest or counsel against certain medical procedures' on the sidewalks and streets surrounding health care facilities.

"The Court is unpersuasive in its attempt to equate the present restriction with content-neutral regulation of demonstrations and picketing—as one may immediately suspect from the opinion's wildly expansive definitions of demonstrations as 'public display[s] of sentiment for or against a person or cause,' 'and of picketing as an effort 'to persuade or otherwise influence.' '(On these terms, Nathan Hale was a demonstrator and Patrick Henry a picket.)' When the government regulates 'picketing,' or 'demonstrating,' it restricts a particular manner of expression that is, as the author of today's opinion has several times explained, 'a mixture of conduct and communication.' '[Today], of course, Justice Stevens gives us an opinion restricting not only handbilling but even one-on-one conversation of a particular content.' * * *

"As for the Court's appeal to the fact that we often 'examine the content of a communication' to determine whether it 'constitutes a threat, blackmail, an agreement to fix prices, a copyright violation, a public offering of securities, or an offer to sell goods,' ante, at 16, the distinction is almost too obvious to bear mention: Speech of a certain content is constitutionally proscribable. The Court has not yet taken the step of consigning 'protest, education, and counseling' to that category.* * *

"The Court makes too much of the statement in *Ward* that '[t]he principal inquiry in determining content neutrality ... is whether the government has adopted a regulation of speech because of disagreement with the message it conveys.' That is indeed 'the *principal* inquiry'—suppression of uncongenial ideas is the worst offense against the First Amendment—but it is not the *only* inquiry. Even a law that has as its purpose something unrelated to the suppression of particular content cannot irrationally single out that content for its prohibition. An ordinance directed at the suppression of noise (and therefore 'justified without reference to the content of regulated speech') cannot be applied only to sound trucks delivering messages of 'protest.' Our very first use of the 'justified by reference to content' language made clear that it is a prohibition *in addition to*, rather than in place of, the prohibition of facially content-based restrictions. 'Selective exclusions from a public forum' we said, 'may not be based on content alone, and may not be justified by reference to content alone.' *Mosley*.[2]"

Scalia, J., argued that the statute could not pass muster even if it were content neutral: "Just three Terms ago, in upholding an injunction against

---

2. The Court's contention that the statute is content-neutral because it is not a "regulation of speech" but a "regulation of the places where some speech may occur," First, because the proposition that a restriction upon the places where speech may occur is not a restriction upon speech is both absurd and contradicted by innumerable cases. And second, because the fact that a restriction is framed as a "regulation of the places where some speech may occur" has nothing whatever to do with whether the restriction is content-neutral—which is why *Boos* held to be content-based the ban on displaying, within 500 feet of foreign embassies, banners designed to "bring into public odium any foreign government."

antiabortion activities, the Court refused to rely on any supposed 'right of the people approaching and entering the facilities to be left alone.' '*Schenck v. Pro-Choice Network of Western N.Y.*' It expressed 'doubt' that this 'right . . . accurately reflects our First Amendment jurisprudence.' Finding itself in something of a jam (the State here has passed a regulation that is obviously not narrowly tailored to advance any other interest) the Court today neatly re-packages the repudiated 'right' as an 'interest' the State may decide to protect and then places it onto the scales opposite the right to free speech in a traditional public forum.

"To support the legitimacy of its self-invented state interest, the Court relies upon a bon mot in a 1928 dissent (which we evidently overlooked in *Schenck*). It characterizes the 'unwilling listener's interest in avoiding unwanted communication' as an 'aspect of the broader' 'right to be let alone' 'Justice Brandeis coined in his dissent in *Olmstead v. United States*.' The amusing feature is that even this slim reed contradicts rather than supports the Court's position. The right to be let alone that Justice Brandeis identified was a right the Constitution 'conferred, *as against the government*;' it was *that* right, not some generalized 'common-law right' or 'interest' to be free from hearing the unwanted opinions of one's fellow citizens, which he called the 'most comprehensive' and 'most valued by civilized men.' To the extent that there can be gleaned from our cases a 'right to be let alone' in the sense that Justice Brandeis intended, it is the right of the *speaker* in the public forum to be free from government interference of the sort Colorado has imposed here.'

"In any event, the Court's attempt to disguise the 'right to be let alone' as a 'governmental interest in protecting the right to be let alone' is unavailing for the simple reason that this is not an interest that may be legitimately weighed against the speakers' First Amendment rights (which the Court demotes to the status of First Amendment 'interests') We have consistently held that 'the Constitution does not permit the government to decide which types of otherwise protected speech are sufficiently offensive to require protection *for the unwilling listener or viewer.' Erznoznik.* * * *

"The Court nonetheless purports to derive from our cases a principle limiting the protection the Constitution affords the speaker's right to direct 'offensive messages' at 'unwilling' audiences in the public forum. Ante, at 10. There is no such principle. We have upheld limitations on a speaker's exercise of his right to speak on the public streets *when that speech intrudes into the privacy of the home. Frisby.* * * * As the universally understood state of First Amendment law is described in a leading treatise: 'Outside the home, the burden is generally on the observer or listener to avert his eyes or plug his ears against the verbal assaults, lurid advertisements, tawdry books and magazines, and other 'offensive' intrusions which increasingly attend urban life.' L. Tribe, *American Constitutional Law* § 12–19, p. 948 (2d ed. 1988). The Court today elevates the abortion clinic to the status of the home. * * *

"[T]he Court's extensive reliance upon *American Steel Foundries* [is misplaced], The First Amendment was not at issue, and was not so much as mentioned in the opinion, so the case is scant authority for the point the Court wishes to make. The case is also irrelevant because it was 'clear from the evidence that from the outset, violent methods were pursued from time to time in such a way as to characterize the attitude of the picketers as continuously threatening. "No such finding was made, or could be made, here. More importantly, however, as far as our future labor cases are concerned: If a 'right to be free' from 'persistence, importunity, following and dogging,' short of actual intimidation was part of our infant First Amendment law in 1921, I am shocked to think that it is there today. The Court's assertion that '[n]one of our decisions has minimized the enduring importance of 'the right to be free' from persistent "importunity, following and dogging' after an offer to communicate has been declined' is belied by the fact that this passage from *American Steel Foundries* has never—not once—found its way into any of the many First Amendment cases this Court has decided since 1921. We will have cause to regret today's injection of this irrelevant anachronism into the mainstream of our First Amendment jurisprudence. * * *

"The burdens this law imposes upon the right to speak are substantial, despite an attempt to minimize them that is not even embarrassed to make the suggestion that they might actually 'assist * * * the speakers' efforts to communicate their messages.' (Compare this with the Court's statement in a nonabortion case, joined by the author of today's opinion: 'The First Amendment mandates that we presume that speakers, not the government, know best both what they want to say and how to say it.') *Riley*. The Court displays a willful ignorance of the type and nature of communication affected by the statute's restrictions. It seriously asserts, for example, that the 8-foot zone allows a speaker to communicate at a 'normal conversational distance.' I have certainly held conversations at a distance of eight feet seated in the quiet of my chambers, but I have never walked along the public sidewalk—and have not seen others do so—'conversing' at an 8-foot remove. The suggestion is absurd. So is the suggestion that the opponents of abortion can take comfort in the fact that the statute 'places no limitation on the number of speakers or the noise level, including the use of amplification equipment.' That is good enough, I suppose, for 'protesting'; but the Court must know that most of the 'counseling' and 'educating' likely to take place outside a health care facility cannot be done at a distance and at a high-decibel level. The availability of a powerful amplification system will be of little help to the woman who hopes to forge, in the last moments before another of her sex is to have an abortion, a bond of concern and intimacy that might enable her to persuade the woman to change her mind and heart. The counselor may wish to walk alongside and to say, sympathetically and as softly as the circumstances allow, something like: 'My dear, I know what you are going through. I've been through it myself. You're not alone and you do not have to do this. There are other alternatives. Will you let me help you? May I show you a picture of what your child looks like at this stage of her human development?' The Court would have us believe that this can be done effectively—yea, perhaps even *more* effectively—by shouting through a bullhorn at a distance of eight feet.

"The Court seems prepared, if only for a moment, to take seriously the magnitude of the burden the statute imposes on simple handbilling and leafletting. That concern is fleeting, however, since it is promptly assuaged by the realization that a leafletter may, without violating the statute, stand 'near the path' of oncoming pedestrians and make his 'proffe[r] * * * which the pedestrians can easily accept.' It does not take a veteran labor organizer to recognize—although surely any would, see Brief for American Federation of Labor and Congress of Industrial Organization as Amicus Curiae—that leafletting will be rendered utterly ineffectual by a requirement that the leafletter obtain from each subject permission to approach, or else man a stationary post (one that does not obstruct access to the facility, lest he violate subsection (2) of statute) and wait for passersby voluntarily to approach an outstretched hand. That simply is not how it is done, and the Court knows it—or should. A leafletter, whether he is working on behalf of Operation Rescue, Local 109, or Bubba's Bar-B-Que, stakes out the best piece of real estate he can, and then walks a few steps toward individuals passing in his vicinity, extending his arm and making it *as easy as possible* for the passerby, whose natural inclination is generally not to seek out such distributions, to simply accept the offering. Few pedestrians are likely to give their 'consent' to the approach of a handbiller (indeed, by the time he requested it they would likely have passed by), and even fewer are likely to walk over in order to pick up a leaflet. In the abortion context, therefore, ordinary handbilling, which we have in other contexts recognized to be a 'classic for[m] of speech that lie[s] at the heart of the First Amendment,' will in its most effective locations be rendered futile, the Court's implausible assertions to the contrary notwithstanding.''

Scalia, J., also questioned the breadth of the statute: '' 'The fact,' the Court says, 'that the coverage of a statute is broader than the specific concern that led to its enactment is of no constitutional significance.' That is true enough ordinarily, but it is not true with respect to restraints upon speech, which is what the doctrine of overbreadth is all about. [Again], the Court says that the overbreadth doctrine is not applicable because this law simply 'does not "ban" any signs, literature, or oral statements,' but 'merely regulates the places where communications may occur.' I know of no precedent for the proposition that time, place, and manner restrictions are not subject to the doctrine of overbreadth. Our decision in *Grace* demonstrates the contrary: Restriction of speech on the sidewalks around the Supreme Court was invalidated because it went further than the needs of security justified. Surely New York City cannot require a parade permit and a security bond for any individual who carries a sign on the sidewalks of Fifth Avenue. * * *

''The foregoing discussion of overbreadth was written before the Court, in responding to Justice Kennedy, abandoned any pretense at compliance with that doctrine, and acknowledged—indeed, boasted—that the statute it approves 'takes a prophylactic approach,' and adopts '[a] bright-line prophylactic rule.'[5] I scarcely know how to respond to such an unabashed repudiation of our First Amendment doctrine. Prophylaxis is the antithesis of narrow tailoring. [If] the Court were going to make this concession, it could simply have dispensed with its earlier (unpersuasive) attempt to show that the statute was narrowly tailored. So one can add to the casualties of our whatever-it-takes proabortion jurisprudence the First Amendment doctrine of narrow tailoring and overbreadth. R. I. P.

''Before it effectively threw in the towel on the narrow-tailoring point, the Court asserted the importance of taking into account 'the place to which the regulations apply in determining whether these restrictions burden more speech than necessary.' 'A proper regard for the "place" involved in this case should result in, if anything, a commitment by this Court to adhere to and rigorously enforce our speech-protective standards.' The public forum involved here—the public spaces outside of health care facilities—has become, by necessity and by virtue of this Court's decisions, a forum of last resort for those who oppose abortion. [For] those who share an abiding moral or religious conviction (or, for that matter, simply a biological appreciation) that abortion is the taking of a human life, there is no option but to persuade women, one by one, not to make that choice. And as a general matter, the most effective place, if not the only place,

---

5. Of course the Court greatly understates the scope of the prophylaxis, saying that ''the statute's prophylactic aspect is justified by the great difficulty of protecting, say, a pregnant woman from physical harassment with legal rules that focus exclusively on the individual impact of each instance of behavior.'' But the statute prevents the ''physically harassing'' act of (shudder!) approaching within closer than eight feet not only when it is directed against pregnant women, but also (just to be safe) when it is directed against 300–pound, male, and unpregnant truck drivers—surely a distinction that is not ''difficult to make accurately.''

where that persuasion can occur, is outside the entrances to abortion facilities. By upholding these restrictions on speech in this place the Court ratifies the State's attempt to make even that task an impossible one.

"Those whose concern is for the physical safety and security of clinic patients, workers, and doctors should take no comfort from today's decision. Individuals or groups intent on bullying or frightening women out of an abortion, or doctors out of performing that procedure, will not be deterred by Colorado's statute; bullhorns and screaming from eight feet away will serve their purposes well. But those who would accomplish their moral and religious objectives by peaceful and civil means, by trying to persuade individual women of the rightness of their cause, will be deterred; and that is not a good thing in a democracy."

KENNEDY, J., dissented: "The Court's holding contradicts more than a half century of well-established First Amendment principles. For the first time, the Court approves a law which bars a private citizen from passing a message, in a peaceful manner and on a profound moral issue, to a fellow citizen on a public sidewalk. If from this time forward the Court repeats its grave errors of analysis, we shall have no longer the proud tradition of free and open discourse in a public forum. * * *

"The Court errs in asserting the Colorado statute is no different from laws sustained as content neutral in earlier cases. The prohibitions against 'picketing' and/or 'leafleting' upheld in *Frisby*, *Grace*, and *Mosley*, the Court says are no different from the restrictions on 'protest, education, or counseling' imposed by the Colorado statute. The parallel the Court sees does not exist. No examination of the content of a speaker's message is required to determine whether an individual is picketing, or distributing a leaflet, or impeding free access to a building. Under the Colorado enactment, however, the State must review content to determine whether a person has engaged in criminal 'protest, education, or counseling.' When a citizen approaches another on the sidewalk in a disfavored-speech zone, an officer of the State must listen to what the speaker says. If, in the officer's judgment, the speaker's words stray too far toward 'protest, education, or counseling'—the boundaries of which are far from clear—the officer may decide the speech has moved from the permissible to the criminal. The First Amendment does not give the government such power.

"The statute is content based for an additional reason: It restricts speech on particular topics. [If] oral protest, education, or counseling on every subject within an 8–foot zone present a danger to the public, the statute should apply to every building entrance in the State. It does not. It applies only to a special class of locations: entrances to buildings with health care facilities. We would close our eyes to reality were we to deny that 'oral protest, education, or counseling' outside the entrances to medical facilities concern a narrow range of topics—indeed, one topic in particular. [If], just a few decades ago, a State with a history of enforcing racial discrimination had enacted a statute like this one, regulating 'oral protest, education, or counseling' within 100 feet of the entrance to any lunch counter, our predecessors would not have hesitated to hold it was content based or viewpoint based. [To] say that one citizen can approach another to ask the time or the weather forecast or the directions to Main Street but not to initiate discussion on one of the most basic moral and political issues in all of contemporary discourse, a question touching profound ideas in philosophy and theology, is an astonishing view of the First Amendment. For the majority to examine the statute under rules applicable to content-neutral regulations is an affront to First Amendment teachings. * * *

"In a further glaring departure from precedent we learn today that citizens have a right to avoid unpopular speech in a public forum. [*Rowan*] did not hold, contrary to statements in today's opinion that the First Amendment permits the government to restrict private speech in a public forum. Indeed, the Court in [*Rowan*] recognized what everyone, before today, understood to be true: '[W]e are often "captives" outside the sanctuary of the home and subject to objectionable speech and other sound.' * * *

"[A]nd *Lehman v. Shaker Heights* [did] not, contrary to the majority's assertions, suggest that government is free to enact categorical measures restricting traditional, peaceful communications among citizens in a public forum. Instead, the Court admonished that citizens usually bear the burden of disregarding unwelcome messages. Today's decision is an unprecedented departure from this Court's teachings respecting unpopular speech in public fora."

"The Colorado statute offends settled First Amendment principles in another fundamental respect. It violates the constitutional prohibitions against vague or overly broad criminal statutes regulating speech." Kennedy, J., argued that the terms "protest," "counseling," "education," and "consent" were undefined and unduly vague. "The statute's vagueness [becomes] as well one source of its overbreadth. The only sure way to avoid violating the law is to refrain from picketing, leafleting, or oral advocacy altogether. Scienter cannot save so vague a statute as this."

Kennedy, J., also argued that the statute burdened more speech than necessary under the *Ward* test: "Both the State and the Court attempt to sidestep the enactment's obvious content-based restriction by praising the statute's breadth, by telling us all topics of conversation, not just discourse on abortion, are banned within the statutory proscription. The saving feature the Court tries to grasp simply creates additional free speech infirmity. Our precedents do not permit content censoring to be cured by taking even more protected speech within a statute's reach. The statute before us, as construed by the majority, would do just that. If it indeed proscribes 'oral protest, education, or counseling' on all subjects across the board, it by definition becomes 'substantially broader than necessary to achieve the government's interest.' "

"The whimsical, arbitrary nature of the statute's operation is further demonstration of a restriction upon more speech than necessary. The happenstance of a dental office being located in a building brings the restricted-speech zone into play. If the same building also houses an organization dedicated, say, to environmental issues, a protest against the group's policies would be barred. Yet if, on the next block there were a public interest enterprise in a building with no health care facility, the speech would be unrestricted. The statute is a classic example of a proscription not narrowly tailored and resulting in restrictions of far more speech than necessary to achieve the legislature's object. * * *

"The majority insists the statute aims to protect distraught women who are embarrassed, vexed, or harassed as they attempt to enter abortion clinics. If these are punishable acts, they should be prohibited in those terms. In the course of praising Colorado's approach, the majority does not pause to tell us why, in its view, substantially less restrictive means cannot be employed to ensure citizens access to health care facilities or to prevent physical contact between citizens. The Court's approach is at odds with the rigor demanded by *Ward*. * * *

"The means of expression at stake here are of controlling importance. Citizens desiring to impart messages to women considering abortions likely do not have resources to use the mainstream media for their message, much less resources to locate women contemplating the option of abortion. Lacking the aid of the government or the media, they seek to resort to the time honored method of leafleting and the display of signs. Nowhere is the speech more important than at the time and place where the act is about to occur. As the named plaintiff, Leila Jeanne Hill, explained, 'I engage in a variety of activities designed to impart information to abortion-bound women and their friends and families.' 'In my many years of sidewalk counseling I have seen a number of [these] women change their minds about aborting their unborn children as a result of my sidewalk counseling, and God's grace.' * * *

"The Court now strikes at the heart of the reasoned, careful balance I had believed was the basis for the joint opinion in *Casey*. The vital principle of the opinion was that in defined instances the woman's decision whether to abort her child was in its essence a moral one, a choice the State could not dictate. Foreclosed from using the machinery of government to ban abortions in early term, those who oppose it are remitted to debate the issue in its moral dimensions. In a cruel way, the Court today turns its back on that balance. It in effect tells us the moral debate is not so important after all and can be conducted just as well through a bullhorn from an 8–foot distance as it can through a peaceful, face-to-face exchange of a leaflet. The lack of care with which the Court sustains the Colorado statute reflects a most troubling abdication of our responsibility to enforce the First Amendment."

GOVERNMENT SUPPORT OF SPEECH

SUBSIDIES AND TAX EXPENDITURES

CON LAW: P. 921, after note 4

AMER CON: P. 906, after note 4

RTS & LIB: P. 828, after note 4

In 1989 the National Endowment for the Arts ("NEA") supported two artists whose work sparked controversy: Robert Mapplethorpe's exhibit, *The Perfect Moment*, included homoerotic photographs; Andres Serrano's photograph, *Piss Christ*, showed a crucifix immersed in urine. In reaction, Congress reduced appropriations in 1990 by the amount that had been granted to the two recipients and took a number of steps leading up to the passage of Title 20 U.S.C. § 954(d) which provided that, "No payment shall be made under this section except upon application therefor which is submitted to the National Endowment for the Arts in accordance with regulations issued and procedures established by the Chairperson. In establishing such regulations and procedures, the Chairperson shall ensure that (1) artistic excellence and artistic merit are the criteria by which applications are judged, taking into consideration general standards of decency and respect for the diverse beliefs and values of the American public; and (2) applications are consistent with the purposes of this section. Such regulations and procedures shall clearly indicate that obscenity is without artistic merit, is not protected speech, and shall not be funded."

The National Council on the Arts which advises the NEA Chairperson resolved to implement the provision by ensuring that the panels conducting initial reviews of grant applications represent geographic, ethnic, and aesthetic diversity, and the Chairperson agreed. Several artists, whose grant applications had been approved before the passage of § 954(d), but reconsidered and denied afterwards, brought suit, challenging § 954(d)(1) on its face. The district court and the court of appeals declared § 954(d)(1) unconstitutional.

NATIONAL ENDOWMENT FOR THE ARTS v. FINLEY, 524 U.S. 569, 118 S.Ct. 2168, 141 L.Ed.2d 500, (1998), per O'CONNOR, J., joined by Rehnquist, C.J., and Stevens, Kennedy, and Breyer, JJ.,[a] upheld § 954(d)(1) maintaining that it did not impermissibly discriminate on the basis of point of view and was not unconstitutionally vague: "Respondents argue that the provision is a paradigmatic example of viewpoint discrimination because it rejects any artistic speech that either fails to respect mainstream values or offends standards of decency. The premise of respondents' claim is that § 954(d)(1) constrains the agency's ability to fund certain categories of artistic expression. The NEA, however, reads the provision as merely hortatory, and contends that it stops well short of an absolute restriction. Section 954(d)(1) adds 'considerations' to the grant-making process; it does not preclude awards to projects that might be deemed 'indecent' or 'disrespectful,' nor place conditions on grants, or even specify that those factors must be given any particular weight in reviewing an application. Indeed, the agency asserts that it has adequately implemented § 954(d)(1) merely by ensuring the representation of various backgrounds and points of view on the advisory panels that analyze grant applications. We do not decide whether the NEA's view—that the formulation of diverse advisory panels is sufficient to comply with Congress' command—is in fact a reasonable reading of the statute. It is clear, however, that the text of § 954(d)(1) imposes no categorical requirement. The advisory language stands in sharp contrast to congressional efforts to prohibit the funding of certain classes of speech. When Congress has in fact intended to affirmatively constrain the NEA's grant-making authority, it has done so in no uncertain terms. See § 954(d)(2) ('[O]bscenity is without artistic merit, is not protected speech, and shall not be funded').

"Furthermore, like the plain language of § 954(d), the political context surrounding the adoption of the 'decency and respect' clause is inconsistent with respondents' assertion that the provision compels the NEA to deny funding on the basis of viewpoint discriminatory criteria. The legislation was a bipartisan proposal introduced as a counterweight to amendments aimed at eliminating the NEA's funding or substantially constraining its grant-making authority. [B]efore the vote on § 954(d)(1), one of its sponsors stated: 'If we have done one important thing in this amendment, it is this. We have maintained the integrity of freedom of expression in the United States.'

"That § 954(d)(1) admonishes the NEA merely to take 'decency and respect' into consideration, and that the legislation was aimed at reforming procedures rather than precluding speech, undercut respondents' argument that the provision inevitably will be utilized as a tool for invidious viewpoint discrimination.

"Respondents' claim that the provision is facially unconstitutional may be reduced to the argument that the criteria in § 954(d)(1) are sufficiently subjective that the agency could utilize them to engage in viewpoint discrimination. Given the varied interpretations of the criteria and the vague exhortation to take them into consideration, it seems unlikely that this provision will introduce any greater element of selectivity than the determination of 'artistic excellence' itself. * * *

"Any content-based considerations that may be taken into account in the grant-making process are a consequence of the nature of arts funding. The NEA

a. Ginsburg, J., also joined O'Connor, J.'s opinion except for the paragraph accompanying footnote b infra.

has limited resources and it must deny the majority of the grant applications that it receives, including many that propose 'artistically excellent' projects. The agency may decide to fund particular projects for a wide variety of reasons, 'such as the technical proficiency of the artist, the creativity of the work, the anticipated public interest in or appreciation of the work, the work's contemporary relevance, its educational value, its suitability for or appeal to special audiences (such as children or the disabled), its service to a rural or isolated community, or even simply that the work could increase public knowledge of an art form.'

"Respondent's reliance on our decision in *Rosenberger v. Rector and Visitors of Univ. of Va.*, 515 U.S. 819, 115 S.Ct. 2510, 132 L.Ed.2d 700 (1995), is therefore misplaced. In *Rosenberger*, a public university declined to authorize disbursements from its Student Activities Fund to finance the printing of a Christian student newspaper. We held that by subsidizing the Student Activities Fund, the University had created a limited public forum, from which it impermissibly excluded all publications with religious editorial viewpoints. Although the scarcity of NEA funding does not distinguish this case from *Rosenberger*, the competitive process according to which the grants are allocated does. In the context of arts funding, in contrast to many other subsidies, the Government does not indiscriminately 'encourage a diversity of views from private speakers.' The NEA's mandate is to make aesthetic judgments, and the inherently content-based 'excellence' threshold for NEA support sets it apart from the subsidy at issue in *Rosenberger*—which was available to all student organizations that were 'related to the educational purpose of the University'—and from comparably objective decisions on allocating public benefits, such as access to a school auditorium or a municipal theater, see *Lamb's Chapel v. Center Moriches Union Free School Dist.*, 508 U.S. 384, 386, 113 S.Ct. 2141, 124 L.Ed.2d 352 (1993); *Southeastern Promotions, Ltd. v. Conrad*, 420 U.S. 546, 555, 95 S.Ct. 1239, 43 L.Ed.2d 448 (1975), or the second class mailing privileges available to 'all newspapers and other periodical publications,' see *Hannegan v. Esquire, Inc.*, 327 U.S. 146, 148, n. 1, 66 S.Ct. 456, 90 L.Ed. 586 (1946).

"Respondents do not allege discrimination in any particular funding decision. * * * Thus, we have no occasion here to address an as-applied challenge in a situation where the denial of a grant may be shown to be the product of invidious viewpoint discrimination. If the NEA were to leverage its power to award subsidies on the basis of subjective criteria into a penalty on disfavored viewpoints, then we would confront a different case. We have stated that, even in the provision of subsidies, the Government may not 'ai[m] at the suppression of dangerous ideas,' and if a subsidy were 'manipulated' to have a 'coercive effect,' then relief could be appropriate. * * * Unless and until § 954(d)(1) is applied in a manner that raises concern about the suppression of disfavored viewpoints, however, we uphold the constitutionality of the provision.

"Finally, although the First Amendment certainly has application in the subsidy context, we note that the Government may allocate competitive funding according to criteria that would be impermissible were direct regulation of speech or a criminal penalty at stake. So long as legislation does not infringe on other constitutionally protected rights, Congress has wide latitude to set spending priorities. See *Regan v. Taxation with Representation of Wash.*, 461 U.S. 540, 549, 103 S.Ct. 1997, 76 L.Ed.2d 129 (1983). In the 1990 Amendments that incorporated § 954(d)(1), Congress modified the declaration of purpose in the NEA's enabling act to provide that arts funding should 'contribute to public support and confidence in the use of taxpayer funds,' and that '[p]ublic funds [must] ultimately serve public purposes the Congress defines.' § 951(5). And as we held in *Rust*,

Congress may 'selectively fund a program to encourage certain activities it believes to be in the public interest, without at the same time funding an alternative program which seeks to deal with the problem in another way.' In doing so, 'the Government has not discriminated on the basis of viewpoint; it has merely chosen to fund one activity to the exclusion of the other.'[b]

"The lower courts also erred in invalidating § 954(d)(1) as unconstitutionally vague. * * * The terms of the provision are undeniably opaque, and if they appeared in a criminal statute or regulatory scheme, they could raise substantial vagueness concerns. It is unlikely, however, that speakers will be compelled to steer too far clear of any 'forbidden area' in the context of grants of this nature. But when the Government is acting as patron rather than as sovereign, the consequences of imprecision are not constitutionally severe.

"In the context of selective subsidies, it is not always feasible for Congress to legislate with clarity. Indeed, if this statute is unconstitutionally vague, then so too are all government programs awarding scholarships and grants on the basis of subjective criteria such as 'excellence.' To accept respondents' vagueness argument would be to call into question the constitutionality of these valuable government programs and countless others like them.

"Section 954(d)(1) merely adds some imprecise considerations to an already subjective selection process. It does not, on its face, impermissibly infringe on First or Fifth Amendment rights.

SCALIA, J., joined by Thomas, J., concurred in the judgment: " 'The operation was a success, but the patient died.' What such a procedure is to medicine, the Court's opinion in this case is to law. It sustains the constitutionality of 20 U.S.C. § 954(d)(1) by gutting it. The most avid congressional opponents of the provision could not have asked for more. I write separately because, unlike the Court, I think that § 954(d)(1) must be evaluated as written, rather than as distorted by the agency it was meant to control. By its terms, it establishes content-and viewpoint-based criteria upon which grant applications are to be evaluated. And that is perfectly constitutional.

"[The statute means what it says. Under the statute, the] application reviewers must take into account 'general standards of decency' and 'respect for the diverse beliefs and values of the American public' when evaluating artistic excellence and merit. One can regard this as either suggesting that decency and respect are elements of what Congress regards as artistic excellence and merit, or as suggesting that decency and respect are factors to be taken into account in addition to artistic excellence and merit. But either way, it is entirely, 100% clear that decency and respect are to be taken into account in evaluating applications.

"This is so apparent that I am at a loss to understand what the Court has in mind (other than the gutting of the statute) when it speculates that the statute is merely 'advisory.' General standards of decency and respect for Americans' beliefs and values *must* (for the statute says that the Chairperson 'shall ensure' this result) be taken into account [in] evaluating all applications. This does not mean that those factors must always be dispositive, but it *does* mean that they must always be considered. The method of compliance proposed by the National Endowment for the Arts (NEA)—selecting diverse review panels of artists and nonartists that reflect a wide range of geographic and cultural perspectives—is so

b. Ginsburg, J., joined O'Connor, J.'s opinion with the exception of the paragraph accompanying this footnote.

obviously inadequate that it insults the intelligence. A diverse panel membership increases the odds that, *if and when* the panel takes the factors into account, it will reach an accurate assessment of what they demand. But it in no way increasés the odds that the panel will take the factors into consideration—much less *ensures* that the panel will do so, which is the Chairperson's duty under the statute. Moreover, the NEA's fanciful reading of § 954(d)(1) would make it wholly superfluous. Section 959(c) already requires the Chairperson to 'issue regulations and establish procedures [to] ensure that all panels are composed, to the extent practicable, of individuals reflecting * * * diverse artistic and cultural points of view.

"I agree with the Court that § 954(d)(1) 'imposes no categorical requirement' in the sense that it does not require the denial of all applications that violate general standards of decency or exhibit disrespect for the diverse beliefs and values of Americans. Compare § 954(d)(2) ('[O]bscenity * * * shall not be funded'). But the factors need not be conclusive to be discriminatory. To the extent a particular applicant exhibits disrespect for the diverse beliefs and values of the American public or fails to comport with general standards of decency, the likelihood that he will receive a grant diminishes. In other words, the presence of the 'tak[e] into consideration' clause 'cannot be regarded as mere surplusage; it means something.' And the 'something' is that the decisionmaker, all else being equal, will favor applications that display decency and respect, and disfavor applications that do not.

"This unquestionably constitutes viewpoint discrimination.[1] That conclusion is not altered by the fact that the statute does not 'compe[l]' the denial of funding any more than a provision imposing a five-point handicap on all black applicants for civil service jobs is saved from being race discrimination by the fact that it does not compel the rejection of black applicants. If viewpoint discrimination in this context is unconstitutional (a point I shall address anon), the law is invalid unless there are some situations in which the decency and respect factors *do not constitute viewpoint discrimination*. And there is none. [T]he conclusion of viewpoint discrimination is not affected by the fact that what constitutes 'decency' or 'the diverse beliefs and values of the American people' is difficult to pin down—any more than a civil-service preference in favor of those who display 'Republican-party values' would be rendered nondiscriminatory by the fact that there is plenty of room for argument as to what Republican-party values might be ...

"The 'political context surrounding the adoption of the "decency and respect" clause,' [does] not change its meaning or affect its constitutionality. All that is proved by the various statements [from] the floor debates is (1) that the provision was not meant categorically to exclude any particular viewpoint (which I have conceded, and which is plain from the text), and (2) that the language was not meant to do anything that is unconstitutional. That in no way propels the Court's leap to the countertextual conclusion that the provision was merely 'aimed at reforming procedures,' and cannot be 'utilized as a tool for invidious viewpoint discrimination.' It is evident in the legislative history that § 954(d)(1) was prompted by, and directed at, the public funding of such offensive productions as Serrano's 'Piss Christ,' the portrayal of a crucifix immersed in urine, and Mapplethorpe's show of lurid homoerotic photographs. Thus, even if one strays beyond the plain text it is perfectly clear that the statute was meant to disfavor—

---

1. [O]ne might argue that the decency and respect factors constitute content discrimination rather than viewpoint discrimination, which would render them easier to uphold. Since I believe this statute must be upheld in either event, I pass over this conundrum and assume the worst.

that is, to discriminate against—such productions. Not to ban their funding absolutely, to be sure (though as I shall discuss, that also would not have been unconstitutional); but to make their funding more difficult.

"More fundamentally, of course, all this legislative history has no valid claim upon our attention at all. It is a virtual certainty that very few of the Members of Congress who voted for this language both (1) knew of, and (2) agreed with, the various statements that the Court has culled from * * * the floor debate (probably conducted on an almost empty floor). And it is wholly irrelevant that the statute was a 'bipartisan proposal introduced as a counterweight' to an alternative proposal that would directly restrict funding on the basis of viewpoint. We do not judge statutes as if we are surveying the scene of an accident; each one is reviewed, not on the basis of how much worse it could have been, but on the basis of what it says. It matters not whether this enactment was the product of the most partisan alignment in history or whether, upon its passage, the Members all linked arms and sang, 'The more we get together, the happier we'll be.' It is 'not consonant with our scheme of government for a court to inquire into the motives of legislators.' The law at issue in this case is to be found in the text of § 954(d)(1), which passed both Houses and was signed by the President. And that law unquestionably disfavors—discriminates against—indecency and disrespect for the diverse beliefs and values of the American people. * * *

"With the enactment of § 954(d)(1), Congress did not *abridge* the speech of those who disdain the beliefs and values of the American public, nor did it *abridge* indecent speech. Those who wish to create indecent and disrespectful art are as unconstrained now as they were before the enactment of this statute. *Avant-garde artistes* such as respondents remain entirely free to *epater les bourgeois*; they are merely deprived of the additional satisfaction of having the bourgeoisie taxed to pay for it. * * *

"As we noted in *Rust*, when Congress chose to establish the National Endowment for Democracy it was not constitutionally required to fund programs encouraging competing philosophies of government—an example of funding discrimination that cuts much closer than this one to the core of political speech which is the primary concern of the First Amendment. It takes a particularly high degree of chutzpah for the NEA to contradict this proposition, since the agency itself discriminates—and is required by law to discriminate—in favor of artistic (as opposed to scientific, or political, or theological) expression. Not all the common folk, or even all great minds, for that matter, think that is a good idea. In 1800, when John Marshall told John Adams that a recent immigration of Frenchmen would include talented artists, 'Adams denounced all Frenchmen, but most especially "schoolmasters, painters, poets, & C." He warned Marshall that the fine arts were like germs that infected healthy constitutions.' J. Ellis, *After the Revolution: Profiles of Early American Culture* 36 (1979). Surely the NEA itself is nothing less than an institutionalized discrimination against that point of view. Nonetheless it is constitutional, as is the congressional determination to favor decency and respect for beliefs and values over the opposite.[3]

"The nub of the difference between me and the Court is that I regard the distinction between 'abridging' speech and funding it as a fundamental divide, on this side of which the First Amendment is inapplicable. The Court, by contrast,

---

3. I suppose it would be unconstitutional for the government to give money to an organization devoted to the promotion of candidates nominated by the Republican party—but it would be just as unconstitutional for the government itself to promote candidates nominated by the Republican party, and I do not think that that unconstitutionality has anything to do with the First Amendment.

seems to believe that the First Amendment, despite its words, has some ineffable effect upon funding, imposing constraints of an indeterminate nature which it announces (without troubling to enunciate any particular test) are not violated by the statute here—or, more accurately, are not violated by the quite different, emasculated statute that it imagines.''

SOUTER, J., dissented: "The decency and respect proviso mandates viewpoint-based decisions in the disbursement of government subsidies, and the Government has wholly failed to explain why the statute should be afforded an exemption from the fundamental rule of the First Amendment that viewpoint discrimination in the exercise of public authority over expressive activity is unconstitutional. * * *[2]

"[An argument] for avoiding unconstitutionality that the Court appears to regard with some favor is the Government's argument that the NEA may comply with § 954(d) merely by populating the advisory panels that analyze grant applications with members of diverse backgrounds. Would that it were so easy; this asserted implementation of the law fails *even* to 'reflec[t] a plausible construction of the plain language of the statute.' *Rust v. Sullivan*, 500 U.S. 173, 184, 111 S.Ct. 1759, 114 L.Ed.2d 233 (1991).

"The Government notes that § 954(d) actually provides that '[i]n establishing * * * regulations and procedures, the Chairperson [of the NEA] shall ensure that (1) artistic excellence and artistic merit are the criteria by which applications are judged, taking into consideration general standards of decency and respect for the diverse beliefs and values of the American public.' According to the Government, this language requires decency and respect to be considered not in judging applications, but in making regulations. If, then, the Chairperson takes decency and respect into consideration through regulations ensuring diverse panels, the statute is satisfied. But it would take a great act of will to find any plausibility in this reading. The reference to considering decency and respect occurs in the subparagraph speaking to the 'criteria by which applications are judged,' not in the preamble directing the Chairperson to adopt regulations; it is in judging applications that decency and respect are most obviously to be considered. * * *

"[Another] try at avoiding constitutional problems is the Court's disclaimer of any constitutional issue here because '[s]ection 954(d)(1) adds "considerations" to the grant-making process; it does not preclude awards to projects that might be deemed "indecent" or "disrespectful," nor place conditions on grants, or even specify that those factors must be given any particular weight in reviewing an application.' * * *

"That is not a fair reading. Just as the statute cannot be read as anything but viewpoint based, or as requiring nothing more than diverse review panels, it cannot be read as tolerating awards to spread indecency or disrespect, so long as the review panel, the National Counsel on the Arts, and the Chairperson have given some thought to the offending qualities and decided to underwrite them anyway. That, after all, is presumably just what prompted the congressional outrage in the first place, and there was nothing naive about the Representative who said he voted for the bill because it does 'not tolerate wasting Federal funds for sexually explicit photographs [or] sacrilegious works.'

2. [Congress] has no obligation to support artistic enterprises that many people detest. The First Amendment speaks up only when Congress decides to participate in the Nation's artistic life by legal regulation, as it does through a subsidy scheme like the NEA. If Congress does choose to spend public funds in this manner, it may not discriminate by viewpoint in deciding who gets the money.

"But even if I found the Court's view of 'consideration' plausible, that would make no difference at all on the question of constitutionality. What if the statute required a panel to apply criteria 'taking into consideration the centrality of Christianity to the American cultural experience,' or 'taking into consideration whether the artist is a communist,' or 'taking into consideration the political message conveyed by the art,' or even 'taking into consideration the superiority of the white race'? Would the Court hold these considerations facially constitutional, merely because the statute had no requirement to give them any particular, much less controlling, weight? I assume not.

"A second basic strand in the Court's treatment of today's question and the heart of Justice Scalia's in effect assumes that whether or not the statute mandates viewpoint discrimination, there is no constitutional issue here because government art subsidies fall within a zone of activity free from First Amendment restraints. The Government calls attention to the roles of government-as-speaker [in] which the government is of course entitled to engage in viewpoint discrimination: if the Food and Drug Administration launches an advertising campaign on the subject of smoking, it may condemn the habit without also having to show a cowboy taking a puff on the opposite page; and if the Secretary of Defense wishes to buy a portrait to decorate the Pentagon, he is free to prefer George Washington over George the Third.

"The Government freely admits, however, that it neither speaks through the expression subsidized by the NEA,[6] nor buys anything for itself with its NEA grants. On the contrary, believing that '[t]he arts * * * reflect the high place accorded by the American people to the nation's rich cultural heritage,' § 951(6), and that '[i]t is vital to a democracy * * * to provide financial assistance to its artists and the organizations that support their work,' § 951(10), the Government acts as a patron, financially underwriting the production of art by private artists and impresarios for independent consumption. Accordingly, the Government would have us liberate government-as-patron from First Amendment strictures not by placing it squarely within the categories of government-as-buyer or government-as-speaker, but by recognizing a new category by analogy to those accepted ones. The analogy is, however, a very poor fit, and this patronage falls embarrassingly on the wrong side of the line between government-as-buyer or-speaker and government-as-regulator-of-private-speech.

"[*Rosenberger*] controls here. The NEA, like the student activities fund in *Rosenberger*, is a subsidy scheme created to encourage expression of a diversity of views from private speakers. Congress brought the NEA into being to help all Americans 'achieve a better understanding of the past, a better analysis of the present, and a better view of the future.' § 951(3). The NEA's purpose is to 'support new ideas' and 'to help create and sustain [a] climate encouraging freedom of thought, imagination, and inquiry.' §§ 951(10),(7). Given this congressional choice to sustain freedom of expression, *Rosenberger* teaches that the First Amendment forbids decisions based on viewpoint popularity. So long as Congress chooses to subsidize expressive endeavors at large, it has no business requiring the NEA to turn down funding applications of artists and exhibitors who devote their 'freedom of thought, imagination, and inquiry' to defying our tastes, our beliefs, or our values. It may not use the NEA's purse to 'suppres[s] dangerous ideas.' *Regan v. Taxation with Representation.*

---

6. Here, the "communicative element inherent in the very act of funding itself," Rosenberger (Souter, J., dissenting), is an endorsement of the importance of the arts collectively, not an endorsement of the individual message espoused in a given work of art.

"The Court says otherwise, claiming to distinguish *Rosenberger* on the ground that the student activities funds in that case were generally available to most applicants, whereas NEA funds are disbursed selectively and competitively to a choice few. But the Court in *Rosenberger* anticipated and specifically rejected just this distinction when it held in no uncertain terms that '[t]he government cannot justify viewpoint discrimination among private speakers on the economic fact of scarcity.'[8] Scarce money demands choices, of course, but choices 'on some acceptable [viewpoint] neutral principle,' like artistic excellence and artistic merit;[9] 'nothing in our decision[s] indicate[s] that scarcity would give the State the right to exercise viewpoint discrimination that is otherwise impermissible.'[[10]]."

BROADCAST REGULATION AND ACCESS TO THE MASS MEDIA

ACCESS TO THE MASS MEDIA

CON LAW: P. 953, after Turner

AMER CON: P. 939, after Turner

RTS & LIB: P. 861, after Turner

After remand, TURNER BROADCASTING SYSTEM, INC. v. FCC, 520 U.S. 180, 117 S.Ct. 1174, 137 L.Ed.2d 369 (1997), per KENNEDY, J., joined by Rehnquist, C.J., Stevens, and Souter, JJ., upheld the must-carry provisions. Applying the *O'Brien* test, he emphasized the importance of deferring to Congress so long as it had "drawn reasonable inferences based upon substantial evidence." He found that the legislation was narrowly tailored to preserve the benefits of local broadcast television, to promote widespread dissemination of information from a multiplicity of sources, and to promote fair competition.

BREYER, J., concurring, joined Kennedy, J.'s opinion except for his discussion and conclusion regarding the fair competition rationale.[a]

O'CONNOR, J., joined by Scalia, Thomas, and Ginsburg, JJ., dissenting, argued again that strict scrutiny should apply, agreed that deference was owed to Congress "in its predictive judgments and its evaluation of complex economic questions," but maintained that even under intermediate scrutiny, the Court had an independent duty to examine with care the Congressional interests, the

---

8. The Court's attempt to avoid *Rosenberger* by describing NEA funding in terms of competition, not scarcity, will not work. Competition implies scarcity, without which there is no exclusive prize to compete for; the Court's 'competition' is merely a surrogate for 'scarcity.'

9. While criteria of 'artistic excellence and artistic merit' may raise intractable issues about the identification of artistic worth, and could no doubt be used covertly to filter out unwanted ideas, there is nothing inherently viewpoint discriminatory about such merit-based criteria. [Decency] and respect, on the other hand, are inherently and facially viewpoint based, and serve no legitimate and permissible end. The Court's assertion that the mere fact that grants must be awarded according to artistic merit precludes 'absolute neutrality' on the part of the NEA is therefore misdirected. It is not to the point that the government necessarily makes choices among competing applications, or even that its judgments about artistic quality may be branded as subjective to some greater or lesser degree; the question here is whether the government may apply patently viewpoint-based criteria in making those choices.

10. [Leaving] aside the proper application of forum analysis to the NEA and its projects, I cannot agree that the holding of *Rosenberger* turned on characterizing its metaphorical forum as public in some degree. Like this case, *Rosenberger* involved viewpoint discrimination, and we have made it clear that such discrimination is impermissible in all forums, even non-public [ones].

a. Stevens, J., also filed a concurring opinion.

findings, and the fit between the goals and consequences. She criticized the Court for being too deferential even on the assumption that the legislation was content neutral.

On O'Connor, J.'s analysis, the record did not support either the conclusion that cable posed a significant threat to local broadcast markets or that the act was narrowly tailored to deal with anti-competitive conduct.

———

ARKANSAS EDUCATIONAL TELEVISION COMMISSION v. FORBES, 523 U.S. 666, 118 S.Ct. 1633, 140 L.Ed.2d 875 (1998), per KENNEDY, J., concluded that a candidate debate sponsored by a state-owned public television broadcaster was a nonpublic forum subject to constitutional restraints, but that the broadcaster's decision to exclude the candidate was reasonable: "A state-owned public television broadcaster [Arkansas Educational Television Commission 'AETC'] sponsored a candidate debate from which it excluded an independent congressional candidate [Ralph Forbes] with little popular support. The issue before us is whether, by reason of its state ownership, the station had a constitutional obligation to allow every candidate access to the debate. We conclude that, unlike most other public television programs, the candidate debate was subject to constitutional constraints applicable to nonpublic fora under our forum precedents. Even so, the broadcaster's decision to exclude the candidate was a reasonable, viewpoint-neutral exercise of journalistic discretion. * * *

"Although public broadcasting as a general matter does not lend itself to scrutiny under the forum doctrine, candidate debates present the narrow exception to the rule. For two reasons, a candidate debate like the one at issue here is different from other programming. First, unlike AETC's other broadcasts, the debate was by design a forum for political speech by the candidates. Consistent with the long tradition of candidate debates, the implicit representation of the broadcaster was that the views expressed were those of the candidates, not its own. The very purpose of the debate was to allow the candidates to express their views with minimal intrusion by the broadcaster. In this respect the debate differed even from a political talk show, whose host can express partisan views and then limit the discussion to those ideas.

"Second, in our tradition, candidate debates are of exceptional significance in the electoral process. [Deliberation] on the positions and qualifications of candidates is integral to our system of government, and electoral speech may have its most profound and widespread impact when it is disseminated through televised debates. * * *

"Under our precedents, the AETC debate was not a designated public forum. [T]he government creates a designated public forum when it makes its property generally available to a certain class of speakers, as the university made its facilities generally available to student groups in *Widmar*. On the other hand, the government does not create a designated public forum when it does no more than reserve eligibility for access to the forum to a particular class of speakers, whose members must then, as individuals, 'obtain permission,' to use it. For instance, the Federal Government did not create a designated public forum in Cornelius when it reserved eligibility for participation in the CFC drive to charitable agencies, and then made individual, non-ministerial judgments as to which of the eligible agencies would participate.

"The [distinction] between general and selective access furthers First Amendment interests. By recognizing the distinction, we encourage the government to open its property to some expressive activity in cases where, if faced with an all-or-nothing choice, it might not open the property at all.[a] That this distinction turns on governmental intent does not render it unprotective of speech. Rather, it reflects the reality that, with the exception of traditional public fora, the government retains the choice of whether to designate its property as a forum for specified classes of speakers.

"Here, the debate did not have an open-microphone format. [AETC] did not make its debate generally available to candidates for Arkansas' Third Congressional District seat. Instead, just as the Federal Government in *Cornelius* reserved eligibility for participation in the CFC program to certain classes of voluntary agencies, AETC reserved eligibility for participation in the debate to candidates for the Third Congressional District seat (as opposed to some other seat). At that point, just as the Government in *Cornelius* made agency-by-agency determinations as to which of the eligible agencies would participate in the CFC, AETC made candidate-by-candidate determinations as to which of the eligible candidates would participate in the debate. 'Such selective access, unsupported by evidence of a purposeful designation for public use, does not create a public forum.' Thus the debate was a nonpublic forum.

"The debate's status as a nonpublic forum, however, did not give AETC unfettered power to exclude any candidate it wished. [To] be consistent with the First Amendment, the exclusion of a speaker from a nonpublic forum must not be based on the speaker's viewpoint and must otherwise be reasonable in light of the purpose of the property. *Cornelius.* * * *

"There is no substance to Forbes' suggestion that he was excluded because his views were unpopular or out of the mainstream. * * * Nor did AETC exclude Forbes in an attempted manipulation of the political process. The evidence provided powerful support for the jury's express finding that AETC's exclusion of Forbes was not the result of 'political pressure from anyone inside or outside [AETC].' There is no serious argument that AETC did not act in good faith in this case. AETC excluded Forbes because the voters lacked interest in his candidacy, not because AETC itself did. The broadcaster's decision to exclude Forbes was a reasonable, viewpoint-neutral exercise of journalistic discretion consistent with the First Amendment.

STEVENS, J., joined by Souter and Ginsburg, JJ., dissented: "The official action that led to the exclusion of respondent Forbes from a debate with the two major-party candidates for election to one of Arkansas' four seats in Congress does not adhere to well-settled constitutional principles. The ad hoc decision of the staff of

a. In a later section, the Court stated: "In each of the 1988, 1992, and 1996 Presidential elections, for example, no fewer than 22 candidates appeared on the ballot in at least one State. In the 1996 congressional elections, it was common for 6 to 11 candidates to qualify for the ballot for a particular seat. In the 1993 New Jersey gubernatorial election, to illustrate further, sample ballot mailings included the written statements of 19 candidates. On logistical grounds alone, a public television editor might, with reason, decide that the inclusion of all ballot-qualified candidates would 'actually undermine the educational value and quality of debates.'

"Were it faced with the prospect of cacophony, on the one hand, and First Amendment liability, on the other, a public television broadcaster might choose not to air candidates' views at [all]. These concerns are more than speculative. As a direct result of the Court of Appeals' decision in this case, the Nebraska Educational Television Network canceled a scheduled debate between candidates in Nebraska's 1996 United States Senate race. A First Amendment jurisprudence yielding these results does not promote speech but represses it."

[AETC] raises precisely the concerns addressed by 'the many decisions of this Court over the last 30 years, holding that a law subjecting the exercise of First Amendment freedoms to the prior restraint of a license, without narrow, objective, and definite standards to guide the licensing authority, is unconstitutional.' *Shuttlesworth v. Birmingham.*

"Given the fact that the Republican winner in the Third Congressional District race in 1992 received only 50.22% of the vote and the Democrat received 47.20%, it would have been necessary for Forbes, who had made a strong showing in recent Republican primaries, to divert only a handful of votes from the Republican candidate to cause his defeat. Thus, even though the AETC staff may have correctly concluded that Forbes was 'not a serious candidate,' their decision to exclude him from the debate may have determined the outcome of the election in the Third District.

"If a comparable decision were made today by a privately owned network, it would be subject to scrutiny under the Federal Election Campaign Act unless the network used 'pre-established objective criteria to determine which candidates may participate in [the] debate.' 11 CFR § 110.13(c) (1997). No such criteria governed AETC's refusal to permit Forbes to participate in the debate. Indeed, whether that refusal was based on a judgment about 'newsworthiness'—as AETC has argued in this Court—or a judgment about 'political viability'—as it argued in the Court of Appeals—the facts in the record presumably would have provided an adequate basis either for a decision to include Forbes in the Third District debate or a decision to exclude him * * *.

"The apparent flexibility of AETC's purported standard suggests the extent to which the staff had nearly limitless discretion to exclude Forbes from the debate based on ad hoc justifications. Thus, the Court of Appeals correctly concluded that the staff's appraisal of 'political viability' was 'so subjective, so arguable, so susceptible of variation in individual opinion, as to provide no secure basis for the exercise of governmental power consistent with the First Amendment.' * * *

"The reasons that support the need for narrow, objective, and definite standards to guide licensing decisions apply directly to the wholly subjective access decisions made by the staff of AETC.[18] The importance of avoiding arbitrary or viewpoint-based exclusions from political debates militates strongly in favor of requiring the controlling state agency to use (and adhere to) pre-established, objective criteria to determine who among qualified candidates may participate. A constitutional duty to use objective standards—i.e., 'neutral principles'—for determining whether and when to adjust a debate format would impose only a modest requirement that would fall far short of a duty to grant every multiple-party request. Such standards would also have the benefit of providing the public with some assurance that state-owned broadcasters cannot select debate participants on arbitrary grounds."

18. Ironically, it is the standardless character of the decision to exclude Forbes that provides the basis for the Court's conclusion that the debates were a nonpublic forum rather than a limited public forum. [T]he Court explains that "[a] designated public forum is not created when the government allows selective access for individual speakers rather than general access for a class of speakers." If, as AETC claims, it did invite either the entire class of 'viable' candidates, or the entire class of 'newsworthy' candidates, under the Court's reasoning, it created a designated public forum.

BROADCASTING AND CONTENT REGULATION:
INDECENT SPEECH

CON LAW: P. 963, after note 3
AMER CON: P. 948, after note 3
RTS & LIB: P. 870, after note 3

Cable operators are required under federal law to reserve channels for commercial lease ("leased access channels") and are routinely required by their franchise agreements with municipalities to reserve channels for public, educational, and governmental access ("public access channels" or "pegs"). For some years federal law prevented cable operators from employing any editorial control over the content of leased access or public access channels. The Cable Television Consumer Protection and Competition of 1992, however, permitted cable operators to prohibit the broadcast of material that the cable operator "reasonably believes describes or depicts sexual or excretory activities or organs in a patently offensive manner" on leased access channels (47 U.S.C. § 10(a)) and public access channels (47 U.S.C. § 10(c)). In addition, if the cable operator did not prohibit such material from being broadcast on leased access channels, the Act required the cable operator to provide a separate channel for the material, to scramble or otherwise block its presentation, and to permit its viewing only upon written request (47 U.S.C. § 10(b))(the "block and segregate requirements"). After the adoption of § 10(b), Congress passed block and segregate requirements for channels primarily dedicated to sexual programming and required cable operators to honor a subscriber's request to block any undesired programs.

DENVER AREA EDUCATIONAL TELECOMMUNICATIONS CONSORTIUM, INC. v. FCC, 518 U.S. 727, 116 S.Ct. 2374, 135 L.Ed.2d 888 (1996) upheld the constitutionality of § 10(a), but invalidated §§ 10(b) and (c). BREYER, J., joined by Stevens, O'Connor, Kennedy, and Souter, JJ., held that the segregate and block requirements (§ 10(b)) were invalid: "We agree with the Government that protection of children is a 'compelling interest.' But we do not agree that the 'segregate and block' requirements properly accommodate the speech restrictions they impose and the legitimate objective they seek to attain. Nor need we here determine whether, or the extent to which, *Pacifica* does, or does not, impose some lesser standard of review where indecent speech is at issue, compare (opinion of Stevens, J.)(indecent materials enjoy lesser First Amendment protection), with (Powell, J., concurring in part and concurring in judgment)(refusing to accept a lesser standard for nonobscene, indecent material). That is because once one examines this governmental restriction, it becomes apparent that, not only is it not a 'least restrictive alternative,' and is not 'narrowly tailored' to meet its legitimate objective, it also seems considerably 'more extensive than necessary.' That is to say, it fails to satisfy this Court's formulations of the First Amendment's 'strictest,' as well as its somewhat less 'strict,' requirements. * * *

"The record does not explain why, under the new Act, blocking alone—without written access-requests—adequately protects children from exposure to regular sex-dedicated channels, but cannot adequately protect those children from programming on similarly sex-dedicated channels that are leased. It does not explain why a simple subscriber blocking request system, perhaps a phone-call based system, would adequately protect children from 'patently offensive' material broadcast on ordinary non-sex-dedicated channels (i.e., almost all channels) but a far more restrictive segregate/block/written-access system is needed to protect children from similar broadcasts on what (in the absence of the segregation requirement) would be non-sex-dedicated channels that are leased. Nor is there any indication Congress thought the new ordinary channel protections less than adequate.

In a portion of his opinion joined by Stevens, O'Connor, and Souter, JJ., Breyer, J., concluded that § 10(a) was valid, but, in a portion of his opinion joined by Stevens and Souter, JJ., he concluded that § 10(c) was invalid. As to § 10(a), BREYER, J., observed: "Justices Kennedy and Thomas would have us decide this case simply by transferring and applying literally categorical standards this Court has developed in other contexts. For Justice Kennedy, leased access channels are like a common carrier, cablecast is a protected medium, strict scrutiny applies, § 10(a) fails this test, and, therefore, § 10(a) is invalid. For Justice Thomas, the case is simple because the cable operator who owns the system over which access channels are broadcast, like a bookstore owner with respect to what it displays on the shelves, has a predominant First Amendment interest. Both categorical approaches suffer from the same flaws: they import law developed in very different contexts into a new and changing environment, and they lack the flexibility necessary to allow government to respond to very serious practical problems without sacrificing the free exchange of ideas the First Amendment is designed to protect. * * *

"Over the years, this Court has restated and refined [basic] First Amendment principles, adopting them more particularly to the balance of competing interests and the special circumstances of each field of application. [This] tradition teaches that the First Amendment embodies an overarching commitment to protect speech from Government regulation through close judicial scrutiny, thereby enforcing the Constitution's constraints, but without imposing judicial formulae so rigid that they become a straightjacket that disables Government from responding to serious problems. This Court, in different contexts, has consistently held that the Government may directly regulate speech to address extraordinary problems, where its regulations are appropriately tailored to resolve those problems without imposing an unnecessarily great restriction on speech. Justices Kennedy and Thomas would have us further declare which, among the many applications of the general approach that this Court has developed over the years, we are applying here. But no definitive choice among competing analogies (broadcast, common carrier, bookstore) allows us to declare a rigid single standard, good for now and for all future media and purposes. That is not to say that we reject all the more specific formulations of the standard—they appropriately cover the vast majority of cases involving Government regulation of speech. Rather, aware as we are of the changes taking place in the law, the technology, and the industrial structure, related to telecommunications, we believe it unwise and unnecessary definitively to pick one analogy or one specific set of words now.

"[W]e can decide this case more narrowly, by closely scrutinizing § 10(a) to assure that it properly addresses an extremely important problem, without imposing, in light of the relevant interests, an unnecessarily great restriction on speech. The importance of the interest at stake here—protecting children from exposure to patently offensive depictions of sex; the accommodation of the interests of programmers in maintaining access channels and of cable operators in editing the contents of their channels; the similarity of the problem and its solution to those at issue in *Pacifica*, and the flexibility inherent in an approach that permits private cable operators to make editorial decisions, lead us to conclude that § 10(a) is a sufficiently tailored response to an extraordinarily important problem. * * *

"[W]e part company with Justice Kennedy on two issues. First, Justice Kennedy's focus on categorical analysis forces him to disregard the cable system operators' interests. We, on the other hand, recognize that in the context of cable broadcast that involves an access requirement (here, its partial removal), and unlike in most cases where we have explicitly required 'narrow tailoring,' the expressive interests of cable operators do play a legitimate role. Cf. *Turner*. While we cannot agree with Justice Thomas that everything turns on the rights of the cable owner, we also cannot agree with Justice Kennedy that we must ignore the expressive interests of cable operators altogether. Second, Justice Kennedy's application of a very strict 'narrow tailoring' test depends upon an analogy with a category ('the public forum cases'), which has been distilled over time from the similarities of many cases. Rather than seeking an analogy to a category of cases, however, we have looked to the cases themselves. And, [we find] that *Pacifica* provides the closest analogy. * * *

"The Court's distinction in *Turner*, [between] cable and broadcast television, relied on the inapplicability of the spectrum scarcity problem to cable. While that distinction was relevant in *Turner* to the justification for structural regulations at issue there (the 'must carry' rules), it has little to do with a case that involves the effects of television viewing on children. Those effects are the result of how parents and children view television programming, and how pervasive and intrusive that programming is. In that respect, cable and broadcast television differ little, if at all.

"[I]f one wishes to view the permissive provisions before us through a 'public forum' lens, one should view those provisions as limiting the otherwise totally open nature of the forum that leased access channels provide for communication of other than patently offensive sexual material—taking account of the fact that the limitation was imposed in light of experience gained from maintaining a totally open 'forum.' One must still ask whether the First Amendment forbids the limitation. But unless a label alone were to make a critical First Amendment difference (and we think here it does not), the features of this case that we have already discussed—the government's interest in protecting children, the 'permissive' aspect of the statute, and the nature of the medium—sufficiently justify the 'limitation' on the availability of this forum.

Breyer, J., argued that the balance was different in § 10(c): "[C]able operators have traditionally agreed to reserve channel capacity for public, governmental, and educational channels as part of the consideration they give municipalities that award them cable franchises. [Thus] these are channels over which cable operators have not historically exercised editorial control. Unlike § 10(a) therefore, § 10(c) does not restore to cable operators editorial rights that they once had, and the countervailing First Amendment interest is nonexistent, or at least much diminished.

"[A] second difference is the institutional background that has developed as a result of the historical difference. When a 'leased channel' is made available by the operator to a private lessee, the lessee has total control of programming during the leased time slot. Public access channels, on the other hand, are normally subject to complex supervisory systems of various sorts, often with both public and private elements. [G]iven present supervisory mechanisms, the need for this particular provision, aimed directly at public access channels, is not obvious."

STEVENS, J., concurring, agreed with Breyer, J., that it was unwise to characterize leased channels as public fora: "When the Federal Government opens cable channels that would otherwise be left entirely in private hands, it deserves more deference than a rigid application of the public forum doctrine would allow. At this early stage in the regulation of this developing industry, Congress should not be put to an all or nothing-at-all choice in deciding whether to open certain cable channels to programmers who would otherwise lack the resources to participate in the marketplace of ideas.

With respect to § 10(c), Stevens, J., stated: "What is of critical importance to me, however, is that if left to their own devices, those authorities may choose to carry some programming that the Federal Government has decided to restrict. As I read § 10(c), the federal statute would disable local governments from making that choice. It would inject federally authorized private censors into forums from which they might otherwise be excluded, and it would therefore limit local forums that might otherwise be open to all constitutionally protected speech.[3]

SOUTER, J., concurred: "All of the relevant characteristics of cable are presently in a state of technological and regulatory flux. Recent and far-reaching legislation not only affects the technical feasibility of parental control over children's access to undesirable material but portends fundamental changes in the competitive structure of the industry and, therefore, the ability of individual entities to act as bottlenecks to the free flow of information. As cable and telephone companies begin their competition for control over the single wire that will carry both their services, we can hardly settle rules for review of regulation on the assumption that cable will remain a separable and useful category of First Amendment scrutiny. And as broadcast, cable, and the cyber-technology of the Internet and the World Wide Web approach the day of using a common receiver, we can hardly assume that standards for judging the regulation of one of them will not have immense, but now unknown and unknowable, effects on the others. * * *

"The upshot of appreciating the fluidity of the subject that Congress must regulate is simply to accept the fact that not every nuance of our old standards will necessarily do for the new technology, and that a proper choice among existing doctrinal categories is not obvious. Rather than definitively settling the issue now, Justice Breyer wisely reasons by direct analogy rather than by rule, concluding that the speech and the restriction at issue in this case may usefully be measured against the ones at issue in *Pacifica*. If that means it will take some time before reaching a final method of review for cases like this one, there may be consolation in recalling that 16 years passed, from *Roth* to *Miller*, before the modern obscenity rule jelled; that it took over 40 years, from *Hague v. CIO* to *Perry*, for the public forum category to settle out; and that a round half-century passed before the clear and present danger of *Schenck* evolved into the modern incitement rule of *Brandenburg*.

"I cannot guess how much time will go by until the technologies of communication before us today have matured and their relationships become known. But until a category of indecency can be defined both with reference to the new technology and with a prospect of durability, the job of the courts will be just what Justice Breyer does today: recognizing established First Amendment interests through a close analysis that constrains the Congress, without wholly incapacitating it in all matters of the significance apparent here, maintaining the high value of open communication, measuring the costs of regulation by exact attention to fact, and compiling a pedigree of experience with the changing subject. These are familiar judicial responsibilities in times when we know too little to risk the

---

3. Although in 1984 Congress essentially barred cable operators from exercising editorial control over PEG channels, see 47 U.S.C. § 531(e), Section 10(c) does not merely restore the status quo ante. Section 10(c) authorizes private operators to exercise editorial discre- tion over "indecent" programming even if the franchising authority objects. Under the pre– 1984 practice, local franchising authorities were free to exclude operators from exercising any such control on PEG channels.

finality of precision, and attention to them will probably take us through the communications revolution. Maybe the judicial obligation to shoulder these responsibilities can itself be captured by a much older rule, familiar to every doctor of medicine: 'First, do no harm.' "

O'CONNOR, J., concurring in part and dissenting in part, agreed with Breyer, J.'s assessment that § 10(a) was valid and § 10(b) invalid. She argued, however, that Breyer, J.'s distinctions regarding § 10(c) were insufficiently weighty: "The interest in protecting children remains the same, whether on a leased access channel or a public access channel, and allowing the cable operator the option of prohibiting the transmission of indecent speech seems a constitutionally permissible means of addressing that interest. Nor is the fact that public access programming may be subject to supervisory systems in addition to the cable operator sufficient in my mind to render § 10(c) so ill-tailored to its goal as to be unconstitutional."

KENNEDY, J., joined by Ginsburg, J., concurring in part and dissenting in part, agreed that § 10(b) and (c) were invalid, but faulted the plurality opinion for its upholding of § 10(a): "The plurality opinion, insofar as it upholds § 10(a) [is] adrift. The opinion treats concepts such as public forum, broadcaster, and common carrier as mere labels rather than as categories with settled legal significance; it applies no standard, and by this omission loses sight of existing First Amendment doctrine. When confronted with a threat to free speech in the context of an emerging technology, we ought to have the discipline to analyze the case by reference to existing elaborations of constant First Amendment principles. This is the essence of the case-by-case approach to ensuring protection of speech under the First Amendment, even in novel settings. * * *

"The plurality begins its flight from standards with a number of assertions nobody disputes. I agree, of course, that it would be unwise 'to declare a rigid single standard, good for now and for all future media and purposes.' I do think it necessary, however, to decide what standard applies to discrimination against indecent programming on cable access channels in the present state of the industry. We owe at least that much to public and leased access programmers whose speech is put at risk nationwide by these laws. * * *

"The plurality claims its resistance to standards is in keeping with our case law, where we have shown a willingness to be flexible in confronting novel First Amendment problems. [W]e have developed specialized or more or less stringent standards when certain contexts demanded them; we did not avoid the use of standards altogether. Indeed, the creation of standards and adherence to them, even when it means affording protection to speech unpopular or distasteful, is the central achievement of our First Amendment jurisprudence. Standards are the means by which we state in advance how to test a law's validity, rather than letting the height of the bar be determined by the apparent exigencies of the day. They also provide notice and fair warning to those who must predict how the courts will respond to attempts to suppress their speech. Yet formulations like strict scrutiny, used in a number of constitutional settings to ensure that the inequities of the moment are subordinated to commitments made for the long run mean little if they can be watered down whenever they seem too strong. They mean still less if they can be ignored altogether when considering a case not on all fours with what we have seen before."

"The plurality seems distracted by the many changes in technology and competition in the cable industry. The laws challenged here, however, do not retool the structure of the cable industry or (with the exception of § 10(b)) involve intricate technologies. The straightforward issue here is whether the Government can deprive certain speakers, on the basis of the content of their speech, of protections afforded all others. There is no reason to discard our existing First Amendment jurisprudence in answering this question.

"While it protests against standards, the plurality does seem to favor one formulation of the question in this case: namely, whether the Act 'properly addresses an extremely important problem, without imposing, in light of the relevant interests, an unnecessarily great restriction on speech.' [This] description of the question accomplishes little, save to clutter our First Amendment case law by adding an untested rule with an uncertain relationship to the others we use to evaluate laws restricting speech. * * *

"Justice Souter recommends to the Court the precept 'First, do no harm.' 'The question, though, is whether the harm is in sustaining the law or striking it down. If the plurality is concerned about technology's direction, it ought to begin by allowing speech, not suppressing it. We have before us an urgent claim for relief against content-based discrimination, not a dry run.

"The constitutionality under *Turner Broadcasting* of requiring a cable operator to set aside leased access channels is not before us. For purposes of this case, we should treat the cable operator's rights in these channels as extinguished, and address the issue these petitioners present: namely, whether the Government can discriminate on the basis of content in affording protection to certain programmers. I cannot agree with Justice Thomas that the cable operator's rights inform this analysis.

"Laws requiring cable operators to provide leased access are the practical equivalent of making them common carriers, analogous in this respect to telephone companies: They are obliged to provide a conduit for the speech of others. [Laws] removing common-carriage protection from a single form of speech based on its content should be reviewed under the same standard as content-based restrictions on speech in a public forum. Making a cable operator a common carrier does not create a public forum in the sense of taking property from private control and dedicating it to public use; rather, regulations of a common carrier dictate the manner in which private control is exercised. A common-carriage mandate, nonetheless, serves the same function as a public forum. It ensures open, nondiscriminatory access to the means of communication.

"*Pacifica* did not purport, however, to apply a special standard for indecent broadcasting. Emphasizing the narrowness of its holding, the Court in *Pacifica* conducted a context-specific analysis of the FCC's restriction on indecent programming during daytime hours. It relied on the general rule that 'broadcasting * * * has received the most limited First Amendment protection.' We already have rejected the application of this lower broadcast standard of review to infringements on the liberties of cable operators, even though they control an important communications medium. *Turner.*' * * *

"[Indecency] often is inseparable from the ideas and viewpoints conveyed, or separable only with loss of truth or expressive power. Under our traditional First Amendment jurisprudence, factors perhaps justifying some restriction on indecent cable programming may all be taken into account without derogating this category of protected speech as marginal.

"Congress does have, however, a compelling interest in protecting children from indecent speech. So long as society gives proper respect to parental choices, it may, under an appropriate standard, intervene to spare children exposure to material not suitable for minors. This interest is substantial enough to justify some regulation of indecent speech even under, I will assume, the [strict scrutiny standard].

"Sections 10(a) and (c) nonetheless are not narrowly tailored to protect children from indecent programs on access channels. First, to the extent some operators may allow indecent programming, children in localities those operators serve will be left unprotected. Partial service of a compelling interest is not narrow tailoring. Put another way, the interest in protecting children from indecency only at the caprice of the cable operator is not compelling. Perhaps Congress drafted the law this way to avoid the clear constitutional difficulties of banning indecent speech from access channels, but the First Amendment does not permit this sort of ill fit between a law restricting speech and the interest it is said to serve.

"Second, to the extent cable operators prohibit indecent programming on access channels, not only children but adults will be deprived of it."

THOMAS, J., joined by Rehnquist, C.J., and Scalia, J., concurring in part and dissenting in part, argued that §§ 10(a),(b), and (c) validly protected the constitutional rights of cable operators: "It is one thing to compel an operator to carry leased and public access speech, in apparent violation of *Tornillo*, but it is another thing altogether to say that the First Amendment forbids Congress to give back part of the operators' editorial discretion, which all recognize as fundamentally protected, in favor of a broader access right. It is no answer to say that leased and public access are content neutral and that §§ 10(a) and (c) are not, for that does not change the fundamental fact, which petitioners never address, that it is the operators' journalistic freedom that is infringed, whether the challenged restrictions be content neutral or content based.

"Because the access provisions are part of a scheme that restricts the free speech rights of cable operators, and expands the speaking opportunities of access programmers, who have no underlying constitutional right to speak through the cable medium, I do not believe that access programmers can challenge the scheme, or a particular part of it, as an abridgment of their 'freedom of speech.' Outside the public forum doctrine, government intervention that grants access programmers an opportunity to speak that they would not otherwise enjoy—and which does not directly limit programmers' underlying speech rights—cannot be an abridgement of the same programmers' First Amendment rights, even if the new speaking opportunity is content-based.

"The permissive nature of §§ 10(a) and (c) is important in this regard. If Congress had forbidden cable operators to carry indecent programming on leased and public access channels, that law would have burdened the programmer's right, recognized in *Turner* to compete for space on an operator's system. The Court would undoubtedly strictly scrutinize such a law. * * *

"Petitioners argue that public access channels are public fora in which they have First Amendment rights to speak and that § 10(c) is invalid because it imposes content-based burdens on those rights. * * *

"Cable systems are not public property. Cable systems are privately owned and privately managed, and petitioners point to no case in which we have held that government may designate private property as a public forum.

"Pursuant to federal and state law, franchising authorities require cable operators to create public access channels, but nothing in the record suggests that local franchising authorities take any formal easement or other property interest in those channels that would permit the government to designate that property as a public forum.

"Public access channels are not public fora, and, therefore, petitioners' attempt to redistribute cable speech rights in their favor must fail. For this reason, and the other reasons articulated earlier, I would sustain both § 10(a) and § 10(c).

"Unlike §§ 10(a) and (c), § 10(b) clearly implicates petitioners' free speech rights. Though § 10(b) by no means bans indecent speech, it clearly places content-based restrictions on the transmission of private speech by requiring cable operators to block and segregate indecent programming that the operator has agreed to carry. Consequently, § 10(b) must be subjected to strict scrutiny and can be upheld only if it furthers a compelling governmental interest by the least restrictive means available.

"The Court strikes down § 10(b) by pointing to alternatives, such as reverse-blocking [that] it says are less restrictive than segregation and blocking. Though these methods attempt to place in parents' hands the ability to permit their children to watch as little, or as much, indecent programming as the parents think proper, they do not effectively support parents' authority to direct the moral upbringing of their children. The FCC recognized that leased-access programming comes 'from a wide variety of independent sources, with no single editor controlling [its] selection and presentation.' Thus, indecent programming on leased access channels is 'especially likely to be shown randomly or intermittently between non-indecent programs.' Rather than being able to simply block out certain channels at certain times, a subscriber [must] carefully monitor all leased-access programming. [The Court's alternative is] largely ineffective."

---

§ 505 of the Telecommunications Act of 1996 requires that cable television operators who provide channels "primarily dedicated to sexually-oriented programming" either "fully scramble or otherwise fully block" the channels so that non-subscribers to the programming would not be able to hear or see it. The art of scrambling has not been perfected, however. "Signal bleed" occurs on many channels, allowing some of the visual and audio aspects of the programming to be heard or seen. In the case of signal bleed, the act requires that the programming be blocked except during hours when children are unlikely to be viewing. The F.C.C.'s regulations provide that those hours are between 10 p.m. and 6 a.m ("the safe harbor provision"). § 504 of the same act required operators to block other programming upon a subscriber's request. A cable television programmer challenged § 505.

UNITED STATES v. PLAYBOY ENTERTAINMENT GROUP, ___ U.S. ___, 120 S.Ct. 1878, ___ L.Ed.2d ___ (2000), per KENNEDY, J., declared the restriction to be content-based with a serious impact on protected speech and held that it did not survive strict scrutiny. Kennedy, J., doubted that signal bleed was sufficiently substantial to imperil children and argued that the government had not demonstrated that a requirement to block upon request with notice of the option provided to the subscriber could not be an effective, but less restrictive alternative: "When the statute became operative, most cable operators had 'no practical choice but to curtail [the targeted] programming during the [regulated] sixteen hours or risk the penalties imposed [if] any audio or video signal bleed occur[red] during [those] times.' The majority of operators–[in one survey, 69%]—complied with § 505 by time channeling the targeted programmers. Since '30 to 50% of all adult programming is viewed by households prior to 10 p.m.,' the result was a significant restriction of communication, with a corresponding reduction in Play-boy's revenues. * * *

"Our zoning cases * * * are irrelevant to the question here. We have made clear that the lesser scrutiny afforded regulations targeting the secondary effects of crime or declining property values has no application to content-based regula-tions targeting the primary effects of protected speech. The statute now before us burdens speech because of its content; it must receive strict scrutiny.

"[A] key difference between cable television and the broadcasting media [is] the point on which this case turns: Cable systems have the capacity to block unwanted channels on a household-by-household basis. The option to block reduces the likelihood, so concerning to the Court in *Pacifica*, that traditional First Amendment scrutiny would deprive the Government of all authority to address this sort of problem. The corollary, of course, is that targeted blocking enables the Government to support parental authority without affecting the First Amendment interests of speakers and willing listeners—listeners for whom, if the speech is unpopular or indecent, the privacy of their own homes may be the optimal place of receipt. Simply put, targeted blocking is less restrictive than banning, and the Government cannot ban speech if targeted blocking is a feasible and effective means of furthering its compelling interests. [When] a plausible, less restrictive alternative is offered to a content-based speech restriction, it is the Government's obligation to prove that the alternative will be ineffective to achieve its goals. The Government has not met that burden here."

STEVENS, J., concurred: "Because Justice Scalia has advanced an argument that the parties have not addressed, a brief response is in order. Relying on *Ginzburg v. United States*, Justice Scalia would treat programs whose content is, he assumes, protected by the First Amendment as though they were obscene because of the way they are advertised. The [*Ginzburg*] theory of obscenity is a legal fiction premised upon a logical bait-and-switch; advertising a bareheaded dancer as 'topless' might be deceptive, but it would not make her performance obscene."[a]

SCALIA, J., dissenting, thought that obscenity law was relevant even if none of the programming was obscene: "We have recognized that commercial entities which engage in 'the sordid business of pandering' by 'deliberately emphasiz[ing] the sexually provocative aspects of [their nonobscene products], in order to catch the salaciously disposed,' engage in constitutionally unprotected behavior. *Ginz-burg* . We are more permissive of government regulation in these circumstances because it is clear from the context in which exchanges between such businesses and their customers occur that neither the merchant nor the buyer is interested in the work's literary, artistic, political, or scientific value.

"Section 505 regulates just this sort of business. [It] is conceivable, I suppose, that a channel which is primarily dedicated to sex might not hold itself forth as primarily dedicated to sex—in which case its productions which contain 'serious literary, artistic, political, or scientific value' (if any) would be as entitled to First Amendment protection as the statuary rooms of the National Gallery. But in the competitive world of cable programming, the possibility that a channel devoted to sex would not advertise itself as such is sufficiently remote, and the number of such channels sufficiently small (if not indeed nonexistent), as not to render the provision substantially overbroad."[2]

---

a. Thomas, J., concurring, indicated that the case would be different if the government had proceeded against aspects of the program-ming that were obscene.

2. Justice Stevens misapprehends in sever-al respects the nature of the test I would apply.

BREYER, J., joined by Rehnquist, C.J., O'Connor & Scalia, JJ., dissenting, argued that the section was justified by the compelling interest in protecting children. He maintained that the suggested alternative of having subscribers ask for blocking if they wished was impractical: "As the majority observes, during the 14 months the Government was enjoined from enforcing § 505, 'fewer than 0.5% of cable subscribers requested full blocking' under § 504. The majority describes this public reaction as 'a collective yawn,' adding that the Government failed to prove that the 'yawn' reflected anything other than the lack of a serious signal bleed problem or a lack of notice which better information about § 504 might cure. The record excludes the first possibility—at least in respect to exposure, as discussed above. And I doubt that the public, though it may well consider the viewing habits of adults a matter of personal choice, would 'yawn' when the exposure in question concerns young children, the absence of parental consent, and the sexually explicit material here at issue.

"Neither is the record neutral in respect to the curative power of better notice. [An] opt-out right works only when parents (1) become aware of their [rights], (2) discover that their children are watching sexually-explicit signal 'bleed,' (3) reach their cable operator and ask that it block the sending of its signal to their home, (4) await installation of an individual blocking device, and, perhaps (5) (where the block fails or the channel number changes) make a new request. Better notice of [blocking rights] does little to help parents discover their children's viewing habits (step two). And it does nothing at all in respect to steps three through five. Yet the record contains considerable evidence that those problems matter, i.e., evidence of endlessly delayed phone call responses, faulty installations, blocking failures, and other mishaps, leaving those steps as significant [obstacles]."

———

Two provisions of the Communications Decency Act ("CDA") seek to protect minors from material on the Internet. 47 U.S.C. § 223(a) prohibits the knowing transmission of indecent messages to any recipient under 18 years of age. 47 U.S.C. § 223(d) prohibits the knowing sending or displaying of patently offensive messages in a manner that is available to a person under 18 years of age. Patently offensive is defined as any "image or other communication that in context, depicts or describes, in terms patently offensive as measured by contemporary community standards, sexual or excretory activities or organs * * *."

RENO v. AMERICAN CIVIL LIBERTIES UNION, 521 U.S. 844, 117 S.Ct. 2329, 138 L.Ed.2d 874 (1997), per STEVENS, J., held that both provisions were too vague and overbroad to withstand first amendment scrutiny.[a] After providing a lengthy description of the Internet focussing on e-mail, automatic mailing list services, newsgroups, chatrooms, and the WORLD Wide Web, Stevens, J., distinguished prior cases: "In four important respects, the statute upheld in *Ginsberg* was narrower than the CDA. First, we noted in *Ginsberg* that 'the prohibition

First, he mistakenly believes that the nature of the advertising controls the obscenity analysis, regardless of the nature of the material being advertised. I entirely agree with him that "advertising a bareheaded dancer as 'topless' might be deceptive, but it would not make her performance obscene.' I believe, however, that if the material is 'patently offensive' and it is being advertised as such, we have little reason to think it is being proffered for its socially redeeming value. * * *"

    a. The CDA also prohibited obscenity on the Internet. That portion of the statute was not challenged, and the Court specifically noted that it had not struck down that part of the statute.

against sales to minors does not bar parents who so desire from purchasing the magazines for their children.' Under the CDA, by contrast, neither the parents' consent—nor even their participation—in the communication would avoid the application of the statute.[32] Second, the New York statute applied only to commercial transactions, whereas the CDA contains no such limitation. Third, the New York statute cabined its definition of material that is harmful to minors with the requirement that it be 'utterly without redeeming social importance for minors.' The CDA fails to provide us with any definition of the term 'indecent' as used in § 223(a)(1) and, importantly, omits any requirement that the 'patently offensive' material covered by § 223(d) lack serious literary, artistic, political, or scientific value. Fourth, the New York statute defined a minor as a person under the age of 17, whereas the CDA, in applying to all those under 18 years, includes an additional year of those nearest majority. * * *

"[S]ome of our cases have recognized special justifications for regulation of the broadcast media that are not applicable to other speakers. In these cases, the Court relied on the history of extensive government regulation of the broadcast medium, see, e.g., *Red Lion;* the scarcity of available frequencies at its inception, see, e.g., *Turner Broadcasting System, Inc. v. FCC;* and its 'invasive' nature, see *Sable Communications of Cal., Inc. v. FCC.*

"Those factors are not present in cyberspace. Neither before nor after the enactment of the CDA have the vast democratic fora of the Internet been subject to the type of government supervision and regulation that has attended the broadcast industry. Moreover, the Internet is not as 'invasive' as radio or television. The District Court specifically found that '[c]ommunications over the Internet do not "invade" an individual's home or appear on one's computer screen unbidden. Users seldom encounter content "by accident." 'It also found that '[a]lmost all sexually explicit images are preceded by warnings as to the content,' and cited testimony that 'odds are slim' that a user would come across a sexually explicit sight by accident. * * *

"Finally, unlike the conditions that prevailed when Congress first authorized regulation of the broadcast spectrum, the Internet can hardly be considered a 'scarce' expressive commodity. It provides relatively unlimited, low-cost capacity for communication of all kinds. The Government estimates that '[a]s many as 40 million people use the Internet today, and that figure is expected to grow to 200 million by 1999.' This dynamic, multifaceted category of communication includes not only traditional print and news services, but also audio, video, and still images, as well as interactive, real-time dialogue. Through the use of chat rooms, any person with a phone line can become a town crier with a voice that resonates farther than it could from any soapbox. Through the use of Web pages, mail exploders, and newsgroups, the same individual can become a pamphleteer. As the District Court found, 'the content on the Internet is as diverse as human thought.' We agree with its conclusion that our cases provide no basis for qualifying the level of First Amendment scrutiny that should be applied to this medium.

"Regardless of whether the CDA is so vague that it violates the Fifth Amendment, the many ambiguities concerning the scope of its coverage render it problematic for purposes of the First Amendment. For instance, each of the two parts of the CDA uses a different linguistic form. The first uses the word

---

32. Given the likelihood that many E-mail transmissions from an adult to a minor are conversations between family members, it is therefore incorrect for the dissent to suggest that the provisions of the CDA, even in this narrow area, "are no different from the law we sustained in *Ginsberg*."

'indecent,' 47 U.S.C.A. § 223(a), while the second speaks of material that 'in context, depicts or describes, in terms patently offensive as measured by contemporary community standards, sexual or excretory activities or organs,' § 223(d). Given the absence of a definition of either term,[35] this difference in language will provoke uncertainty among speakers about how the two standards relate to each other and just what they mean.[37] Could a speaker confidently assume that a serious discussion about birth control practices, homosexuality, the First Amendment issues raised by the Appendix to our *Pacifica* opinion, or the consequences of prison rape would not violate the CDA? This uncertainty undermines the likelihood that the CDA has been carefully tailored to the congressional goal of protecting minors from potentially harmful materials.

"The vagueness of the CDA is a matter of special concern for two reasons. First, the CDA is a content-based regulation of speech. [Second,] the CDA is a criminal statute. In addition to the opprobrium and stigma of a criminal conviction, the CDA threatens violators with penalties including up to two years in prison for each act of violation. The severity of criminal sanctions may well cause speakers to remain silent rather than communicate even arguably unlawful words, ideas, and images. As a practical matter, this increased deterrent effect, coupled with the 'risk of discriminatory enforcement' of vague regulations, poses greater First Amendment concerns than those implicated by the civil regulation reviewed in *Denver Area Ed. Telecommunications Consortium, Inc. v. FCC*. * * *

"Because the CDA's 'patently offensive' standard (and, we assume arguendo, its synonymous 'indecent' standard) is one part of the three-prong *Miller* test, the Government reasons, it cannot be unconstitutionally vague. [The] Government's assertion is incorrect as a matter of fact. The second prong of the *Miller* test—the purportedly analogous standard—contains a critical requirement that is omitted from the CDA: that the proscribed material be 'specifically defined by the applicable state law.' This requirement reduces the vagueness inherent in the open-ended term 'patently offensive' as used in the CDA. Moreover, the *Miller* definition is limited to 'sexual conduct,' whereas the CDA extends also to include (1) 'excretory activities' as well as (2) 'organs' of both a sexual and excretory nature.

"The Government's reasoning is also flawed. Just because a definition including three limitations is not vague, it does not follow that one of those limitations, standing by itself, is not vague. Each of *Miller's* additional two prongs—(1) that, taken as a whole, the material appeal to the 'prurient' interest, and (2) that it 'lac[k] serious literary, artistic, political, or scientific value'—critically limits the uncertain sweep of the obscenity definition. The second requirement is particularly important because, unlike the 'patently offensive' and 'prurient interest' criteria, it is not judged by contemporary community standards. This 'societal value' requirement, absent in the CDA, allows appellate courts to impose some limitations and regularity on the definition by setting, as a matter of law, a national floor for socially redeeming value. The Government's contention that courts will be able to give such legal limitations to the CDA's standards is belied

---

35. "Indecent" does not benefit from any textual embellishment at all. "Patently offensive" is qualified only to the extent that it involves "sexual or excretory activities or organs" taken "in context" and "measured by contemporary community standards."

37. The statute does not indicate whether the "patently offensive" and "indecent" deter-

minations should be made with respect to minors or the population as a whole. The Government asserts that the appropriate standard is "what is suitable material for minors." But the Conferees expressly rejected amendments that would have imposed such a "harmful to minors" standard.

by Miller's own rationale for having juries determine whether material is 'patently offensive' according to community standards: that such questions are essentially ones of fact.

"In contrast to *Miller* and our other previous cases, the CDA thus presents a greater threat of censoring speech that, in fact, falls outside the statute's scope. Given the vague contours of the coverage of the statute, it unquestionably silences some speakers whose messages would be entitled to constitutional protection. That danger provides further reason for insisting that the statute not be overly broad. The CDA's burden on protected speech cannot be justified if it could be avoided by a more carefully drafted statute. * * *

"It is true that we have repeatedly recognized the governmental interest in protecting children from harmful materials. But that interest does not justify an unnecessarily broad suppression of speech addressed to adults. [In] arguing that the CDA does not so diminish adult communication, the Government relies on the incorrect factual premise that prohibiting a transmission whenever it is known that one of its recipients is a minor would not interfere with adult-to-adult communication. The findings of the District Court make clear that this premise is untenable. Given the size of the potential audience for most messages, in the absence of a viable age verification process, the sender must be charged with knowing that one or more minors will likely view it. Knowledge that, for instance, one or more members of a 100–person chat group will be [a] minor—and therefore that it would be a crime to send the group an indecent message—would surely burden communication among adults.[42]

"The District Court found that at the time of trial existing technology did not include any effective method for a sender to prevent minors from obtaining access to its communications on the Internet without also denying access to adults. The Court found no effective way to determine the age of a user who is accessing material through e-mail, mail exploders, newsgroups, or chat rooms. As a practical matter, the Court also found that it would be prohibitively expensive for noncommercial—as well as some commercial—speakers who have Web sites to verify that their users are adults. These limitations must inevitably curtail a significant amount of adult communication on the Internet. By contrast, the District Court found that '[d]espite its limitations, currently available user-based software suggests that a reasonably effective method by which parents can prevent their children from accessing sexually explicit and other material which parents may believe is inappropriate for their children will soon be widely available.'

"The breadth of the CDA's coverage is wholly unprecedented. Unlike the regulations upheld in *Ginsberg* and *Pacifica,* the scope of the CDA is not limited to commercial speech or commercial entities. Its open-ended prohibitions embrace all nonprofit entities and individuals posting indecent messages or displaying them on their own computers in the presence of minors. The general, undefined terms 'indecent' and 'patently offensive' cover large amounts of nonpornographic material with serious educational or other value. Moreover, the 'community standards' criterion as applied to the Internet means that any communication available to a nation-wide audience will be judged by the standards of the community most likely to be offended by the message. The regulated subject matter includes any of the seven 'dirty words' used in the *Pacifica* monologue, the use of which the Government's expert acknowledged could constitute a felony. It may also extend

---

42. The Government agrees that these provisions are applicable whenever "a sender transmits a message to more than one recipient, knowing that at least one of the specific persons receiving the message is a minor."

to discussions about prison rape or safe sexual practices, artistic images that include nude subjects, and arguably the card catalogue of the Carnegie Library.

"For the purposes of our decision, we need neither accept nor reject the Government's submission that the First Amendment does not forbid a blanket prohibition on all 'indecent' and 'patently offensive' messages communicated to a 17–year old—no matter how much value the message may contain and regardless of parental approval. It is at least clear that the strength of the Government's interest in protecting minors is not equally strong throughout the coverage of this broad statute. Under the CDA, a parent allowing her 17–year–old to use the family computer to obtain information on the Internet that she, in her parental judgment, deems appropriate could face a lengthy prison term. Similarly, a parent who sent his 17–year–old college freshman information on birth control via e-mail could be incarcerated even though neither he, his child, nor anyone in their home community, found the material 'indecent' or 'patently offensive,' if the college town's community thought otherwise.

"The breadth of this content-based restriction of speech imposes an especially heavy burden on the Government to explain why a less restrictive provision would not be as effective as the CDA. It has not done so. The arguments in this Court have referred to possible alternatives such as requiring that indecent material be 'tagged' in a way that facilitates parental control of material coming into their homes, making exceptions for messages with artistic or educational value, providing some tolerance for parental choice, and regulating some portions of the Internet—such as commercial web sites—differently than others, such as chat rooms. Particularly in the light of the absence of any detailed findings by the Congress, or even hearings addressing the special problems of the CDA, we are persuaded that the CDA is not narrowly tailored if that requirement has any meaning at all."

O'CONNOR, J., joined by Rehnquist, C.J., concurred in the judgment in part and dissented in part: "Given the present state of cyberspace, I agree with the Court that the 'display' provision cannot pass muster. Until gateway technology is available throughout cyberspace, and it is not in 1997, a speaker cannot be reasonably assured that the speech he displays will reach only adults because it is impossible to confine speech to an 'adult zone.' Thus, the only way for a speaker to avoid liability under the CDA is to refrain completely from using indecent speech. But this forced silence impinges on the First Amendment right of adults to make and obtain this speech and, for all intents and purposes, 'reduce[s] the adult population [on the Internet] to reading only what is fit for children.'

"The 'indecency transmission' and 'specific person' provisions present a closer issue, for they are not unconstitutional in all of their applications. [T]he 'indecency transmission' provision makes it a crime to transmit knowingly an indecent message to a person the sender knows is under 18 years of age. The 'specific person' provision proscribes the same conduct, although it does not as explicitly require the sender to know that the intended recipient of his indecent message is a minor. Appellant urges the Court to construe the provision to impose such a knowledge requirement, and I would do so.

"So construed, both provisions are constitutional as applied to a conversation involving only an adult and one or more minors—e.g., when an adult speaker sends an e-mail knowing the addressee is a minor, or when an adult and minor converse by themselves or with other minors in a chat room. In this context, these provisions are no different from the law we sustained in *Ginsberg*. Restricting what the adult may say to the minors in no way restricts the adult's ability to communicate with other adults. He is not prevented from speaking indecently to other adults in a chat room (because there are no other adults participating in the conversation) and he remains free to send indecent e-mails to other adults. The relevant universe contains only one adult, and the adult in that universe has the power to refrain from using indecent speech and consequently to keep all such speech within the room in an 'adult' zone.

"The analogy to *Ginsberg* breaks down, however, when more than one adult is a party to the conversation. If a minor enters a chat room otherwise occupied by adults, the CDA effectively requires the adults in the room to stop using indecent speech. If they did not, they could be prosecuted under the 'indecency transmission' and 'specific person' provisions for any indecent statements they make to the group, since they would be transmitting an indecent message to specific persons, one of whom is a minor. The CDA is therefore akin to a law that makes it a crime for a bookstore owner to sell pornographic magazines to anyone once a minor enters his store. Even assuming such a law might be constitutional in the physical world as a reasonable alternative to excluding minors completely from the store, the absence of any means of excluding minors from chat rooms in cyberspace restricts the rights of adults to engage in indecent speech in those rooms. The 'indecency transmission' and 'specific person' provisions share this defect. * * *

"Whether the CDA substantially interferes with the First Amendment rights of minors, and thereby runs afoul of the second characteristic of valid zoning laws, presents a closer question. [The] Court neither 'accept[s] nor reject[s]' the argument that the CDA is facially overbroad because it substantially interferes with the First Amendment rights of minors. I would reject it. [In] my view, the universe of speech constitutionally protected as to minors but banned by the CDA—i.e., the universe of material that is 'patently offensive,' but which nonetheless has some redeeming value for minors or does not appeal to their prurient interest—is a very small one. Appellees cite no examples of speech falling within this universe and do not attempt to explain why that universe is substantial 'in relation to the statute's plainly legitimate sweep.' That the CDA might deny minors the right to obtain material that has some 'value' is largely beside the point. While discussions about prison rape or nude art, may have some redeeming education value for adults, they do not necessarily have any such value for minors, and under *Ginsberg,* minors only have a First Amendment right to obtain patently offensive material that has 'redeeming social importance for minors.' There is also no evidence in the record to support the contention that 'many [e]-mail transmissions from an adult to a minor are conversations between family members,' and no support for the legal proposition that such speech is absolutely immune from regulation. Accordingly, in my view, the CDA does not burden a substantial amount of minors' constitutionally protected speech.

"Thus, the constitutionality of the CDA as a zoning law hinges on the extent to which it substantially interferes with the First Amendment rights of adults. Because the rights of adults are infringed only by the 'display' provision and by the 'indecency transmission' and 'specific person' provisions as applied to communications involving more than one adult, I would invalidate the CDA only to that extent. Insofar as the 'indecency transmission' and 'specific person' provisions prohibit the use of indecent speech in communications between an adult and one or more minors, however, they can and should be sustained. The Court reaches a contrary conclusion, and from that holding that I respectfully dissent."[b]

b. Stevens, J., argued that Congress had not provided guidance as to where lines should be drawn if the statute were otherwise to be struck down. Lacking guidance, he declined to find that the statute was readily subject to a

THE RIGHT NOT TO SPEAK, THE RIGHT TO ASSOCIATE, AND THE RIGHT NOT TO ASSOCIATE

THE RIGHT NOT TO BE ASSOCIATED WITH PARTICULAR IDEAS

CON LAW: P. 970, add to note 6

AMER CON: P. 955, add to note 6

RTS & LIB: P. 877, add to note 6

Buckley v. American Constitutional Law Foundation, 525 U.S. 182, 119 S.Ct. 636, 142 L.Ed.2d 599 (1999), per Ginsburg, J., held unconstitutional a Colorado statute requiring that circulators of initiatives wear identification badges bearing their names and that sponsors of the initiative report the names and addresses of all paid circulators. By contrast, the Court was satisfied that the requirement of the filing of an affidavit containing the name and address of the circulator of petitions was consistent with the first amendment.

FREEDOM OF ASSOCIATION AND EMPLOYMENT

CON LAW: P. 974, addition to fn. b

AMER CON: P. 959, addition to fn. b

RTS & LIB: P. 881, addition to fn. b

Should *Elrod* and *Branti* be extended to independent contractors? See *O'Hare Truck Service v. City of Northlake,* 518 U.S. 712, 116 S.Ct. 2353, 135 L.Ed.2d 874 (1996).

CON LAW: P. 978, addition to fn. 5

AMER CON: P. 963, addition to fn. 5

RTS & LIB: P. 885, addition to fn. 5

[Should *Pickering* be extended to independent contractors? See *Board of County Commissioners v. Umbehr,* 518 U.S. 668, 116 S.Ct. 2342, 135 L.Ed.2d 843 (1996)].

CON LAW: P. 985, addition to fn. c

AMER CON: P. 970, addition to fn. c

RTS & LIB: P. 892, addition to fn. c

For light on the application of *Abood* to a mandatory university student activity fee, see Board of Regents v. Southworth, ___ U.S. ___, 120 S.Ct. 1346, ___ L.Ed.2d ___ (2000) (no refund required so long as allocation of funding is viewpoint neutral; interest in stimulating diverse ideas on campus outweighs the interests of objecting students).

CON LAW: P. 987, after note 4

AMER CON: P. 972, after note 4

RTS & LIB: P. 894, after note 4

5. *Beyond employment: The scope of Abood.* The Agricultural Marketing Agreement Act of 1937 enables committees of producers appointed by the Secre-

narrowing construction.

tary of Agriculture to issue certain marketing orders without violating the antitrust laws provided that two thirds of the producers who market at least two thirds of the volume of a product approve. The purpose of such orders is to establish and maintain orderly marketing conditions and fair prices for agricultural commodities. Such orders, which are restricted to the smallest practicable production area, range from price fixing, joint research projects, standardized packaging, and joint advertising. Expenses of administering an order are paid from funds collected pursuant to the marketing order.

Some producers of California nectarines, plums, and peaches brought a proceeding challenging marketing orders requiring them to pay for generic advertising. They invoked a first amendment right not to be compelled to subsidize the speech of others.

GLICKMAN v. WILEMAN BROTHERS & ELLIOT, INC., 521 U.S. 457, 117 S.Ct. 2130, 138 L.Ed.2d 585 (1997), per Stevens, J., held that the compelled funding of generic advertising did not violate the first amendment: "The legal question that we address is whether being compelled to fund this advertising raises a First Amendment issue for us to resolve, or rather is simply a question of economic policy for Congress and the Executive to resolve.

"Three characteristics of the regulatory scheme at issue distinguish it from laws that we have found to abridge the freedom of speech protected by the First Amendment. First, the marketing orders impose no restraint on the freedom of any producer to communicate any message to any audience. Second, they do not compel any person to engage in any actual or symbolic speech. Third, they do not compel the producers to endorse or to finance any political or ideological views. Indeed, since all of the respondents are engaged in the business of marketing California nectarines, plums, and peaches, it is fair to presume that they agree with the central message of the speech that is generated by the generic program.[a] Thus, none of our First Amendment jurisprudence provides any support for the suggestion that the promotional regulations should be scrutinized under a different standard than that applicable to the other anticompetitive features of the marketing orders. * * *

"Respondents argue that the assessments for generic advertising impinge on their First Amendment rights because they reduce the amount of money that producers have available to conduct their own advertising. This is equally true, however, of assessments to cover employee benefits, inspection fees, or any other activity that is authorized by a marketing order. * * *

"None of the advertising in this record promotes any particular message other than encouraging consumers to buy California tree fruit. Neither the fact that respondents may prefer to foster that message independently in order to promote and distinguish their own products, nor the fact that they think more or less money should be spent fostering it, makes this case comparable to those in which an objection rested on political or ideological disagreement with the content of the message. The mere fact that objectors believe their money is not being well spent 'does not mean [that] they have a First Amendment complaint.' * * *

"As with other features of the marketing orders, individual producers may not share the views or the interests of others in the same market. But decisions that are made by the majority, if acceptable for other regulatory programs, should

---

a. The producers objected to the content of some of the advertisements. Stevens, J., stated that these concerns might call into question portions of the program, but had no bearing on the entire program. He also stated that these concerns were more properly addressed to the Secretary.

be equally so for promotional advertising. Perhaps more money may be at stake when a generic advertising program is adopted than for other features of the cooperative endeavor, but that fact does not transform this question of business judgment into a constitutional issue. In sum, what we are reviewing is a species of economic regulation that should enjoy the same strong presumption of validity that we accord to other policy judgments made by Congress. The mere fact that one or more producers 'do not wish to foster' generic advertising of their product is not a sufficient reason for overriding the judgment of the majority of market participants, bureaucrats, and legislators who have concluded that such programs are beneficial.''

SOUTER, J., joined by Rehnquist, C.J., and Scalia, J., and Thomas, J., in part, dissented: ''The Court's first mistaken conclusion lies in treating *Abood* as permitting any enforced subsidy for speech that is germane to permissible economic regulation, in the sense that it relates to the subject matter of the regulation and tends to further its objectives. But *Abood* and its subsequent line of cases is not nearly so permissive as the Court makes out. In *Abood,* we recognized that even in matters directly related to collective bargaining, compulsory funding of union activities has an impact on employees' First Amendment interests, since the employees might disagree with positions taken by the union on issues such as the inclusion of abortion in a medical benefit plan, or negotiating no-strike agreements, or even the desirability of unionism in general. To be sure, we concluded that any interference with such interests was 'constitutionally justified by the legislative assessment of the important contribution of the union shop to the system of labor relations established by Congress.' But this was simply a way of saying that the government's objective of guaranteeing the opportunity for a union shop, the importance and legitimacy of which were already settled, could not be attained without the incidental infringements of the interests in unfettered speech and association that petitioners there claimed. * * *

''Decisions postdating *Abood* have made clear, however, that its limited sanction for laws affecting First Amendment interests may not be expanded to cover every imposition that is in some way 'germane' to a regulatory program in the sense of relating sympathetically to it. Rather, to survive scrutiny under *Abood*, a mandatory fee must not only be germane to some otherwise legitimate regulatory scheme; it must also be justified by vital policy interests of the government and not add significantly to the burdening of free speech inherent in achieving those interests. *Lehnert v. Ferris Faculty Assn.*

''Thus, in *Lehnert* eight Justices concluded that a teachers' union could not constitutionally charge objecting employees for a public relations campaign meant to raise the esteem for teachers in the public mind and so increase the public's willingness to pay for public education. 'Expression of this kind extends beyond the negotiation and grievance-resolution contexts and imposes a substantially greater burden upon First Amendment rights than do [collective-bargaining functions].' The advertising campaigns here suffer from the same defect as the public relations effort to stimulate demand for the teachers' product: a local union can negotiate a particular contract for the benefit of a shop's whole labor force without globally espousing the virtues of teachers, and (in the absence of further explanation) produce markets can be directly regulated in the interest of stability and growth without espousing the virtues of fruit. They were, indeed, for a quarter century, and still are under the many agricultural marketing orders that authorize no advertising schemes. In each instance, the challenged burden on dissenters' First Amendment rights is substantially greater than anything inherent in regulation of the commercial transactions. Thus, the *Abood* line does not permit this program merely because it is germane to the marketing orders.

"The Court's second misemployment of *Abood* and its successors is its reliance on them for the proposition that when government neither forbids speech nor attributes it to an objector, it may compel subsidization for any objectionable message that is not political or ideological. * * * While it is perfectly true that cases like *Abood* and *Keller* did involve political or ideological speech, and the Court made reference to that character in explaining the gravity of the First Amendment interests at stake, nothing in those cases suggests that government has free rein to compel funding of nonpolitical speech (which might include art, for example, as well as commercial advertising). * * * The fact that no prior case of this Court has applied this principle to commercial and nonideological speech simply reflects the fortuity that this is the first commercial-speech subsidy case to come before us.

"An apparent third ground for the Court's conclusion that the First Amendment is not implicated here is its assumption that respondents do not disagree with the advertisements they object to subsidizing.[b] * * *

"What counts [here] is not whether respondents fail to disagree with the generalized message of the generic ads that California fruit is good, but that they do indeed deny that the general message is as valuable and worthy of their support as more particular claims about the merits of their own brands. One need not 'disagree' with an abstractionist when buying a canvas from a representational painter; one merely wishes to support a different act of expression.

"The Secretary of Agriculture has a further argument for minimizing or eliminating scrutiny of this subsidization mandate, which deserves some mention even though the Court does not adopt it. The Secretary calls for lesser scrutiny of forced payments for truthful advertising and promotion than for restrictions on commercial speech, on the ground that the effect of compelled funding is to increase the sum of information to the consuming public. This argument rests, however, on the assumption that regulation of commercial speech is justified solely or largely on preservation of public access to truthful information, an assumption we have already seen to be inaccurate. Truth is indeed a justifiable objective of commercial speech protection, but so is nonmisleading persuasion directed to the advertiser's own choice of what to promote."[c]

THOMAS, J., joined by Scalia, J., dissenting observed: "What we are now left with, if we are to take the majority opinion at face value, is one of two disturbing consequences: Either (1) paying for advertising is not speech at all, while such activities as draft card burning, flag burning, armband wearing, public sleeping, and nude dancing are, or (2) compelling payment for third party communication does not implicate speech, and thus the Government would be free to force payment for a whole variety of expressive conduct that it could not restrict. In either case, surely we have lost our way."

b. Souter, J., pointed out that the producers did object to some of the advertisements and whether these objections seemed "trivial to the Court, they in fact relate directly to a vendor's recognized First Amendment interest in touting his wares as he sees fit so long as he does not mislead."

c. Souter, J., proceeded to argue that the government's order did not meet the *Central Hudson* test. Thomas, J., did not join this section of the opinion because he maintained, as he had in *Liquormart,* that more stringent standards should apply to commercial speech.

INTIMATE ASSOCIATION AND EXPRESSIVE ASSOCIATION

CON LAW: P. 992, after note
AMER CON: P. 977, after note
RTS & LIB: P. 899, after note

James Dale's position as an assistant scoutmaster of a New Jersey troop of the Boy Scouts of America was revoked when the Boy Scouts learned that he, an Eagle Scout, was gay, and the co-President of the Rutgers University Lesbian/Gay Alliance, who had been publicly quoted on the importance in his own life on the need for gay role models. Dale sued, and the New Jersey Supreme Court ultimately held that New Jersey's anti-discrimination public accommodation law required that the Scouts readmit him.

BOY SCOUTS OF AMERICA v. DALE, ___ U.S. ___, 120 S.Ct. 2446, ___ L.Ed.2d ___, (2000), per REHNQUIST,C.J., held that the New Jersey accommodations law violated the expressive association rights of the Boy Scouts: "To determine whether a group is protected by the First Amendment's expressive associational right, we must determine whether the group engages in 'expressive association.' The First Amendment's protection of expressive association is not reserved for advocacy groups. But to come within its ambit, a group must engage in some form of expression, whether it be public or private.

"Because this is a First Amendment case where the ultimate conclusions of law are virtually inseparable from findings of fact, we are obligated to independently review the factual record to ensure that the state court's judgment does not unlawfully intrude on free expression. The record reveals the following. The Boy Scouts is a private, nonprofit organization. According to its mission statement:

"It is the mission of the Boy Scouts of America to serve others by helping to instill values in young people and, in other ways, to prepare them to make ethical choices over their lifetime in achieving their full potential.

"The values we strive to instill are based on those found in the Scout Oath and Law"

Rehnquist, C.J., cited a portion of the Scout Oath requiring Scouts to be "morally straight" and a portion of Scout law requiring Scouts to be "Clean": "Thus, the general mission of the Boy Scouts is clear: '[T]o instill values in young people.' The Boy Scouts seeks to instill these values by having its adult leaders spend time with the youth members, instructing and engaging them in activities like camping, archery, and fishing. During the time spent with the youth members, the scoutmasters and assistant scoutmasters inculcate them with the Boy Scouts' values—both expressly and by example. It seems indisputable that an association that seeks to transmit such a system of values engages in expressive activity. * * *

"Obviously, the Scout Oath and Law do not expressly mention sexuality or sexual orientation. And the terms 'morally straight' and 'clean' are by no means self-defining. Different people would attribute to those terms very different meanings. For example, some people may believe that engaging in homosexual conduct is not at odds with being 'morally straight' and 'clean.' And others may believe that engaging in homosexual conduct is contrary to being 'morally straight' and 'clean.' The Boy Scouts says it falls within the latter category.

"The Boy Scouts asserts that it 'teach[es] that homosexual conduct is not morally straight,' Brief for Petitioners 39, and that it does 'not want to promote homosexual conduct as a legitimate form of behavior,' Reply Brief for Petitioners 5. We accept the Boy Scouts' assertion. We need not inquire further to determine the nature of the Boy Scouts' expression with respect to homosexuality. But because the record before us contains written evidence of the Boy Scouts' viewpoint, we look to it as instructive, if only on the question of the sincerity of the professed beliefs."

Rehnquist, C.J., recounted a 1978 position statement to the Boy Scouts' Executive Committee, signed by the President of the Boy Scouts and the Chief Scout Executive, expressing the 'official position' that openly declared homosexuals could not be Scout leaders, a 1991 public position statement (issued after Dale's membership revocation, but before the litigation) asserting that homosexual conduct was inconsistent with being morally straight and clean, a 1993 public position statement maintaining that homosexual role models did not reflect the expectations that scouting families have had for the organization, and the Scouts' participation in litigation throughout the 80's and the 90's defending its position in litigation: "We cannot doubt that the Boy Scouts sincerely holds this view. We must then determine whether Dale's presence as an assistant scoutmaster would significantly burden the Boy Scouts' desire to not 'promote homosexual conduct as a legitimate form of behavior.' As we give deference to an association's assertions regarding the nature of its expression, we must also give deference to an association's view of what would impair its expression. [That] is not to say that an expressive association can erect a shield against antidiscrimination laws simply by asserting that mere acceptance of a member from a particular group would impair its message. But here Dale, by his own admission, is one of a group of gay Scouts who have 'become leaders in their community and are open and honest about their sexual orientation.' Dale was the copresident of a gay and lesbian organization at college and remains a gay rights activist. Dale's presence in the Boy Scouts would, at the very least, force the organization to send a message, both to the youth members and the world, that the Boy Scouts accepts homosexual conduct as a legitimate form of behavior. * * *

"*Hurley* is illustrative on this point. There we considered whether the application of Massachusetts' public accommodations law to require the organizers of a private St. Patrick's Day parade to include among the marchers an Irish–American gay, lesbian, and bisexual group, GLIB, violated the parade organizers' First Amendment rights. We noted that the parade organizers did not wish to exclude the GLIB members because of their sexual orientations, but because they wanted to march behind a GLIB banner. We observed: '[A] contingent marching behind the organization's banner would at least bear witness to the fact that some Irish are gay, lesbian, or bisexual, and the presence of the organized marchers would suggest their view that people of their sexual orientations have as much claim to unqualified social acceptance as heterosexuals. * * * The parade's organizers may not believe these facts about Irish sexuality to be so, or they may object to unqualified social acceptance of gays and lesbians or have some other reason for wishing to keep GLIB's message out of the parade. But whatever the reason, it boils down to the choice of a speaker not to propound a particular point of view, and that choice is presumed to lie beyond the government's power to control.'

"Here, we have found that the Boy Scouts believes that homosexual conduct is inconsistent with the values it seeks to instill in its youth members; it will not 'promote homosexual conduct as a legitimate form of behavior.' Reply Brief for Petitioners 5. As the presence of GLIB in Boston's St. Patrick's Day parade would have interfered with the parade organizers' choice not to propound a particular point of view, the presence of Dale as an assistant scoutmaster would just as surely interfere with the Boy Scout's choice not to propound a point of view contrary to its beliefs.

"[A]ssociations do not have to associate for the 'purpose' of disseminating a certain message in order to be entitled to the protections of the First Amendment. An association must merely engage in expressive activity that could be impaired in order to be entitled to protection. For example, the purpose of the St. Patrick's Day parade in Hurley was not to espouse any views about sexual orientation, but we held that the parade organizers had a right to exclude certain participants nonetheless.

"[E]ven if the Boy Scouts discourages Scout leaders from disseminating views on sexual issues—a fact that the Boy Scouts disputes with contrary evidence—the First Amendment protects the Boy Scouts' method of expression. If the Boy Scouts wishes Scout leaders to avoid questions of sexuality and teach only by example, this fact does not negate the sincerity of its belief discussed above. * * *

"Dale makes much of the claim that the Boy Scouts does not revoke the membership of heterosexual Scout leaders that openly disagree with the Boy Scouts' policy on sexual orientation. But if this is true, it is irrelevant. The presence of an avowed homosexual and gay rights activist in an assistant scout-master's uniform sends a distinctly different message from the presence of a heterosexual assistant scoutmaster who is on record as disagreeing with Boy Scouts policy. The Boy Scouts has a First Amendment right to choose to send one message but not the other. The fact that the organization does not trumpet its views from the housetops, or that it tolerates dissent within its ranks, does not mean that its views receive no First Amendment protection. * * *

"We recognized in cases such as *Roberts* and *Duarte* that States have a compelling interest in eliminating discrimination against women in public accommodations. But in each of these cases we went on to conclude that the enforcement of these statutes would not materially interfere with the ideas that the organization sought to express. * * *

"Dale contends that we should apply the intermediate standard of review enunciated in *O'Brien* to evaluate the competing interests. [But] New Jersey's public accommodations law directly and immediately affects associational rights, in this case associational rights that enjoy First Amendment protection. Thus, *O'Brien* is inapplicable.

"In *Hurley*, we applied traditional First Amendment analysis to hold that the application of the Massachusetts public accommodations law to a parade violated the First Amendment rights of the parade organizers. Although we did not explicitly deem the parade in Hurley an expressive association, the analysis we applied there is similar to the analysis we apply here. We have already concluded that a state requirement that the Boy Scouts retain Dale as an assistant scoutmaster would significantly burden the organization's right to oppose or disfavor homosexual conduct. The state interests embodied in New Jersey's public accommodations law do not justify such a severe intrusion on the Boy Scouts' rights to freedom of expressive association. That being the case, we hold that the First Amendment prohibits the State from imposing such a requirement through the application of its public accommodations law."

STEVENS, J., joined by Souter, Ginsburg, and Breyer, J., dissenting, argued that nothing in in the Scout Oath or Scout Law spoke of sexual orientation even in the definitions of morally straight and clean. Moreover, he observed that Scoutmasters are instructed not to instruct Scouts in any formalized manner regarding sex because it is not 'Scouting's proper area' and they are advised to steer questions about sexual matters to spiritual leaders, family, or doctors, if possible, otherwise 'you may just have to do the best you can. Stevens, J., observed that the 1978 statement (made before Dale entered scouting) was never distributed to the public and itself stated that termination of an individual because of homosexuality should ensue unless a law to the contrary existed. In that case the Scouts should obey the law. Stevens, J., added that statements issued in 1991 and a similar statement in 1992 about the relationship between homosexuality and morality and cleanliness was abondoned by the 1993 sttement focusing on family expectations and could not ground an adequate claim of expressive association: ''[E]ven during the brief period in 1991 and 1992, when BSA tried to connect its exclusion of homosexuals to its definition of terms found in the Oath and Law, there is no evidence that Scouts were actually taught anything about homosexuality's alleged inconsistency with those principles. Beyond the single sentence in these policy statements, there is no indication of any shared goal of teaching that homosexuality is incompatible with being 'morally straight' and 'clean.' Neither BSA's mission statement nor its official membership policy was altered; no Boy Scout or Scoutmaster Handbook was amended to reflect the policy statement; no lessons were imparted to Scouts; no change was made to BSA's policy on limiting discussion of sexual matters; and no effort was made to restrict acceptable religious affiliations to those that condemn homosexuality. In short, there is no evidence that this view was part of any collective effort to foster beliefs about homosexuality.

"[BSA] never took any clear and unequivocal position on homosexuality. Though the 1991 and 1992 policies state one interpretation of 'morally straight' and 'clean,' the group's published definitions appearing in the Boy Scout and Scoutmaster Handbooks take quite another view. And BSA's broad religious tolerance combined with its declaration that sexual matters are not its 'proper area' render its views on the issue equivocal at best and incoherent at worst. We have never held, however, that a group can throw together any mixture of contradictory positions and then invoke the right to associate to defend any one of those views. At a minimum, a group seeking to prevail over an antidiscrimination law must adhere to a clear and unequivocal view.

"[A]t most the 1991 and 1992 statements declare only that BSA believed 'homosexual conduct is inconsistent with the requirement in the Scout Oath that a Scout be morally straight and in the Scout Law that a Scout be clean in word and deed.' But New Jersey's law prohibits discrimination on the basis of sexual *orientation*. And when Dale was expelled from the Boy Scouts, BSA said it did so because of his sexual orientation, not because of his sexual conduct.

"It is clear, then, that nothing in these policy statements supports BSA's claim. The only policy written before the revocation of Dale's membership was an equivocal, undisclosed statement that evidences no connection between the group's discriminatory intentions and its expressive interests. The later policies demonstrate a brief—though ultimately abandoned—attempt to tie BSA's exclusion to its expression, but other than a single sentence, BSA fails to show that it ever taught Scouts that homosexuality is not 'morally straight' or 'clean,' or that

such a view was part of the group's collective efforts to foster a belief. Furthermore, BSA's policy statements fail to establish any clear, consistent, and unequivocal position on homosexuality. Nor did BSA have any reason to think Dale's sexual conduct, as opposed to his orientation, was contrary to the group's values.
* * *

"It speaks volumes about the credibility of BSA's claim to a shared goal that homosexuality is incompatible with Scouting that since at least 1984 it had been aware of this issue—indeed, concerned enough to twice file amicus briefs before this Court—yet it did nothing in the intervening six years (or even in the years after Dale's expulsion) to explain clearly and openly why the presence of homosexuals would affect its expressive activities, or to make the view of 'morally straight' and 'clean' taken in its 1991 and 1992 policies a part of the values actually instilled in Scouts through the Handbook, lessons, or otherwise.

"Several principles are made perfectly clear by *Jaycees* and *Rotary Club*. First, to prevail on a claim of expressive association in the face of a State's antidiscrimination law, it is not enough simply to engage in *some kind* of expressive activity. Both the Jaycees and the Rotary Club engaged in expressive activity protected by the First Amendment, yet that fact was not dispositive. Second, it is not enough to adopt an openly avowed exclusionary membership policy. Both the Jaycees and the Rotary Club did that as well. Third, it is not sufficient merely to articulate *some* connection between the group's expressive activities and its exclusionary policy. The Rotary Club, for example, justified its male-only membership policy by pointing to the 'aspect of fellowship ... that is enjoyed by the [exclusively] male membership' and by claiming that only with an exclusively male membership could it 'operate effectively' in foreign countries.

"Rather, in *Jaycees*, we asked whether Minnesota's Human Rights Law requiring the admission of women 'impose[d] any *serious burdens*' on the group's 'collective effort on behalf of [its] *shared goals*.' Notwithstanding the group's obvious publicly stated exclusionary policy, we did not view the inclusion of women as a 'serious burden' on the Jaycees' ability to engage in the protected speech of its choice. Similarly, in *Rotary Club*, we asked whether California's law would 'affect in any *significant* way the existing members' ability' to engage in their protected speech, or whether the law would require the clubs 'to abandon their basic goals.' * * *

"The evidence before this Court makes it exceptionally clear that BSA has, at most, simply adopted an exclusionary membership policy and has no shared goal of disapproving of homosexuality. BSA's mission statement and federal charter say nothing on the matter; its official membership policy is silent; its Scout Oath and Law—and accompanying definitions—are devoid of any view on the topic; its guidance for Scouts and Scoutmasters on sexuality declare that such matters are 'not construed to be Scouting's proper area,' but are the province of a Scout's parents and pastor; and BSA's posture respecting religion tolerates a wide variety of views on the issue of homosexuality. Moreover, there is simply no evidence that BSA otherwise teaches anything in this area, or that it instructs Scouts on matters involving homosexuality in ways not conveyed in the Boy Scout or Scoutmaster Handbooks. In short, Boy Scouts of America is simply silent on homosexuality. There is no shared goal or collective effort to foster a belief about homosexuality at all—let alone one that is significantly burdened by admitting homosexuals. * * *

"The majority pretermits this entire analysis. It finds that BSA in fact 'teach[es] that homosexual conduct is not morally straight.' This conclusion, remarkably, rests entirely on statements in BSA's briefs. Moreover, the majority insists that we must 'give deference to an association's assertions regarding the nature of its expression' and 'we must also give deference to an association's view of what would impair its expression.' So long as the record 'contains written evidence' to support a group's bare assertion, '[w]e need not inquire further.' Once the organization 'asserts' that it engages in particular expression, '[w]e cannot doubt' the truth of that assertion.

"This is an astounding view of the law. I am unaware of any previous instance in which our analysis of the scope of a constitutional right was determined by looking at what a litigant asserts in his or her brief and inquiring no further. It is even more astonishing in the First Amendment area, because, as the majority itself acknowledges, 'we are obligated to independently review the factual record.' It is an odd form of independent review that consists of deferring entirely to whatever a litigant claims. But the majority insists that our inquiry must be 'limited' because 'it is not the role of the courts to reject a group's expressed values because they disagree with those values or find them internally inconsistent.'

"But nothing in our cases calls for this Court to do any such thing. An organization can adopt the message of its choice, and it is not this Court's place to disagree with it. But we must inquire whether the group is, in fact, expressing a message (whatever it may be) and whether that message (if one is expressed) is significantly affected by a State's antidiscrimination law. More critically, that inquiry requires our *independent* analysis, rather than deference to a group's litigating posture. Reflection on the subject dictates that such an inquiry is required. * * *

"If this Court were to defer to whatever position an organization is prepared to assert in its briefs, there would be no way to mark the proper boundary between genuine exercises of the right to associate, on the one hand, and sham claims that are simply attempts to insulate nonexpressive private discrimination, on the other hand. Shielding a litigant's claim from judicial scrutiny would, in turn, render civil rights legislation a nullity, and turn this important constitutional right into a farce. Accordingly, the Court's prescription of total deference will not do. * * *

"In its briefs, BSA implies, even if it does not directly argue, that Dale would use his Scoutmaster position as a 'bully pulpit' to convey immoral messages to his troop, and therefore his inclusion in the group would compel BSA to include a message it does not want to impart. Even though the majority does not endorse that argument, I think it is important to explain why it lacks merit, before considering the argument the majority does accept. BSA has not contended, nor does the record support, that Dale had ever advocated a view on homosexuality to his troop before his membership was revoked. Accordingly, BSA's revocation could only have been based on an assumption that he would do so in the future. * * *

"But there is no basis for BSA to presume that a homosexual will be unable to comply with BSA's policy not to discuss sexual matters any more than it would presume that politically or religiously active members could not resist the urge to proselytize or politicize during troop meetings. As BSA itself puts it, its rights are 'not implicated unless a prospective leader presents himself as a role model inconsistent with Boy Scouting's understanding of the Scout Oath and Law.'

"The majority, though, does not rest its conclusion on the claim that Dale will use his position as a bully pulpit. Rather, it contends that Dale's mere presence among the Boy Scouts will itself force the group to convey a message about homosexuality—even if Dale has no intention of doing so. The majority holds that '[t]he presence of an avowed homosexual and gay rights activist in an assistant scoutmaster's uniform sends a distinc[t] ... message,' and, accordingly, BSA is entitled to exclude that message. In particular, 'Dale's presence in the Boy Scouts would, at the very least, force the organization to send a message, both to the youth members and the world, that the Boy Scouts accepts homosexual conduct as a legitimate form of behavior.'

"The majority's argument relies exclusively on *Hurley*. [Though] *Hurley* has a superficial similarity to the present case, a close inspection reveals a wide gulf between that case and the one before us today.

"First, it was critical to our analysis that GLIB was actually conveying a message by participating in the parade—otherwise, the parade organizers could hardly claim that they were being forced to include any unwanted message at all. Our conclusion that GLIB was conveying a message was inextricably tied to the fact that GLIB wanted to march in a parade, as well as the manner in which it intended to march. * * * Indeed, we expressly distinguished between the members of GLIB, who marched as a unit to express their views about their own sexual orientation, on the one hand, and homosexuals who might participate as individuals in the parade without intending to express anything about their sexuality by doing so.

"Second, we found it relevant that GLIB's message 'would likely be perceived' as the parade organizers' own speech. That was so because '[p]arades and demonstrations * * * are not understood to be so neutrally presented or selectively viewed' as, say, a broadcast by a cable operator, who is usually considered to be 'merely "a conduit" for the speech' produced by others. Rather, parade organizers are usually understood to make the 'customary determination about a unit admitted to the parade.'

"Dale's inclusion in the Boy Scouts is nothing like the case in *Hurley*. His participation sends no cognizable message to the Scouts or to the world. Unlike GLIB, Dale did not carry a banner or a sign; he did not distribute any fact sheet; and he expressed no intent to send any message. If there is any kind of message being sent, then, it is by the mere act of joining the Boy Scouts. Such an act does not constitute an instance of symbolic speech under the First Amendment.

"It is true, of course, that some acts are so imbued with symbolic meaning that they qualify as 'speech' under the First Amendment. At the same time, however, '[w]e cannot accept the view that an apparently limitless variety of conduct can be labeled 'speech' whenever the person engaging in the conduct intends thereby to express an idea.' *O'Brien*. [Indeed], if merely joining a group did constitute symbolic speech; and such speech were attributable to the group being joined; and that group has the right to exclude that speech (and hence, the right to exclude that person from joining), then the right of free speech effectively becomes a limitless right to exclude for every organization, whether or not it engages in any expressive activities. That cannot be, and never has been, the law.

"The only apparent explanation for the majority's holding, then, is that homosexuals are simply so different from the rest of society that their presence alone—unlike any other individual's—should be singled out for special First Amendment treatment. Under the majority's reasoning, an openly gay male is irreversibly affixed with the label 'homosexual.' That label, even though unseen, communicates a message that permits his exclusion wherever he goes. His openness is the sole and sufficient justification for his ostracism. Though unintended, reliance on such a justification is tantamount to a constitutionally prescribed symbol of inferiority. As counsel for the Boy Scouts remarked, Dale 'put a banner around his neck when he * * * got himself into the newspaper * * * He created a reputation. * * * He can't take that banner off. He put it on himself and, indeed, he has continued to put it on himself.'

"Another difference between this case and *Hurley* lies in the fact that *Hurley* involved the parade organizers' claim to determine the content of the message they wish to give at a particular time and place. The standards governing such a claim are simply different from the standards that govern BSA's claim of a right of expressive association. Generally, a private person or a private organization has a right to refuse to broadcast a message with which it disagrees, and a right to refuse to contradict or garble its own specific statement at any given place or time by including the messages of others. An expressive association claim, however, normally involves the avowal and advocacy of a consistent position on some issue over time. This is why a different kind of scrutiny must be given to an expressive association claim, lest the right of expressive association simply turn into a right to discriminate whenever some group can think of an expressive object that would seem to be inconsistent with the admission of some person as a member or at odds with the appointment of a person to a leadership position in the group."[a]

POLITICAL ASSOCIATION AND POLITICAL PARTIES

CON LAW: P. 1011, after note 2

AMER CON: P. 996, after note 2

RTS & LIB: P. 918, after note 2

Minnesota's "antifusion" laws prohibit political candidates from appearing on the ballot as candidates for more than one party. Twin Cities Area New Party ("New Party") named a candidate for state representative, Andy Dawkins, who also was a candidate of the Minnesota–Democratic–Farmer–Labor Party ("DFL"). Dawkins signed an affidavit for the New Party, but local election officials refused to accept it since his affidavit of candidacy for DFL had already been filed.[a] The New Party brought suit maintaining that the antifusion laws violated the party's rights of association.

TIMMONS v. TWIN CITIES AREA NEW PARTY, 520 U.S. 351, 117 S.Ct. 1364, 137 L.Ed.2d 589 (1997), per Rehnquist, C.J., upheld the antifusion laws: "The First Amendment protects the right of citizens to associate and to form political parties for the advancement of common political goals and ideas. * * * [On] the other hand, it is also clear that States may, and inevitably must, enact reasonable regulations of parties, elections, and ballots to reduce election-and campaign-related disorder. * * * When deciding whether a state election law

a. Souter, J., joined by Ginsburg, J., and Breyer, J., also dissented.   **a.** The DFL did not object.

violates First and Fourteenth Amendment associational rights, we weigh the ' "character and magnitude" 'of the burden the State's rule imposes on those rights against the interests the State contends justify that burden, and consider the extent to which the State's concerns make the burden necessary. Regulations imposing severe burdens on plaintiffs' rights must be narrowly tailored and advance a compelling state interest. Lesser burdens, however, trigger less exacting review, and a State's ' "important regulatory interests" ' will usually be enough to justify ' "reasonable, nondiscriminatory restrictions." ' No bright line separates permissible election-related regulation from unconstitutional infringements on First Amendment freedoms.

"The New Party's claim that it has a right to select its own candidate is uncontroversial, so far as it goes. That is, the New Party, and not someone else, has the right to select the New Party's 'standard bearer.' It does not follow, though, that a party is absolutely entitled to have its nominee appear on the ballot as that party's candidate. A particular candidate might be ineligible for office, unwilling to serve, or, as here, another party's candidate. That a particular individual may not appear on the ballot as a particular party's candidate does not severely burden that party's association rights.

"The New Party relies on *Eu v. San Francisco County Democratic Central Comm.*, 489 U.S. 214, 109 S.Ct. 1013, 103 L.Ed.2d 271 (1989) and *Tashjian v. Republican Party of Conn.*, 479 U.S. 208, 107 S.Ct. 544, 93 L.Ed.2d 514 (1986). In *Eu*, we struck down California election provisions that prohibited political parties from endorsing candidates in party primaries and regulated parties' internal affairs and structure. And in *Tashjian*, we held that Connecticut's closed-primary statute, which required voters in a party primary to be registered party members, interfered with a party's associational rights by limiting 'the group of registered voters whom the Party may invite to participate in the basic function of selecting the Party's candidates.' But while *Tashjian* and *Eu* involved regulation of political parties' internal affairs and core associational activities, Minnesota's fusion ban does not. The ban, which applies to major and minor parties alike, simply precludes one party's candidate from appearing on the ballot, as that party's candidate, if already nominated by another party. Respondent is free to try to convince Representative Dawkins to be the New Party's, not the DFL's, candidate. * * *

"The New Party contends that the fusion ban burdens its 'right . . . to communicate its choice of nominees on the ballot on terms equal to those offered other parties, and the right of the party's supporters and other voters to receive that information,' and insists that communication on the ballot of a party's candidate choice is a 'critical source of information for the great majority of voters [who] rely upon party "labels" as a voting guide.'

"It is true that Minnesota's fusion ban prevents the New Party from using the ballot to communicate to the public that it supports a particular candidate who is already another party's candidate. In addition, the ban shuts off one possible avenue a party might use to send a message to its preferred *candidate* because, with fusion, a candidate who wins an election on the basis of two parties' votes will likely know more—if the parties' votes are counted separately—about the particular wishes and ideals of his constituency. We are unpersuaded, however, by the Party's contention that it has a right to use the ballot itself to send a particularized message, to its candidate and to the voters, about the nature of its support for the candidate. Ballots serve primarily to elect candidates, not as fora for political expression. Like all parties in Minnesota, the New Party is able to use the ballot to communicate information about itself and its candidate to the voters, so long as that candidate is not already someone else's candidate. * * *

"In sum, Minnesota's laws do not restrict the ability of the New Party and its members to endorse, support, or vote for anyone they like. The laws do not directly limit the Party's access to the ballot. They are silent on parties' internal structure, governance, and policy-making. Instead, these provisions reduce the universe of potential candidates who may appear on the ballot as the Party's nominee only by ruling out those few individuals who both have already agreed to be another party's candidate and also, if forced to choose, themselves prefer that other party. They also limit, slightly, the Party's ability to send a message to the voters and to its preferred candidates. We conclude that the burdens Minnesota imposes on the Party's First and Fourteenth Amendment associational rights—though not trivial—are not severe.

"[Therefore,] the State's asserted regulatory interests need only be 'sufficiently weighty to justify the limitation' imposed on the Party's rights. Nor do we require elaborate, empirical verification of the weightiness of the State's asserted justifications. * * *

"Minnesota argues here that its fusion ban is justified by its interests in avoiding voter confusion, promoting candidate competition (by reserving limited ballot space for opposing candidates), preventing electoral distortions and ballot manipulations, and discouraging party splintering and 'unrestrained factionalism.' States certainly have an interest in protecting the integrity, fairness, and efficiency of their ballots and election processes as means for electing public officials. Petitioners contend that a candidate or party could easily exploit fusion as a way of associating his or its name with popular slogans and catch phrases. For example, members of a major party could decide that a powerful way of 'sending a message' via the ballot would be for various factions of that party to nominate the major party's candidate as the candidate for the newly-formed 'No New Taxes,' 'Conserve Our Environment,' and 'Stop Crime Now' parties. In response, an opposing major party would likely instruct its factions to nominate that party's candidate as the 'Fiscal Responsibility,' 'Healthy Planet,' and 'Safe Streets' parties' candidate.

"Whether or not the putative 'fusion' candidates' names appeared on one or four ballot lines, such maneuvering would undermine the ballot's purpose by transforming it from a means of choosing candidates to a billboard for political advertising. The New Party responds to this concern, ironically enough, by insisting that the State could avoid such manipulation by adopting more demanding ballot-access standards rather than prohibiting multiple-party nomination. However, [because] the burdens the fusion ban imposes on the Party's associational rights are not severe, the State need not narrowly tailor the means it chooses to promote ballot integrity. The Constitution does not require that Minnesota compromise the policy choices embodied in its ballot-access requirements to accommodate the New Party's fusion strategy.

"Relatedly, petitioners urge that permitting fusion would undercut Minnesota's ballot-access regime by allowing minor parties to capitalize on the popularity of another party's candidate, rather than on their own appeal to the voters, in order to secure access to the ballot. That is, voters who might not sign a minor party's nominating petition based on the party's own views and candidates might do so if they viewed the minor party as just another way of nominating the same person nominated by one of the major parties. * * * The State surely has a valid interest in making sure that minor and third parties who are granted access to the ballot are bona fide and actually supported, on their own merits, by those who have provided the statutorily required petition or ballot support.

"States also have a strong interest in the stability of their political systems.[10] This interest does not permit a State to completely insulate the two-party system from minor parties' or independent candidates' competition and influence, nor is it a paternalistic license for States to protect political parties from the consequences of their own internal disagreements. That said, the States' interest permits them to enact reasonable election regulations that may, in practice, favor the traditional two-party system, and that temper the destabilizing effects of party-splintering and excessive factionalism. The Constitution permits the Minnesota Legislature to decide that political stability is best served through a healthy two-party system. And while an interest in securing the perceived benefits of a stable two-party system will not justify unreasonably exclusionary restrictions, States need not remove all of the many hurdles third parties face in the American political arena today.

"In *Storer v. Brown,* 415 U.S. 724, 94 S.Ct. 1274, 39 L.Ed.2d 714 (1974), we upheld a California statute that denied ballot positions to independent candidates who had voted in the immediately preceding primary elections or had a registered party affiliation at any time during the year before the same primary elections.[11] After surveying the relevant caselaw, we 'ha[d] no hesitation in sustaining' the party-disaffiliation provisions. We recognized that the provisions were part of a 'general state policy aimed at maintaining the integrity of [the] ballot,' and noted that the provision did not discriminate against independent candidates. We concluded that while a 'State need not take the course California [has], California apparently believes with the Founding Fathers that splintered parties and unrestrained factionalism may do significant damage to the fabric of government. It appears obvious to us that the one-year disaffiliation provision furthers the State's interest in the stability of its political system.'[12]

"Our decision in *Burdick v. Takushi,* 504 U.S. 428, 112 S.Ct. 2059, 119 L.Ed.2d 245 (1992) is also relevant. There, we upheld Hawaii's ban on write-in voting against a claim that the ban unreasonably infringed on citizens' First and Fourteenth Amendment rights. In so holding, we rejected the petitioner's argument that the ban 'deprive[d] him of the opportunity to cast a meaningful ballot,' emphasizing that the function of elections is to elect candidates and that

10. The dissents state that we may not consider "what appears to be the true basis for [our] holding—the interest in preserving the two-party system," because Minnesota did not defend this interest in its briefs and "expressly rejected" it at oral argument. In fact, at oral argument, the State contended that it has an interest in the stability of its political system and that, even if certain election-related regulations, such as those requiring single-member districts, tend to work to the advantage of the traditional two-party system, the "States do have a permissible choice [there], as long as they don't go so far as to close the door to minor part[ies]." We agree.

11. A similar provision applied to party candidates, and imposed a "flat disqualification upon any candidate seeking to run in a party primary if he has been 'registered as affiliated with a political party other than that political

party the nomination of which he seeks within 12 months immediately prior to the filing of the declaration.' " Another provision stated that "no person may file nomination papers for a party nomination and an independent nomination for the same office. . . . "

12. The dissent insists that New York's experience with fusion politics undermines Minnesota's contention that its fusion ban promotes political stability. California's experiment with cross-filing, on the other hand, provides some justification for Minnesota's concerns. In 1946, for example, Earl Warren was the nominee of both major parties, and was therefore able to run unopposed in California's general election. It appears to be widely accepted that California's cross-filing system stifled electoral competition and undermined the role of distinctive political parties.

'we have repeatedly upheld reasonable, politically neutral regulations that have the effect of channeling expressive activit[ies] at the polls.'

"Minnesota's fusion ban is far less burdensome than the disaffiliation rule upheld in *Storer,* and is justified by similarly weighty state interests. By reading *Storer* as dealing only with 'sore-loser candidates,' the dissent, in our view, fails to appreciate the case's teaching. Under the California disaffiliation statute at issue in *Storer, any* person affiliated with a party at any time during the year leading up to the primary election was absolutely precluded from appearing on the ballot as an independent or as the candidate of another party. Minnesota's fusion ban is not nearly so restrictive; the challenged provisions say nothing about the previous party affiliation of would-be candidates but only require that, in order to appear on the ballot, a candidate not be the nominee of more than one party. California's disaffiliation rule limited the field of candidates by thousands; Minnesota's precludes only a handful who freely choose to be so limited. It is also worth noting that while California's disaffiliation statute absolutely banned many candidacies, Minnesota's fusion ban only prohibits a candidate from being named twice.

"We conclude that the burdens Minnesota's fusion ban imposes on the New Party's associational rights are justified by 'correspondingly weighty' valid state interests in ballot integrity and political stability.[13] In deciding that Minnesota's fusion ban does not unconstitutionally burden the New Party's First and Fourteenth Amendment rights, we express no views on the New Party's policy-based arguments concerning the wisdom of fusion. It may well be that, as support for new political parties increase, these arguments will carry the day in some States' legislatures. But the Constitution does not require Minnesota, and the approximately 40 other States that do not permit fusion, to allow it."

STEVENS, J., joined in part by Ginsburg and Souter, JJ., dissented: "The Court's conclusion that the Minnesota statute prohibiting multiple-party candidacies is constitutional rests on three dubious premises: (1) that the statute imposes only a minor burden on the Party's right to choose and to support the candidate of its choice; (2) that the statute significantly serves the State's asserted interests in avoiding ballot manipulation and factionalism; and (3) that, in any event, the interest in preserving the two-party system justifies the imposition of the burden at issue in this case. I disagree with each of these premises. * * *

"The members of a recognized political party unquestionably have a constitutional right to select their nominees for public office and to communicate the identity of their nominees to the voting public. Both the right to choose and the right to advise voters of that choice are entitled to the highest respect.

"The Minnesota statutes place a significant burden on both of those rights. The Court's recital of burdens that the statute does not inflict on the Party does nothing to minimize the severity of the burdens that it does impose. The fact that the Party may nominate its second choice surely does not diminish the significance of a restriction that denies it the right to have the name of its first choice appear on the ballot. Nor does the point that it may use some of its limited resources to publicize the fact that its first choice is the nominee of some other party provide an adequate substitute for the message that is conveyed to every person who actually votes when a party's nominees appear on the ballot.[1] [T]he

---

13. The dissent rejects the argument that Minnesota's fusion ban serves its alleged paternalistic interest in "avoiding voter confusion." Although this supposed interest was discussed below, and in the parties' briefs before this Court, it plays no part in our analysis today.

1. The burden on the Party's right to nominate its first-choice candidate, by limiting the Party's ability to convey through its nominee right to be on the election ballot is precisely what separates a political party from any other interest group.

"The majority rejects as unimportant the limits that the fusion ban may impose on the Party's ability to express its political views, relying on our decision in *Burdick v. Takushi,* in which we noted that 'the purpose of casting, counting, and recording votes is to elect public officials, not to serve as a general forum for political expression.' But in *Burdick* we concluded simply that an individual voter's interest in expressing his disapproval of the single candidate running for office in a particular election did not require the State to finance and provide a mechanism for tabulating write-in votes. Our conclusion that the ballot is not principally a forum for the individual expression of political sentiment through the casting of a vote does not justify the conclusion that the ballot serves no expressive purpose for the parties who place candidates on the ballot. Indeed, the long-recognized right to choose a '"standard bearer who best represents the party's ideologies and preferences," '*Eu,* is inescapably an expressive right. 'To the extent that party labels provide a shorthand designation of the views of party candidates on matters of public concern, the identification of candidates with particular parties plays a role in the process by which voters inform themselves for the exercise of the franchise.' *Tashjian v. Republican Party of Conn.*

"In this case, and presumably in most cases, the burden of a statute of this kind is imposed upon the members of a minor party, but its potential impact is much broader. Popular candidates like Andy Dawkins sometimes receive nation-wide recognition. Fiorello LaGuardia, Earl Warren, Ronald Reagan, and Franklin D. Roosevelt, are names that come readily to mind as candidates whose reputations and political careers were enhanced because they appeared on election ballots as fusion candidates. A statute that denied a political party the right to nominate any of those individuals for high office simply because he had already been nominated by another party would, in my opinion, place an intolerable burden on political expression and association.

"[E]ven accepting the majority's view that the burdens imposed by the law are not weighty, the State's asserted interests must at least bear some plausible relationship to the burdens it places on political parties. Although the Court today suggests that the State does not have to support its asserted justifications for the fusion ban with evidence that they have any empirical validity, we have previously required more than a bare assertion that some particular state interest is served by a burdensome election requirement.

"While the State describes some imaginative theoretical sources of voter confusion that could result from fusion candidacies, in my judgment the argument that the burden on First Amendment interests is justified by this concern is meritless and severely underestimates the intelligence of the typical voter. We have noted more than once that ' "[a] State's claim that it is enhancing the ability of its citizenry to make wise decisions by restricting the flow of information to them must be viewed with some skepticism." ' *Eu; Tashjian.*

what the Party represents, risks impinging on another core element of any political party's associational rights—the right to "broaden the base of public participation in and support for its activities." A fusion ban burdens the right of a minor party to broaden its base of support because of the political reality that the dominance of the major parties frequently makes a vote for a minor party or independent candidate a "wasted" vote. When minor parties can nominate a candidate also nominated by a major party, they are able to present their members with an opportunity to cast a vote for a candidate who will actually be elected. Although this aspect of a party's effort to broaden support is distinct from the ability to nominate the candidate who best represents the party's views, it is important to note that the party's right to broaden the base of its support is burdened in both ways by the fusion ban.

"The State's concern about ballot manipulation, readily accepted by the majority, is similarly farfetched. The possibility that members of the major parties will begin to create dozens of minor parties with detailed, issue-oriented titles for the sole purpose of nominating candidates under those titles is entirely hypothetical.[3] The majority dismisses out-of-hand the Party's argument that the risk of this type of ballot manipulation and crowding is more easily averted by maintaining reasonably stringent requirements for the creation of minor parties. In fact, though, the Party's point merely illustrates the idea that a State can place some kinds—but not every kind—of limitation on the abilities of small parties to thrive. If the State wants to make it more difficult for any group to achieve the legal status of being a political party, it can do so within reason and still not run up against the First Amendment. 'The State has the undoubted right to require candidates to make a preliminary showing of substantial support in order to qualify for a place on the ballot, because it is both wasteful and confusing to encumber the ballot with the names of frivolous candidates.' *Anderson,* 460 U.S., at 788–789, n. 9, 103 S.Ct., at 1570, n. 9. See also *Jenness v. Fortson,* 403 U.S. 431, 442, 91 S.Ct. 1970, 1976, 29 L.Ed.2d 554 (1971). But once the State has established a standard for achieving party status, forbidding an acknowledged party from putting on the ballot its chosen candidate clearly frustrates core associational rights.[5]

"The State argues that the fusion ban promotes political stability by preventing intra-party factionalism and party raiding. States do certainly have an interest in maintaining a stable political system. But the State has not convincingly articulated how the fusion ban will prevent the factionalism it fears. Unlike the law at issue in *Storer v. Brown,* for example, this law would not prevent sore-loser candidates from defecting with a disaffected segment of a major party and running as an opposition candidate for a newly formed minor party. Nor does this law, like those aimed at requiring parties to show a modicum of support in order to secure a place on the election ballot, prevent the formation of numerous small parties. Indeed, the activity banned by Minnesota's law is the formation of coalitions, not the division and dissension of ' "splintered parties and unrestrained factionalism" ' * * *

"[The interest in preserving the two-party system is not] sufficient to justify the fusion ban.[b] In most States, perhaps in all, there are two and only two major political parties. It is not surprising, therefore, that most States have enacted election laws that impose burdens on the development and growth of third parties.

---

3. [T]he parade of horribles that the majority appears to believe might visit Minnesota should fusion candidacies be allowed is fantastical, given the evidence from New York's experience with fusion. Thus, the evidence that actually is available diminishes, rather than strengthens, Minnesota's claims. The majority asserts that California's cross-filing system, in place during the first half of this century, provides a compelling counter-example. But cross-filing, which "allowed candidates to file in the primary of any or all parties without specifying party affiliation." D. Mazmanian, *Third Parties in Presidential Elections* 132–133 (1974) is simply not the same as fusion politics, and the problems suffered in California do not provide empirical support for Minnesota's position.

5. A second "ballot manipulation" argument accepted by the majority is that minor parties will attempt to "capitalize on the popularity of another party's candidate, rather than on their own appeal to the voters, in order to secure access to the ballot." What the majority appears unwilling to accept is that *Andy Dawkins was the New Party's chosen candidate.* The Party was not trying to capitalize on his status as someone else's candidate, but to identify him as their own choice.

b. Stevens, J., maintained that the majority should not have considered the interest in maintaining the two-party system because it was not argued in the briefs and was rejected by the state at oral arguments. Ginsburg and Souter, JJ., did not join the section of Stevens, J.'s opinion about the two-party system.

The law at issue in this case is undeniably such a law. The fact that the law was both intended to disadvantage minor parties and has had that effect is a matter that should weigh against, rather than in favor of, its constitutionality.

"Our jurisprudence in this area reflects a certain tension: on the one hand, we have been clear that political stability is an important state interest and that incidental burdens on the formation of minor parties are reasonable to protect that interest, see *Storer;* on the other, we have struck down state elections laws specifically because they give 'the two old, established parties a decided advantage over any new parties struggling for existence,' *Williams v. Rhodes,* 393 U.S. 23, 89 S.Ct. 5, 21 L.Ed.2d 24 (1968).[7] * * * *[c]

"Nothing in the Constitution prohibits the States from maintaining single-member districts with winner-take-all voting arrangements. And these elements of an election system do make it significantly more difficult for third parties to thrive. But these laws are different in two respects from the fusion bans at issue here. First, the method by which they hamper third-party development is not one that impinges on the associational rights of those third parties; minor parties remain free to nominate candidates of their choice, and to rally support for those candidates. The small parties' relatively limited likelihood of ultimate success on election day does not deprive them of the right to try. Second, the establishment of single-member districts correlates directly with the States' interests in political stability. Systems of proportional representation, for example, may tend toward factionalism and fragile coalitions that diminish legislative effectiveness. In the context of fusion candidacies, the risks to political stability are extremely attenuated.[8] Of course, the reason minor parties so ardently support fusion politics is because it allows the parties to build up a greater base of support, as potential minor party members realize that a vote for the smaller party candidate is not necessarily a 'wasted' vote. Eventually, a minor party might gather sufficient strength that—were its members so inclined—it could successfully run a candidate not endorsed by any major party, and legislative coalition-building will be made more difficult by the presence of third party legislators. But the risks to political stability in that scenario are speculative at best. * * *

"The strength of the two-party system—and of each of its major components—is the product of the power of the ideas, the traditions, the candidates, and the voters that constitute the parties. It demeans the strength of the two-party system to assume that the major parties need to rely on laws that discriminate against independent voters and minor parties in order to preserve their positions of power.[12] Indeed, it is a central theme of our jurisprudence that the entire

---

7. In *Anderson v. Celebrezze,* 460 U.S. 780, 103 S.Ct. 1564, 75 L.Ed.2d 547 (1983) the State argued that its interest in political stability justified the early filing deadline for presidential candidates at issue in the case. We recognized that the "asserted interest in political stability amounts to a desire to protect existing political parties from competition," and rejected that interest.

c. *Williams* dealt with ballot access requirements making it virtually impossible for new political parties, even ones with hundreds of thousands of members, to gain access to the ballot. In Presidential elections, for example, Ohio had required new parties to submit petitions totaling 15% of the number of ballots cast in the prior gubernatorial election. (Most states require less than 1% of the ballots cast).

The result was to confine the ballot to the two major parties. The Court struck down the statute on equal protection grounds: "There is, of course, no reason why two parties should retain a permanent monopoly on the right to have people vote for or against them."

8. Even in a system that allows fusion, a candidate for election must assemble majority support, so the State's concern cannot logically be about risks to political stability in the particular election in which the fusion candidate is running.

12. The experience in New York with fusion politics provides considerable evidence that neither political stability nor the ultimate strength of the two major parties is truly risked by the existence of successful minor parties.

electorate, which necessarily includes the members of the major parties, will benefit from robust competition in ideas and governmental policies that ' "is at the core of our electoral process and of the First Amendment freedoms." ' '* * *

SOUTER, J., dissenting, was willing to "judge the challenged statutes only on the interests the State has raised in their defense and would hold them unconstitutional. I am, however, unwilling to go the further distance of considering and rejecting the majority's 'preservation of the two-party system' rationale. For while Minnesota has made no such argument before us, I cannot discount the possibility of a forceful one. There is considerable consensus that party loyalty among American voters has declined significantly in the past four decades and that the overall influence of the parties in the political process has decreased considerably. [I]t may not be unreasonable to infer that the two-party system is in some jeopardy.

"Surely the majority is right that States 'have a strong interest in the stability of their political systems,' that is, in preserving a political system capable of governing effectively. If it could be shown that the disappearance of the two-party system would undermine that interest, and that permitting fusion candidacies poses a substantial threat to the two-party scheme, there might well be a sufficient predicate for recognizing the constitutionality of the state action presented by this case. Right now, however, no State has attempted even to make this argument, and I would therefore leave its consideration for another day.

California by initiative proposition 198 adopted a blanket primary system, permitting citizens to vote in the primary of any party for any office regardless of their party membership. Thus, voters could vote in the democratic party primary for governor while voting in the Republican party primary for senator or vice versa. Several political parties challenged these arrangements on the ground that their freedom of association was violated.

CALIFORNIA DEMOCRATIC PARTY v. JONES, ___ U.S. ___, 120 S.Ct. 2402, ___ L.Ed.2d ___, (2000) per SCALIA, J., invalidated the blanket primary on first amendment grounds: "[W]e have not held [that] the processes by which political parties select their nominees are, as respondents would have it, wholly public affairs that States may regulate freely. [Representative] democracy in any populous unit of governance is unimaginable without the ability of citizens to band together in promoting among the electorate candidates who espouse their political views. Consistent with this tradition, the Court has recognized that the First Amendment protects 'the freedom to join together in furtherance of common political beliefs,' *Tashjian*, which 'necessarily presupposes the freedom to identify the people who constitute the association, and to limit the association to those people only,' That is to say, a corollary of the right to associate is the right not to associate. * * *

"In no area is the political association's right to exclude more important than in the process of selecting its nominee. That process often determines the party's positions on the most significant public policy issues of the day, and even when those positions are predetermined it is the nominee who becomes the party's ambassador to the general electorate in winning it over to the party's views. * * *

"California's blanket primary violates the principles set forth in these cases. Proposition 198 forces political parties to associate with—to have their nominees, and hence their positions, determined by—those who, at best, have refused to affiliate with the party, and, at worst, have expressly affiliated with a rival. In this respect, it is qualitatively different from a closed primary. Under that system, even when it is made quite easy for a voter to change his party affiliation the day of the primary, and thus, in some sense, to 'cross over,' at least he must formally become a member of the party; and once he does so, he is limited to voting for candidates of that party.

"The evidence in this case demonstrates that under California's blanket primary system, the prospect of having a party's nominee determined by adherents of an opposing party is far from remote—indeed, it is a clear and present danger. For example, in one 1997 survey of California voters 37 percent of Republicans said that they planned to vote in the 1998 Democratic gubernatorial primary, and 20 percent of Democrats said they planned to vote in the 1998 Republican United States Senate primary. * * *

"The record also supports the obvious proposition that these substantial numbers of voters who help select the nominees of parties they have chosen not to join often have policy views that diverge from those of the party faithful. [One] expert went so far as to describe it as 'inevitable [under Proposition 198] that parties will be forced in some circumstances to give their official designation to a candidate who's not preferred by a majority or even plurality of party members.' (expert testimony of Bruce Cain).

"In sum, Proposition 198 forces petitioners to adulterate their candidate-selection process—the 'basic function of a political party,'—by opening it up to persons wholly unaffiliated with the party. Such forced association has the likely outcome—indeed, in this case the intended outcome—of changing the parties' message. We can think of no heavier burden on a political party's associational freedom. Proposition 198 is therefore unconstitutional unless it is narrowly tailored to serve a compelling state interest.

"The aspect of fairness addressed by Proposition 198 is presumably the supposed inequity of not permitting nonparty members in 'safe' districts to determine the party nominee. If that is unfair at all (rather than merely a consequence of the eminently democratic principle that—except where constitutional imperatives intervene—the majority rules), it seems to us less unfair than permitting nonparty members to hijack the party. As for affording voters greater choice, it is obvious that the net effect of this scheme—indeed, its avowed purpose—is to reduce the scope of choice, by assuring a range of candidates who are all more 'centrist.' This may well be described as broadening the range of choices favored by the majority—but that is hardly a compelling state interest, if indeed it is even a legitimate one. The interest in increasing voter participation is just a variation on the same theme (more choices favored by the majority will produce more voters), and suffers from the same defect. As for the protection of privacy: The specific privacy interest at issue is not the confidentiality of medical records or personal finances, but confidentiality of one's party affiliation. Even if (as seems unlikely) a scheme for administering a closed primary could not be devised in which the voter's declaration of party affiliation would not be public information, we do not think that the State's interest in assuring the privacy of this piece of information in all cases can conceivably be considered a 'compelling' one. * * *

"Finally, we may observe that even if all these state interests were compelling ones, Proposition 198 is not a narrowly tailored means of furthering them. Respondents could protect them all by resorting to a nonpartisan blanket primary. Generally speaking, under such a system, the State determines what qualifications it requires for a candidate to have a place on the primary ballot—which may include nomination by established parties and voter-petition requirements for independent candidates. Each voter, regardless of party affiliation, may then vote for any candidate, and the top two vote getters (or however many the State prescribes) then move on to the general election. This system has all the characteristics of the partisan blanket primary, save the constitutionally crucial one: Primary voters are not choosing a party's nominee. Under a nonpartisan blanket primary, a State may ensure more choice, greater participation, increased 'privacy,' and a sense of 'fairness'—all without severely burdening a political party's First Amendment right of association."[a]

STEVENS, J., joined by Ginsburg, J., dissented: "[T]he associational rights of political parties are neither absolute nor as comprehensive as the rights enjoyed by wholly private associations. [I] think it clear—though the point has never been decided by this Court—'that a State may require parties to use the primary format for selecting their nominees.' The reason a State may impose this significant restriction on a party's associational freedoms is that both the general election and the primary are quintessential forms of state action.

"The so-called 'right not to associate' that the Court relies upon, then, is simply inapplicable to participation in a state election. A political party, like any other association, may refuse to allow non-members to participate in the party's decisions when it is conducting its own affairs * * *. California's blanket primary system does not infringe this principle. But an election, unlike a convention or caucus, is a public affair. Although it is true that we have extended First Amendment protection to a party's right to invite independents to participate in its primaries, *Tashjian*, neither that case nor any other has held or suggested that the 'right not to associate' imposes a limit on the State's power to open up its primary elections to all voters eligible to vote in a general election. In my view, while state rules abridging participation in its elections should be closely scrutinized, the First Amendment does not inhibit the State from acting to broaden voter access to state-run, state-financed elections. When a State acts not to limit democratic participation but to expand the ability of individuals to participate in the democratic process, it is acting not as a foe of the First Amendment but as a friend and ally.[b]

"[A]nyone can 'join' a political party merely by asking for the appropriate ballot at the appropriate time or (at most) by registering within a state-defined reasonable period of time before an election; neither past voting history nor the voter's race, religion, or gender can provide a basis for the party's refusal to 'associate' with an unwelcome new member. There is an obvious mismatch between a supposed constitutional right 'not to associate' and a rule that turns on

a. Kennedy, J., concurred.

b. Later in his opinion Stevens, J., stated: "The Court's glib rejection of the State's interest in increasing voter participation is particularly regrettable. In an era of dramatically declining voter participation, States should be free to experiment with reforms designed to make the democratic process more robust by involving the entire electorate in the process of selecting those who will serve as government officials. Opening the nominating process to all and encouraging voters to participate in any election that draws their interest is one obvious means of achieving this goal."

nothing more than the state-defined timing of the new associate's application for membership."[c]

The Virginia Republican Party required those who wished to become delegates to the 1994 state nominating convention for United States Senator to pay a registration fee. Morse filed suit contending that the fee violated the Voting Rights Act including the provision that changes in voting requirements in particular jurisdictions be submitted to the Attorney General for preclearance. The Republican Party denied the application of the statute to the fee requirement, but, argued, alternatively, that such an interpretation would violate the right of political association.

MORSE v. REPUBLICAN PARTY OF VIRGINIA, 517 U.S. 186, 116 S.Ct. 1186, 134 L.Ed.2d 347 (1996), held that application of the preclearance requirement did not violate political association rights. STEVENS, J., joined by Ginsburg, J., announcing the judgment of the Court, recognized that curtailment of party association rights must be subject to the "closest scrutiny." Nonetheless, he observed that the Act's purpose was to prevent racial discrimination and that Morse had not argued that immunity from the particular fee was protected under the first amendment: "We leave consideration of hypothetical concerns for another day."

BREYER, J., joined by O'Connor and Souter, JJ., concurring, concluded that the fees at issue were "well outside the area of greatest 'associational' concern."

SCALIA, J., joined by Thomas, J., dissenting, not only faulted the majority for ignoring vagueness and overbreadth doctrine, but also argued that the case involved a "classic prior restraint" because the party could make no changes affecting a voter's capacity to elect a candidate without governmental clearance: "A freedom of political association that must await the Government's favorable response to a 'Mother, may I?' is no freedom of political association at all."

THOMAS, J., joined by Rehnquist, C.J., and Scalia, J., dissenting, argued that the act was inapplicable, but further contended that charging each delegate a fee rather than funding the convention with major donors was a constitutionally protected choice. Moreover, to refuse preclearance "would in effect be requiring the Party to include persons who could not, or would not, pay the registration fee for its convention," violating the right to decide with whom to associate.[a]

WEALTH AND THE POLITICAL PROCESS: CONCERNS FOR EQUALITY

CON LAW: P. 1023, after note 4
AMER CON: P. 1008, after note 4
RTS & LIB: P. 930, after note 4

5. *Expenditure limitations and political parties.* COLORADO REPUBLICAN FEDERAL CAMPAIGN COMMITTEE v. FEDERAL ELECTION COMMITTEE, 518 U.S. 604, 116 S.Ct. 2309, 135 L.Ed.2d 795 (1996), ruled that the Federal

c. Stevens, J., also thought the initiative raised additional constitutional issues. Ginsburg, J., did not join that portion of Stevens, J.'s opinion.

a. Kennedy, J., joined by Rehnquist, C.J., dissenting, argued that first amendment and other concerns justified a narrow construction of the statute.

Election Campaign Act's limitation on independent expenditures by political parties was unconstitutional. BREYER, J., joined by O'Connor and Souter, JJ., announced the judgment of the Court, but did not reach the question whether the Act's prohibition of expenditures coordinated with the candidate were similarly unconstitutional.

KENNEDY, J., joined by Scalia, J., concurring in part and dissenting in part, argued that the prohibition on coordinated expenditures between political parties and their candidates was also unconstitutional: "We have a constitutional tradition of political parties and their candidates engaging in joint first amendment activity. [Congress] may have authority, consistent with the first amendment, to restrict undifferentiated political party contributions [as discussed in] *Buckley*, but that type of regulation is not at issue here." Kennedy, J., dissented from the judgment's failure to reach the question of coordinated expenditures.[a]

STEVENS, J., joined by Ginsburg, J., dissenting, maintained that independent expenditures by parties were contributions and that federal limits were justified by the need to level "the electoral playing field," and to avoid corruption or its appearance.

Shrink Missouri Government PAC, a political action committee and "Jay" Nixon, an unsuccessful candidate in the primary for Missouri state auditor brought suit challenging provisions of Missouri's campaign finance law limiting the amount of contributions to candidates. NIXON v. SHRINK MISSOURI GOVERNMENT PAC, ___ U.S. ___, 120 S.Ct. 897, 145 L.Ed.2d 886 (2000), per SOUTER, J., joined by Rehnquist, C.J., and Stevens, O'Connor, Ginsburg, and Breyer, JJ., reaffirmed *Buckley,* and upheld the restrictions on campaign contributions despite the fact that the limits were lower in real dollar value than those upheld in *Buckley*: "The particular provision challenged here reads that '[t]o elect an individual to the office of governor, lieutenant governor, secretary of state, state treasurer, state auditor or attorney general, [[t]he amount of contributions made by or accepted from any person other than the candidate in any one election shall not exceed] one thousand dollars.' The statutory dollar amounts are baselines for an adjustment each even-numbered year, to be made 'by multiplying the base year amount by the cumulative consumer' price index * * * and rounded to the nearest twenty-five-dollar amount, for all years since January 1, 1995.' * * *

"Precision about the relative rigor of the standard to review contribution limits was not a pretense of the *Buckley* per curiam opinion. To be sure, in addressing the speech claim, we explicitly rejected both *O'Brien* intermediate scrutiny for communicative action and the similar standard applicable to merely time, place, and manner restrictions. In distinguishing these tests, the discussion referred generally to 'the exacting scrutiny required by the First Amendment,' and added that 'the constitutional guarantee has its fullest and most urgent application precisely to the conduct of campaigns for political office.'

"We then, however, drew a line between expenditures and contributions, treating expenditure restrictions as direct restraints on speech * * *. [While] we did not then say in so many words that different standards might govern expenditure and contribution limits affecting associational rights, [i]t has [been]

a. Thomas, J., joined by Rehnquist, C.J., and Scalia, J., would also have reached the question, arguing that *Buckley*'s anti-corruption rationale did not apply to associations between political parties and candidates. Thomas, J., on his own, additionally argued that the distinction between contributions and expenditures was generally unsatisfactory and that both should receive first amendment protection.

plain ever since *Buckley* that contribution limits would more readily clear the hurdles before them. [Thus], under *Buckley's* standard of scrutiny, a contribution limit involving 'significant interference' with associational rights could survive if the Government demonstrated that contribution regulation was 'closely drawn' to match a 'sufficiently important interest' though the dollar amount of the limit need not be 'fine tun[ed].'

"While we did not attempt to parse distinctions between the speech and association standards of scrutiny for contribution limits, we did make it clear that those restrictions bore more heavily on the associational right than on freedom to speak. Id., at 24–25, 96 S.Ct. 612. We consequently proceeded on the understanding that a contribution limitation surviving a claim of associational abridgment would survive a speech challenge as well, and we held the standard satisfied by the contribution limits under review.

"[T]he prevention of corruption and the appearance of corruption,' was found to be a 'constitutionally sufficient justification,' * * * In speaking of 'improper influence' and 'opportunities for abuse' in addition to 'quid pro quo arrangements,' we recognized a concern not confined to bribery of public officials, but extending to the broader threat from politicians too compliant with the wishes of large contributors. These were the obvious points behind our recognition that the Congress could constitutionally address the power of money 'to influence governmental action' in ways less 'blatant and specific' than bribery. *Buckley.*[4]

"Although respondents [do not call] for any reconsideration of *Buckley*, they take the State to task, as the Court of Appeals did, for failing to justify the invocation of those interests with empirical evidence of actually corrupt practices or of a perception among Missouri voters that unrestricted contributions must have been exerting a covertly corrosive influence. The state statute is not void, however, for want of evidence.

"The quantum of empirical evidence needed to satisfy heightened judicial scrutiny of legislative judgments will vary up or down with the novelty and plausibility of the justification raised. *Buckley* demonstrates that the dangers of large, corrupt contributions and the suspicion that large contributions are corrupt are neither novel nor implausible. [While] *Buckley's* evidentiary showing [relying on the Court of Appeals] exemplifies a sufficient justification for contribution limits, it does not speak to what may be necessary as a minimum.

"[T]his case does not present a close call requiring further definition of whatever the State's evidentiary obligation may be. While the record does not show that the Missouri Legislature relied on the evidence and findings accepted in *Buckley*, the evidence introduced into the record by respondents or cited by the lower courts in this action is enough to show that the substantiation of the congressional concerns reflected in *Buckley* has its counterpart supporting the Missouri law. * * *

"There might, of course, be need for a more extensive evidentiary documentation if petitioners had made any showing of their own to cast doubt on the apparent implications of Buckley's evidence and the record here, but the closest respondents come to challenging these conclusions is their invocation of academic studies said to indicate that large contributions to public officials or candidates do not actually result in changes in candidates' positions. Given the conflict among

---

4. In arguing that the *Buckley* standard should not be relaxed, respondents Shrink Missouri and Fredman suggest that a candidate like Fredman suffers because contribution lim-its favor incumbents over challengers. [N]othing in the record here gives respondents a stronger argument than the *Buckley* petitioners made.

these publications, and the absence of any reason to think that public perception has been influenced by the studies cited by respondents, there is little reason to doubt that sometimes large contributions will work actual corruption of our political system, and no reason to question the existence of a corresponding suspicion among voters.

"Nor do we see any support for respondents' various arguments that in spite of their striking resemblance to the limitations sustained in *Buckley*, those in Missouri are so different in kind as to raise essentially a new issue about the adequacy of the Missouri statute's tailoring to serve its purposes. Here, as in *Buckley*, '[t]here is no indication ... that the contribution limitations imposed by the [law] would have any dramatic[ally] adverse effect on the funding of campaigns and political associations,' and thus no showing that 'the limitations prevented the candidates and political committees from amassing the resources necessary for effective advocacy.' [Even] if we were to assume that the contribution limits affected respondent Fredman's ability to wage a competitive campaign (no small assumption given that Fredman only identified one contributor, Shrink Missouri, that would have given him more than $1,075 per election), a showing of one affected individual does not point up a system of suppressed political advocacy that would be unconstitutional under *Buckley*.

"The dissenters in this case think our reasoning evades the real issue. Justice Thomas chides us for 'hiding behind' *Buckley*, and Justice Kennedy faults us for seeing this case as 'a routine application of our analysis' in *Buckley* instead of facing up to what he describes as the consequences of *Buckley*. Each dissenter would overrule *Buckley* and thinks we should do the same.

"The answer is that we are supposed to decide this case. Shrink and Fredman did not request that *Buckley* be overruled; the furthest reach of their arguments about the law was that subsequent decisions already on the books had enhanced the State's burden of justification beyond what *Buckley* required, a proposition we [reject] as mistaken."

STEVENS, J., concurred: "Justice Kennedy suggests that the misuse of soft money tolerated by this Court's misguided decision in *Colorado Republican Federal Campaign Comm. v. Federal Election Comm'n*, 518 U.S. 604, 116 S.Ct. 2309, 135 L.Ed.2d 795 (1996), demonstrates the need for a fresh examination of the constitutional issues raised by Congress' enactment of the Federal Election Campaign Acts of 1971 and 1974 and this Court's resolution of those issues in *Buckley*. In response to his call for a new beginning, therefore, I make one simple point. Money is property; it is not speech.

" Speech has the power to inspire volunteers to perform a multitude of tasks on a campaign trail, on a battleground, or even on a football field. Money, meanwhile, has the power to pay hired laborers to perform the same tasks. It does not follow, however, that the First Amendment provides the same measure of protection to the use of money to accomplish such goals as it provides to the use of ideas to achieve the same results.*

"Our Constitution and our heritage properly protect the individual's interest in making decisions about the use of his or her own property. Governmental regulation of such decisions can sometimes be viewed either as 'deprivations of

---

* Unless, of course, the prohibition entirely forecloses a channel of communication, such as the use of paid petition circulators. See, e.g., *Meyer v. Grant*, 486 U.S. 414, 424, 108 S.Ct. 1886, 100 L.Ed.2d 425 (1988) ("Colorado's pro-hibition of paid petition circulators restricts access to the most effective, fundamental, and perhaps economical avenue of political discourse, direct one-on-one communication * * * ").

liberty' or as 'deprivations of property,' see, e.g., *Moore v. East Cleveland* (Stevens, J., concurring in judgment). [Because] I did not participate in the Court's decision in Buckley, I did not have the opportunity to suggest then that those property and liberty concerns adequately explain the Court's decision to invalidate the expenditure limitations in the 1974 Act. * * *

"The right to use one's own money to hire gladiators, or to fund 'speech by proxy,' certainly merits significant constitutional protection. These property rights, however, are not entitled to the same protection as the right to say what one pleases."

BREYER, J., joined by Ginsburg, J., concurred: "The dissenters accuse the Court of weakening the First Amendment. [But] this is a case where constitutionally protected interests lie on both sides of the legal equation. For that reason there is no place for a strong presumption against constitutionality, of the sort often thought to accompany the words 'strict scrutiny.'

"On the one hand, a decision to contribute money to a campaign is a matter of First Amendment concern—not because money is speech (it is not); but because it enables speech. Through contributions the contributor associates himself with the candidate's cause, helps the candidate communicate a political message with which the contributor agrees, and helps the candidate win by attracting the votes of similarly minded voters. *Buckley.* Both political association and political communication are at stake.

"On the other hand, restrictions upon the amount any one individual can contribute to a particular candidate seek to protect the integrity of the electoral process—the means through which a free society democratically translates political speech into concrete governmental action. Moreover, by limiting the size of the largest contributions, such restrictions aim to democratize the influence that money itself may bring to bear upon the electoral process. In doing so, they seek to build public confidence in that process and broaden the base of a candidate's meaningful financial support, encouraging the public participation and open discussion that the First Amendment itself presupposes.

"In service of these objectives, the statute imposes restrictions of degree. It does not deny the contributor the opportunity to associate with the candidate through a contribution, though it limits a contribution's size. Nor does it prevent the contributor from using money (alone or with others) to pay for the expression of the same views in other ways. Instead, it permits all supporters to contribute the same amount of money, in an attempt to make the process fairer and more democratic.

"Under these circumstances, a presumption against constitutionality is out of place. I recognize that *Buckley* used language that could be interpreted to the contrary. It said, for example, that it rejected 'the concept that government may restrict the speech of some elements of our society in order to enhance the relative voice of others.' But those words cannot be taken literally. The Constitution often permits restrictions on the speech of some in order to prevent a few from drowning out the many—in Congress, for example, where constitutionally protected debate, Art. I, § 6, is limited to provide every Member an equal opportunity to express his or her views. Or in elections, where the Constitution tolerates numerous restrictions on ballot access, limiting the political rights of some so as to make effective the political rights of the entire electorate. Regardless, as the result in *Buckley* made clear, the statement does not automatically invalidate a statute that seeks a fairer electoral debate through contribution limits, nor should it forbid the Court to take account of the competing constitutional interests just mentioned.

"In such circumstances—where a law significantly implicates competing constitutionally protected interests in complex ways—the Court has closely scrutinized the statute's impact on those interests, but refrained from employing a simple test that effectively presumes unconstitutionality. Rather, it has balanced interests. [Where] a legislature has significantly greater institutional expertise, as, for example, in the field of election regulation, the Court in practice defers to empirical legislative judgments—at least where that deference does not risk such constitutional evils as, say, permitting incumbents to insulate themselves from effective electoral challenge.

"Applying this approach to the present case, I would uphold the statute essentially for the reasons stated by the Court. I agree that the legislature understands the problem—the threat to electoral integrity, the need for democratization—better than do we. We should defer to its political judgment that unlimited spending threatens the integrity of the electoral process. But we should not defer in respect to whether its solution, by imposing too low a contribution limit, significantly increases the reputation-related or media-related advantages of incumbency and thereby insulates legislators from effective electoral challenge. The statutory limit here, $1,075 (or 378, 1976 dollars), is low enough to raise such a question. But given the empirical information presented—the type of election at issue; the record of adequate candidate financing post-reform; and the fact that the statute indexes the amount for inflation—I agree with the Court that the statute does not work disproportionate harm. The limit may have prevented the plaintiff, Zev David Fredman, from financing his own campaign for office, for Fredman's support among potential contributors was not sufficiently widespread. But any contribution statute (like any statute setting ballot eligibility requirements will narrow the field of conceivable challengers to some degree. * * *

"The *Buckley* decision, as well, might be interpreted as embodying sufficient flexibility for the problem at hand. After all, *Buckley*'s holding seems to leave the political branches broad authority to enact laws regulating contributions that take the form of 'soft money.' It held public financing laws constitutional. It says nothing one way or the other about such important proposed reforms as reduced-price media time. [Alternatively], it might prove possible to reinterpret aspects of *Buckley* in light of the post-*Buckley* experience stressed by Justice Kennedy, making less absolute the contribution/expenditure line, particularly in respect to independently wealthy candidates, whose expenditures might be considered contributions to their own campaigns.

"But what if I am wrong about *Buckley*? Suppose *Buckley* denies the political branches sufficient leeway to enact comprehensive solutions to the problems posed by campaign finance. If so, like Justice Kennedy, I believe the Constitution would require us to reconsider *Buckley*. With that understanding I join the Court's opinion."

KENNEDY, J., dissented: "[T]he Court [perpetuates] and compounds a serious distortion of the First Amendment resulting from our own intervention in *Buckley*. The Court is concerned about voter suspicion of the role of money in politics. Amidst an atmosphere of skepticism, however, it hardly inspires confidence for the Court to abandon the rigors of our traditional First Amendment structure. * * * The plain fact is that the compromise the Court invented in *Buckley* set the stage for a new kind of speech to enter the political system. It is covert speech. The Court has forced a substantial amount of political speech underground, as contributors and candidates devise ever more elaborate methods of avoiding contribution limits, limits which take no account of rising campaign costs. The preferred method has been to conceal the real purpose of the speech. Soft money may be contributed to political parties in unlimited amounts, and is used often to fund so-called issue advocacy, advertisements that promote or attack a candidate's positions without specifically urging his or her election or defeat. Briffault, *Issue Advocacy: Redrawing the Elections/Politics Line*, 77 Tex. L.Rev. 1751, 1752–1753 (1999). Issue advocacy, like soft money, is unrestricted, while straightforward speech in the form of financial contributions paid to a candidate, speech subject to full disclosure and prompt evaluation by the public, is not. Thus has the Court's decision given us covert speech. This mocks the First Amendment. The current system would be unfortunate, and suspect under the First Amendment, had it evolved from a deliberate legislative choice; but its unhappy origins are in our earlier decree in *Buckley*, which by accepting half of what Congress did (limiting contributions) but rejecting the other (limiting expenditures) created a misshapen system, one which distorts the meaning of speech. * * *

"The wrong goes deeper, however. By operation of the *Buckley* rule, a candidate cannot oppose this system in an effective way without selling out to it first. Soft money must be raised to attack the problem of soft money. In effect, the Court immunizes its own erroneous ruling from change. Rulings of this Court must never be viewed with more caution than when they provide immunity from their own correction in the political process and in the forum of unrestrained speech. The melancholy history of campaign finance in *Buckley*'s wake shows what can happen when we intervene in the dynamics of speech and expression by inventing an artificial scheme of our own.

"The case in one sense might seem unimportant. It appears that Mr. Fredman was an outsider candidate who may not have had much of a chance. Yet, by binding him to the outdated limit of $1075 per contribution in a system where parties can raise soft money without limitation and a powerful press faces no restrictions on use of its own resources to back its preferred candidates, the Court tells Mr. Fredman he cannot challenge the status quo unless he first gives into it. This is not the First Amendment with which I am familiar.

"To defend its extension of *Buckley* to present times, the Court, of course, recites the dangers of corruption, or the appearance of corruption, when an interested person contributes money to a candidate. What the Court does not do is examine and defend the substitute it has encouraged, covert speech funded by unlimited soft money. In my view that system creates dangers greater than the one it has replaced. [For example,] we have an indirect system of accountability that is confusing, if not dispiriting, to the voter. The very disaffection or distrust that the Court cites as the justification for limits on direct contributions has now spread to the entire political discourse. *Buckley* has not worked. * * *

"Among the facts the Court declines to take into account is the emergence of cyberspace communication by which political contributions can be reported almost simultaneously with payment. The public can then judge for itself whether the candidate or the officeholder has so overstepped that we no longer trust him or her to make a detached and neutral judgment. This is a far more immediate way to assess the integrity and the performance of our leaders than through the hidden world of soft money and covert speech.

"To this point my view may seem to be but a reflection of what Justice Thomas has written, and [I] may well come out as he does, for his reasoning and my own seem to point to the conclusion that the legislature can do little by way of imposing limits on political speech of this sort. For now, however, I would leave open the possibility that Congress, or a state legislature, might devise a system in which there are some limits on both expenditures and contributions, thus permitting officeholders to concentrate their time and efforts on official duties rather than on fundraising. * * * I would overrule *Buckley* and then free Congress or state legislatures to attempt some new reform, if, based upon their own considered view of the First Amendment, it is possible to do so. * * * The First Amendment ought to be allowed to take its own course without further obstruction from the artificial system we have imposed. It suffices here to say that the law in question does not come even close to passing any serious scrutiny."

THOMAS, J., joined by Scalia, J., dissented: "For nearly half a century, this Court has extended First Amendment protection to a multitude of forms of 'speech,' such as making false defamatory statements, filing lawsuits, dancing nude, exhibiting drive-in movies with nudity, burning flags, and wearing military uniforms. Not surprisingly, the Courts of Appeals have followed our lead and concluded that the First Amendment protects, for example, begging, shouting obscenities, erecting tables on a sidewalk, and refusing to wear a necktie. In light of the many cases of this sort, today's decision is a most curious anomaly. Whatever the proper status of such activities under the First Amendment, I am confident that they are less integral to the functioning of our Republic than campaign contributions. Yet the majority today, rather than going out of its way to protect political speech, goes out of its way to avoid protecting it. * * *

"At bottom, the majority's refusal to apply strict scrutiny to contribution limits rests upon Buckley's discounting of the First Amendment interests at stake. [*Buckley*] noted that '[w]hile contributions may result in political expression if spent by a candidate or an association to present views to the voters, the transformation of contributions into political debate involves speech by someone other than the contributor.'

"But this was a faulty distinction ab initio because it ignored the reality of how speech of all kinds is disseminated: 'Even in the case of a direct expenditure, there is usually some go-between that facilitates the dissemination of the spender's message—for instance, an advertising agency or a television station. To call a contribution 'speech by proxy' thus does little to differentiate it from an expenditure. The only possible difference is that contributions involve an extra step in the proxy chain. But again, that is a difference in form, not substance.' *Colorado Republican* (Thomas, J., concurring in judgment and dissenting in part). * * *

"Without the assistance of the speech-by-proxy argument, the remainder of *Buckley's* rationales founder. Those rationales—that the 'quantity of communication by the contributor does not increase perceptibly with the size of his contribution,' that 'the size of the contribution provides a very rough index of the intensity of the contributor's support for the candidate,' and that '[a] contribution serves as a general expression of support for the candidate and his views, but does not communicate the underlying basis for the support,'—still rest on the proposition that speech by proxy is not fully protected. These contentions simply ignore that a contribution, by amplifying the voice of the candidate, helps to ensure the dissemination of the messages that the contributor wishes to convey. Absent the ability to rest on the denigration of contributions as mere 'proxy speech,' the arguments fall apart.

"The decision of individuals to speak through contributions rather than through independent expenditures is entirely reasonable.[4] Political campaigns are largely candidate focused and candidate driven. Citizens recognize that the best advocate for a candidate (and the policy positions he supports) tends to be the candidate himself. * * *

"In the end, *Buckley*'s claim that contribution limits 'd[o] not in any way infringe the contributor's freedom to discuss candidates and issues,' ignores the distinct role of candidate organizations as a means of individual participation in the Nation's civic dialogue. The result is simply the suppression of political speech. * * *

"In the case at hand, the Missouri scheme has a clear and detrimental effect on a candidate such as petitioner Fredman, who lacks the advantages of incumbency, name recognition, or substantial personal wealth, but who has managed to attract the support of a relatively small number of dedicated supporters: It forbids his message from reaching the voters. And the silencing of a candidate has consequences for political debate and competition overall. See *Arkansas Ed. Television Comm'n v. Forbes* (Stevens, J., dissenting) (noting that the suppression of a minor candidate's speech may directly affect the outcome of an election). * * *

"Apart from its endorsement of Buckley's rejection of the intermediate standards of review used to evaluate expressive conduct and time, place, and manner restrictions, the Court makes no effort to justify its deviation from the tests we traditionally employ in free speech cases. [After] hiding behind *Buckley's* discredited reasoning and invoking '*Buckley's* standard of scrutiny,' the Court proceeds to significantly extend the holding in that case. * * *

"The majority today [separates] 'corruption' from its quid pro quo roots and gives it a new, far-reaching (and speech-suppressing) definition, something like '[t]he perversion of anything from an original state of purity.' And the Court proceeds to define that state of purity, casting aspersions on 'politicians too compliant with the wishes of large contributors.' [Presumably], the majority does not mean that politicians should be free of attachments to constituent groups. And the majority does not explicitly rely upon the 'harm' that the Court in *Buckley* rejected out of hand, namely, that speech could be regulated to equalize the voices of citizens. Instead, without bothering to offer any elaboration, much less justification, the majority permits vague and unenumerated harms to suffice as a compelling reason for the government to smother political speech.

"In refashioning *Buckley*, the Court then goes on to weaken the requisite precision in tailoring, while at the same time representing that its fiat 'do [es] not

---

4. Justice Stevens asserts that "[m]oney is property; it is not speech," and contends that there is no First Amendment right "to hire mercenaries" and "to hire gladiators." These propositions are directly contradicted by many of our precedents. For example, in *Meyer v. Grant*, this Court confronted a state ban on payments to petition circulators [and] held that '[t]he refusal to permit appellees to pay petition circulators restricts political expression' by 'limit[ing] the number of voices who will convey appellees' message and the hours they can speak and, therefore, limits the size of the audience they can reach.' In short, the Court held that the First Amendment protects the right to pay others to help get a message out. In other cases, this Court extended such protection, holding that the First Amendment prohibits laws that do not ban, but instead only regulate, the terms upon which so-called mercenaries and gladiators are retained. See *Riley v. National Federation of Blind of N.C., Inc.* (holding that the First Amendment prohibits state restriction on the amount a charity may pay a professional fundraiser); *Chicago Teachers Union v. Hudson* (holding that the First Amendment restrains government-compelled exactions of money); *Abood v. Detroit Bd. of Ed.* (same). In these cases, the Court did not resort to Justice Stevens' assertion that money 'is not speech' to dismiss challenges to monetary regulations. Instead, the Court properly examined the impact of the regulations on free expression.

relax *Buckley*'s standard.' The fact is that the majority ratifies a law with a much broader sweep than that approved in *Buckley*. In *Buckley*, the Court upheld contribution limits of $1,000 on individuals and $5,000 on political committees (in 1976 dollars). Here, by contrast, the Court approves much more restrictive contribution limitations, ranging from $250 to $1,000 (in 1995 dollars) for both individuals and political committees. The disparity between Missouri's caps and those upheld in *Buckley* is more pronounced when one takes into account some measure of inflation. See *Shrink Missouri Government PAC v. Adams*, 161 F.3d 519, 523, and n. 4 (8th Cir. 1998) (noting that, according to the Consumer Price Index, a dollar today purchases about a third of what it did in 1976 when Buckley was decided). Yet the Court's opinion gives not a single indication that the two laws may differ in their tailoring. I cannot fathom how a $251 contribution could pose a substantial risk of 'secur [ing] a political quid pro quo.' Thus, contribution caps set at such levels could never be 'closely drawn' to preventing quid pro quo corruption. The majority itself undertakes no such defense. * * *

"Because the Court unjustifiably discounts the First Amendment interests of citizens and candidates, and consequently fails to strictly scrutinize the inhibition of political speech and competition, I respectfully dissent."

CON LAW: P. 1030, add to note 1(b)

AMER CON: P. 1015, add to note 1(b)

RTS & LIB: P. 937, add to note 1(b)

See also *Buckley v. American Constitutional Law Foundation*, 525 U.S. 182, 119 S.Ct. 636, 142 L.Ed.2d 599 (1999) (extending *Meyer* to a requirement that paid circulators be registered voters).

FREEDOM OF RELIGION

ESTABLISHMENT CLAUSE

FINANCIAL AID TO RELIGION

CON LAW: P. 1076, add at end of fn. b

AMER CON: P. 1053, add at end of fn. b

RTS & LIB: P. 983, add at end of fn. b

See *Agostini v. Felton*, below, holding that "later Establishment Clause cases have so undermined *Aguilar* that it is no longer good law."

CON LAW: P. 1077, at end

AMER CON: P. 1054, after *Zobrest*

RTS & LIB: P. 984, at end

AGOSTINI v. FELTON, 521 U.S. 203, 117 S.Ct. 1997, 138 L.Ed.2d 391 (1997), per O'CONNOR, J., "overruled *Aguilar* and those portions of *Grand Rapids* inconsistent with our most recent decisions." The case involved Title I of the Elementary and Secondary Education Act of 1965, the statute at issue in *Aguilar*. Congress enacted Title I "to 'provid[e] full educational opportunity to every child regardless of economic background.' Toward that end, Title I channels federal funds, through the States, to 'local educational agencies' (LEA's). The LEA's spend these funds to provide remedial education, guidance, and job counseling to eligible students. An eligible student is one (i) who resides within the attendance boundaries of a public school located in a low-income area; and (ii) who is failing, or is at risk of failing, the State's student performance standards. [T]he LEA must retain complete control over Title I funds; retain title to all materials used to provide Title I services; and provide those services through public employees or other persons independent of the private school and any religious institution. The Title I services themselves must be 'secular, neutral, and nonideological,' and must 'supplement, and in no case supplant, the level of services' already provided by the private school."

The plan in *Aguilar* "called for the provision of Title I services on private school premises during school hours. Under the plan, only public employees could serve as Title I instructors and counselors. Assignments to private schools were made on a voluntary basis and without regard to the religious affiliation of the employee or the wishes of the private school. [A] large majority of Title I teachers worked in nonpublic schools with religious affiliations different from their own [and] moved among the private schools, spending fewer than five days a week at the same school. [All] religious symbols were to be removed from classrooms used for Title I services. The rules acknowledged that it might be necessary for Title I teachers to consult with a student's regular classroom teacher to assess the student's particular needs and progress, but admonished instructors to limit those consultations to mutual professional concerns regarding the student's education. To ensure compliance with these rules, a publicly employed field supervisor was to attempt to make at least one unannounced visit to each teacher's classroom every month. * * *

"Our more recent cases have undermined the assumptions upon which *Grand Rapids* and *Aguilar* relied [respecting] whether aid to religion has an impermissible effect. * * * First, we have abandoned the presumption erected in *Meek* and *Grand Rapids* that the placement of public employees on parochial school grounds inevitably results in the impermissible effect of state-sponsored indoctrination[a] or constitutes a symbolic union between government and religion. [*Zobrest*][b] Second, we have departed from the rule relied on in *Grand Rapids* that all government aid that directly aids the educational function of religious schools is invalid. [*Witters*] [Moreover,] as in *Zobrest*, Title I services are by law supplemental to the regular curricula [and] do not, therefore, 'reliev[e] sectarian schools of costs they otherwise would have borne in educating their students.' [Further, no] Title I funds ever reach the coffers of religious schools. [Finally], where the aid is allocated on the basis of neutral, secular criteria that neither favor nor disfavor religion, and is made available to both religious and secular beneficiaries on a nondiscriminatory basis[, the] aid is less likely to have the effect of advancing religion. See *Widmar*."

[handwritten margin note: Not the controlling test but overall is in this case]

SOUTER, J., joined by Stevens, Ginsburg and Breyer, JJ., dissented: "Instead of aiding isolated individuals within a school system, New York City's Title I program before *Aguilar* served about 22,000 private school students, all but 52 of whom attended religious schools. Instead of serving individual blind or deaf students, as such, Title I as administered in New York City before *Aguilar* (and as now to be revived) funded instruction in core subjects (remedial reading, reading skills, remedial mathematics, English as a second language) and provided guidance services. Instead of providing a service the school would not otherwise furnish, the Title I services necessarily relieved a religious school of 'an expense that it otherwise would have assumed,' and freed its funds for other, and sectarian uses.

"Finally, [in] *Zobrest* and *Witters,* it was fair to say that individual students were themselves applicants for individual benefits on a scale that could not amount to a systemic supplement. But under Title I, a local educational agency (which in New York City is the Board of Education) may receive federal funding by proposing programs approved to serve individual students who meet the criteria of need, which it then uses to provide such programs at the religious schools."

CON LAW: P. 1085, add at end of Sec. II

AMER CON: P. 1059, add at end of Sec. II

RTS & LIB: P. 992, add at end of Sec. II

MITCHELL v. HELMS, ___ U.S. ___, 120 S.Ct. 2530, ___ L.Ed.2d ___ (2000), involved the federal government's "Chapter 2" loan of educational materials

a. "Since we have abandoned the assumption that properly instructed public employees will fail to discharge their duties faithfully, we must also discard the assumption that pervasive monitoring of Title I teachers is required. [Moreover,] we have not found excessive entanglement in cases in which States imposed far more onerous burdens on religious institutions than the monitoring system at issue here."

b. "We do not see any perceptible (let alone dispositive) difference in the degree of symbolic union between a student receiving remedial instruction in a classroom on his sectarian school's campus and one receiving instruction in a van parked just at the school's curbside. To draw this line based solely on the location of the public employee is neither 'sensible' nor 'sound.' "

(mainly for libraries and computers)—which could not "supplant funds from non-Federal sources"—to elementary and secondary schools. The "services, materials, and equipment" for participating private schools (which were required to be nonprofit) must be "secular, neutral and nonideological." There being no challenge to the program's "secular purpose" or its creation of "excessive entanglement," THOMAS, J., joined by Rehnquist, C.J., and Scalia and Kennedy, JJ.,—overruling *Meek* and *Wolman* (with the concurrence of O'Connor and Breyer, JJ., infra)—upheld it because, as stated in *Agostini*, "it neither results in religious indoctrination by the government nor defines its recipients by reference to religion. * * *

"As we indicated in *Agostini*, [the] question whether governmental aid to religious schools results in governmental indoctrination is ultimately a question whether any religious indoctrination that occurs in those schools could reasonably be attributed to governmental action. * * * We have also indicated that the answer to the question of indoctrination will resolve the question whether a program of educational aid 'subsidizes' religion, as our religion cases use that term.

"In distinguishing between indoctrination that is attributable to the State and indoctrination that is not, we have consistently turned to the principle of neutrality, upholding aid that is offered to a broad range of groups or persons without regard to their religion. If the religious, irreligious, and a religious are all alike eligible for governmental aid, no one would conclude that any indoctrination that any particular recipient conducts has been done at the behest of the government. [To] put the point differently, if the government, seeking to further some legitimate secular purpose, offers aid on the same terms, without regard to religion, to all who adequately further that purpose, then it is fair to say that any aid going to a religious recipient only has the effect of furthering that secular purpose. The government, in crafting such an aid program, has had to conclude that a given level of aid is necessary to further that purpose among secular recipients and has provided no more than that same level to religious recipients.

"As a way of assuring neutrality, we have repeatedly considered whether any governmental aid that goes to a religious institution does so 'only as a result of the genuinely independent and private choices of individuals.' [For] if numerous private choices, rather than the single choice of a government, determine the distribution of aid pursuant to neutral eligibility criteria, then a government cannot, or at least cannot easily, grant special favors that might lead to a religious establishment. Private choice also helps guarantee neutrality by mitigating the preference for pre-existing recipients that is arguably inherent in any governmental aid program, see, e.g., Gilder, *The Revitalization of Everything: The Law of the Microcosm*, Harv. Bus. Rev. 49 (Mar./Apr. 1988), and that could lead to a program inadvertently favoring one religion or favoring religious private schools in general over nonreligious ones. * * *

"*Agostini's* [second] criterion requires a court to consider whether an aid program 'define[s] its recipients by reference to religion' [—i.e.] whether the criteria for allocating the aid 'creat[e] a financial incentive to undertake religious indoctrination.' [For] to say that a program does not create an incentive to choose religious schools is to say that the private choice is truly 'independent.' When such an incentive does exist, there is a greater risk that one could attribute to the government any indoctrination by the religious schools.

"We hasten to add, what should be obvious from the rule itself, that simply because an aid program offers private schools, and thus religious schools, a benefit that they did not previously receive does not mean that the program, by reducing the cost of securing a religious education, creates, under *Agostini*'s second criterion, an 'incentive' for parents to choose such an education for their children. For any aid will have some such effect.

"Respondents [argue] first, and chiefly, that 'direct, nonincidental' aid to the primary educational mission of religious schools is always impermissible.[7]

"Although some of our earlier cases, particularly *Grand Rapids*, did emphasize the distinction between direct and indirect aid, the purpose of this distinction was merely to prevent 'subsidization' of religion. [*Agostini*] made clear that private choice and neutrality would resolve the concerns formerly addressed by the rule in *Grand Rapids*. It was undeniable in *Witters* that the aid (tuition) would ultimately go to the Inland Empire School of the Bible and would support religious education. We viewed this arrangement, however, as no different from a government issuing a paycheck to one of its employees knowing that the employee would direct the funds to a religious institution. Both arrangements would be valid * * *. Whether one chooses to label this program 'direct' or 'indirect' is a rather arbitrary choice, one that does not further the constitutional analysis.

"Of course, we have seen 'special Establishment Clause dangers,' *Rosenberger*, when money is given to religious schools or entities directly rather than, as in *Witters* and *Mueller*, indirectly.[8] But direct payments of money are not at issue in this case, and we refuse to allow a 'special' case to create a rule for all cases.

"Respondents also contend that the Establishment Clause requires that aid to religious schools not be impermissibly religious in nature or be divertible to religious use. We agree with the first part of this argument but not the second. Respondents' 'no divertibility' rule is inconsistent with our more recent case law and is unworkable. So long as the governmental aid is not itself 'unsuitable for use in the public schools because of religious content,' and eligibility for aid is determined in a constitutionally permissible manner, any use of that aid to indoctrinate cannot be attributed to the government and is thus not of constitutional concern [discussing *Zobrest* and *Witters*]. [J]ust as a government interpreter does not herself inculcate a religious message—even when she is conveying one—so also a government computer or overhead projector does not itself inculcate a religious message, even when it is conveying one.[9] * * *

7. Respondents also contend that Chapter 2 aid supplants, rather than supplements, the core educational function of parochial schools and therefore has the effect of furthering religion. Our case law does provide some indication that this distinction may be relevant to determining whether aid results in governmental indoctrination, but we have never delineated the distinction's contours or held that it is constitutionally required. Nor, [do] we need to resolve the distinction's constitutional status today, [for] Chapter 2 itself requires that aid may only be supplemental. * * *

8. The reason for such concern is not that the form per se is bad, but that such a form creates special risks that governmental aid will have the effect of advancing religion (or, even more, a purpose of doing so). An indirect form of payment reduces these risks. It is arguable, however, at least after *Witters*, that the principles of neutrality and private choice would be adequate to address those special risks, for it is hard to see the basis for deciding *Witters* differ-

ently simply if the State had sent the tuition check directly to whichever school Witters chose to attend. Similarly, we doubt it would be unconstitutional if, to modify *Witters*'s hypothetical, a government employer directly sent a portion of an employee's paycheck to a religious institution designated by that employee pursuant to a neutral charitable program. [Finally,] at least some of our prior cases striking down direct payments involved serious concerns about whether the payments were truly neutral. See, e.g., *Nyquist*.

9. The dissent would find an establishment of religion if a government-provided projector were used in a religious school to show a privately purchased religious film, even though a public school that possessed the same kind of projector would likely be constitutionally barred from refusing to allow a student bible club to use that projector in a classroom to show the very same film, where the classrooms and projectors were generally available to student groups. See *Lamb's Chapel*.

"A concern for divertibility, as opposed to improper content, is misplaced not only because it fails to explain why the sort of aid that we have allowed is permissible, but also because it is boundless—enveloping all aid, no matter how trivial—and thus has only the most attenuated (if any) link to any realistic concern for preventing an 'establishment of religion.' Presumably, for example, government-provided lecterns, chalk, crayons, pens, paper, and paintbrushes would have to be excluded from religious schools under respondents' proposed rule. But we fail to see how indoctrination by means of (i.e., diversion of) such aid could be attributed to the government. In fact, the risk of improper attribution is less when the aid lacks content, for there is no risk (as there is with books), of the government inadvertently providing improper content. See *Allen* (Douglas, J., dissenting). Finally, any aid, with or without content, is 'divertible' in the sense that it allows schools to 'divert' resources. Yet we have 'not accepted the recurrent argument that all aid is forbidden because aid to one aspect of an institution frees it to spend its other resources on religious ends.'

"It is perhaps conceivable that courts could take upon themselves the task of distinguishing among the myriad kinds of possible aid based on the ease of diverting each kind. But it escapes us how a court might coherently draw any such line. It not only is far more workable, but also is actually related to real concerns about preventing advancement of religion by government, simply to require, as did *Zobrest*, *Agostini*, and *Allen*, that a program of aid to schools not provide improper content and that it determine eligibility and allocate the aid on a permissible basis.

"The dissent serves up a smorgasbord of 11 factors that, depending on the facts of each case 'in all its particularity,' could be relevant to the constitutionality of a school-aid program. * * *

"One of the dissent's factors deserves special mention: whether a school that receives aid (or whose students receive aid) is pervasively sectarian. The dissent is correct that there was a period when this factor mattered, particularly if the pervasively sectarian school was a primary or secondary school. But that period is one that the Court should regret, and it is thankfully long past [discussing *Witters*, *Zobrest* and *Agostini*].

"[T]he religious nature of a recipient should not matter to the constitutional analysis, so long as the recipient adequately furthers the government's secular purpose. If a program offers permissible aid to the religious (including the pervasively sectarian), the areligious, and the irreligious, it is a mystery which view of religion the government has established, and thus a mystery what the constitutional violation would be. The pervasively sectarian recipient has not received any special favor, and it is most bizarre that the Court would, as the dissent seemingly does, reserve special hostility for those who take their religion seriously, who think that their religion should affect the whole of their lives, or who make the mistake of being effective in transmitting their views to children.

"[T]he inquiry into the recipient's religious views required by a focus on whether a school is pervasively sectarian is not only unnecessary but also offensive. It is well established, in numerous other contexts, that courts should refrain from trolling through a person's or institution's religious beliefs. [In] addition, and related, the application of the 'pervasively sectarian' factor collides with our decisions that have prohibited governments from discriminating in the distribution of public benefits based upon religious status or sincerity. See *Rosenberger*; *Lamb's Chapel*; *Widmar*.[19]

"Finally, hostility to aid to pervasively sectarian schools has a shameful pedigree * * *. Opposition to aid to 'sectarian' schools acquired prominence in the 1870's with Congress's consideration (and near passage) of the Blaine Amendment, which would have amended the Constitution to bar any aid to sectarian institutions. Consideration of the amendment arose at a time of pervasive hostility to the Catholic Church and to Catholics in general, and it was an open secret that 'sectarian' was code for 'Catholic.' Notwithstanding its history, of course, 'sectarian' could, on its face, describe the school of any religious sect, but the Court eliminated this possibility of confusion when, in *Hunt v. McNair*, it coined the term 'pervasively sectarian'—a term which, at that time, could be applied almost exclusively to Catholic parochial schools and which even today's dissent exemplifies chiefly by reference to such schools. [This] doctrine, born of bigotry, should be buried now. * * *

"[W]e agree with the dissent that there is evidence of actual diversion [in this case from Jefferson Parish, La.] and that, were the safeguards anything other than anemic, there would almost certainly be more such evidence. In any event, for reasons we discussed supra, the evidence of actual diversion and the weakness of the safeguards against actual diversion are not relevant to the constitutional inquiry * * *.

"Respondents do, however, point to some religious books that [were] improperly allowed to be loaned to several religious schools, and they contend that the monitoring programs [are] insufficient to prevent such errors. The evidence, however, establishes just the opposite, for the improper lending of library books occurred—and was discovered and remedied—before this litigation began almost 15 years [ago]. We are unwilling to elevate scattered de minimis statutory violations, discovered and remedied by the relevant authorities themselves prior to any litigation, to such a level as to convert an otherwise unobjectionable parish-wide program into a law that has the effect of advancing religion."

O'CONNOR, joined by Breyer, J., concurred in the judgment: "I write separately because, in my view, the plurality announces a rule of unprecedented breadth for the evaluation of Establishment Clause challenges to government school-aid programs. Reduced to its essentials, the plurality's rule states that government aid to religious schools does not have the effect of advancing religion so long as the aid is offered on a neutral basis and the aid is secular in content. [First,] the plurality's treatment of neutrality comes close to assigning that factor singular importance in the future adjudication of Establishment Clause challenges to government school-aid programs. Second, the plurality's approval of actual diversion of government aid to religious indoctrination is in tension with our precedents and, in any event, unnecessary to decide the instant case.

"[W]e have never held that a government-aid program passes constitutional muster solely because of the neutral criteria it employs as a basis for distributing aid. For example, in *Agostini*, neutrality was only one of several factors we considered * * *. I agree with Justice Souter's conclusion that our 'most recent use of 'neutrality' to refer to generality or evenhandedness of distribution [is] relevant in judging whether a benefit scheme so characterized should be seen as

---

19. Indeed, [to] require exclusion of religious schools from such a program would raise serious questions under the Free Exercise Clause. See, e.g., *Church of Lukumi Babalu Aye, Inc. v. Hialeah*, [Casebooks, infra]; *Everson*.

aiding a sectarian school's religious mission, but this neutrality is not alone sufficient to qualify the aid as constitutional.'

"[At] least two of the decisions at the heart of today's case [*Agostini* and *Allen*] demonstrate that we have long been concerned that secular government aid not be diverted to the advancement of religion. * * *

"The plurality bases its holding that actual diversion is permissible on *Witters* and *Zobrest*. Those decisions, however, rested [on] the understanding that the aid was provided directly to the individual student who, in turn, made the choice of where to put that aid to use. This characteristic of both programs made them less like a direct subsidy, which would be impermissible under the Establishment Clause, and more akin to the government issuing a paycheck to an employee who, in turn, donates a portion of that check to a religious institution. [Like] Justice Souter, I do not believe that we should treat a per-capita-aid program the same as the true private-choice programs considered in *Witters* and *Zobrest*. First, when the government provides aid directly to the student beneficiary, that student can attend a religious school and yet retain control over whether the secular government aid will be applied toward the religious education. The fact that aid flows to the religious school and is used for the advancement of religion is therefore wholly dependent on the student's private decision.

"Second, [i]n terms of public perception, a government program of direct aid to religious schools based on the number of students attending each school differs meaningfully from the government distributing aid directly to individual students who, in turn, decide to use the aid at the same religious schools. In the former example, if the religious school uses the aid to inculcate religion in its students, it is reasonable to say that the government has communicated a message of endorsement. Because the religious indoctrination is supported by government assistance, the reasonable observer would naturally perceive the aid program as government support for the advancement of religion. That the amount of aid received by the school is based on the school's enrollment does not separate the government from the endorsement of the religious message. The aid formula does not—and could not—indicate to a reasonable observer that the inculcation of religion is endorsed only by the individuals attending the religious school, who each affirmatively choose to direct the secular government aid to the school and its religious mission. No such choices have been made. In contrast, when government aid supports a school's religious mission only because of independent decisions made by numerous individuals to guide their secular aid to that [school,] endorsement of the religious message is reasonably attributed to the individuals who select the path of the aid.

"[If,] as the plurality contends, a per-capita-aid program is identical in relevant constitutional respects to a true private-choice program, then there is no reason that, under the plurality's reasoning, the government should be precluded from providing direct money payments to religious organizations (including churches) based on the number of persons belonging to each organization. And, because actual diversion is permissible under the plurality's holding, the participating religious organizations (including churches) could use that aid to support religious indoctrination. * * *

"[Under *Agostini*], we need ask only whether the program results in governmental indoctrination or defines its recipients by reference to religion. * * *

"The Chapter 2 program at issue here bears the same hallmarks of the New York City Title I program that we found important in *Agostini*. [First,] Chapter 2 aid is distributed on the basis of neutral, secular criteria. The aid is available to assist students regardless of whether they attend public or private nonprofit religious schools. [Second,] Chapter 2 funds must in no case be used to supplant funds from non-Federal sources. Third, no Chapter 2 funds ever reach the coffers of a religious school.[a] [Finally,] the statute provides that all Chapter 2 materials and equipment must be 'secular, neutral, and nonideological.' * * *

"Because divertibility fails to explain the distinction our cases have drawn between textbooks and instructional materials and equipment, there remains the question of which of the two irreconcilable strands of our Establishment Clause jurisprudence we should now follow. Between the two, I would adhere to the rule that we have applied in the context of textbook lending programs: To establish a First Amendment violation, plaintiffs must prove that the aid in question actually is, or has been, used for religious purposes. [In] *Agostini*, we repeatedly emphasized that it would be inappropriate to presume inculcation of religion; rather, plaintiffs raising an Establishment Clause challenge must present evidence that the government aid in question has resulted in religious indoctrination. * * *

"Respondents note that in *Agostini* we did not overrule that portion of *Grand Rapids* holding the Community Education program unconstitutional. Under that program, the government paid religious-school teachers to operate as part-time public teachers at their religious schools by teaching secular classes at the conclusion of the regular school day. Relying on both the majority opinion and my separate opinion in *Grand Rapids*, respondents therefore contend that we must presume that religious-school teachers will inculcate religion in their students. If that is so, they argue, we must also presume that religious-school teachers will be unable to follow secular restrictions on the use of instructional materials and equipment lent to their schools by the government.

"I disagree, however, that the latter proposition follows from the former. [When] a religious school receives textbooks or instructional materials and equipment lent with secular restrictions, the school's teachers need not refrain from teaching religion altogether. Rather, the instructors need only ensure that any such religious teaching is done without the instructional aids provided by the government. We have always been willing to assume that religious-school instructors can abide by such restrictions when the aid consists of textbooks. [The] same assumption should extend to instructional materials and equipment.

"For the same reason, my position in *Grand Rapids* is distinguishable. [In] that context, I was willing to presume that the religious-school teacher who works throughout the day to advance the school's religious mission would also do so, at least to some extent, during the supplemental classes provided at the end of the day. Because the government financed the entirety of such classes, any religious indoctrination taking place therein would be directly attributable to the government. In the instant case, because the Chapter 2 aid concerns only teaching tools that must remain supplementary, the aid comprises only a portion of the teacher's educational efforts during any single class.* * *

"The plurality and Justice Souter direct the primary thrust of their arguments at the alleged inadequacy of the program's safeguards. Respondents, the plurality, and Justice Souter all appear to proceed from the premise that, so long

a. O'Connor, J.'s opinion stated further: "[T]he most important reason for according special treatment to direct money grants is that this form of aid falls precariously close to the original object of the Establishment Clause's prohibition. Statements concerning the constitutionally suspect status of direct cash aid, accordingly, provide no justification for applying an absolute rule against divertibility when the aid consists instead of instructional materials and equipment."

as actual diversion presents a constitutional problem, the government must have a failsafe mechanism capable of detecting any instance of diversion. We rejected that very assumption, however, in *Agostini*. There, we explained that because we had 'abandoned the assumption that properly instructed public employees will fail to discharge their duties faithfully, we must also discard the assumption that pervasive monitoring of Title I teachers is required.' Because I believe that the Court should abandon the presumption adopted in *Meek* and *Wolman* respecting the use of instructional materials and equipment by religious-school teachers, I see no constitutional need for pervasive monitoring under the Chapter 2 program. * * *

"Justice Souter contends that any evidence of actual diversion requires the Court to declare the Chapter 2 program unconstitutional as applied in Jefferson Parish [but] I know of no case in which we have declared an entire aid program unconstitutional on Establishment Clause grounds solely because of violations on the miniscule scale of those at issue here."

SOUTER, J., joined by Stevens and Ginsburg, JJ., dissented: "In all the years of its effort, the Court has isolated no single test of constitutional sufficiency, and the question in every case [is]: what reasons are there to characterize this benefit as aid to the sectarian school in discharging its religious mission? Particular factual circumstances control, and the answer is a matter of judgment.

"[The] Court's decisions demonstrate its repeated attempts to isolate considerations relevant in classifying particular benefits as between those that do not discernibly support or threaten support of a school's religious mission, and those that cross or threaten to cross the line into support for religion.

"The most deceptively familiar of those considerations is 'neutrality' * * *.

"There is, of course, good reason for considering the generality of aid and the evenhandedness of its distribution in making close calls between benefits that in purpose or effect support a school's religious mission and those that do not. [T]he breadth of evenhanded distribution is one pointer toward the law's purpose, since on the face of it aid distributed generally and without a religious criterion is less likely to be meant to aid religion than a benefit going only to religious institutions or people. And, depending on the breadth of distribution, looking to evenhandedness is a way of asking whether a benefit can reasonably be seen to aid religion in fact; we do not regard the postal system as aiding religion, even though parochial schools get mail. Given the legitimacy of considering evenhandedness, then, there is no reason to avoid the term 'neutrality' to refer to it. But one crucial point must be borne in mind [:If] we looked no further than evenhandedness, and failed to ask what activities the aid might support, or in fact did support, religious schools could be blessed with government funding as massive as expenditures made for the benefit of their public school counterparts, and religious missions would thrive on public money. This is why the consideration of less than universal neutrality has never been recognized as dispositive and has always been teamed with attention to other facts bearing on the substantive prohibition of support for a school's religious objective.

"At least three main lines of enquiry addressed particularly to school aid have emerged to complement evenhandedness neutrality. First, we have noted that two types of aid recipients heighten Establishment Clause concern: pervasively religious schools and primary and secondary religious schools. Second, we have identified two important characteristics of the method of distributing aid: directness or indirectness of distribution and distribution by genuinely independent choice. Third, we have found relevance in at least five characteristics of the aid itself: its religious content; its cash form; its divertibility or actual diversion to religious support;[13] its supplantation of traditional items of religious school expense; and its substantiality. * * *

"The plurality, however, would reject that lesson. The majority misapplies it. * * *

"First, the plurality treats an external observer's attribution of religious support to the government as the sole impermissible effect of a government aid scheme. While perceived state endorsement of religion is undoubtedly a relevant concern under the Establishment Clause, it is certainly not the only [one.] State aid not attributed to the government would still violate a taxpayer's liberty of conscience, threaten to corrupt religion, and generate disputes over [aid.]¹⁹

"Second, the plurality apparently assumes as a fact that equal amounts of aid to religious and nonreligious schools will have exclusively secular and equal effects, on both external perception and on incentives to attend different schools. But there is no reason to believe that this will be the [case].

"Third, the plurality assumes that per capita distribution rules safeguard the same principles as independent, private choices. But [a] per capita aid program is a far cry from awarding scholarships to individuals, one of whom makes an independent private choice. Not the least of the significant differences [is] the right and genuine opportunity of the recipient to choose not to give the aid. To hold otherwise would be to license the government to donate funds to churches based on the number of their members, on the patent fiction of independent private choice. * * *

"The plurality's conception of evenhandedness does not, however, control the case, whose disposition turns on the misapplication of accepted categories of school aid analysis. The facts most obviously relevant to the Chapter 2 scheme in Jefferson Parish are those showing divertibility and actual diversion in the circumstance of pervasively sectarian religious schools. The type of aid, the structure of the program, and the lack of effective safeguards clearly demonstrate the divertibility of the aid. While little is known about its use, owing to the anemic enforcement system in the parish, even the thin record before us reveals that actual diversion occurred.

"[First,] the record shows actual diversion in the library book program. [D]iscovery revealed that under Chapter 2, nonpublic schools requested and the government purchased at least 191 religious books with taxpayer funds by December 1985. Books such as *A Child's Book of Prayers* and *The Illustrated Life of Jesus* were discovered among others that had been ordered under the program.

---

13. I reject the plurality's argument that divertibility is a boundless principle. Our long experience of evaluating this consideration demonstrates its practical limits. Moreover, the Establishment Clause charges us with making such enquiries, regardless of their difficulty. Finally, the First Amendment's rule permitting only aid with fixed secular content seems no more difficult to apply than the plurality's rule prohibiting only aid with fixed religious content.

19. Adopting the plurality's rule would permit practically any government aid to religion so long as it could be supplied on terms ostensibly comparable to the terms under which aid was provided to nonreligious recipients. As a principle of constitutional sufficiency, the manipulability of this rule is breathtaking. A legislature would merely need to state a secular objective in order to legalize massive aid to all religions, one religion, or even one sect, to which its largess could be directed through the easy exercise of crafting facially neutral terms under which to offer aid favoring that religious group. Short of formally replacing the Establishment Clause, a more dependable key to the public fisc or a cleaner break with prior law would be difficult to imagine.

"The evidence persuasively suggests that other aid was actually diverted as well. The principal of one religious school testified, for example, that computers lent with Chapter 2 funds were joined in a network with other non-Chapter 2 computers in some schools, and that religious officials and teachers were allowed to develop their own unregulated software for use on this network. She admitted that the Chapter 2 computer took over the support of the computing system whenever there was a breakdown of the master computer purchased with the religious school's own funds. [Moreover,] comparing the records of considerable federal funding of audiovisual equipment in religious schools with records of the schools' use of unidentified audiovisual equipment in religion classes strongly suggests that film projectors and videotape machines purchased with public funds were used in religious indoctrination over a period of at least seven years. [The] Court has no choice but to hold that the program as applied violated the Establishment Clause. [28]

"The plurality would break with the law. [Its] choice to employ imputations of bigotry and irreligion as terms in the Court's debate makes one point clear: that in rejecting the principle of no aid to a school's religious mission the plurality is attacking the most fundamental assumption underlying the Establishment Clause * * *."

OFFICIAL ACKNOWLEDGMENT OF RELIGION

CON LAW: P. 1101, at end of note 2

AMER CON: P. 1073, at end of note 2

RTS & LIB: P. 1008, at end of note 2

Prayer at other school activities—issues of government purpose and involvement. SANTA FE IND. SCHOOL DIST. v. DOE, ___ U.S. ___, 120 S.Ct. 2266, ___ L.Ed.2d ___ (2000), per STEVENS, J., relied on *Lee* to hold "invalid on its face" the school district's policy authorizing a student election (1) to determine whether to have a student "deliver a brief invocation and/or message [at] varsity football games to solemnize the event, to promote good sportsmanship and student safety, and to establish the appropriate environment for the competition," and (2) to select "a student volunteer who is [to] decide what statement or invocation to deliver, consistent with the goals and purposes of this policy. Any message and/or invocation delivered by a student must be nonsectarian and nonproselytizing." The Court found "the evolution of the current policy [to be] most striking," pointing to the earlier practice of having an elected "Student Chaplain [deliver] a prayer over the public address system before each varsity football game for the entire season," and to the title—"Prayer at Football Games"—of the most recent preceding policy, which was similar to the school's policy for prayer at graduations. The Court also emphasized the parties' stipulation that "the district's high school students voted to determine whether a student would deliver prayer at varsity football games," all of which led it "to infer that the specific purpose of the policy was to preserve a popular 'state-sponsored religious practice.'"

"[T]he District first argues that [the] messages are private student speech, not public speech. [But] these invocations are authorized by a government policy and take place on government property at government-sponsored school-related

---

28. Since the divertibility and diversion require a finding of unconstitutionality, I will not explore other grounds, beyond noting the like-lihood that unconstitutional supplantation occurred as well. * * *

events. [Unlike] the type of forum discussed in [*Rosenberger* and similar cases, here,] the school allows only one student, the same student for the entire season, to give the invocation. [T]he majoritarian process implemented by the District guarantees, by definition, that minority candidates will never prevail and that their views will be effectively silenced. [This] encourages divisiveness along religious lines in a public school setting, a result at odds with the Establishment Clause.

"[Further], the policy, by its terms, invites and encourages religious messages. The policy itself states that the purpose of the message is 'to solemnize the event.' A religious message is the most obvious method of solemnizing an event. Moreover, the requirements that the message 'promote good citizenship' and 'establish the appropriate environment for competition' further narrow the types of message deemed appropriate, suggesting that a solemn, yet nonreligious, message, such as commentary on United States foreign policy, would be prohibited. Indeed, the only type of message that is expressly endorsed in the text is an 'invocation'—a term that primarily describes an appeal for divine assistance. In fact, as used in the past at Santa Fe High School, an 'invocation' has always entailed a focused religious message. [In the context of a] broadcast over the school's public address system [at all varsity football games,] the members of the listening audience must perceive the pregame message as a public expression of the views of the majority of the student body delivered with the approval of the school administration."

As for the issue of "coercion," "we may assume that the District is correct in arguing that the informal pressure to attend an athletic event is not as strong as a senior's desire to attend her own graduation ceremony. [But] to assert that [many] high school students do not feel immense social pressure, or have a truly genuine desire, to be involved in the extracurricular event that is American high school football is 'formalistic in the extreme.' "

As for the District's argument of "premature facial challenge" because the policy had yet to be implemented: "Under the *Lemon* standard, a court must invalidate a statute if it lacks 'a secular legislative purpose.' [E]ven if no Santa Fe High School student were ever to offer a religious message, [the] attempt by the District to encourage prayer is also at issue. Government efforts to endorse religion cannot evade constitutional reproach based solely on the remote possibility that those attempts may fail."

REHNQUIST, C.J., joined by Scalia and Thomas, JJ., dissented: "Even if it were appropriate to apply the *Lemon* test here, the district's student-message policy should not be invalidated on its face. [I]t is possible that the students might vote not to have a pregame speaker, in which case there would be no threat of a constitutional violation. It is also possible that the election would not focus on prayer, but on public speaking ability or social popularity. And if student campaigning did begin to focus on prayer, the school might decide to implement reasonable campaign restrictions.

"[A]ny speech that may occur as a result of the election process here would be private, not government, speech. [Unlike *Lee*, the] elected student, not the government, would choose what to say. [A] newly elected prom king or queen, could use opportunities for public speaking to say prayers. Under the Court's view, the mere grant of power to the students to vote for such offices, in light of the fear that those elected might publicly pray, violates the Establishment

Clause.[a]

"[T]he Court dismisses the [policy's 'plausible secular purpose'] of solemnization.[b] [But] it is easy to think of solemn messages that are not religious in nature, for example urging that a game be fought fairly. And sporting events often begin with a solemn rendition of our national anthem, with its concluding verse 'And this be our motto: "In God is our trust." Under the Court's logic, a public school that sponsors the singing of the national anthem before football games violates the Establishment Clause.' "

FREE EXERCISE CLAUSE AND RELATED PROBLEMS

CONFLICT WITH STATE REGULATION

CON LAW: P. 1121, at end of 1st ¶

AMER CON: P. 1086, at end of 2d full ¶

RTS & LIB: P. 1028, at end of 1st ¶

[In *Boerne v. Flores*, p. 222 of this Supplement, O'Connor, J., joined by Breyer, J., argued that "the historical evidence [bears] out the conclusion that, at the time the Bill of Rights was ratified, it was accepted that government should, when possible, accommodate religious practice." Scalia, J., joined by Stevens, J., disagreed: "The historical evidence put forward by the dissent does nothing to undermine the conclusion we reached in *Smith*." For an extensive review, see Michael W. McConnell, *Freedom From Persecution or Protection of the Rights of Conscience?: A Critique of Justice Scalia's Historical Arguments*, 39 Wm. & M. L. Rev. 819 (1998)].

CON LAW: P. 1126, at end of note 3

AMER CON: P. 1090, at end of note 2

RTS & LIB: P. 1033, at end of note 3

RFRA was held unconstitutional in *Boerne v. Flores*, p. 222 of this Supplement.

a. The Court responded: "If instead of a choice between an invocation and no pregame message, the first election determined whether a political speech should be made, and the second election determined whether the speaker should be a Democrat or a Republican, it would be rather clear that the public address system was being used to deliver a partisan message reflecting the viewpoint of the majority rather than a random statement by a private individual."

"The fact that the District's policy provides for the election of the speaker only after the majority has voted on her message identifies an obvious distinction between this case and the typical election of a 'student body president, or even a newly elected prom king or queen.'

b. The Court responded: "When a governmental entity professes a secular purpose for an arguably religious policy, the government's characterization is, of course, entitled to some deference. But it is nonetheless the duty of the courts to 'distinguis[h] a sham secular purpose from a sincere one.' (O'Connor, J., concurring in judgment)."

EQUAL PROTECTION

RACE AND ETHNIC ANCESTRY

CON LAW: P. 1167, after fn.f
AMER CON: P. 1125, after note 2
RTS & LIB: P. 1074, after fn. f

DISCRIMINATION AGAINST RACIAL AND ETHNIC MINORITIES

RICE v. CAYETANO, __ U.S. __, 120 S.Ct. 1044, 145 L.Ed.3d 1007 (2000), per KENNEDY, J., invalidated Hawaii's granting only to "Hawaiians" (descendants of those inhabiting the Islands in 1778) the right to vote for trustees of a state agency that administers programs for "Hawaiians": "The ancestral inquiry mandated by the State implicates the same grave concerns as a classification specifying a particular race by name. One of the principal reasons race is treated as a forbidden classification is that it demeans the dignity and worth of a person to be judged by ancestry instead of by his or her own merit and essential qualities. An inquiry into ancestral lines is not consistent with respect based on the unique personality each of us possesses, a respect the Constitution itself secures in its concern for persons and citizens.

"The ancestral inquiry mandated by the State is forbidden by the Fifteenth Amendment for the further reason that the use of racial classifications is corruptive of the whole legal order democratic elections seek to preserve."

STEVENS, J., joined by Ginsburg, J., relying on *Morton v. Mancari,* dissented because of the "compelling similarity, fully supported by our precedent, between the once subjugated, indigenous peoples of the continental United States and the peoples of the Hawaiian Islands whose historical sufferings and status parallel those of the continental Native Americans."

DE JURE vs. DE FACTO DISCRIMINATION

CON LAW: P. 1184, before note 1(b)
AMER CON: P. 1091, before note 1(b)
RTS & LIB: P. 1138, before note 1(b)

Selective prosecution. In order to make out a prima facie case of intentional racial discrimination, UNITED STATES v. ARMSTRONG, 517 U.S. 456, 116 S.Ct. 1480, 134 L.Ed.2d 687 (1996), per REHNQUIST, C.J., reasoned that "the claimant must show that similarly situated individuals of a different race were not prosecuted." The fact (among several)[a] that all 24 defendants in "crack" cocaine cases

---

a. Defendants also submitted "an affidavit alleging that an intake coordinator at a drug treatment center had told her that there are 'an equal number of caucasian users and dealers to minority users and dealers,' [an] affidavit from a criminal defense attorney alleging closed by the Federal Public Defender in the previous year were black did not establish the defendants' "entitlement to discovery." STEVENS, J., dissented: "I am persuaded that the District Judge did not abuse her discretion when she concluded that the factual showing was sufficiently disturbing to require some response from the United States Attorney's Office."

REPEALS OF REMEDIES AND RESTRUCTURINGS OF THE POLITICAL PROCESS THAT BURDEN MINORITIES

CON LAW: P. 1226, after note 2

AMER CON: P. 1173, after note 2

RTS & LIB: P. 1133, after note 2

3. *Applicability to non-suspect classes.* *Romer v. Evans*, 517 U.S. 620, 116 S.Ct. 1620, 134 L.Ed.2d 855 (1996), included as a principal case p. 204 of this Supplement, invalidated an amendment to the Colorado constitution that forbade the state and its subdivisions to "enact, adopt or enforce any statute, regulation, ordinance or policy" protecting homosexuals against public or private discrimination. The amendment had the effect of nullifying several local ordinances and an executive order by the governor of Colorado, and the Colorado Supreme Court, whose judgement the Court affirmed, had relied on "precedents involving discriminatory restructuring of governmental decisionmaking" such as *Hunter v. Erickson* and *Washington v. Seattle School District No. 1*. But the Court, per KENNEDY, J., without further discussion of the Colorado Supreme Court's ground for decision, rested on the different rationale that the challenged amendment, which "declar[ed] that in general it shall be more difficult for one group of citizens than for all others to seek aid from the government," was too broad and undifferentiated to be rationally related to any legitimate state purpose. The amendment's very breadth "raise[d] the inevitable inference that the disadvantage imposed is born of animosity toward the class of persons affected." Scalia, J., joined by Rehnquist, C.J., and Thomas, J., dissented.

AFFIRMATIVE ACTION AND "BENIGN" DISCRIMINATION

CON LAW: P. 1244, at the end of note 7

AMER CON: P. 1190, at the end of note 7

RTS & LIB: P. 1151, at the end of note 7

In *Hopwood v. Texas*, 78 F.3d 932 (5th Cir.1996), the court of appeals, in invalidating an affirmative action plan implemented by the University of Texas Law School, explicitly rejected Justice Powell's *Bakke* opinion and held that the use of race as a factor in law school admissions was "per se proscribed." According to the two-judge majority, "Justice Powell's view in *Bakke* is not binding precedent," because much of his opinion "was joined by no other justice," and his argument in *Bakke* never garnered a majority. Did the court of appeals fail to account for the significance of Part V–C of Powell, J.'s *Bakke* opinion, which a majority of the Court did join?

The Supreme Court denied certiorari in *Hopwood* on the last day of its 1995 Term. 518 U.S. 1033, 116 S.Ct. 2580, 135 L.Ed.2d 1094 (1996). In a statement

[handwritten margin note: they changed the policy so its moot.]

that in his experience many nonblacks are prosecuted in state court for crack offenses, and a newspaper article reporting that Federal 'crack criminals [are] being punished far more severely than if they had been caught with powder cocaine, and almost every single one of them is black.' "

accompanying the denial, Ginsburg, J., joined by Souter, J., noted that the University of Texas Law School had announced its abandonment of the affirmative action program challenged in the lower courts, under which it evaluated minority applicants under separate processes and standards from those used to evaluate others. Although the Law School had propounded a new policy, which considers the race of minority applicants on a more individualized basis, that policy had not been a specific subject of the court of appeals' judgment. Although Texas officials challenged "the rationale relied on by the Court of Appeals," the Court "reviews judgments, not opinions." "Accordingly, we must await a final judgment on a program genuinely in controversy before addressing the important issue raised in this petition."

DISCRIMINATIONS BASED ON GENDER

DEFINING THE LEVEL OF SCRUTINY

CON LAW: P. 1279, after note 3

AMER CON: P. 1216, after note 3

RTS & LIB: P. 1186, after note 3

4. *Requirement of "an exceedingly persuasive justification."* In *United States v. Virginia*, 518 U.S. 515, 116 S.Ct. 2264, 135 L.Ed.2d 735 (1996), p. 197 of this Supplement, the Court, per Ginsburg, J., quoted the *Craig* formulation that gender-based classifications must serve "important governmental objectives" and be "substantially related to the achievement of those objectives." But the Court preceded its recitation of that standard with what it identified as the "core instruction of this Court's pathmarking decisions in *J.E.B. v. Alabama ex rel. T.B.*, [CON LAW, p. 1289, RTS & LIB, p. 1196] and *Mississippi Univ. for Women*, [CON LAW, p. 1295; AMER CON, p. 1226, RTS & LIB, p. 1202]: Parties who seek to defend gender-based government action must demonstrate an 'exceedingly persuasive justification' for that action." In holding that Virginia violated the Equal Protection Clause by excluding women from the Virginia Military Institute, the Court repeatedly invoked the "exceedingly persuasive justification" requirement. Rehnquist, C.J., who concurred in the judgment only, specifically objected that the Court introduced "an element of uncertainty" in equal protection doctrine by relying on this new formulation. Scalia, J., who dissented, protested that no authority supported departure from the *Craig* standard—which, he argued, the state of Virginia had met, since provision of all-male education via the "adversative" method was "substantially related" to the "important" state interest in educational diversity.[a]

DIFFERENCES—REAL AND IMAGINED

CON LAW: P. 1288, at the end of note 5

AMER CON: P. 1221, after Geduldig v. Aiello

RTS & LIB: P. 1195, at the end of note 5

MILLER v. ALBRIGHT, 523 U.S. 420, 118 S.Ct. 1428, 140 L.Ed.2d 575 (1998), upheld a provision of the Immigration and Naturalization Act that provides automatic naturalization for illegitimate children who are born abroad to mothers who are American citizens, but establishes various procedural require-

a. Thomas, J., took no part.

ments, which must be completed before the child turns 18 or 21, for the illegitimate children of citizen fathers and non-citizen mothers, such as the plaintiff Miller, to become American citizens. STEVENS, J., announcing the judgment of the Court in an opinion that was joined only by Rehnquist, C.J, found that the statute distinguished unmarried fathers from unmarried mothers based on gender, but was justified by important governmental interests. Although Stevens, J., concluded that deference to the political branches' immigration powers dictated a narrow standard of review, he believed that the statute would also survive "the heightened scrutiny that normally governs gender discrimination claims." SCALIA, J., joined by Thomas, J., concurred that the plaintiff's claim must fail, but did not reach the question whether the statute worked an unconstitutional discrimination: "The complaint must be dismissed because the Court has no power to provide the relief requested: conferral of citizenship on a basis other than that prescribed by Congress." O'CONNOR, J., joined by Kennedy, J., also concurred in the judgment, on the ground that the statutory distinction between children of illegitimate mothers and children of illegitimate fathers was supported by a rational basis. According to O'Connor, J., rational basis review applied because the plaintiff—an illegitimate child claiming citizenship—lacked standing to assert the rights of fathers of illegitimate children to be free from gender-based discrimination in transferring citizenship to their offspring. Although upholding the provision under a rational basis standard, O'Connor and Kennedy, JJ., did "not share Justice Stevens' assessment that the [challenged] provision withstands heightened scrutiny." BREYER, J., joined by Souter and Ginsburg, JJ., believed that the statute did discriminate on the basis of gender, reasoned that heightened scrutiny therefore applied, and concluded that the statutory discrimination should be invalidated. Noting that O'Connor and Kennedy, JJ., had also opined that the statute could not withstand heightened scrutiny (if heightened scrutiny were properly brought to bear), Breyer, J., concluded that "a majority of the Court agrees [that] '[i]t is unlikely [that] any gender classifications based on stereotypes can survive heightened scrutiny.'" If Breyer, J., is correct, have *Parham v. Hughes* and *Lehr v. Robertson* ceased to be good law?

CON LAW: P. 1291, after J.E.B.

AMER CON: P. 1221, after Notes and Questions

RTS & LIB: P. 1178, after J.E.B.

UNITED STATES v. VIRGINIA

518 U.S. 515, 116 S.Ct. 2264, 135 L.Ed.2d 735 (1996).

JUSTICE GINSBURG delivered the opinion of the Court.

Virginia's public institutions of higher learning include an incomparable military college, Virginia Military Institute (VMI). The United States maintains that the Constitution's equal protection guarantee precludes Virginia from reserving exclusively to men the unique educational opportunities VMI affords. We agree.

Founded in 1839, VMI is today the sole single-sex school among Virginia's 15 public institutions of higher learning. VMI's distinctive mission is to produce "citizen-soldiers." [Assigning] prime place to character development, VMI uses an "adversative method" modeled on English public schools and once characteristic of military instruction. [This model] features "physical rigor, mental stress, absolute equality of treatment, absence of privacy, minute regulation of behavior, and indoctrination in desirable values." [VMI] cadets live in spartan barracks where surveillance is constant and privacy nonexistent. [Entering] students are incessantly exposed to the rat line, "an extreme form of the adversative model," [which] bonds new cadets to their fellow sufferers and, when they have completed the 7–month experience, to their former tormentors.

In 1990, prompted by a complaint filed with the Attorney General by a female high-school student seeking admission to VMI, the United States sued the Commonwealth of Virginia and VMI, alleging that VMI's exclusively male admission policy violated the Equal Protection Clause of the Fourteenth Amendment. [The district court upheld the policy, but the court of appeals reversed, finding an equal protection violation. Following the remand, the state of Virginia proposed a remedial plan, under which the state would adopt] a parallel program for women: Virginia Women's Institute for Leadership (VWIL). The 4–year, state-sponsored undergraduate program would be located at Mary Baldwin College, a private liberal arts school for women, and would be open, initially, to about 25 to 30 students. Although VWIL would share VMI's mission—to produce "citizen-soldiers"—the VWIL program would differ, as does Mary Baldwin College, from VMI in academic offerings, methods of education, and financial resources.

The average combined SAT score of entrants at Mary Baldwin is about 100 points lower than the score for VMI freshmen. [While] VMI offers degrees in liberal arts, the sciences, and engineering, Mary Baldwin, at the time of trial, offered only bachelor of arts degrees. [Under the proposed remedial plan,] VWIL students would participate in ROTC programs [but in] lieu of VMI's adversative method, [VWIL would offer] "a cooperative method which reinforces self-esteem."

Virginia represented that it will provide equal financial support for in-state VWIL students and VMI cadets, and the VMI Foundation agreed to supply a $5.4625 million endowment for the VWIL program. Mary Baldwin's own endowment is about $19 million; VMI's is $131 million. Mary Baldwin will add $35 million to its endowment based on future commitments; VMI will add $220 million.

[Both the district court and the court of appeals held that the proposed remedial plan satisfied the Equal Protection Clause.]

The cross-petitions in this case present two ultimate issues. First, does Virginia's exclusion of women from the educational opportunities provided by VMI—extraordinary opportunities for military training and civilian leadership development—deny to women "capable of all of the individual activities required of VMI cadets," the equal protection of the laws guaranteed by the Fourteenth Amendment? Second, if VMI's "unique" situation—as Virginia's sole single-sex public institution of higher education—offends the Constitution's equal protection principle, what is the remedial requirement?

We note, once again, the core instruction of this Court's pathmarking decisions in *J.E.B. v. Alabama ex rel. T.B.*, [CON LAW p. 1289; RTS & LIB. p. 1196] and *Mississippi Univ. for Women*, [CON LAW p. 1295; AMER CON p. 1226; RTS & LIB p. 1202]: Parties who seek to defend gender-based government action must demonstrate an "exceedingly persuasive justification" for that action. [The] burden of justification is demanding and it rests entirely on the State. The State must show "at least that the [challenged] classification serves 'important governmental objectives and that the discriminatory means employed' are 'substantially related to the achievement of those objectives.'" The justification must be genuine, not hypothesized or invented post hoc in response to litigation. And it must not rely on overbroad generalizations about the different talents, capacities, or preferences of males and females.

The heightened review standard our precedent establishes does not make sex a proscribed classification. Supposed "inherent differences" are no longer accepted as a ground for race or national origin classifications. See *Loving v. Virginia*. Physical differences between men and women, however, are enduring. [Sex] classifications may be used to compensate women "for particular economic disabilities [they have] suffered," *Califano v. Webster*, [CON LAW p. 1293, AMER CON p. 1223, RTS & LIB p. 1200], to "promote equal employment opportunity," see *California Federal Sav. & Loan Assn. v. Guerra*, [CON LAW p. 1298, AMER CON p. 1228, RTS & LIB p. 1205], [and] to advance full development of the talent and capacities of our Nation's people.[7] But such classifications may not be used, as they once were, to create or perpetuate the legal, social, and economic inferiority of women. [Measuring] the record in this case against the review standard just described, we conclude that Virginia has shown no "exceedingly persuasive justification" for excluding all women from the citizen-soldier training afforded by VMI.

[Single-sex] education affords pedagogical benefits to at least some students, Virginia emphasizes, and that reality is uncontested in this litigation. Similarly, it is not disputed that diversity among public educational institutions can serve the public good. But Virginia has not shown that VMI was established, or has been maintained, with a view to diversifying, by its categorical exclusion of women, educational opportunities within the State. In cases of this genre, our precedent instructs that "benign" justifications proffered in defense of categorical exclusions will not be accepted automatically; a tenable justification must describe actual state purposes, not rationalizations for actions in fact differently grounded.

[Neither] recent nor distant history bears out Virginia's alleged pursuit of diversity through single-sex educational options. In 1839, when the State established VMI, a range of educational opportunities for men and women was scarcely contemplated. [In] admitting no women, VMI followed the lead of [the] University of Virginia, founded in 1819. [Beginning in 1894,] Virginia eventually provided for several women's seminaries and colleges. [By] the mid–1970's, [however,] all [had] become coeducational. [The] University of Virginia introduced coeducation [in 1970] and, in 1972, began to admit women on an equal basis with men.

Virginia describes the current absence of public single-sex higher education for women as "an historical anomaly." But the historical record indicates action more deliberate than anomalous: First, protection of women against higher education; next, schools for women far from equal in resources and stature to schools for men; finally, conversion of the separate schools to coeducation. [In] sum, we find no persuasive evidence in this record that VMI's male-only admission policy "is in furtherance of a state policy of 'diversity.' "

[Virginia] next argues that VMI's adversative method of training provides educational benefits that cannot be made available, unmodified, to women. Alterations to accommodate women would necessarily be "radical," so "drastic,"

7. Several amici have urged that diversity in educational opportunities is an altogether appropriate governmental pursuit and that single-sex schools can contribute importantly to such diversity. Indeed, it is the mission of some single-sex schools "to dissipate, rather than perpetuate, traditional gender classifications." We do not question the State's prerogative evenhandedly to support diverse educational opportunities. We address specifically and only an educational opportunity recognized by the District Court and the Court of Appeals as "unique," an opportunity available only at Virginia's premier military institute, the State's sole single-sex public university or college.

Virginia asserts, as to transform, indeed "destroy," VMI's program. [The] District Court [found] that coeducation would materially affect "at least these three aspects of VMI's program—physical training, the absence of privacy, and the adversative approach." And it is uncontested that women's admission would require accommodations, primarily in arranging housing assignments and physical training programs for female cadets. It is also undisputed, however, that "the VMI methodology could be used to educate women."

The notion that admission of women would downgrade VMI's stature, destroy the adversative system and, with it, even the school, is a judgment hardly proved, a prediction hardly different from other "self-fulfilling prophecies" once routinely used to deny rights or opportunities. [Women's] successful entry into the federal military academies, and their participation in the Nation's military forces, indicate that Virginia's fears for the future of VMI may not be solidly grounded. [Virginia], in sum, "has fallen far short of establishing the 'exceedingly persuasive justification'" that must be the solid base for any gender-defined classification.

In the second phase of the litigation, Virginia presented its remedial plan—maintain VMI as a male-only college and create VWIL as a separate program for women.

[Having] violated the Constitution's equal protection requirement, Virginia was obliged to show that its remedial proposal "directly addressed and related to" the violation, i.e., the equal protection denied to women ready, willing, and able to benefit from educational opportunities of the kind VMI offers. Virginia described VWIL as a "parallel program," and asserted that VWIL shares VMI's mission of producing "citizen-soldiers" and VMI's goals of providing "education, military training, mental and physical discipline, character * * * and leadership development." [But] VWIL affords women no opportunity to experience the rigorous military training for which VMI is famed. Instead, the VWIL program "deemphasizes" military education, and uses a "cooperative method" of education "which reinforces self-esteem."

[Virginia] maintains that these methodological differences are "justified pedagogically," based on "important differences between men and women in learning and developmental needs," "psychological and sociological differences" Virginia describes as "real" and "not stereotypes." [As] earlier stated, [however], generalizations about "the way women are," estimates of what is appropriate for most women, no longer justify denying opportunity to women whose talent and capacity place them outside the average description. "[S]ome women, at least, would want to attend [VMI] if they had the opportunity"; "some women are capable of all of the individual activities required of VMI cadets" and "can meet the physical standards [VMI] now imposes on men". It is [for] these women [that] a remedy must be crafted.[19]

[In] myriad respects other than military training, VWIL does not qualify as VMI's equal. VWIL's student body, faculty, course offerings, and facilities hardly match VMI's. Nor can the VWIL graduate anticipate the benefits associated with VMI's 157–year history, the school's prestige, and its influential alumni network.

[Virginia's] VWIL solution is reminiscent of the remedy Texas proposed 50 years ago, in response to a state trial court's 1946 ruling that, given the equal protection guarantee, African Americans could not be denied a legal education at a

---

19. Admitting women to VMI would undoubtedly require alterations necessary to afford members of each sex privacy from the other sex in living arrangements, and to adjust aspects of the physical training programs. Experience [at the United States military academies] shows such adjustments are manageable.

state facility. See *Sweatt v. Painter,* [CON LAW p. 1172, AMER CON p. 1129, RTS & LIB p. 1079]. Reluctant to admit African Americans to its flagship University of Texas Law School, the State set up a separate school for Herman Sweatt and other black law students. [This] Court contrasted resources at the new school with those at the school from which Sweatt had been excluded [and held that] the Equal Protection Clause required Texas to admit African Americans to the University of Texas Law School. In line with *Sweatt,* we rule here that Virginia has not shown substantial equality in the separate educational opportunities the State supports at VWIL and VMI. * * *

JUSTICE THOMAS took no part in the consideration or decision of this case.

CHIEF JUSTICE REHNQUIST, concurring in the judgment.

Two decades ago in *Craig v. Boren,* we announced that "to withstand constitutional challenge, * * * classifications by gender must serve important governmental objectives and must be substantially related to achievement of those objectives." [While] the majority adheres to this test today, it also says that the State must demonstrate an " 'exceedingly persuasive justification' " to support a gender-based classification. [To] avoid introducing potential confusion, I would have adhered more closely to our traditional [standard].

[I] agree with the Court that there is scant evidence in the record that [diversity] was the real reason that Virginia decided to maintain VMI as men only. [Even] if diversity in educational opportunity were the State's actual objective, [however,] the State's position would still be problematic. The difficulty [is] that the diversity benefited only one sex.

[Virginia] offers a second justification for the single-sex admissions policy: maintenance of the adversative method. [But a] State does not have substantial interest in the adversative methodology unless it is pedagogically beneficial. While considerable evidence shows that a single-sex education is pedagogically beneficial for some students, and hence a State may have a valid interest in promoting that methodology, there is no similar evidence in the record that an adversative method is pedagogically beneficial or is any more likely to produce character traits than other methodologies.

The Court defines the constitutional violation in this case as "the categorical exclusion of women from an extraordinary educational opportunity afforded to men." By defining the violation in this way, [the] Court necessarily implies that the only adequate remedy would be the admission of women to the all-male institution. [I] would not define the violation in this way; it is not the "exclusion of women" that violates the Equal Protection Clause, but the maintenance of an all-men school without providing any—much less a comparable—institution for women. * * *

JUSTICE SCALIA, dissenting.

* * * Much of the Court's opinion is devoted to deprecating the closed-mindedness of our forebears with regard to women's education, and even with regard to the treatment of women in areas that have nothing to do with education. Closed-minded they were—as every age is, including our own, with regard to matters it cannot guess, because it simply does not consider them debatable. The virtue of a democratic system with a First Amendment is that it readily enables the people, over time, to be persuaded that what they took for granted is not so, and to change their laws accordingly. That system is destroyed if the smug assurances of each age are removed from the democratic process and written into the Constitution. So to counterbalance the Court's criticism of our

Scalia is really mad

ancestors, let me say a word in their praise: they left us free to change. The same cannot be said of this most illiberal Court, which has embarked on a course of inscribing one after another of the current preferences of the society (and in some cases only the counter-majoritarian preferences of the society's law-trained elite) into our Basic Law. Today it enshrines the notion that no substantial educational value is to be served by an all-men's military academy—so that the decision by the people of Virginia to maintain such an institution denies equal protection to women who cannot attend that institution but can attend others.

[In] my view the function of this Court is to preserve our society's values regarding (among other things) equal protection, not to revise them. [Whatever] abstract tests we may choose to devise, they cannot supersede—and indeed ought to be crafted so as to reflect—those constant and unbroken national traditions that embody the people's understanding of ambiguous constitutional texts. More specifically, it is my view that "when a practice not expressly prohibited by the text of the Bill of Rights bears the endorsement of a long tradition of open, widespread, and unchallenged use that dates back to the beginning of the Republic, we have no proper basis for striking it down."

p.c trend vs. tradition

The all-male constitution of VMI comes squarely within such a governing tradition. For almost all of VMI's more than a century and a half of existence, its single-sex status reflected the uniform practice for government-supported military colleges.

[To] reject the Court's disposition today, however, it is [only] necessary to apply honestly the test the Court has been applying to sex-based classifications for the past two decades. [Only] the amorphous "exceedingly persuasive justification" phrase, and not the standard elaboration of intermediate scrutiny, can be made to yield [the] conclusion that VMI's single-sex composition is unconstitutional because there exist several women (or, one would have to conclude under the Court's reasoning, a single woman) willing and able to undertake VMI's program. Intermediate scrutiny has never required a least-restrictive-means analysis, but only a "substantial relation" between the classification and the state interests that it serves.

[It] is beyond question that Virginia has an important state interest in providing effective college education for its citizens. That single-sex instruction is an approach substantially related to that interest should be evident enough from the long and continuing history in this country of men's and women's colleges. But beyond that, [there was] "virtually uncontradicted" [expert evidence introduced in this case tending to show the benefits of single-sex education].

[Besides] its single-sex constitution, VMI [employs] a "distinctive educational method," sometimes referred to as the "adversative, or doubting, model of education." [It] was uncontested that "if the state were to establish a women's VMI-type [i.e., adversative] program, the program would attract an insufficient number of participants to make the program work"; and it was found by the District Court that if Virginia were to include women in VMI, the school "would eventually find it necessary to drop the adversative system altogether." Thus, Virginia's options were an adversative method that excludes women or no adversative method at all.

There can be no serious dispute that single-sex education and a distinctive educational method "represent legitimate contributions to diversity in the Virginia higher education system." As a theoretical matter, Virginia's educational interest would have been best served (insofar as the two factors we have mentioned are concerned) by six different types of public colleges—an all-men's, an all-women's, and a coeducational college run in the "adversative method," and an all-men's, an all-women's, and a coeducational college run in the "traditional method." But as a practical matter, of course, Virginia's financial resources, like any State's, are not limitless, and the Commonwealth must select among the available options. [In] these circumstances, Virginia's election to fund one public all-male institution and one on the adversative model—and to concentrate its resources in a single entity that serves both these interests in diversity—is substantially related to the State's important educational interests.

[The] Court argues that VMI would not have to change very much if it were to admit women. The principal response to that argument is that it is irrelevant: If VMI's single-sex status is substantially related to the government's important educational objectives, as I have demonstrated above and as the Court refuses to discuss, that concludes the inquiry. [But] if such a debate were relevant, the Court would certainly be on the losing side.

[Finally], the absence of a precise "all-women's analogue" to VMI is irrelevant. [VWIL] was carefully designed by professional educators who have long experience in educating young women. [None] of the United States' own experts in the remedial phase of this case was willing to testify that VMI's adversative method was an appropriate methodology for educating women.

[The] Court's decision today will have consequences that extend far beyond the parties to the case. [Under] the constitutional principles announced and applied today, single-sex public education is unconstitutional. [Although] the Court [purports] to have said nothing of relevance to other public schools [and to have considered] only an educational opportunity recognized * * * as "unique," [footnote 7, supra] * * * I suggest that the single-sex program that will not be capable of being characterized as "unique" is not only unique but nonexistent.

[A broader] potential of today's decision for widespread disruption of existing institutions lies in its application to private single-sex education. Government support is immensely important to private educational institutions. [When government funding is challenged, the] issue will be not whether government assistance turns private colleges into state actors, but whether the government itself would be violating the Constitution by providing state support to single-sex colleges. For example, in *Norwood v. Harrison*, [CON LAW p. 1446, AMER CON p. 1364, RTS & LIB p. 1353], we saw no room to distinguish between state operation of racially segregated schools and state support of privately run segregated schools. [The] only hope for state-assisted single-sex private schools is that the Court will not apply in the future the principles of law it has applied today.
* * *

"BENIGN"—"COMPENSATORY"—"REMEDIAL" DISCRIMINATION

CON LAW: P. 1295, at end of note 3

AMER CON: P. 1225, at end of note 3

RTS & LIB: P. 1202, at end of note 3

Consider the relevance to these questions of *United States v. Virginia*, p. 197 of this Supplement.

CON LAW: P. 1298, at end of note 1

AMER CON: P. 1228, at end of note 1

RTS & LIB: P. 1204, at end of note 1

Does *United States v. Virginia*, p. 197 of this Supplement, establish that single-gender education is never permissible? Compare footnote 7 of the majority opinion with the assertions of Scalia, J., dissenting.

SPECIAL SCRUTINY FOR OTHER CLASSIFICATIONS

OTHER, CHALLENGED BASES FOR DISCRIMINATION

CON LAW: P. 1306, at the end of note 5(a)

AMER CON: P. 1237, at the end of note 5(a)

RTS & LIB: P. 1213, at the end of note 5(a)

See also *Reno v. American–Arab Anti–Discrimination Committee*, 525 U.S. 471, 119 S.Ct. 936, 142 L.Ed.2d 940 (1999) (finding that no constitutional issue was presented by a statute denying illegal aliens a forum in which to challenge their impending deportations on "selective enforcement" grounds, because "an alien unlawfully in this country [generally] has no constitutional right" to freedom from selective enforcement).

CON LAW: P. 1321, after note 2

AMER CON: P. 1251, after note 2

RTS & LIB: P. 1228, after note 2

ROMER v. EVANS

517 U.S. 620, 116 S.Ct. 1620, 134 L.Ed.2d 855 (1996).

JUSTICE KENNEDY delivered the opinion of the Court.

One century ago, the first Justice Harlan admonished this Court that the Constitution "neither knows nor tolerates classes among citizens." *Plessy v. Ferguson* (dissenting opinion). Unheeded then, those words are now understood to state a commitment to the law's neutrality where the rights of persons are at stake. The Equal Protection Clause enforces this principle and today requires us to hold invalid a provision of Colorado's Constitution.

* * * The enactment challenged in this case is an amendment to the Constitution of the State of Colorado, adopted in a 1992 statewide referendum [and referred to] as "Amendment 2," its designation when submitted to the voters. [The] amendment reads: "No Protected Status Based on Homosexual, Lesbian, or Bisexual Orientation. Neither the State of Colorado, through any of its branches or departments, nor any of its agencies, political subdivisions, municipalities or school districts, shall enact, adopt or enforce any statute, regulation, ordinance or policy whereby homosexual, lesbian or bisexual orientation, conduct, practices or relationships shall constitute or otherwise be the basis of or entitle any person or class of persons to have or claim any minority status, quota preferences, protected status or claim of discrimination. This Section of the Constitution shall be in all respects self-executing."

[The] State's principal argument in defense of Amendment 2 is that it puts gays and lesbians in the same position as all other persons. So, the State says, the measure does no more than deny homosexuals special rights. This reading of the amendment's language is implausible. We rely not upon our own interpretation of the amendment but upon the authoritative construction of Colorado's Supreme Court, [which held that] "The immediate objective of Amendment 2 is, at a minimum, to repeal existing statutes, regulations, ordinances, and policies of state and local entities that barred discrimination based on sexual orientation." [Under Amendment 2 as thus construed, homosexuals], by state decree, are put in a solitary class with respect to transactions and relations in both the private and governmental spheres. The amendment withdraws from homosexuals, but no others, specific legal protection from the injuries caused by discrimination, and it forbids reinstatement of these laws and policies.

The change that Amendment 2 works in the legal status of gays and lesbians in the private sphere is far-reaching, both on its own terms and when considered in light of the structure and operation of modern antidiscrimination laws. That structure is well illustrated by contemporary statutes and ordinances prohibiting discrimination by providers of public accommodations. "At common law, innkeepers, smiths, and others who 'made profession of a public employment,' were prohibited from refusing, without good reason, to serve a customer." The duty was a general one and did not specify protection for particular groups. The common law rules, however, proved insufficient in many instances, and [most] States have chosen to counter discrimination by enacting detailed statutory schemes.

Colorado's state and municipal laws typify this emerging tradition of statutory protection and follow a consistent pattern. The laws first enumerate the persons or entities subject to a duty not to discriminate. The list goes well beyond the entities covered by the common law. The Boulder ordinance, for example, has a comprehensive definition of entities deemed places of "public accommodation." They include "any place of business engaged in any sales to the general public and any place that offers services, facilities, privileges, or advantages to the general public or that receives financial support through solicitation of the general public or through governmental subsidy of any kind."

These statutes and ordinances also depart from the common law by enumerating the groups or persons within their ambit of protection. [In] following this approach, Colorado's state and local governments have not limited anti-discrimination laws to groups that have so far been given the protection of heightened equal protection scrutiny under our cases. Rather, they set forth an extensive catalogue of traits which cannot be the basis for discrimination, including age, military status, marital status, pregnancy, parenthood, custody of a minor child, political affiliation, physical or mental disability of an individual or of his or her associates—and, in recent times, sexual orientation.

Amendment 2 bars homosexuals from securing protection against the injuries that these public-accommodations laws address. That in itself is a severe consequence, but there is more. Amendment 2, in addition, nullifies specific legal protections for this targeted class in all transactions in housing, sale of real estate, insurance, health and welfare services, private education, and employment.

[Not] confined to the private sphere, Amendment 2 also operates to repeal and forbid all laws or policies providing specific protection for gays or lesbians from discrimination by every level of Colorado government. The State Supreme Court cited two examples of protections in the governmental sphere that are now rescinded and may not be reintroduced. The first is [an] Executive Order which forbids employment discrimination against " 'all state employees, classified and exempt' on the basis of sexual orientation." Also repealed, and now forbidden, are "various provisions prohibiting discrimination based on sexual orientation at state colleges."

Amendment 2's reach may not be limited to specific laws passed for the benefit of gays and lesbians. It is a fair, if not necessary, inference from the broad language of the amendment that it deprives gays and lesbians even of the protection of general laws and policies that prohibit arbitrary discrimination [such as statutes subjecting agency action to judicial review under the arbitrary and capricious standard and making it a criminal offense for a public servant knowingly, arbitrarily, or capriciously to refrain from performing a duty imposed by law]. At some point in the systematic administration of these laws, an official must determine whether homosexuality is an arbitrary and thus forbidden basis for decision. Yet a decision to that effect would itself amount to a policy prohibiting discrimination on the basis of homosexuality, and so would appear to be no more valid under Amendment 2 than the specific prohibitions against discrimination the state court held invalid.

[The] state court did not decide whether the amendment has this effect, however, and neither need we. [Even] if, as we doubt, homosexuals could find some safe harbor in laws of general application, we cannot accept the view that Amendment 2's prohibition on specific legal protections does no more than deprive homosexuals of special rights. To the contrary, the amendment imposes a special disability upon those persons alone. Homosexuals are forbidden the safeguards that others enjoy or may seek without constraint. They can obtain specific protection against discrimination only by enlisting the citizenry of Colorado to amend the state constitution or perhaps, on the State's view, by trying to pass helpful laws of general applicability. This is so no matter how local or discrete the harm, no matter how public and widespread the injury. We find nothing special in the protections Amendment 2 withholds. These are protections taken for granted by most people either because they already have them or do not need them; these are protections against exclusion from an almost limitless number of transactions and endeavors that constitute ordinary civic life in a free society.

[If] a law neither burdens a fundamental right nor targets a suspect class, we will uphold the legislative classification so long as it bears a rational relation to some legitimate end. Amendment 2 fails, indeed defies, even this conventional inquiry. [Even] in the ordinary equal protection case calling for the most deferential of standards, we insist on knowing the relation between the classification adopted and the object to be attained. [By] requiring that the classification bear a rational relationship to an independent and legitimate legislative end, we ensure that classifications are not drawn for the purpose of disadvantaging the group burdened by the law.

Amendment 2 confounds this normal process of judicial review. It is at once too narrow and too broad. It identifies persons by a single trait and then denies them protection across the board. [It] is not within our constitutional tradition to enact laws of this sort. Central both to the idea of the rule of law and to our own Constitution's guarantee of equal protection is the principle that government and each of its parts remain open on impartial terms to all who seek its assistance. [Respect] for this principle explains why laws singling out a certain class of citizens for disfavored legal status or general hardships are rare. A law declaring that in general it shall be more difficult for one group of citizens than for all others to seek aid from the government is itself a denial of equal protection of the laws in the most literal sense. * * *

Davis v. Beason, 133 U.S. 333, 10 S.Ct. 299, 33 L.Ed. 637 (1890), not cited by the parties but relied upon by the dissent, is not evidence that Amendment 2 is within our constitutional tradition, and any reliance upon it as authority for sustaining the amendment is misplaced. In *Davis*, the Court approved an Idaho territorial statute denying Mormons, polygamists, and advocates of polygamy the right to vote and to hold office. [To] the extent *Davis* held that persons advocating a certain practice may be denied the right to vote, it is no longer good law. *Brandenburg v. Ohio*, [CON LAW p. 656, AMER CON p. 666, RTS & LIB p. 563]. To the extent it held that the groups designated in the statute may be deprived of the right to vote because of their status, its ruling could not stand without surviving strict scrutiny, a most doubtful outcome. *Dunn v. Blumstein*, [CON LAW p. 1375, AMER CON p. 1305, RTS & LIB p. 1282].

[A] second and related point is that laws of the kind now before us raise the inevitable inference that the disadvantage imposed is born of animosity toward the class of persons affected. "[I]f the constitutional conception of 'equal protection of the laws' means anything, it must at the very least mean that a bare * * * desire to harm a politically unpopular group cannot constitute a *legitimate* governmental interest." *Moreno*, [CON LAW p. 1158, AMER CON p. 1119, RTS & LIB, p. 1065]. Even laws enacted for broad and ambitious purposes often can be explained by reference to legitimate public policies which justify the incidental disadvantages they impose on certain persons. Amendment 2, however, in making a general announcement that gays and lesbians shall not have any particular protections from the law, inflicts on them immediate, continuing, and real injuries that outrun and belie any legitimate justifications that may be claimed for it.

[The] primary rationale the State offers for Amendment 2 is respect for other citizens' freedom of association, and in particular the liberties of landlords or employers who have personal or religious objections to homosexuality. Colorado also cites its interest in conserving resources to fight discrimination against other groups. The breadth of the Amendment is so far removed from these particular justifications that we find it impossible to credit them. [It] is a status-based enactment divorced from any factual context from which we could discern a relationship to legitimate state interests; it is a classification of persons undertaken for its own sake, something the Equal Protection Clause does not permit. * * *

JUSTICE SCALIA, with whom THE CHIEF JUSTICE and JUSTICE THOMAS join, dissenting.

[In] rejecting the State's arguments that Amendment 2 "puts gays and lesbians in the same position as all other persons," and "does no more than deny homosexuals special rights," [the] Court considers it unnecessary to decide the validity of the State's argument that Amendment 2 does not deprive homosexuals of the "protection [afforded by] general laws and policies that prohibit arbitrary discrimination in governmental and private settings." I agree that we need not resolve that dispute, because the Supreme Court of Colorado has resolved it for us. [The] Colorado court stated: "[I]t is significant to note that Colorado law currently proscribes discrimination against persons who are not suspect classes, including discrimination based on age, marital or family status, veterans' status, and for any legal, off-duty conduct such as smoking tobacco. *Of course Amendment 2 is not intended to have any effect on this legislation, but seeks only to prevent the adoption of antidiscrimination laws intended to protect gays, lesbians, and bisexuals."* (emphasis added). [This] analysis, which is fully in accord with (indeed, follows inescapably from) the text of the constitutional provision, lays to rest such horribles [as] the prospect that assaults upon homosexuals could not be prosecuted.   The amendment prohibits *special treatment* of homosexuals, and nothing more.   It would not affect, for example, a requirement of state law that pensions be paid to all retiring state employees with a certain length of service; homosexual employees, as well as others, would be entitled to that benefit.   But it would prevent the State or any municipality from making death-benefit payments to the "life partner" of a homosexual when it does not make such payments to the long-time roommate of a nonhomosexual employee.

[Despite] all of its hand-wringing about the potential effect of Amendment 2 on general antidiscrimination laws, the Court's opinion ultimately does not dispute all this, but assumes it to be true.   The only denial of equal treatment it contends homosexuals have suffered is this: They may not obtain *preferential* treatment without amending the state constitution. That is to say, the principle underlying the Court's opinion is that one who is accorded equal treatment under the laws, but cannot as readily as others obtain *preferential* treatment under the laws, has been denied equal protection of the laws.   If merely stating this alleged "equal protection" violation does not suffice to refute it, our constitutional jurisprudence has achieved terminal silliness.

The central thesis of the Court's reasoning is that any group is denied equal protection when, to obtain advantage (or, presumably, to avoid disadvantage), it must have recourse to a more general and hence more difficult level of political decisionmaking than others.   The world has never heard of such a principle, which is why the Court's opinion is so long on emotive utterance and so short on relevant legal citation.   And it seems to me most unlikely that any multilevel democracy can function under such a principle.   For *whenever* a disadvantage is imposed, or conferral of a benefit is prohibited, at one of the higher levels of democratic decisionmaking (*i.e.*, by the state legislature rather than local government, or by the people at large in the state constitution rather than the legislature), the affected group has (under this theory) been denied equal protection.   To take the simplest of examples, consider a state law prohibiting the award of municipal contracts to relatives of mayors or city councilmen.   Once such a law is passed, the group composed of such relatives must, in order to get the benefit of city contracts, persuade the state legislature—unlike all other citizens, who need only persuade the municipality.   It is ridiculous to consider this a denial of equal protection, which is why the Court's theory is unheard of.   * * *

I turn next to whether there was a legitimate rational basis for the substance of the constitutional amendment—for the prohibition of special protection for homosexuals.[1]   It is unsurprising that the Court avoids discussion of this question, since the answer is so obviously yes.   The case most relevant to the issue before us today is not even mentioned in the Court's opinion: In *Bowers v. Hardwick*, [CON LAW p. 516, AMER CON p. 591, RTS & LIB p. 422], we held that the Constitution does not prohibit what virtually all States had done from the founding of the Republic until very recent years—making homosexual conduct a crime.   [If] it is constitutionally permissible for a State to make homosexual

---

1.   The Court evidently agrees that "rational basis"—the normal test for compliance with the Equal Protection Clause—is the governing standard.   The trial court rejected respondents' argument that homosexuals constitute a "suspect" or "quasi-suspect" class, and respondents elected not to appeal that ruling to the Supreme Court of Colorado.   And the Court implicitly rejects the Supreme Court of Colorado's holding that Amendment 2 infringes upon a "fundamental right" of "independently identifiable class[es]" to "participate equally in the political process."

conduct criminal, surely it is constitutionally permissible for a State to enact other laws merely *disfavoring* homosexual conduct. [And] a fortiori it is constitutionally permissible for a State to adopt a provision *not even* disfavoring homosexual conduct, but merely prohibiting all levels of state government from bestowing *special protections* upon homosexual conduct. Respondents (who, unlike the Court, cannot afford the luxury of ignoring inconvenient precedent) counter *Bowers* with the argument that a greater-includes-the-lesser rationale cannot justify Amendment 2's application to individuals who do not engage in homosexual acts, but are merely of homosexual "orientation."

[Assuming] that, in Amendment 2, a person of homosexual "orientation" is someone who does not engage in homosexual conduct but merely has a tendency or desire to do so, *Bowers* still suffices to establish a rational basis for the provision. If it is rational to criminalize the conduct, surely it is rational to deny special favor and protection to those with a self-avowed tendency or desire to engage in the conduct. Indeed, where criminal sanctions are not involved, homosexual "orientation" is an acceptable stand-in for homosexual conduct. A State "does not violate the Equal Protection Clause merely because the classifications made by its laws are imperfect." Just as a policy barring the hiring of methadone users as transit employees does not violate equal protection simply because *some* methadone users pose no threat to passenger safety, see *New York City Transit Authority v. Beazer,* [CON LAW p. 1157, AMER CON p. 1118, RTS & LIB p. 1064], [Amendment] 2 is not constitutionally invalid simply because it could have been drawn more precisely so as to withdraw special antidiscrimination protections only from those of homosexual "orientation" who actually engage in homosexual conduct.

[The] Court's opinion contains grim, disapproving hints that Coloradans have been guilty of "animus" or "animosity" toward homosexuality, as though that has been established as Unamerican. Of course it is our moral heritage that one should not hate any human being or class of human beings. But I had thought that one could consider certain conduct reprehensible—murder, for example, or polygamy, or cruelty to animals—and could exhibit even "animus" toward such conduct. Surely that is the only sort of "animus" at issue here: moral disapproval of homosexual conduct, the same sort of moral disapproval that produced the centuries-old criminal laws that we held constitutional in *Bowers.*

[But] though Coloradans are, as I say, *entitled* to be hostile toward homosexual conduct, the fact is that the degree of hostility reflected by Amendment 2 is the smallest conceivable. The Court's portrayal of Coloradans as a society fallen victim to pointless, hate-filled "gay-bashing" is so false as to be comical. Colorado not only is one of the 25 States that have repealed their antisodomy laws, but was among the first to do so. But the society that eliminates criminal punishment for homosexual acts does not necessarily abandon the view that homosexuality is morally wrong and socially harmful; often, abolition simply reflects the view that enforcement of such criminal laws involves unseemly intrusion into the intimate lives of citizens.

There is a problem, however, which arises when criminal sanction of homosexuality is eliminated but moral and social disapprobation of homosexuality is meant to be retained. [Because] those who engage in homosexual conduct tend to reside in disproportionate numbers in certain communities, and of course care about homosexual-rights issues much more ardently than the public at large, they possess political power much greater than their numbers, both locally and statewide. Quite understandably, they devote this political power to achieving not merely a grudging social toleration, but full social acceptance, of homosexuality.

By the time Coloradans were asked to vote on Amendment 2, [three] Colorado cities—Aspen, Boulder, and Denver—had enacted ordinances that listed "sexual orientation" as an impermissible ground for discrimination, equating the moral disapproval of homosexual conduct with racial and religious bigotry[, and] the Governor of Colorado had signed an executive order [directing] state agency-heads to "ensure non-discrimination" in hiring and promotion based on, among other things, "sexual orientation." [I] do not mean to be critical of these legislative successes; homosexuals are as entitled to use the legal system for reinforcement of their moral sentiments as are the rest of society. But they are subject to being countered by lawful, democratic countermeasures as well.

That is where Amendment 2 came in. It sought to counter both the geographic concentration and the disproportionate political power of homosexuals by (1) resolving the controversy at the statewide level, and (2) making the election a single-issue contest for both sides. [The] Court today asserts that this most democratic of procedures is unconstitutional. Lacking any cases to establish that facially absurd proposition, it simply asserts that it *must* be unconstitutional, because it has never happened before. [But, as] I have noted above, this is proved false every time a state law prohibiting or disfavoring certain conduct is passed, because such a law prevents the adversely affected group—whether drug addicts, or smokers, or gun owners, or motorcyclists—from changing the policy thus established in "each of [the] parts" of the State.

[But] there is a much closer analogy, one that involves precisely the effort by the majority of citizens to preserve its view of sexual morality statewide, against the efforts of a geographically concentrated and politically powerful minority to undermine it. The constitutions of the States of Arizona, Idaho, New Mexico, Oklahoma, and Utah *to this day* contain provisions stating that polygamy is "forever prohibited." Polygamists, and those who have a polygamous "orientation," have been "singled out" by these provisions for much more severe treatment than merely denial of favored status; and that treatment can only be changed by achieving amendment of the state constitutions. The Court's disposition today suggests that these provisions are unconstitutional, and that polygamy must be permitted in these States on a state-legislated, or perhaps even local-option, basis—unless, of course, polygamists for some reason have fewer constitutional rights than homosexuals.

[Has] the Court concluded that the perceived social harm of polygamy is a "legitimate concern of government," and the perceived social harm of homosexuality is not? [I] strongly suspect that the answer [to the last question is] yes, which leads me to the last point I wish to make: [To] suggest [that] this constitutional amendment springs from nothing more than " 'a bare * * * desire to harm a politically unpopular group,' " is nothing short of insulting. (It is also nothing short of preposterous to call "politically unpopular" a group which enjoys enormous influence in American media and politics, and which, as the trial court here noted, though composing no more than 4% of the population had the support of 46% of the voters on Amendment 2.) [When] the Court takes sides in the culture wars, it tends to be with the knights rather than the villeins—and more specifically with the Templars, reflecting the views and values of the lawyer class from which the Court's Members are drawn. How that class feels about homosexuality will be evident to anyone who wishes to interview job applicants at virtually any of the Nation's law schools. The interviewer may refuse to offer a job because the applicant is a Republican; because he is an adulterer; [or] because he went to the wrong prep school or belongs to the wrong country club. But if the interviewer should wish not to be an associate or partner of an applicant because he disapproves of the applicant's homosexuality, *then* he will have violated the pledge which the Association of American Law Schools requires all its member-schools to exact from job interviewers: "assurance of the employer's willingness" to hire homosexuals. This law-school view of what "prejudices" must be stamped out may be contrasted with the more plebeian attitudes that apparently still prevail in the United States Congress, which has been unresponsive to repeated attempts to extend to homosexuals the protections of federal civil rights laws.

[Today's] opinion has no foundations in American constitutional law, and barely pretends to. The people of Colorado have adopted an entirely reasonable provision which does not even disfavor homosexuals in any substantive sense, but merely denies them preferential treatment. Amendment 2 is designed to prevent piecemeal deterioration of the sexual morality favored by a majority of Colora-dans, and is not only an appropriate means to that legitimate end, but a means that Americans have employed before. Striking it down is an act, not of judicial judgment, but of political will. * * *

In BOYS SCOUTS OF AMERICA v. DALE, p. 153 of this Supplem Court, per Rehnquist, C.J., held that a New Jersey statute barring discri on grounds of homosexuality violated the Boy Scouts' protected right to of association. Although the case presented no equal protection issue, Stevens, J., in a dissenting opinion joined by Souter, Ginsburg, and Breyer, JJ., described hostile attitudes toward homosexuals as "prejudices."

"FUNDAMENTAL RIGHTS"

VOTING

"DILUTION" OF THE RIGHT: APPORTIONMENT

CON LAW: P. 1368, before notes and questions
AMER CON: P. 1298, before notes and questions
RTS & LIB: P. 1275, before notes and questions

On remand in *Miller,* the plaintiffs amended their complaint to challenge a second of the majority-black districts. The district court held that the district violated *Miller* standards. When the Georgia legislature was unable to produce a plan of its own, the district court produced a plan with only one majority-black district. The plaintiffs did not defend the original district, but protested the failure of the district court to include another majority-black district.

ABRAMS v. JOHNSON, 521 U.S. 74, 117 S.Ct. 1925, 138 L.Ed.2d 285 (1997), per KENNEDY, J., upheld the district court. He found "ample basis in the record" to support the district court's conclusion that a second majority-black district could not have been drawn without allowing race to predominate over traditional districting principles such as protecting incumbents from contests with each other and preserving (1) county lines where possible; (2) district cores; (3) four traditional districts in the corners of the state; and (4) a majority-black district in the center of Atlanta.[a]

---

a. In the same term, *Lawyer v. Department of Justice,* 521 U.S. 567, 117 S.Ct. 2186, 138   L.Ed.2d 669 (1997), per Souter, J., upheld the constitutionality of a Florida state senate dis-

Kennedy, J., therefore, found that strict scrutiny applied. He assumed, but did not decide, that a need to comply with section two of the Voting Rights Act would meet the standard, but concluded that there was no such need.

BREYER, J., joined by Stevens, Souter, and Ginsburg, JJ., dissenting, argued on the facts that a second majority-black district would not have interfered with other important districting objectives and contended that the district court should have deferred to the legislature's reasonable belief that the failure to have a second majority-black district would violate section two of the Voting Rights Act.[b]

CON LAW: P. 1369, after note 4

AMER CON: P. 1299, after note 4

RTS & LIB: P. 1276, after note 4

5.   BUSH v. VERA, 517 U.S. 952, 116 S.Ct. 1941, 135 L.Ed.2d 248 (1996), struck down congressional districts crafted to meet what Texas argued was needed to meet the requirements of the Voting Rights Act. Although race was a factor in drawing the lines, Texas argued that the predominant factor was the protection of incumbents. O'CONNOR, J., joined by Rehnquist, C.J., and Kennedy, J., agreed that avoiding contests between incumbents was a legitimate districting consideration,[a] and she emphasized that the "decision to create majority-minority districts was not objectionable in and of itself." She concluded on the facts, however, that strict scrutiny was appropriate because race had predominated over legitimate districting considerations. Among the findings weighing in favor of the application of strict scrutiny were "that the State substantially neglected traditional districting criteria such as compactness, that it was committed from the outset to creating majority-minority districts, and that it manipulated district lines to exploit unprecedentedly detailed racial data." She observed that none of the findings would independently justify strict scrutiny. O'Connor, J., also concluded that the Texas districts were not narrowly tailored to meet the requirements of the Voting Rights Act because the act does not require a state to create districts

trict that had been approved as a part of a judicial settlement. The district was produced as a replacement for another district that had been challenged on racial grounds, and the lower court found a substantial evidentiary and legal basis for the challenge of the prior district. A non-settling defendant challenged the new district on the ground that it too was motivated by predominantly racial considerations. The new district included two counties, crossed a body of water, was not compact, and was irregular in shape. In addition, it contained a percentage of black voters significantly higher than the percentage in the counties from which the district was drawn. Souter, J., upheld the lower court's determination that the new district was in traditional respects in line with other districts in the state. Moreover, he denied the principle that black residents in a district may not exceed the percentage of black residents in the political subdivisions from which the district is produced.

Scalia, J., joined by O'Connor, Kennedy, and Thomas, JJ., dissenting, did not reach the issue, arguing instead that the district court should have determined the merits of the law suit—as opposed to finding a substantial basis

for it—and should also have given the state legislature an opportunity to reapportion before proceeding with the settlement.

b. Souter, J., found this belief reasonable because of the presence of at least two majority-black districts in the plans that had previously been produced by the Georgia legislature in this census period. Kennedy, J., replied that the presence of such districts represented a response to Justice Department pressure, not the legislature's true preference. Souter, J., did not deny the pressure, but offered what he believed to be independent legislative testimony of a desire for a second or third black-majority district and evidence of a section two violation.

a. The "incumbents" were members of the Texas legislature who had declared their intention to run for Congress. Is protection of these persons a legitimate state interest? Should incumbent protection be a legitimate state interest? In a state where racially polarized voting is prominent, under what circumstances is it possible to protect incumbents without taking race into account in drawing district lines?

that are not reasonably compact:[b] "If, because of the dispersion of the minority population, a reasonably compact majority-minority district cannot be created, the [Voting Rights Act] does not require a majority-minority district; if a reasonably compact district can be created, nothing in [the Voting Rights Act] requires the race-based creation of a district that is far from compact."[c]

In a separate concurring opinion, O'CONNOR, J., summarized "the rules governing the States consideration of race in the districting process[:] First, so long as they do not subordinate traditional districting criteria to the use of race for its own sake or as a proxy, States may intentionally create majority-minority districts,[d] and may otherwise take race into consideration, without coming under strict scrutiny. See (plurality opinion); (Stevens, J., dissenting); (Souter, J., dissenting). Only if traditional districting criteria are neglected and that neglect is predominantly due to the misuse of race does strict scrutiny apply. (plurality opinion).

"Second, where voting is racially polarized, § 2 [of the Voting Rights Act] prohibits States from adopting districting schemes that would have the effect that minority voters 'have less opportunity than other members of the electorate to * * * elect representatives of their choice.' § 2(b). That principle may require a State to create a majority-minority district where the three Gingles factors are present—viz. (i) the minority group 'is sufficiently large and geographically compact to constitute a majority in a single-member district, (ii) it is politically cohesive,' and (iii) the white majority votes sufficiently as a bloc to enable it * * * usually to defeat the minority's preferred candidate.'

"Third, the state interest in avoiding liability under [§ 2] is compelling.[e] If a State has a strong basis in evidence for concluding that the Gingles factors are present, it may create a majority-minority district without awaiting judicial findings. Its 'strong basis in evidence' need not take any particular form, although it cannot simply rely on generalized assumptions about the prevalence of racial bloc voting.'

"Fourth, if a State pursues that compelling interest by creating a district that 'substantially addresses' the potential liability, and does not deviate substantially from a hypothetical court-drawn § 2 district for predominantly racial reasons, its

---

b. The Court reached the same conclusion in the companion case, *Shaw v. Hunt*, 517 U.S. 899, 116 S.Ct. 1894, 135 L.Ed.2d 207 (1996)(districts described in *Shaw v. Reno* not narrowly tailored to meet a compelling state interest even assuming that compliance with the Voting Rights Act was compelling).

c. Thomas, J., joined by Scalia, J., concurring, argued that the intentional creation of majority-minority district should be enough to invoke strict scrutiny. Kennedy, J., concurring, strongly suggested he would join Thomas and Scalia, JJ., on that point if the issue were presented. Stevens, J., joined by Ginsburg and Breyer, JJ., dissenting, denied that race was a predominant consideration in the formation of the Texas districts, maintained that the creation of districts not reasonably compact was consistent with the Voting Rights Act (though he conceded that liability could be imposed only if the state could have created a majority-minority reasonably compact district), and he continued to question *Shaw*. Souter, J., joined by Ginsburg and Breyer, JJ., dissenting, con-

tinued to question *Shaw* and argued that the post-*Shaw* cases had failed to provide a manageable standard.

d. *Hunt v. Cromartie*, 526 U.S. 541, 119 S.Ct. 1545, 143 L.Ed.2d 731 (1999), per Thomas, J., stated that the intentional use of race to create districts with slightly less than a majority of minority citizens could also be subject to an equal protection challenge, but found that summary judgment as to the legislature's intent was inappropriate under the circumstances because there was controversy whether the intent was political or racial. Stevens, J., joined by Souter, Ginsburg and Breyer, JJ., concurring, argued that the inclusion of black voters may well have been motivated by the desire to create a Democratic district, not by a desire to create a district with a black representative.

e. The four dissenters in *Vera* (who also dissented in *Hunt*) together with O'Connor J., supported this proposition.

districting plan will be deemed narrowly tailored. Cf. (plurality opinion)(acknowledging this possibility); (Souter, J., dissenting)(same); (Stevens, J., dissenting)(contending that it is applicable here).

"Finally, however, districts that are bizarrely shaped and non-compact, and that otherwise neglect traditional districting principles and deviate substantially from the hypothetical court-drawn district, for predominantly racial reasons, are unconstitutional. (plurality opinion)."

TRAVEL

CON LAW: P. 1380

AMER CON: P. 1310

RTS & LIB: P. 1286

SAENZ v. ROE, 526 U.S. 489, 119 S.Ct. 1518, 143 L.Ed.2d 689 (1999), per STEVENS, J., shifted equality analysis in right to travel cases from the equal protection to the privilege and immunities and citizenship clauses in section one of the fourteenth amendment: "In 1992, California enacted a statute limiting the maximum welfare benefits available to newly arrived residents. The scheme limits the amount payable to a family that has resided in the State for less than 12 months to the amount payable by the State of the family's prior residence. The questions presented by this case are whether the 1992 statute was constitutional when it was enacted and, if not, whether an amendment to the Social Security Act enacted by Congress in 1996 affects that determination.

"The word 'travel' is not found in the text of the Constitution. Yet the 'constitutional right to travel from one State to another' is firmly embedded in our jurisprudence. [The] 'right to travel' discussed in our cases embraces at least three different components. It protects the right of a citizen of one State to enter and to leave another State, the right to be treated as a welcome visitor rather than an unfriendly alien when temporarily present in the second State, and, for those travelers who elect to become permanent residents, the right to be treated like other citizens of that State.* * *

"What is at issue in this case [is the] third aspect of the right to travel—the right of the newly arrived citizen to the same privileges and immunities enjoyed by other citizens of the same State. That right is protected not only by the new arrival's status as a state citizen, but also by her status as a citizen of the United States. That additional source of protection is plainly identified in the opening words of the Fourteenth Amendment* * *

"Despite fundamentally differing views concerning the coverage of the Privileges or Immunities Clause of the Fourteenth Amendment, most notably expressed in the majority and dissenting opinions in the *Slaughter-House Cases*, it has always been common ground that this Clause protects the third component of the right to travel. Writing for the majority in the *Slaughter-House Cases*, Justice Miller explained that one of the privileges conferred by this Clause 'is that a citizen of the United States can, of his own volition, become a citizen of any State of the Union by a bona fide residence therein, with the same rights as other citizens of that State.' * * *

"Neither mere rationality nor some intermediate standard of review should be used to judge the constitutionality of a state rule that discriminates against some of its citizens because they have been domiciled in the State for less than a year. The appropriate standard may be more categorical than that articulated in *Shapiro*, but it is surely no less strict. * * *

"It is undisputed that respondents and the members of the class that they represent are citizens of California and that their need for welfare benefits is unrelated to the length of time that they have resided in California. We thus have no occasion to consider what weight might be given to a citizen's length of residence if the bona fides of her claim to state citizenship were questioned. Moreover, because whatever benefits they receive will be consumed while they remain in California, there is no danger that recognition of their claim will encourage citizens of other States to establish residency for just long enough to acquire some readily portable benefit, such as a divorce or a college education, that will be enjoyed after they return to their original domicile. See, e.g., *Sosna v. Iowa*; *Vlandis v. Kline*.

"Disavowing any desire to fence out the indigent, California has instead advanced an entirely fiscal justification for its [scheme]. The enforcement of § 11450.03 will save the State approximately $10.9 million a year. The question is not whether such saving is a legitimate purpose but whether the State may accomplish that end by the discriminatory means it has chosen. An evenhanded, across-the-board reduction of about 72 cents per month for every beneficiary would produce the same result. But our negative answer to the question does not rest on the weakness of the State's purported fiscal justification. It rests on the fact that the Citizenship Clause of the Fourteenth Amendment expressly equates citizenship with residence: 'That Clause does not provide for, and does not allow for, degrees of citizenship based on length of residence.' *Zobel*. * * *

"The question that remains is whether congressional approval of durational residency requirements in the 1996 amendment to the Social Security Act somehow resuscitates the constitutionality of § 11450.03. That question is readily answered, for we have consistently held that Congress may not authorize the States to violate the Fourteenth Amendment."

REHNQUIST, C.J., joined by Thomas, J., dissented: "The Court today breathes new life into the previously dormant Privileges or Immunities Clause of the Fourteenth Amendment—a Clause relied upon by this Court in only one other decision, *Colgate v. Harvey*, 296 U.S. 404, 56 S.Ct. 252, 80 L.Ed. 299 (1935), overruled five years later by *Madden v. Kentucky*, 309 U.S. 83, 60 S.Ct. 406, 84 L.Ed. 590 (1940). It uses this Clause to strike down what I believe is a reasonable measure falling under the head of a "good-faith residency requirement." Because I do not think any provision of the Constitution—and surely not a provision relied upon for only the second time since its enactment 130 years ago—requires this result, I dissent. * * *

"I agree with the proposition that a 'citizen of the United States can, of his own volition, become a citizen of any State of the Union by a bona fide residence therein, with the same rights as other citizens of that State.' *Slaughter-House Cases*. But I cannot see how the right to become a citizen of another State is a necessary 'component' of the right to travel, or why the Court tries to marry these separate and distinct rights. A person is no longer 'traveling' in any sense of the word when he finishes his journey to a State which he plans to make his home. Indeed, under the Court's logic, the protections of the Privileges or Immunities Clause recognized in this case come into play only when an individual *stops* traveling with the intent to remain and become a citizen of a new State. [At] most, restrictions on an individual's right to become a citizen indirectly affect his calculus in deciding whether to exercise his right to travel in the first place, but such an attenuated and uncertain relationship is no ground for folding one right into the other.

"No doubt the Court has, in the past 30 years, essentially conflated the right to travel with the right to equal state citizenship in striking down durational residence requirements similar to the one challenged here.* * *

"The Court today tries to clear much of the underbrush created by these prior right-to-travel cases, abandoning its effort to define what residence requirements deprive individuals of 'important rights and benefits' or 'penalize' the right to travel. Under its new analytical framework, a State, outside certain ill-defined circumstances, cannot classify its citizens by the length of their residence in the State without offending the Privileges or Immunities Clause of the Fourteenth Amendment. The Court thus departs from *Shapiro* and its progeny, and, while paying lipservice to the right to travel, the Court does little to explain how the right to travel is involved at all. Instead, as the Court's analysis clearly demonstrates, this case is only about respondents' right to immediately enjoy all the privileges of being a California citizen in relation to that State's ability to test the good-faith assertion of this right. * * *

"In unearthing from its tomb the right to become a state citizen and to be treated equally in the new State of residence, however, the Court ignores a State's need to assure that only persons who establish a bona fide residence receive the benefits provided to current residents of the State.[T]he Court has consistently recognized that while new citizens must have the same opportunity to enjoy the privileges of being a citizen of a State, the States retain the ability to use bona fide residence requirements to ferret out those who intend to take the privileges and run.* * *

"If States can require individuals to reside in-state for a year before exercising the right to educational benefits, the right to terminate a marriage, or the right to vote in primary elections that all other state citizens enjoy, then States may surely do the same for welfare benefits. Indeed, there is no material difference between a 1–year residence requirement applied to the level of welfare benefits given out by a State, and the same requirement applied to the level of tuition subsidies at a state university. The welfare payment here and in-state tuition rates are cash subsidies provided to a limited class of people, and California's standard of living and higher education system make both subsidies quite attractive. Durational residence requirements were upheld when used to regulate the provision of higher education subsidies, and the same deference should be given in the case of welfare payments.

"The Court today recognizes that States retain the ability to determine the bona fides of an individual's claim to residence, but then tries to avoid the issue. It asserts that because respondents' need for welfare benefits is unrelated to the length of time they have resided in California, it has 'no occasion to consider what weight might be given to a citizen's length of residence if the bona fides of her claim to state citizenship were questioned.' But I do not understand how the absence of a link between need and length of residency bears on the State's ability to objectively test respondents' resolve to stay in California. There is no link between the need for an education or for a divorce and the length of residence, and yet States may use length of residence as an objective yardstick to channel their benefits to those whose intent to stay is legitimate. * * *

"The Court tries to distinguish education and divorce benefits by contending that the welfare payment here will be consumed in California, while a college education or a divorce produces benefits that are 'portable' and can be enjoyed after individuals return to their original domicile. But this 'you can't take it with you' distinction is more apparent than real, and offers little guidance to lower courts who must apply this rationale in the future. Welfare payments are a form of insurance, giving impoverished individuals and their families the means to meet the demands of daily life while they receive the necessary training, education, and time to look for a job. The cash itself will no doubt be spent in California, but the benefits from receiving this income and having the opportunity to become employed or employable will stick with the welfare recipient if they stay in California or go back to their true domicile. Similarly, tuition subsidies are 'consumed' instate but the recipient takes the benefits of a college education with him wherever he goes. A welfare subsidy is thus as much an investment in human capital as is a tuition subsidy, and their attendant benefits are just as 'portable.' More importantly, this foray into social economics demonstrates that the line drawn by the Court borders on the metaphysical, and requires lower courts to plumb the policies animating certain benefits like welfare to define their 'essence' and hence their 'portability.' * * *

"I therefore believe that the durational residence requirement challenged here is a permissible exercise of the State's power to 'assur[e] that services provided for its residents are enjoyed only by residents.' "

THOMAS, J., joined by Rehnquist, C.J., dissented: "Unlike the Equal Protection and Due Process Clauses, which have assumed near-talismanic status in modern constitutional law, the Court all but read the Privileges or Immunities Clause out of the Constitution in the *Slaughter-House Cases*. * * *

"Unlike the majority, I would look to history to ascertain the original meaning of the Clause. At least in American law, the phrase (or its close approximation) appears to stem from the 1606 Charter of Virginia, which provided that 'all and every the Persons being our Subjects, which shall dwell and inhabit within every or any of the said several Colonies * * * shall HAVE and enjoy all Liberties, Franchises, and Immunities * * * as if they had been abiding and born, within this our Realme of England.' [The] colonists' repeated assertions that they maintained the rights, privileges and immunities of persons 'born within the realm of England' and 'natural born' persons suggests that, at the time of the founding, the terms 'privileges' and 'immunities' (and their counterparts) were understood to refer to those fundamental rights and liberties specifically enjoyed by English citizens, and more broadly, by all persons. * * * Justice Bushrod Washington's landmark opinion in *Corfield v. Coryell* reflects this historical understanding. * * * Justice Washington's opinion in *Corfield* indisputably influenced the Members of Congress who enacted the Fourteenth Amendment. When Congress gathered to debate the Fourteenth Amendment, members frequently, if not as a matter of course, appealed to *Corfield*, arguing that the Amendment was necessary to guarantee the fundamental rights that Justice Washington identified in his opinion. * * *

"That Members of the 39th Congress appear to have endorsed the wisdom of Justice Washington's opinion does not, standing alone, provide dispositive insight into their understanding of the Fourteenth Amendment's Privileges or Immunities Clause. Nevertheless, their repeated references to the *Corfield* decision, combined with what appears to be the historical understanding of the Clause's operative terms, supports the inference that, at the time the Fourteenth Amendment was adopted, people understood that 'privileges or immunities of citizens' were fundamental rights, rather than every public benefit established by positive law. Accordingly, the majority's conclusion—that a State violates the Privileges or

Immunities Clause when it 'discriminates' against citizens who have been domiciled in the State for less than a year in the distribution of welfare benefit appears contrary to the original understanding and is dubious at best.

"As The Chief Justice points out, it comes as quite a surprise that the majority relies on the Privileges or Immunities Clause at all in this case. [Although] the majority appears to breathe new life into the Clause today, it fails to address its historical underpinnings or its place in our constitutional jurisprudence. Because I believe that the demise of the Privileges or Immunities Clause has contributed in no small part to the current disarray of our Fourteenth Amendment jurisprudence, I would be open to reevaluating its meaning in an appropriate case. Before invoking the Clause, however, we should endeavor to understand what the framers of the Fourteenth Amendment thought that it meant. We should also consider whether the Clause should displace, rather than augment, portions of our equal protection and substantive due process jurisprudence. The majority's failure to consider these important questions raises the specter that the Privileges or Immunities Clause will become yet another convenient tool for inventing new rights, limited solely by the 'predilections of those who happen at the time to be Members of this Court.' "

ACCESS TO THE COURTS

CON LAW: P. 1386, addition to fn. c

AMER CON: P. 1316, addition to fn. c

RTS & LIB: P. 1293, addition to fn. c

To what extent should prisons be required to provide law library facilities for inmates? If a right to adequate law library facilities exists, is it founded in equal protection, due process, or the right to petition the courts for redress of grievances? See *Lewis v. Casey*, 518 U.S. 343, 116 S.Ct. 2174, 135 L.Ed.2d 606 (1996).

CON LAW: P. 1388, before notes and questions

AMER CON: P. 1318, before notes and questions

RTS & LIB: P. 1295, before notes and questions

A Mississippi chancery court terminated M.L.B.'s parental rights to her two young children. M.L.B. tried to appeal, but Mississippi required that she pay record preparation fees of $22,352.36 in advance. She could not afford to do so, and her appeal was dismissed.

M.L.B. v. S.L.J., 519 U.S. 102, 117 S.Ct. 555, 136 L.Ed.2d 473 (1996), per GINSBURG, J., held that "just as the State may not block an indigent petty offender's access to an appeal afforded others, so Mississippi may not deny M.L.B., because of her poverty, appellate review of the sufficiency of the evidence on which the trial court found her unfit to be a parent. [A]s *Ortwein* underscored, this Court has not extended *Griffin* to the broad array of civil cases. But tellingly, the Court has consistently set apart from the mine run of cases those involving state controls or intrusions on family relationships. [T]he Court's decisions concerning access to judicial processes * * * reflect both equal protection and due process concerns. * * * The equal protection concern relates to the legitimacy of fencing out would-be appellants based solely on their inability to pay core costs. The due process concern hones in on the essential fairness of the state-ordered proceedings anterior to adverse state action. * * * Nevertheless, '[m]ost decisions in this area,' we have recognized, 'res[t] on an equal protection framework,

* * * for [due] process does not independently require that the State provide an appeal.

"[Unlike *Washington v. Davis,*] the Mississippi prescription here at issue [is] not merely *disproportionate* in impact. Rather [it is] wholly contingent on one's ability to pay, and thus 'visi[ts] different consequences on two categories of persons;' [it applies] to all indigents and do[es] not reach anyone outside that class. In sum, under [a broad] reading of *Washington v. Davis,* our overruling of the *Griffin* line of cases would be two decades overdue. It suffices to point out that this Court has not so conceived the meaning and effect of our 1976 'disproportionate impact precedent.'

"Respondents and the dissenters urge that we will open floodgates if we do not rigidly restrict *Griffin* to cases typed 'criminal.' But we have repeatedly noticed what sets parental status termination decrees apart from [the] mine run [of] civil actions, even from other domestic relations matters such as divorce, paternity, and child custody. To recapitulate, termination decrees 'wor[k] a unique kind of deprivation.' In contrast to matters modifiable at the parties' will or based on changed circumstances, termination adjudications involve the awesome authority of the State 'to destroy permanently all legal recognition of the parental relationship.' Our [decisions], recognizing that parental termination decrees are among the most severe forms of state action have not served as precedent in other areas. We are therefore satisfied that the label 'civil' should not entice us to leave undisturbed the Mississippi courts' disposition of this case.

"For the reasons stated, we hold that Mississippi may not withhold from M.L.B. 'a "record of sufficient completeness" to permit proper [appellate] consideration of [her] claims.' "[a]

Thomas, J., joined by Scalia, J., and Rehnquist, C.J., in part, dissented: "[M.L.B.] defended against the 'destruction of her family bonds' in the Chancery Court hearing at which she was accorded all the process this Court has required of the States in parental termination cases. She now desires 'state aid to subsidize [her] privately initiated' appeal—an appeal that neither petitioner nor the majority claims Mississippi is required to provide—to overturn the determination that resulted from that hearing. I see no principled difference between a facially neutral rule that serves in some cases to prevent persons from availing themselves of state employment, or a state-funded education, or a state-funded abortion—each of which the State may, but is not required to, provide—and a facially neutral rule that prevents a person from taking an appeal that is available only because the State chooses to provide it.[1]

"The *Griffin* line of cases ascribed to—one might say announced—an equalizing notion of the Equal Protection Clause that would, I think, have startled the Fourteenth Amendment's Framers. In those cases, the Court did not find, nor did it seek, any purposeful discrimination on the part of the state defendants. That their statutes had disproportionate effect on poor persons was sufficient for us to find a constitutional violation. In *Davis,* among other cases, we began to recognize the potential mischief of a disparate impact theory writ large, and

---

a. Kennedy, J., concurring, would have rested on the due process clause "given the existing appellate structure in Mississippi" though he also observed that "the authorities do not hold that an appeal is required even in a criminal case."

1. *Harper v. Virginia Bd. of Elections,* struck down a poll tax that directly restricted the exercise of a right found in that case to be fundamental—the right to vote in state elections. The fee that M.L.B. is unable to pay does not prevent the exercise of a fundamental right directly: The fundamental interest identified by the majority is not the right to a civil appeal, it is rather the right to maintain the parental relationship.

endeavored to contain it. In this case, I would continue that enterprise. Mississippi's requirement of prepaid transcripts in civil appeals seeking to contest the sufficiency of the evidence adduced at trial is facially neutral; it creates no classification. The transcript rule reasonably obliges would-be appellants to bear the costs of availing themselves of a service that the State chooses, but is not constitutionally required, to provide. Any adverse impact that the transcript requirement has on any person seeking to appeal arises not out of the State's action, but out of factors entirely unrelated to it."[b]

b. In another section of his opinion, Thomas, J., argued that he would overrule *Griffin* in a proper case, but would, in any event, confine *Griffin* to criminal cases. Rehnquist, C.J., did not join that section of the opinion.

THE CONCEPT OF STATE ACTION

"GOVERNMENT FUNCTION"

CON LAW: P. 1416, add to fn. b

RTS & LIB: P. 1323, add to fn. b

Would it be "state action" if one of the major political parties imposed a registration fee in order to attend its convention to nominate candidates (assuming this would be barred by the 24th amendment if done by a state)? See *Morse v. Republican Party of Virginia*, p. 171 of this Supplement. Suppose the party excluded African Americans?

CONGRESSIONAL ENFORCEMENT
OF CIVIL RIGHTS

MODERN DEVELOPMENTS

CON LAW: P. 1473, before Notes & Questions

AMER CON: P. 1384, before *Guest*

RTS & LIB: P. 1380, before Notes & Questions

LOPEZ v. MONTEREY COUNTY, 525 U.S. 266, 119 S.Ct. 693, 142 L.Ed.2d 728 (1999), per O'CONNOR, J., held that Congress had power under § 2 of the fifteenth amendment to suspend voting regulations in a California county which was "covered" under the Voting Rights Act of 1965 even though the state legislature of California, which was not "covered," had passed a statute requiring the new voting regulations.

Kennedy, joined by Rehnquist, C.J., concurring, and Thomas, J., dissenting, avoided deciding the constitutional issue, but expressed "grave constitutional concerns."

CON LAW: P. 1498, at end

AMER CON: P. 1405, before *Jones*

RTS & LIB: P. 1405, at end

BOERNE v. FLORES

521 U.S. 507, 117 S.Ct. 2157, 138 L.Ed.2d 624 (1997).

JUSTICE KENNEDY delivered the opinion of the Court.

A decision by local zoning authorities to deny a church a building permit was challenged under the Religious Freedom Restoration Act of 1993 (RFRA). * * *

Congress enacted RFRA in direct response to the Court's decision in *Employment Div. v. Smith*, [CON LAW, P. 1113; AMER CON P. 1079; RTS & LIB, P. 1020]. *Smith* held that neutral, generally applicable laws may be applied to religious practices even when not supported by a compelling governmental interest. [Many] criticized the Court's reasoning, and this disagreement resulted in the passage of RFRA. * * *

RFRA prohibits "[g]overnment" from "substantially burden[ing]" a person's exercise of religion even if the burden results from a rule of general applicability unless the government can demonstrate the burden "(1) is in furtherance of a compelling governmental interest; and (2) is the least restrictive means of furthering that compelling governmental interest." * * *

Congress relied on its Fourteenth Amendment enforcement power in enacting the most far reaching and substantial of RFRA's provisions, those which impose its requirements on the States. [W]e agree with respondent, of course, that

Congress can enact legislation under § 5 enforcing the constitutional right to the free exercise of religion. * * *

Congress' power under § 5, however, extends only to "enforc[ing]" the provisions of the Fourteenth Amendment. The Court has described this power as "remedial," *South Carolina v. Katzenbach.* The design of the Amendment and the text of § 5 are inconsistent with the suggestion that Congress has the power to decree the substance of the Fourteenth Amendment's restrictions on the States. Legislation which alters the meaning of the Free Exercise Clause cannot be said to be enforcing the Clause. Congress does not enforce a constitutional right by changing what the right is. It has been given the power "to enforce," not the power to determine what constitutes a constitutional violation. Were it not so, what Congress would be enforcing would no longer be, in any meaningful sense, the "provisions of [the Fourteenth Amendment]."

While the line between measures that remedy or prevent unconstitutional actions and measures that make a substantive change in the governing law is not easy to discern, and Congress must have wide latitude in determining where it lies, the distinction exists and must be observed. There must be a congruence and proportionality between the injury to be prevented or remedied and the means adopted to that end. Lacking such a connection, legislation may become substantive in operation and effect. * * *

The Fourteenth Amendment's history confirms the remedial, rather than substantive, nature of the Enforcement Clause. [The] objections to the [Joint] Committee's first draft of the Amendment ["The Congress shall have power to make all laws which shall be necessary and proper to secure to the citizens of each State all privileges and immunities of citizens in the several States, and to all persons in the several States equal protection in the rights of life, liberty, and property."] have a direct bearing on the central issue of defining Congress' enforcement power. * * * Members of Congress from across the political spectrum criticized the Amendment, and the criticisms had a common theme: The proposed Amendment gave Congress [a] power to intrude into traditional areas of state responsibility, a power inconsistent with the federal design central to the Constitution. [Under] the revised Amendment, Congress' power was no longer plenary but remedial [and] did not raise the concerns expressed earlier regarding broad congressional power to prescribe uniform national laws with respect to life, liberty, and property.[a] * * *

The design of the Fourteenth Amendment has proved significant also in maintaining the traditional separation of powers between Congress and the Judiciary. The first eight Amendments to the Constitution set forth self-executing prohibitions on governmental action, and this Court has had primary authority to interpret those prohibitions. The [first] draft, some thought, departed from that tradition by vesting in Congress primary power to interpret and elaborate on the meaning of the new Amendment through legislation. Under it, "Congress, and not the courts, was to judge whether or not any of the privileges or immunities were not secured to citizens in the several States." Horace E. Flack, *The Adoption of the Fourteenth Amendment* 64 (1908). While this separation of powers aspect did not occasion the widespread resistance which was caused by the proposal's threat to the federal balance, it nonetheless attracted the attention of various Members.

a. Compare Douglas Laycock, *Conceptual Gulfs in City of Boerne v. Flores*, 39 Wm. & M. L. Rev. 743, 766 (1998): "Senators and representatives argued [that] the enforcement power would add nothing if it were confined to the judicially enforceable meaning of the Amendment."

As enacted, the Fourteenth Amendment confers substantive rights against the States which, like the provisions of the Bill of Rights, are self-executing. The power to interpret the Constitution in a case or controversy remains in the Judiciary.[b] * * *

There is language in our opinion in *Morgan* which could be interpreted as acknowledging a power in Congress to enact legislation that expands the rights contained in § 1 of the Fourteenth Amendment. This is not a necessary interpretation, however, or even the best one. [As] Justice Stewart explained in *Mitchell,* interpreting *Morgan* to give Congress the power to interpret the Constitution "would require an enormous extension of that decision's rationale."

If Congress could define its own powers by altering the Fourteenth Amendment's meaning, no longer would the Constitution be "superior paramount law, unchangeable by ordinary means." It would be "on a level with ordinary legislative acts, and, like other [acts,] alterable when the legislature shall please to alter it." *Marbury v. Madison.* Under this approach, it is difficult to conceive of a principle that would limit congressional power. Shifting legislative majorities could change the Constitution and effectively circumvent the difficult and detailed amendment process contained in Article V. * * *   *Federalism*

Respondent contends that RFRA is a proper exercise of Congress' remedial or preventive power. The Act, it is [said,] prevents and remedies laws which are enacted with the unconstitutional object of targeting religious beliefs and practices. See *Church of the Lukumi Babalu Aye, Inc. v. Hialeah,* [CON LAW P. 1124, AMER CON P. 1088, RTS & LIB P. 1031] To avoid the difficulty of proving such violations, it is said, Congress can simply invalidate any law which imposes a substantial burden on a religious practice unless it is justified by a compelling interest and is the least restrictive means of accomplishing that interest. If Congress can prohibit laws with discriminatory effects in order to prevent racial discrimination in violation of the Equal Protection Clause, then it can do the same, respondent argues, to promote religious liberty.

While preventive rules are sometimes appropriate remedial measures, there must be a congruence between the means used and the ends to be achieved. * * * Strong measures appropriate to address one harm may be an unwarranted response to another, lesser one.

A comparison between RFRA and the Voting Rights Act is instructive. In contrast to the record which confronted Congress and the judiciary in the voting rights cases, RFRA's legislative record lacks examples of modern instances of generally applicable laws passed because of religious bigotry. [Rather,] the emphasis of the hearings was on laws of general applicability which place incidental burdens on religion. * * *

Regardless of the state of the legislative record, RFRA [is] so out of proportion to a supposed remedial or preventive object that it cannot be understood as responsive to, or designed to prevent, unconstitutional behavior. It appears, instead, to attempt a substantive change in constitutional protections. Preventive measures prohibiting certain types of laws may be appropriate when there is reason to believe that many of the laws affected by the congressional enactment have a significant likelihood of being unconstitutional. See *Rome.* * * *

b. The concurring opinion of Scalia, J., joined by Stevens, J., both of whom joined the   Court's opinion, is omitted.

RFRA is not so confined. Sweeping coverage ensures its intrusion at every level of government, displacing laws and prohibiting official actions of almost every description and regardless of subject matter. [Any] law is subject to challenge at any time by any individual who alleges a substantial burden on his or her free exercise of religion.

The reach and scope of RFRA distinguish it from other measures passed under Congress' enforcement power, even in the area of voting rights. In *South Carolina v. Katzenbach,* the challenged provisions were confined to those regions of the country where voting discrimination had been most flagrant, and affected a discrete class of state laws, i.e., state voting laws. Furthermore, to ensure that the reach of the Voting Rights Act was limited to those cases in which constitutional violations were most likely (in order to reduce the possibility of overbreadth), the coverage under the Act would terminate "at the behest of States and political subdivisions in which the danger of substantial voting discrimination has not materialized during the preceding five years." The provisions restricting and banning literacy tests, upheld in *Morgan* attacked a particular type of voting qualification, one with a long history as a "notorious means to deny and abridge voting rights on racial grounds." [This] is not to say, of course, that § 5 legislation requires termination dates, geographic restrictions or egregious predicates. Where, however, a congressional enactment pervasively prohibits constitutional state action in an effort to remedy or to prevent unconstitutional state action, limitations of this kind tend to ensure Congress' means are proportionate to ends legitimate under § 5. * * *

The substantial costs RFRA exacts, both in practical terms of imposing a heavy litigation burden on the States and in terms of curtailing their traditional general regulatory power, far exceed any pattern or practice of unconstitutional conduct under the Free Exercise Clause as interpreted in *Smith.* [In] addition, the Act imposes in every case a least restrictive means requirement—a requirement that was not used in the pre-*Smith* jurisprudence RFRA purported to codify— which also indicates that the legislation is broader than is appropriate if the goal is to prevent and remedy constitutional violations.

When [the] Court has interpreted the Constitution, it has acted within the province of the Judicial Branch, which embraces the duty to say what the law is. When the political branches of the Government act against the background of a judicial interpretation of the Constitution already issued, it must be understood that in later cases and controversies the Court will treat its precedents with the respect due them under settled principles, including stare decisis, and contrary expectations must be disappointed. RFRA was designed to control cases and controversies, such as the one before us; but as the provisions of the federal statute here invoked are beyond congressional authority, it is this Court's precedent, not RFRA, which must control. * * *

JUSTICE STEVENS, concurring.

In my opinion, RFRA is a "law respecting an establishment of religion" that violates the First Amendment * * *.[c]

JUSTICE O'CONNOR, with whom JUSTICE BREYER joins except as to [the first two sentences below].

c. The concurring opinion of Scalia, J., joined by Stevens, J., both of whom joined the Court's opinion, is omitted.

* * * I agree with much of the reasoning set forth in [the] Court's opinion. Indeed, if I agreed with the Court's standard in *Smith,* I would join the opinion. [But] I remain of the view that *Smith* was wrongly decided, and I would use this case to reexamine the Court's holding there. Therefore, I would direct the parties to brief the question whether *Smith* represents the correct understanding of the Free Exercise Clause and set the case for reargument. If the Court were to correct the misinterpretation of the Free Exercise Clause set forth in *Smith,* it would simultaneously put our First Amendment jurisprudence back on course and allay the legitimate concerns of a majority in Congress who believed that *Smith* improperly restricted religious liberty. We would then be in a position to review RFRA in light of a proper interpretation of the Free Exercise Clause. * * *

JUSTICE SOUTER, dissenting.

* * * Justice O'Connor's opinion [raises] very substantial issues about the soundness of the *Smith* rule. [In] order to provide full adversarial consideration, this case should be set down for reargument permitting plenary reexamination of the issue. Since the Court declines to follow that course, our free-exercise law remains marked by an "intolerable tension," *Lukumi,* and the constitutionality of the Act of Congress to enforce the free-exercise right cannot now be soundly decided. I would therefore dismiss the writ of certiorari as improvidently granted * * *.

Equal protection. KIMEL v. FLORIDA BD. OF REGENTS, ___ U.S. ___ 120 S.Ct. 631, 145 L.Ed.2d 522 (2000), per O'CONNOR, J., explored *Boerne's* scope in the context of Congress' exercising its § 5 power—which may be used to abrogate the states' immunity from suits in federal court guaranteed by the eleventh amendment—to make states subject to federal court actions for violating the Age Discrimination in Employment Act: "We have considered claims of unconstitutional age discrimination under the Equal Protection Clause three times [and held that] age is not a suspect classification * * *. Our Constitution permits States to draw lines on the basis of age when they have a rational basis for doing so at a class-based level, even if it 'is probably not true' that those reasons are valid in the majority of cases.

"Judged against the backdrop of our equal protection jurisprudence, it is clear that the ADEA is 'so out of proportion to a supposed remedial or preventive object that it cannot be understood as responsive to, or designed to prevent, unconstitutional behavior.' *Boerne.* The Act, through its broad restriction on the use of age as a discriminating factor, prohibits substantially more state employment decisions and practices than would likely be held unconstitutional under the applicable equal protection, rational basis standard. [Petitioners] contend that the Act's prohibition, considered together with its exceptions, applies only to arbitrary age discrimination, which in the majority of cases corresponds to conduct that violates the Equal Protection Clause. We disagree.

"Petitioners stake their claim [on] the 'bona fide occupational qualification' (BFOQ) defense. [But to] succeed under the BFOQ defense, we held that an employer must demonstrate either 'a substantial basis for believing that all or nearly all employees above an age lack the qualifications required for the position,' or that reliance on the age classification is necessary because 'it is highly impractical for the employer to insure by individual testing that its employees will have the necessary qualifications for the job.' Measured against the rational basis standard of our equal protection jurisprudence, the ADEA plainly imposes substantially higher burdens on state employers [at] a level akin to our heightened scrutiny cases under the Equal Protection Clause. * * *

"That the ADEA prohibits very little conduct likely to be held unconstitutional, while significant, does not alone provide the answer to our § 5 inquiry. Difficult and intractable problems often require powerful remedies, and we have never held that § 5 precludes Congress from enacting reasonably prophylactic legislation. Our task is to determine whether the ADEA is in fact just such an appropriate remedy or, instead, merely an attempt to substantively redefine the States' legal obligations with respect to age discrimination.

"Our examination of the ADEA's legislative record confirms [that] Congress never identified any pattern of age discrimination by the States, much less any discrimination whatsoever that rose to the level of constitutional violation. The evidence compiled by petitioners [consists] almost entirely of isolated sentences clipped from floor debates and legislative reports. * * *

"Our decision today does not signal the end of the line for employees who find themselves subject to age discrimination at the hands of their state employers. [State] employees are protected by state age discrimination statutes, and may recover money damages from their state employers, in almost every State of the Union."

STEVENS, J., joined by Souter, Ginsburg and Breyer, JJ., dissented: "Federalism concerns do make it appropriate for Congress to speak clearly when it regulates state action. But when it does so, as it has in these cases, we can safely presume that the burdens the statute imposes on the sovereignty of the several States were taken into account during the deliberative process leading to the enactment of the measure. [O]nce Congress has made its policy choice, the sovereignty concerns of the several States are satisfied. The importance of respecting the Framers' decision to assign the business of lawmaking to the Congress dictates firm resistance to the present majority's repeated substitution of its own views of federalism for those expressed in statutes enacted by the Congress and signed by the President."[d]

d. The scope of the eleventh amendment is considered in detail in Federal Courts courses. But several recent decisions—by the same 5–4 split as in *Lopez, Morrison, Printz* [pp. 13, 2 of this Supplement], and *Kimel*—have interpreted it to similarly enforce principles of federalism and state sovereignty. *Seminole Tribe v. Florida*, 517 U.S. 44, 116 S.Ct. 1114, 134 L.Ed.2d 252 (1996)—overruling *Pennsylvania v. Union Gas Co.*, 491 U.S. 1, 109 S.Ct. 2273, 105 L.Ed.2d 1 (1989)—per Rehnquist C.J., held that, unlike its § 5 power, Congress has *no* authority under the commerce clause to abrogate state immunity under the eleventh amendment, and *Florida Prepaid Postsecondary Educ. Expense Bd. v. College Savings Bank*, below, extended this limitation to other Art. I powers (patent clause). *Alden v. Maine*, 527 U.S. 706, 119 S.Ct. 2240, 144 L.Ed.2d 636 (1999), per Kennedy, J., while agreeing that the Fair Labor Standards Act could constitutionally be applied to states (see *Garcia*), held that, just as under *Seminole Tribe* private parties could not sue states under such federal statutes in federal court without their consent,

so, too, states could not be sued in their own courts under such circumstances:

"[T]he sovereign immunity of the States neither derives from nor is limited by the terms of the Eleventh Amendment. Rather, as the Constitution's structure, and its history, and the authoritative interpretations by this Court make clear, the States' immunity from suit is a fundamental aspect of the sovereignty which the States enjoyed before the ratification of the Constitution, and which they [retain] except as altered by the plan of the Convention or certain constitutional Amendments."

Souter J., spoke for the dissenters: "[T]oday the Court has no qualms about saying frankly that the federal right to damages afforded by Congress under the FLSA cannot create a concomitant private remedy. [The] Court calls 'immunity from private suits central to sovereign dignity,' [but] this dignity is [not] a quality easily translated from the person of the King to the participatory abstraction of a republican State. [It] would be hard to imagine anything more inimical to the republican conception,

Due process. FLORIDA PREPAID POSTSECONDARY EDUCATION EX-PENSE BOARD v. COLLEGE SAVINGS BANK, 527 U.S. 627, 119 S.Ct. 2199, 144 L.Ed.2d 575 (1999), per REHNQUIST, C.J., concerned Congress' § 5 power to expressly make states subject to federal court actions for patent infringement: Although patents "have long been considered a species [of] 'property' of which no person may be deprived by a State without due process of law [, *Boerne*] held that for Congress to invoke § 5, it must identify conduct transgressing the Fourteenth Amendment's substantive provisions, and must tailor its legislative scheme to remedying or preventing such conduct. * * *

"In enacting the Patent Remedy Act, however, Congress identified no pattern of patent infringement by the States, let alone a pattern of constitutional viola-tions. Unlike the undisputed record of racial discrimination confronting Congress in the voting rights cases, Congress came up with little evidence of infringing conduct on the part of the States. [At] most, Congress heard testimony that patent infringement by States might increase in the future* * *.

"[U]nder the plain terms of the [Due Process] Clause [, only] where the State provides no remedy, or only inadequate remedies, to injured patent owners for its infringement of their patent could a deprivation of property without due process result.

"Congress, however, barely considered the availability of state remedies for patent infringement and hence whether the States' conduct might have amounted to a constitutional violation under the Fourteenth Amendment. It did hear a limited amount of testimony to the effect that the remedies available in some States were uncertain.

"The primary point made by these witnesses, however, was not that state remedies were constitutionally inadequate, but rather that they were less conve-nient than federal remedies, and might undermine the uniformity of patent law.[9] [The] need for uniformity in the construction of patent law is undoubtedly important, but that is a factor which belongs to the Article I patent-power calculus, rather than to any determination of whether a state plea of sovereign immunity deprives a patentee of property without due process of law.* * *

"The legislative record thus suggests that the Patent Remedy Act does not respond to a history of 'widespread and persisting deprivation of constitutional rights' of the sort Congress has faced in enacting proper prophylactic § 5 legisla-tion. [Though] the lack of support in the legislative record is not determinative, identifying the targeted constitutional wrong or evil is still a critical part of our § 5 calculus because '[s]trong measures appropriate to address one harm may be an unwarranted response to another, lesser one.' *Boerne*. Here, the record at best offers scant support for Congress' conclusion that States were depriving patent owners of property without due process of law by pleading sovereign immunity in federal-court patent actions.

"Because of this lack, the provisions of the Patent Remedy Act are 'so out of proportion to a supposed remedial or preventive object that [they] cannot be understood as responsive to, or designed to prevent, unconstitutional behavior.' *Boerne*. Congress did nothing to limit the coverage of the Act to cases involving

which rests on the understanding of its citizens precisely that the government is not above them, but of them, its actions being governed by law just like their own."

9. It is worth mentioning that the State of Florida provides remedies to patent owners for alleged infringement on the part of the State. Aggrieved parties may pursue a legislative remedy through a claims bill for payment in full, or a judicial remedy through a takings or conversion claim.

arguable constitutional violations, such as where a State refuses to offer any state-court remedy for patent owners whose patents it had infringed. Nor did it make any attempt to confine the reach of the Act by limiting the remedy to certain types of infringement, such as nonnegligent infringement or infringement authorized pursuant to state policy; or providing for suits only against States with questionable remedies or a high incidence of infringement."

STEVENS, J., joined by Souter, Ginsburg and Breyer, JJ., dissented: "Sound reasons support both Congress' authority over patents and its subsequent decision in 1800 to vest exclusive jurisdiction over patent infringement litigation in the federal courts. [The] principle that undergirds all aspects of our patent system: national uniformity [supports] the congressional decision in 1982 to consolidate appellate jurisdiction of patent appeals in the Court of Appeals for the Federal Circuit [which] would be undermined by any exception that allowed patent infringement claims to be brought in state court.* * *

"It is quite unfair for the Court to strike down Congress' Act based on an absence of findings supporting a requirement this Court had not yet articulated. * * *

"It is true that, when considering the Patent Remedy Act, Congress did not review the remedies available in each State for patent infringements and surmise what kind of recovery a plaintiff might obtain in a tort suit in all 50 jurisdictions. But, [g]iven that Congress had long ago pre-empted state jurisdiction over patent infringement cases, it was surely reasonable for Congress to assume that such remedies simply did not exist. Furthermore, it is well known that not all States have waived their sovereign immunity from suit, and among those States that have, the contours of this waiver vary widely.

"Even if such remedies might be available in theory, it would have been 'appropriate' for Congress to conclude that they would not guarantee patentees due process in infringement actions against state defendants. State judges have never had the exposure to patent litigation that federal judges have experienced for decades, and, unlike infringement actions brought in federal district courts, their decisions would not be reviewable in the Court of Appeals for the Federal Circuit. * * *

"Even if state courts elected to hear patent infringement cases against state entities, the entire category of such cases would raise questions of impartiality. This concern underlies both the constitutional authorization of diversity jurisdiction and the statutory provisions for removal of certain cases from state to federal [courts.]

"Finally, this Court has never mandated that Congress must find 'widespread and persisting deprivation of constitutional rights,' in order to employ its § 5 authority. It is not surprising, therefore, that Congress did not compile an extensive legislative record analyzing the due process (or lack thereof) that each State might afford for a patent infringement suit retooled as an action in tort. In 1992, Congress had no reason to believe it needed to do such a thing; indeed, it should not have to do so today.

"[The] Court's opinion today threatens to read Congress' power to pass prophylactic legislation out of § 5 altogether; its holding is unsupported by *Boerne* and in fact conflicts with our reasoning in that case. * * *

"The difference between the harm targeted by RFRA and the harm that motivated the enactment of the Patent Remedy Act is striking. In RFRA Congress sought to overrule this Court's interpretation of the First Amendment. The

Patent Remedy Act, however, was passed to prevent future violations of due process, based on the substantiated fear that States would be unable or unwilling to provide adequate remedies for their own violations of patent-holders' rights. Congress' 'wide latitude' in determining remedial or preventive measures, see *Boerne*, has suddenly become very narrow indeed.

"[In *Boerne*,] the sweeping coverage of the statute ensured 'its intrusion at every level of government, displacing laws and prohibiting official actions of almost every description and regardless of subject matter.' [Here, the Act] has no impact whatsoever on any substantive rule of state law, but merely effectuates settled federal policy to confine patent infringement litigation to federal judges. There is precise congruence between 'the means used' (abrogation of sovereign immunity in this narrow category of cases) and 'the ends to be achieved' (elimination of the risk that the defense of sovereign immunity will deprive some patentees of property without due process of law).

"That congruence is equally precise whether infringement of patents by state actors is rare or frequent. If they are indeed unusual, the statute will operate only in those rare cases. But if such infringements are common, or should become common as state activities in the commercial arena increase, the impact of the statute will likewise expand in precise harmony with the growth of the problem that Congress anticipated and sought to prevent. In either event the statute will have no impact on the States' enforcement of their own laws. None of the concerns that underlay our decision in *Boerne* are even remotely implicated in this case."

State action. UNITED STATES v. MORRISON, p. 2 of this Supplement, per REHNQUIST, C.J., held that Congress had no § 5 power to grant a civil remedy to victims of gender-motivated violence despite Congress' (1) receiving "evidence that many participants in state justice systems are perpetuating an array of erroneous stereotypes and assumptions," and (2) concluding "that these discriminatory stereotypes often result in insufficient investigation and prosecution of gender-motivated crime, inappropriate focus on the behavior and credibility of the victims of that crime, and unacceptably lenient punishments for those who are actually convicted of gender-motivated violence": The statute "is directed not at any State or state actor, but at individuals who have committed criminal acts motivated by gender bias. [It] visits no consequence whatever on any Virginia public official involved in investigating or prosecuting Brzonkala's assault. The section is, therefore, unlike any of the § 5 remedies that we have previously upheld"—as in *Morgan, South Carolina v. Katzenbach*, and *Ex parte Virginia*, which were directed at states or state officials. The "remedy is not 'corrective in its character, adapted to counteract and redress the operation of such prohibited state laws or proceedings of state officers.' *Civil Rights Cases*.[a] Or, as we have phrased it in more recent cases, prophylactic legislation under § 5 must have a 'congruence and proportionality between the injury to be prevented or remedied and the means adopted to that end.'[b]

a. "There is abundant evidence [t]o show that the Congresses that enacted the [laws in the *Civil Rights Cases*] had a purpose similar to that of Congress in enacting § 13981: There were state laws on the books bespeaking equality of treatment, but in the administration of these laws there was discrimination against newly freed slaves."

b. As for *Guest*, "it would take more than the naked dicta contained in Justice Clark's opinion, when added to Justice Brennan's opinion, to cast any doubt upon the enduring vitality of the *Civil Rights Cases*."

"Section 13981 is also different from these previously upheld remedies in that it applies uniformly throughout the Nation. Congress' findings indicate that the problem of discrimination against the victims of gender-motivated crimes does not exist in all States, or even most States. By contrast, the § 5 remedy upheld in *Morgan* was directed only to the State where the evil found by Congress existed, and in *South Carolina v. Katzenbach,* the remedy was directed only to those States in which Congress found that there had been discrimination."

BREYER, J., joined by Stevens, J., "doubt[ed] the Court's reasoning," but did not "answer the § 5 question"[c]: "The Federal Government's argument [is] that Congress used § 5 to remedy the actions of *state actors,* namely, those States which, through discriminatory design or the discriminatory conduct of their officials, failed to provide adequate (or any) state remedies for women injured by gender-motivated violence—a failure that the States, and Congress, documented in depth." The *Civil Rights Cases* did not consider "this kind of claim," observing in that case that the statute "did 'not profess to be corrective of any constitutional wrong committed by the States' and that it established 'rules for the conduct of individuals in society towards each other, [without] referring in any manner to any supposed action of the State or its authorities.'

"[W]hy can Congress not provide a remedy against private actors? Those private actors, of course, did not themselves violate the Constitution. But this Court has held that Congress at least sometimes can enact remedial 'legislation [that] prohibits conduct which is not itself unconstitutional.' *Boerne.* The statutory remedy [may] lead state actors to improve their own remedial systems, primarily through example. It restricts private actors only by imposing liability for private conduct that is, in the main, already forbidden by state law. Why is the remedy 'disproportionate'? And given the relation between remedy and violation—the creation of a federal remedy to substitute for constitutionally inadequate state remedies—where is the lack of 'congruence'?

"* * * Congress had before it the task force reports of at least 21 States documenting constitutional violations. And it made its own findings about pervasive gender-based stereotypes hampering many state legal systems, sometimes unconstitutionally so. The record nowhere reveals a congressional finding that the problem 'does not exist' elsewhere. [This] Court has not previously held that Congress must document the existence of a problem in every State prior to proposing a national solution."

Miranda. DICKERSON v. U.S., p. 37 of this Supplement, per REHNQUIST, C.J., invalidated a federal statute which was "intended [to] overrule *Miranda,*" "a constitutional decision of this Court": "Congress [may] not supersede this Court's decisions interpreting and applying the Constitution, see, *Boerne.*" Scalia and Thomas, JJ., dissented.

c. Souter and Ginsburg, JJ., having found the law valid under the commerce clause, felt no occasion to reach the § 5 issue.

LIMITATIONS ON JUDICIAL POWER AND REVIEW

STANDING

THE STRUCTURE OF STANDING DOCTRINE

CON LAW: P. 1517, at the end note 3

AMER CON: P. 1416, at the end of note 3

RTS & LIB: P. 1419, at the end of note 3

The Court again emphasized the linkage between standing and the separation of powers in LEWIS v. CASEY, 518 U.S. 343, 116 S.Ct. 2174, 135 L.Ed.2d 606 (1996), which held that prison inmates lack standing to challenge denials of access to law libraries and other forms of legal assistance unless they can show that denial impedes the presentation of non-frivolous legal claims. The district court had granted a broad injunction, which was affirmed by the court of appeals. Reversing, the Court, per SCALIA, J., observed that the distinction between the judicial role and that of the political branches "would be obliterated if, to invoke intervention of the courts, no actual or imminent harm were needed, but merely the status of being subject to a governmental institution that was not organized or managed properly." Souter, J., joined by Ginsburg and Breyer, J.J., concurred in part and dissented in part. Stevens, J., dissented.

If prisoners lack access to prison libraries or other sources of legal advice, how can they be expected to establish—as a requirement of standing—that their legal claims are non-frivolous?

CON LAW: P. 1518, at the end of footnote i

AMER CON: P. 1416, at the end of footnote i

RTS & LIB: P. 1419, at the end of footnote i

United Food & Commercial Workers Union Local 751 v. Brown Group, Inc., 517 U.S. 544, 116 S.Ct. 1529, 134 L.Ed.2d 758 (1996), held that Congress may override the third requirement of the *Hunt* test for organizational standing and authorize a union to sue for damages on behalf of its members.

TAXPAYER STANDING AND OTHER STATUS-BASED STANDING ISSUES

CON LAW: P. 1528, at the end of note 2

AMER CON: P. 1426, at the end of note 2

RTS & LIB: P. 1429, at the end of note 2

The Court returned to the issues involving "generalized grievances" that are inadequate to support standing in FEC v. AKINS, 524 U.S. 11, 118 S.Ct. 1777, 141 L.Ed.2d 10 (1998). The Court per BREYER, J., upheld the standing of a group of voters to challenge a determination by the Federal Election Commission ("FEC") that the American Israel Public Affairs Committee ("AIPAC") is not a "political committee" as defined by the Federal Election Campaign Act of 1971 and, accordingly, that AIPAC had not violated the Act and was not required to make disclosures concerning its membership, contributions, and expenditures. "The FEC's strongest argument," the Court said, is "that this lawsuit involves only a 'generalized grievance'" inadequate to ground standing. But the "language [disclaiming the justiciability of generalized grievances] to which the FEC points * * * invariably appears in cases where the harm at issue is not only widely shared, but is also of an abstract and indefinite nature—for example, harm to the 'common concern for obedience to law.'" By contrast, the Court concluded, the injury of which the plaintiffs complained, that of being denied information through AIPAC's failure to make disclosures allegedly mandated by the statute, though "widely shared," was nonetheless concrete and specific; the case was analogous to those "where large numbers of voters suffer interference with voting rights" but all affected persons have standing.

SCALIA, J., joined O'Connor and Thomas, JJ., dissented. He thought that *United States v. Richardson* was not distinguishable: "[T]he Court is wrong to think that generalized grievances have only concerned us when they are abstract. One need go no further than *Richardson* to prove that—unless the Court believes that deprivation of information is an abstract injury, in which event this case could be disposed of on that much broader ground." Justice Scalia continued: "What is noticeably lacking in the Court's discussion of our generalized-grievance jurisprudence is all reference to two words that have figured in it prominently: 'particularized' and 'undifferentiated'. 'Particularized' means that 'the injury must affect the plaintiff in a personal and individual way.' If the effect is 'undifferentiated and common to all members of the public,' the plaintiff has a 'generalized grievance' that must be pursued by political rather than judicial means." The harm of being deprived of information fit that description: "The harm caused to Mr. Richardson [and Mr. Akins] * * * was precisely the same as the harm caused to everyone else."

CON LAW: P. 1530, at end of note 5

AMER CON: P. 1427, at end of note 5

RTS & LIB: P. 1430, at end of note 5

See also *Shaw v. Hunt,* 517 U.S. 899, 116 S.Ct. 1894, 135 L.Ed.2d 207 (1996)(holding that plaintiffs lack standing to challenge districting legislation as an unconstitutional racial gerrymander when they neither reside within the challenged district nor present specific evidence that they personally have been subjected to a racial classification). Stevens, J., dissenting, again would have denied standing more generally.

CON LAW: P. 1531, at the end of note 6

AMER CON: P. 1427, at the end of note 6

RTS & LIB: P. 1430, at the end of note 6

RAINES v. BYRD, 521 U.S. 811, 117 S.Ct. 2312, 138 L.Ed.2d 849 (1997), per REHNQUIST, C.J., distinguished *Coleman v. Miller,* which had upheld the standing of state legislators who complained that their votes against a proposed constitutional amendment were rendered nullities when the lieutenant governor impermissibly broke a tie by casting an affirmative vote, and held that members of Congress lacked standing to challenge the constitutionality of the Line Item Veto Act ("the Act"), which authorizes the President to "cancel" certain spending and tax benefit measures after signing them into law: *Coleman* "stands (at most * * *) for the proposition that legislators whose votes would have been sufficient to defeat (or enact) a specific legislative act have standing to sue if that legislative action goes into effect (or does not go into effect), on the ground that their votes have been completely nullified." Although plaintiffs alleged that the Line Item Veto Act diluted the significance of their votes for bills that are subject to presidential cancellation, there was a "vast difference" between the "level of vote nullification" in this case and that in *Coleman*. "We attach some significance to the fact that appellees have not been authorized to represent their respective Houses of Congress, and indeed both Houses actively oppose their suit. [N]or [does the decision] foreclose[ ] the Act from constitutional challenge (by someone who suffers judicially cognizable injury as a result of the Act). Whether the case would be different if any of these circumstances were different we need not now decide."

Souter, J., joined by Ginsburg, J., agreed that the plaintiffs lacked standing. Stevens, J., dissented, as did Breyer, J.

CONGRESSIONAL POWER TO CREATE STANDING

CON LAW: P. 1536, at the end of note 2
AMER CON: P. 1421, at the end of note 8
RTS & LIB: P. 1424, at the end of note 8

In FEC v. AKINS, 524 U.S. 11, 118 S.Ct. 1777, 141 L.Ed.2d 10 (1998), the Court, per BREYER, J., upheld the power of Congress to confer standing on any "aggrieved" person who suffers the harm of "inability to receive information" as a result of a decision by the FEC that reporting and disclosure requirements are not applicable to a private party. Although the interest in acquiring information was not protected at common law, and although "prudential" considerations might have precluded recognition of standing to sue based on so widespread an injury in the absence of a statute, Congress had specifically authorized suit under the Federal Election Campaign Act. Judicially imposed "prudential" limitations on standing therefore had to give way; the "failure to obtain relevant information" is a "concrete" enough injury to satisfy the requirements of Article III.

SCALIA, J., joined by O'Connor and Thomas, JJ., dissented. The asserted injury was too generalized and undifferentiated to support standing, and a statute could not cure the constitutional defect. "If today's decision is correct, it is within the power of Congress to authorize any interested person to manage (through the courts) the Executive's enforcement of any law that includes a requirement for the filing and public availability of a piece of paper. This is not the system we have had, and it is not the system we should desire."

The Court also upheld standing in FRIENDS OF THE EARTH, INC. v. LAIDLAW ENVIRONMENTAL SERVICES (TOC), INC., ___ U.S. ___, 120 S.Ct. 693, 145 L.Ed.2d 610 (2000), this time under the citizen suit provisions of the Clean Water Act. The defendant argued that standing was defeated because the District Court, in imposing a penalty, ruled that the defendant's illegal actions had not been proved to "result in any health risk or environmental harm." But the Court held, per GINSBURG, J., that the relevant injury "is not injury to the environment, but injury to the plaintiff," and that the plaintiffs had suffered injury from their "reasonable concern" that pollution had damaged land that they otherwise would have used. Scalia, J., joined by Thomas, J., dissented.

†